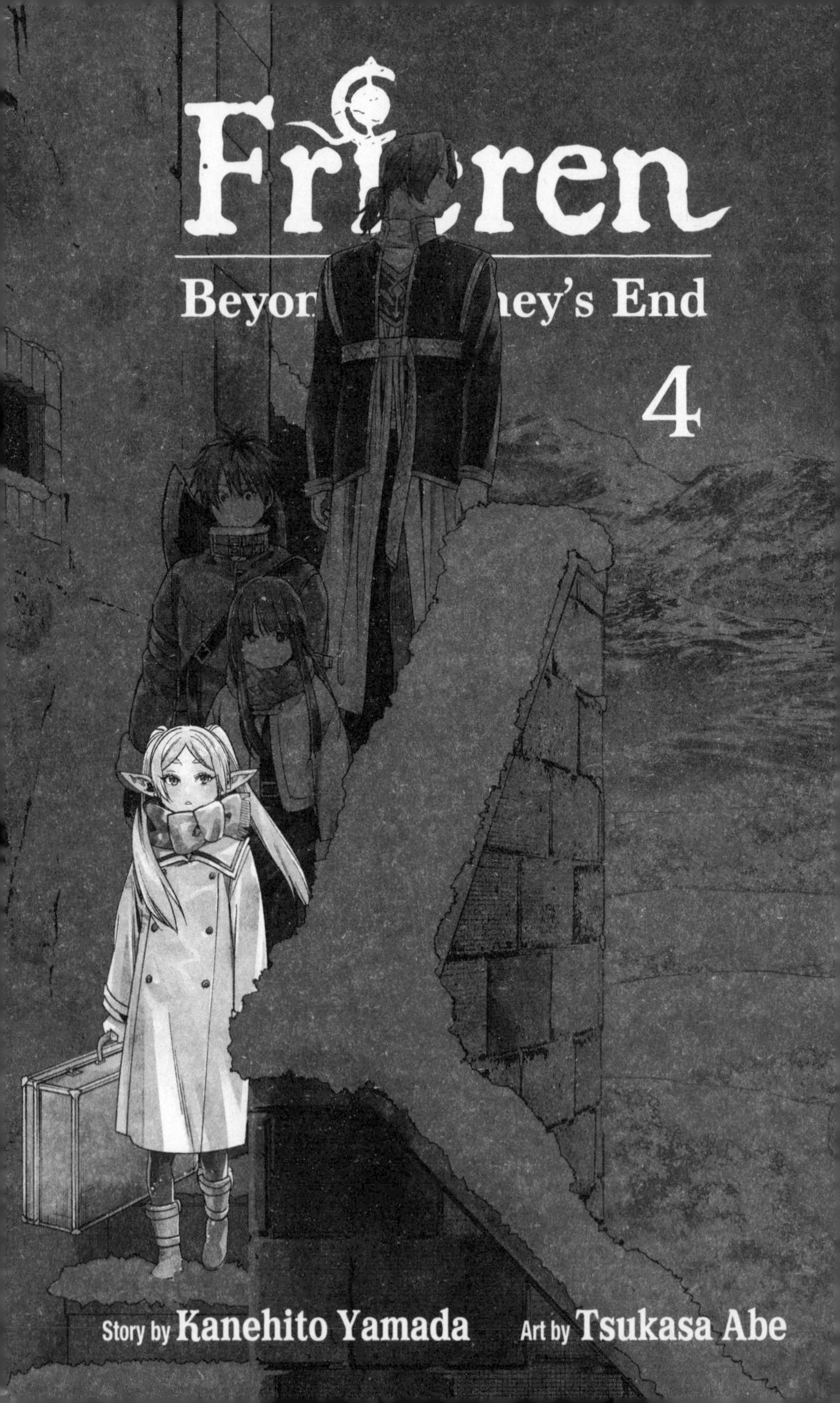
Fri eren
Beyon ney's End
4
Story by Kanehito Yamada
Art by Tsukasa Abe

CONTENTS

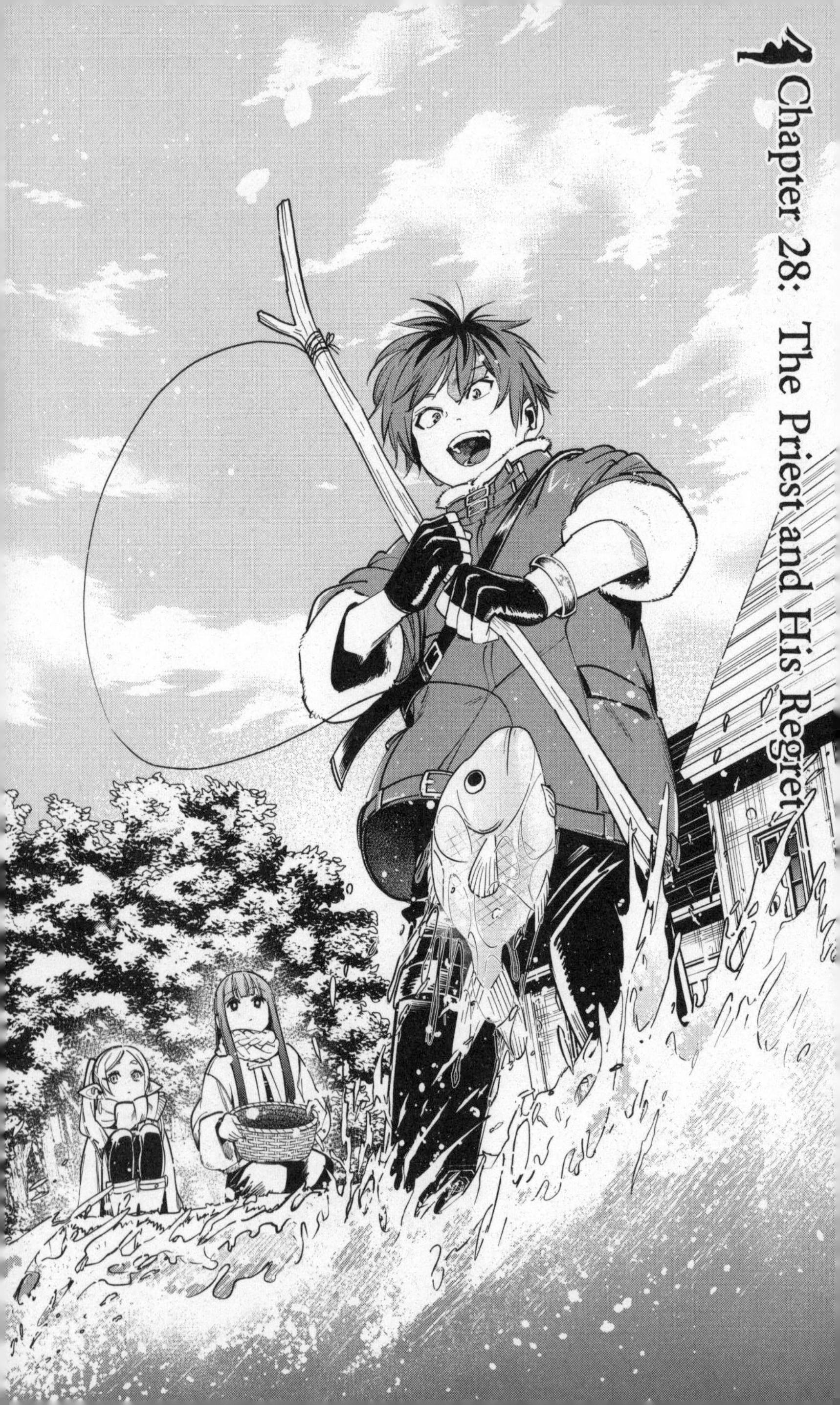
Chapter 28: The Priest and His Regret

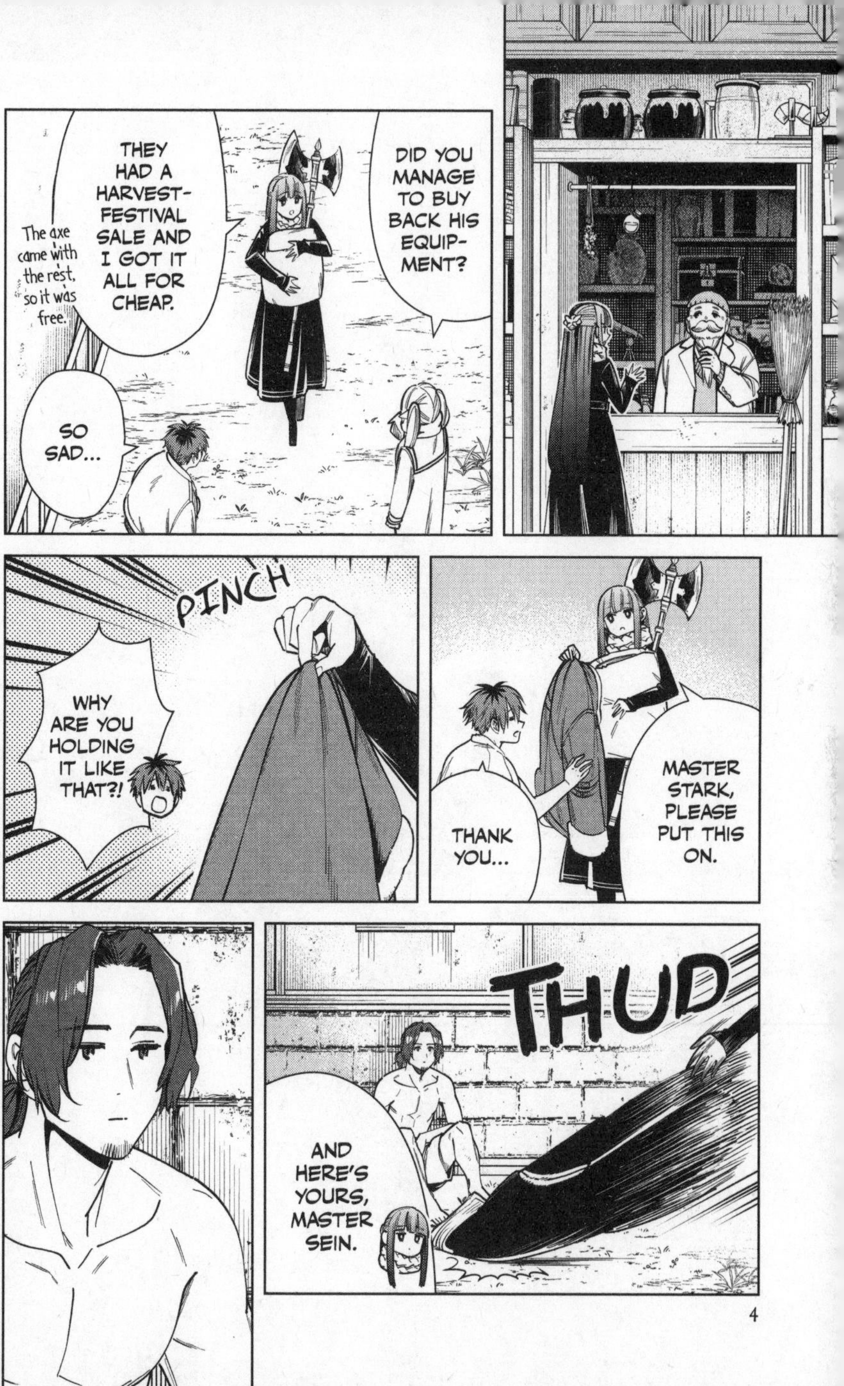
DID YOU MANAGE TO BUY BACK HIS EQUIPMENT?
THEY HAD A HARVEST-FESTIVAL SALE AND I GOT IT ALL FOR CHEAP.
The axe came with the rest, so it was free.
SO SAD...
MASTER STARK, PLEASE PUT THIS ON.
THANK YOU...
PINCH
WHY ARE YOU HOLDING IT LIKE THAT?!
THUD
AND HERE'S YOURS, MASTER SEIN.

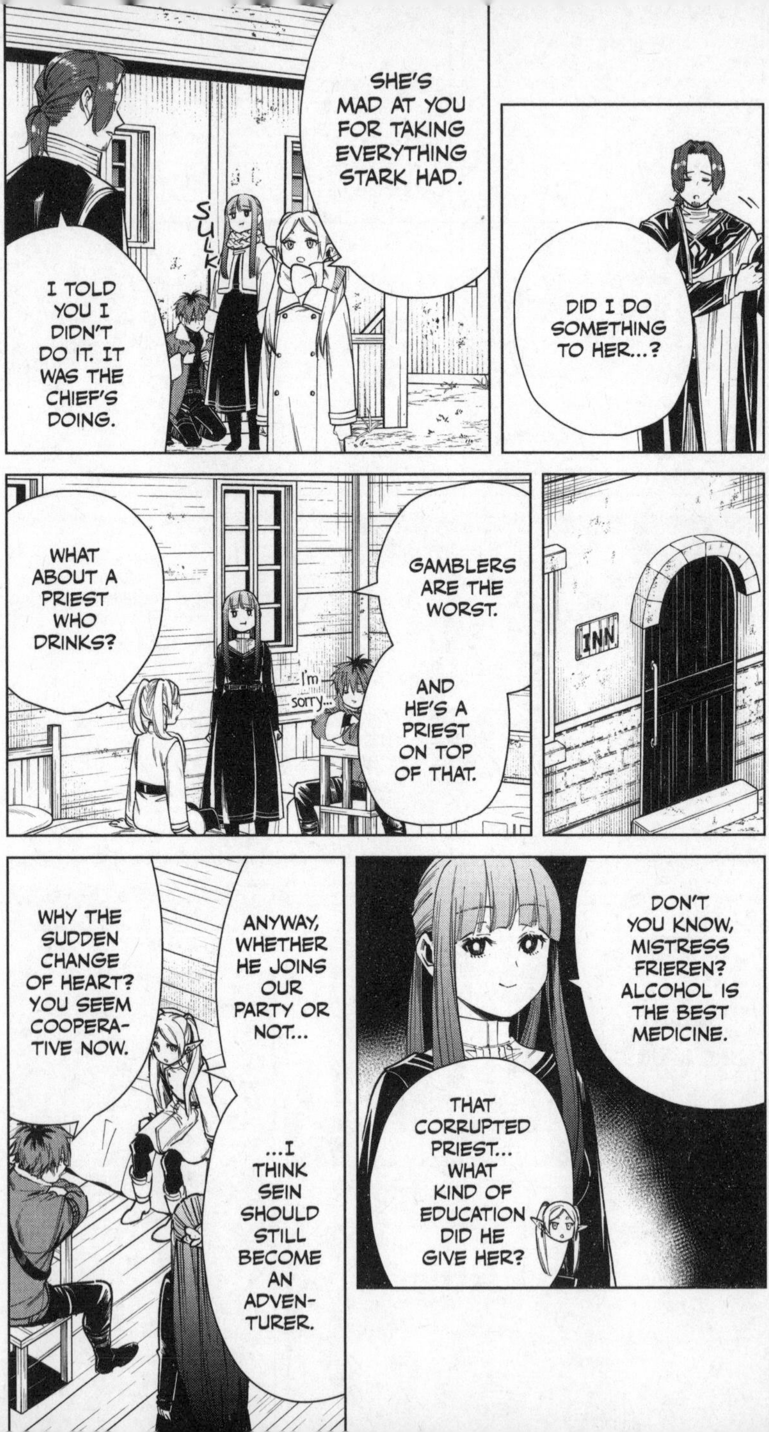
DID I DO SOMETHING TO HER...?
SHE'S MAD AT YOU FOR TAKING EVERYTHING STARK HAD.
SULK
I TOLD YOU I DIDN'T DO IT. IT WAS THE CHIEF'S DOING.
INN
GAMBLERS ARE THE WORST.
AND HE'S A PRIEST ON TOP OF THAT.
I'm sorry...
WHAT ABOUT A PRIEST WHO DRINKS?
DON'T YOU KNOW, MISTRESS FRIEREN? ALCOHOL IS THE BEST MEDICINE.
THAT CORRUPTED PRIEST... WHAT KIND OF EDUCATION DID HE GIVE HER?
ANYWAY, WHETHER HE JOINS OUR PARTY OR NOT...
WHY THE SUDDEN CHANGE OF HEART? YOU SEEM COOPERA-TIVE NOW.
...I THINK SEIN SHOULD STILL BECOME AN ADVEN-TURER.

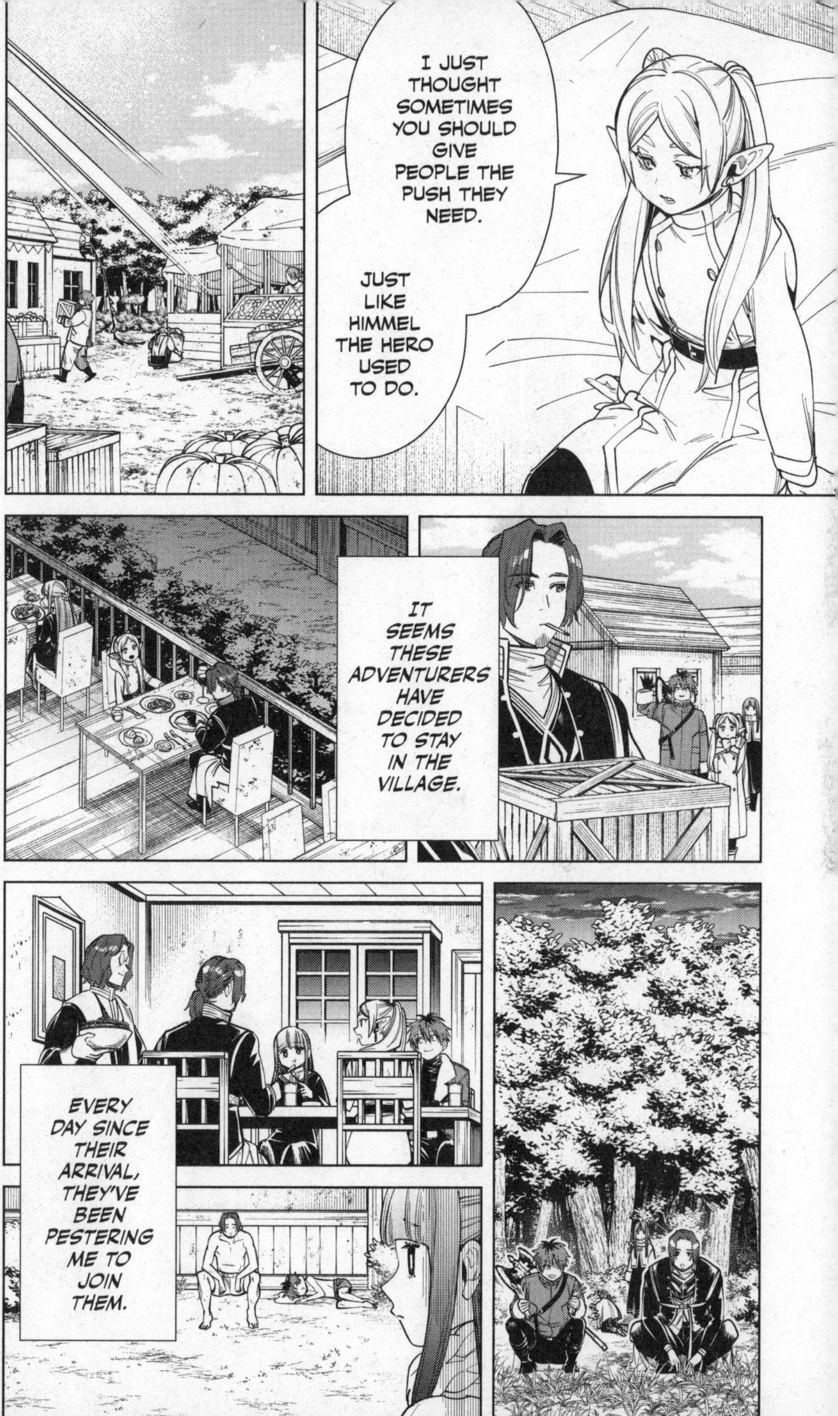
I JUST THOUGHT SOMETIMES YOU SHOULD GIVE PEOPLE THE PUSH THEY NEED.
JUST LIKE HIMMEL THE HERO USED TO DO.
IT SEEMS THESE ADVENTURERS HAVE DECIDED TO STAY IN THE VILLAGE.
EVERY DAY SINCE THEIR ARRIVAL, THEY'VE BEEN PESTERING ME TO JOIN THEM.

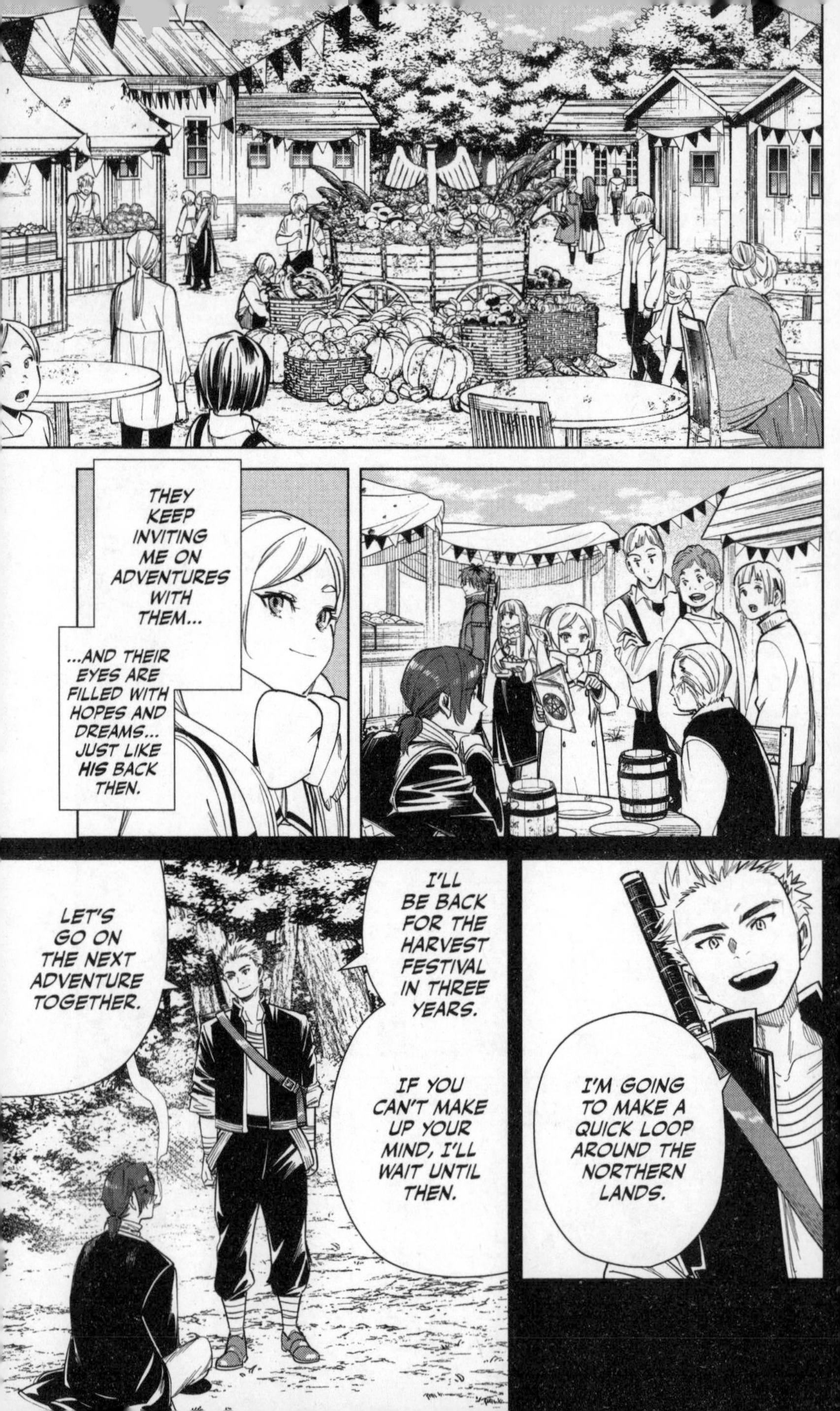
THEY KEEP INVITING ME ON ADVENTURES WITH THEM...
...AND THEIR EYES ARE FILLED WITH HOPES AND DREAMS... JUST LIKE HIS BACK THEN.
I'M GOING TO MAKE A QUICK LOOP AROUND THE NORTHERN LANDS.
I'LL BE BACK FOR THE HARVEST FESTIVAL IN THREE YEARS.
IF YOU CAN'T MAKE UP YOUR MIND, I'LL WAIT UNTIL THEN.
LET'S GO ON THE NEXT ADVENTURE TOGETHER.

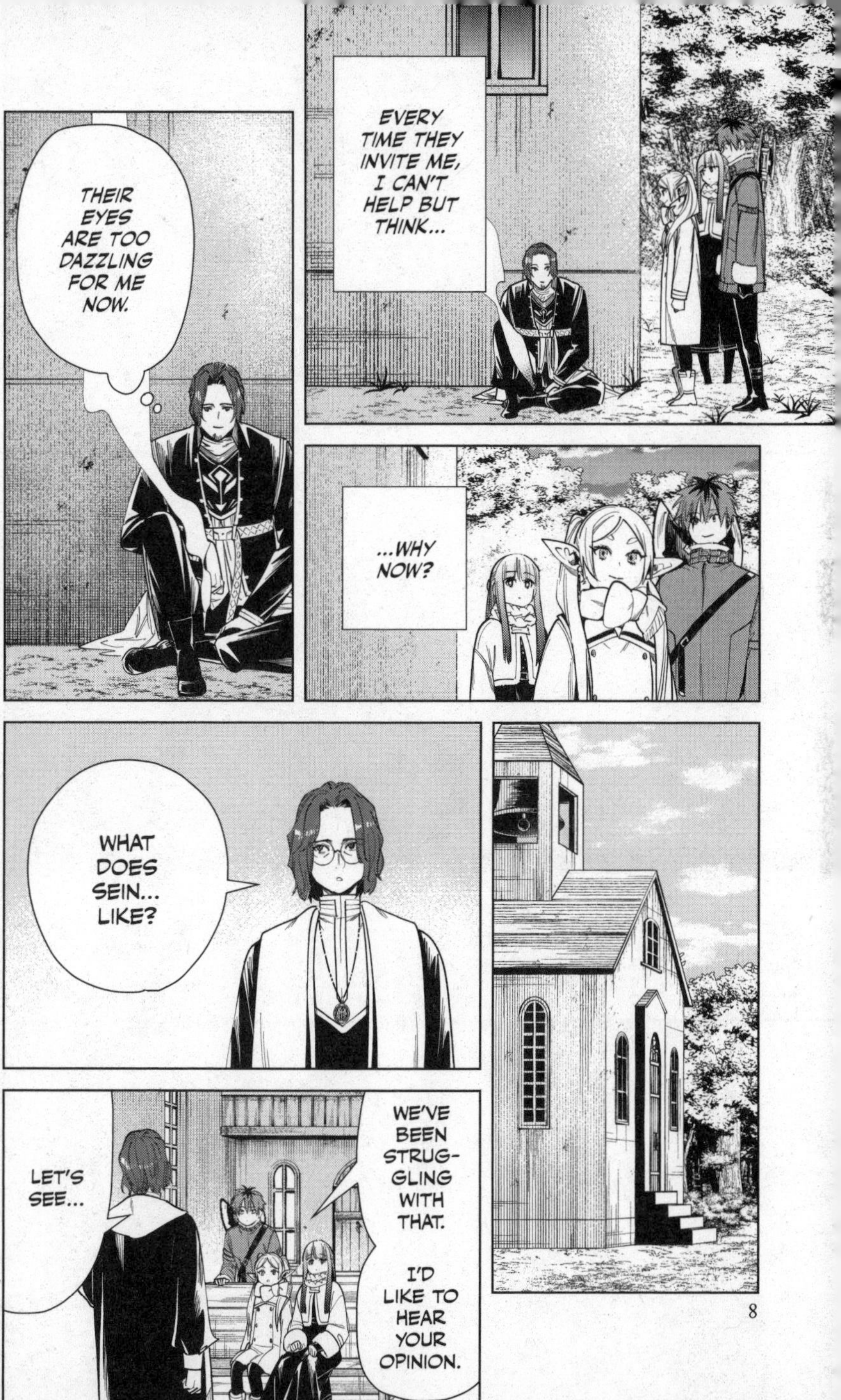
EVERY TIME THEY INVITE ME, I CAN'T HELP BUT THINK...
...WHY NOW?
THEIR EYES ARE TOO DAZZLING FOR ME NOW.
WHAT DOES SEIN... LIKE?
WE'VE BEEN STRUG-GLING WITH THAT.
I'D LIKE TO HEAR YOUR OPINION.
LET'S SEE...

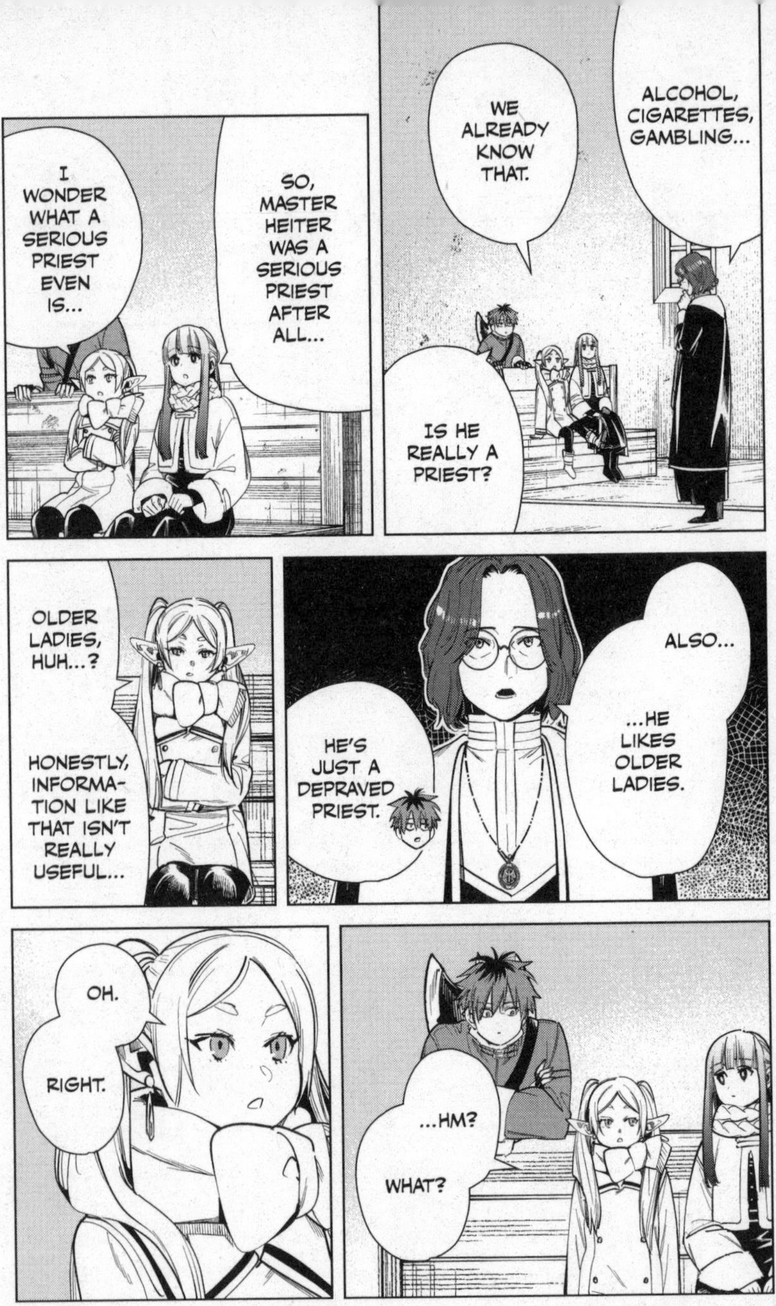
ALCOHOL, CIGARETTES, GAMBLING...
WE ALREADY KNOW THAT.
IS HE REALLY A PRIEST?
SO, MASTER HEITER WAS A SERIOUS PRIEST AFTER ALL...
I WONDER WHAT A SERIOUS PRIEST EVEN IS...
ALSO...
...HE LIKES OLDER LADIES.
HE'S JUST A DEPRAVED PRIEST.
OLDER LADIES, HUH...?
HONESTLY, INFORMATION LIKE THAT ISN'T REALLY USEFUL...
...HM?
WHAT?
OH.
RIGHT.

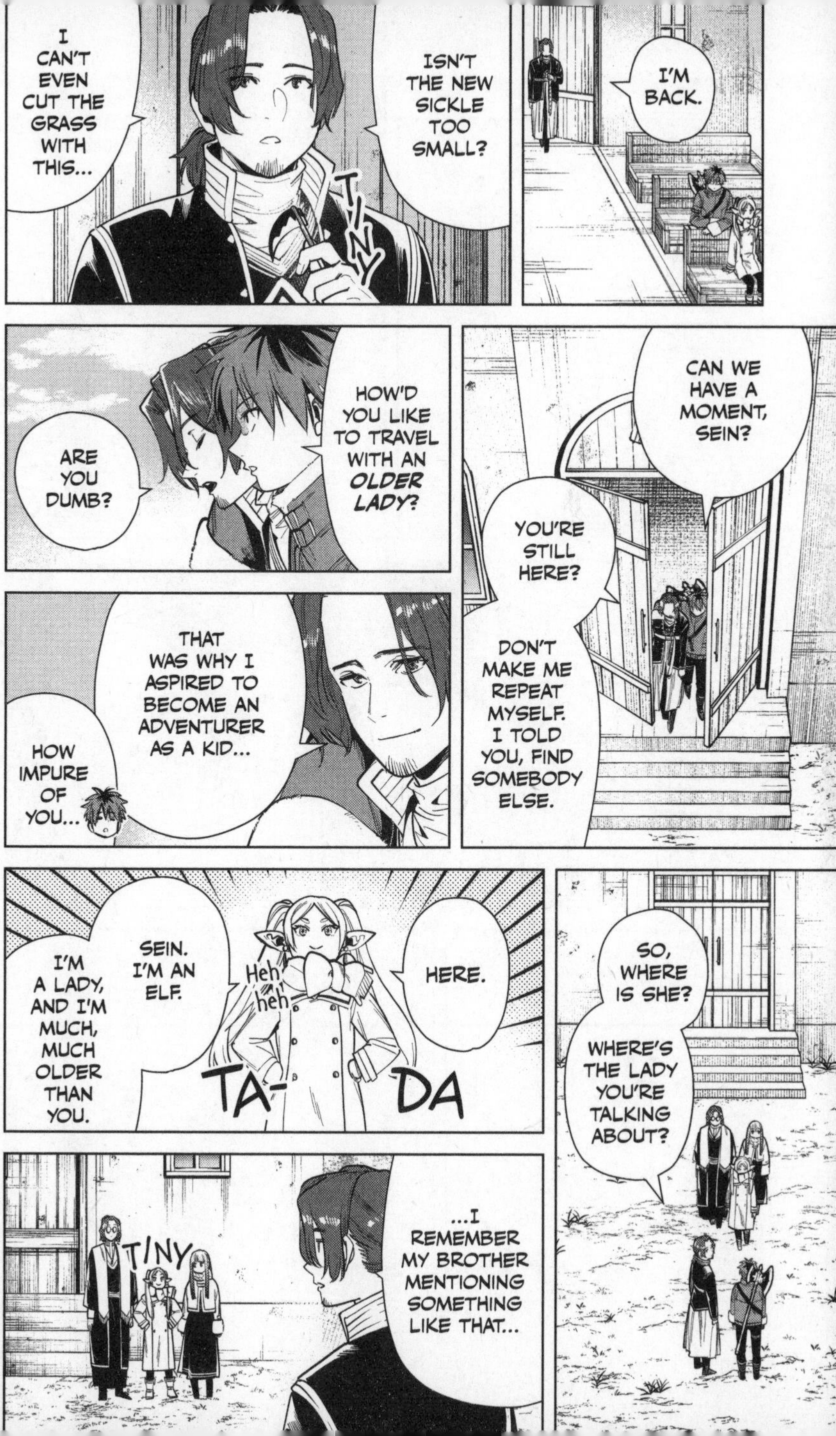
I'M BACK.
ISN'T THE NEW SICKLE TOO SMALL?
TINY
I CAN'T EVEN CUT THE GRASS WITH THIS...
CAN WE HAVE A MOMENT, SEIN?
YOU'RE STILL HERE?
DON'T MAKE ME REPEAT MYSELF. I TOLD YOU, FIND SOMEBODY ELSE.
HOW'D YOU LIKE TO TRAVEL WITH AN *OLDER LADY*?
ARE YOU DUMB?
THAT WAS WHY I ASPIRED TO BECOME AN ADVENTURER AS A KID...
HOW IMPURE OF YOU...
SO, WHERE IS SHE?
WHERE'S THE LADY YOU'RE TALKING ABOUT?
HERE.
Heh heh
TA- DA
SEIN. I'M AN ELF.
I'M A LADY, AND I'M MUCH, MUCH OLDER THAN YOU.
...I REMEMBER MY BROTHER MENTIONING SOMETHING LIKE THAT...
TINY

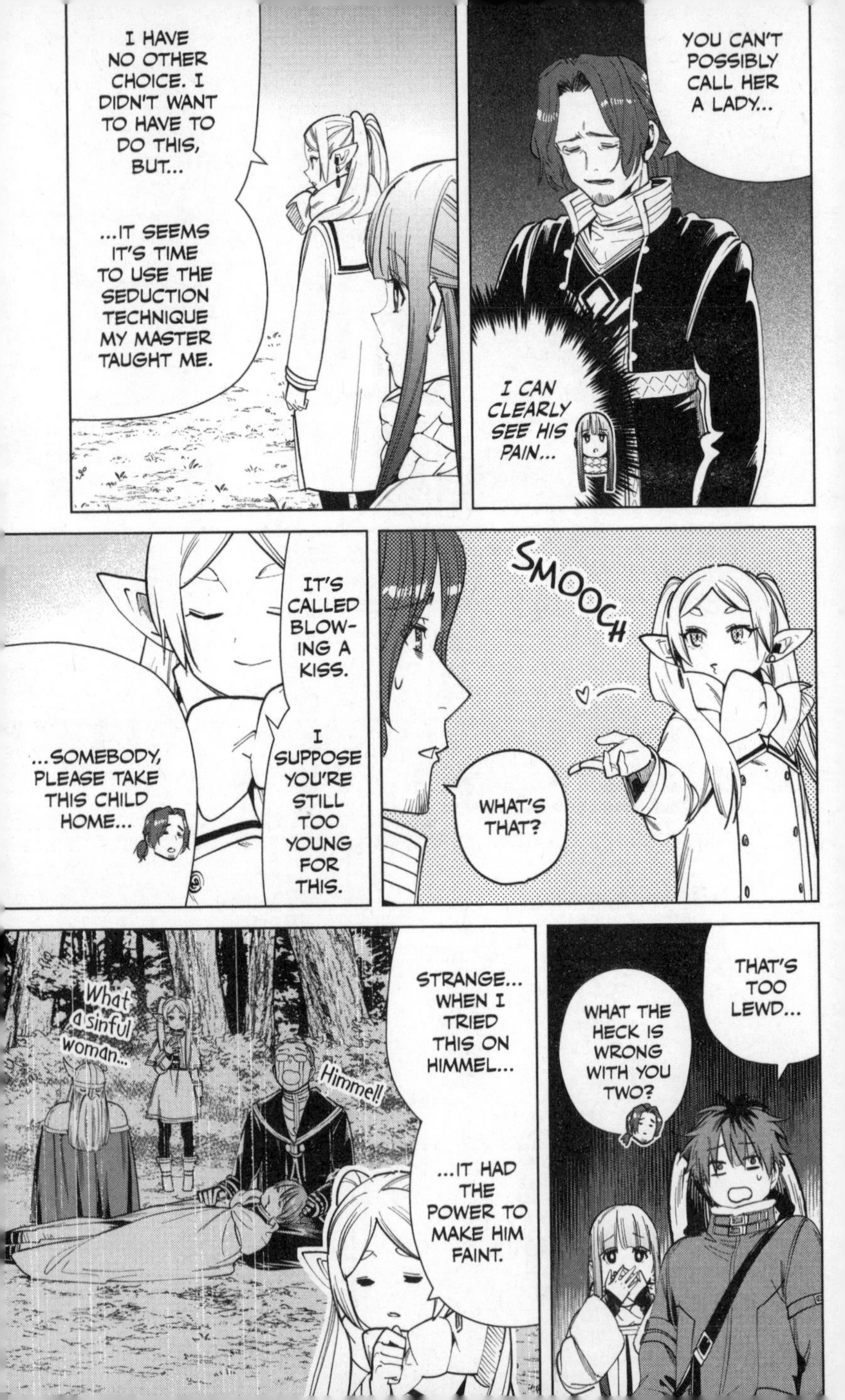
YOU CAN'T POSSIBLY CALL HER A LADY...
I CAN CLEARLY SEE HIS PAIN...
I HAVE NO OTHER CHOICE. I DIDN'T WANT TO HAVE TO DO THIS, BUT...
...IT SEEMS IT'S TIME TO USE THE SEDUCTION TECHNIQUE MY MASTER TAUGHT ME.
SMOOCH
WHAT'S THAT?
IT'S CALLED BLOWING A KISS.
I SUPPOSE YOU'RE STILL TOO YOUNG FOR THIS.
...SOMEBODY, PLEASE TAKE THIS CHILD HOME...
THAT'S TOO LEWD...
WHAT THE HECK IS WRONG WITH YOU TWO?
STRANGE... WHEN I TRIED THIS ON HIMMEL...
...IT HAD THE POWER TO MAKE HIM FAINT.
Himmel!
What a sinful woman...

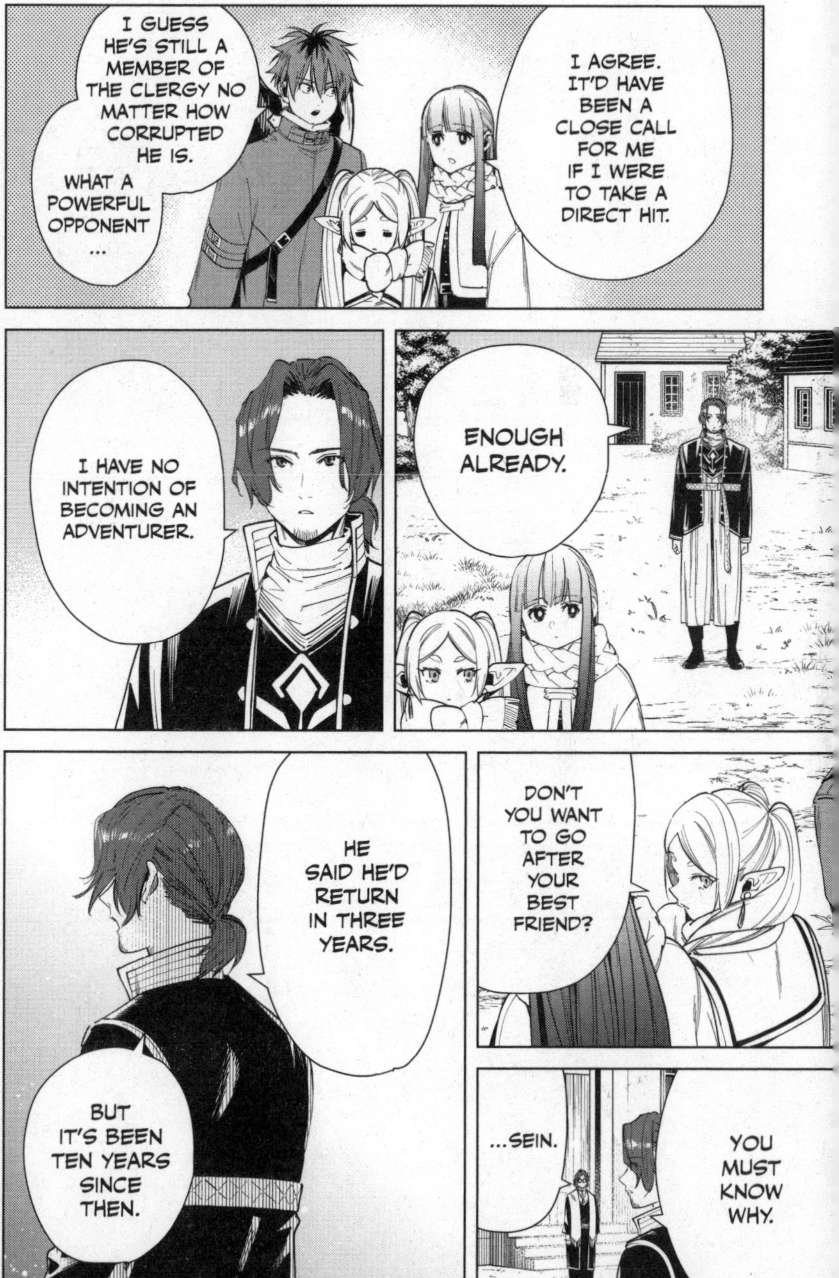
I GUESS HE'S STILL A MEMBER OF THE CLERGY NO MATTER HOW CORRUPTED HE IS.
WHAT A POWERFUL OPPONENT ...
I AGREE. IT'D HAVE BEEN A CLOSE CALL FOR ME IF I WERE TO TAKE A DIRECT HIT.
ENOUGH ALREADY.
I HAVE NO INTENTION OF BECOMING AN ADVENTURER.
DON'T YOU WANT TO GO AFTER YOUR BEST FRIEND?
YOU MUST KNOW WHY.
...SEIN.
HE SAID HE'D RETURN IN THREE YEARS.
BUT IT'S BEEN TEN YEARS SINCE THEN.

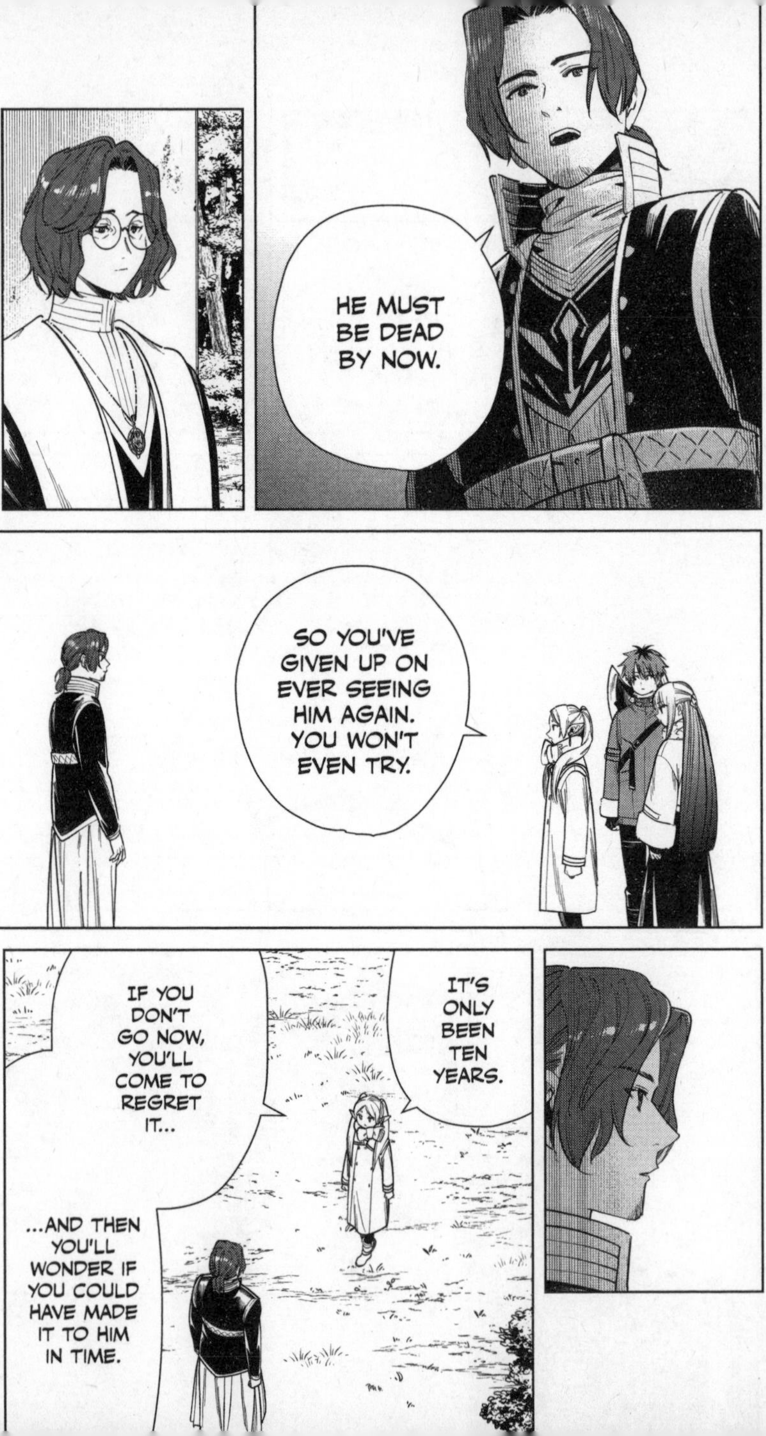
HE MUST BE DEAD BY NOW.
SO YOU'VE GIVEN UP ON EVER SEEING HIM AGAIN. YOU WON'T EVEN TRY.
IT'S ONLY BEEN TEN YEARS.
IF YOU DON'T GO NOW, YOU'LL COME TO REGRET IT...
...AND THEN YOU'LL WONDER IF YOU COULD HAVE MADE IT TO HIM IN TIME.

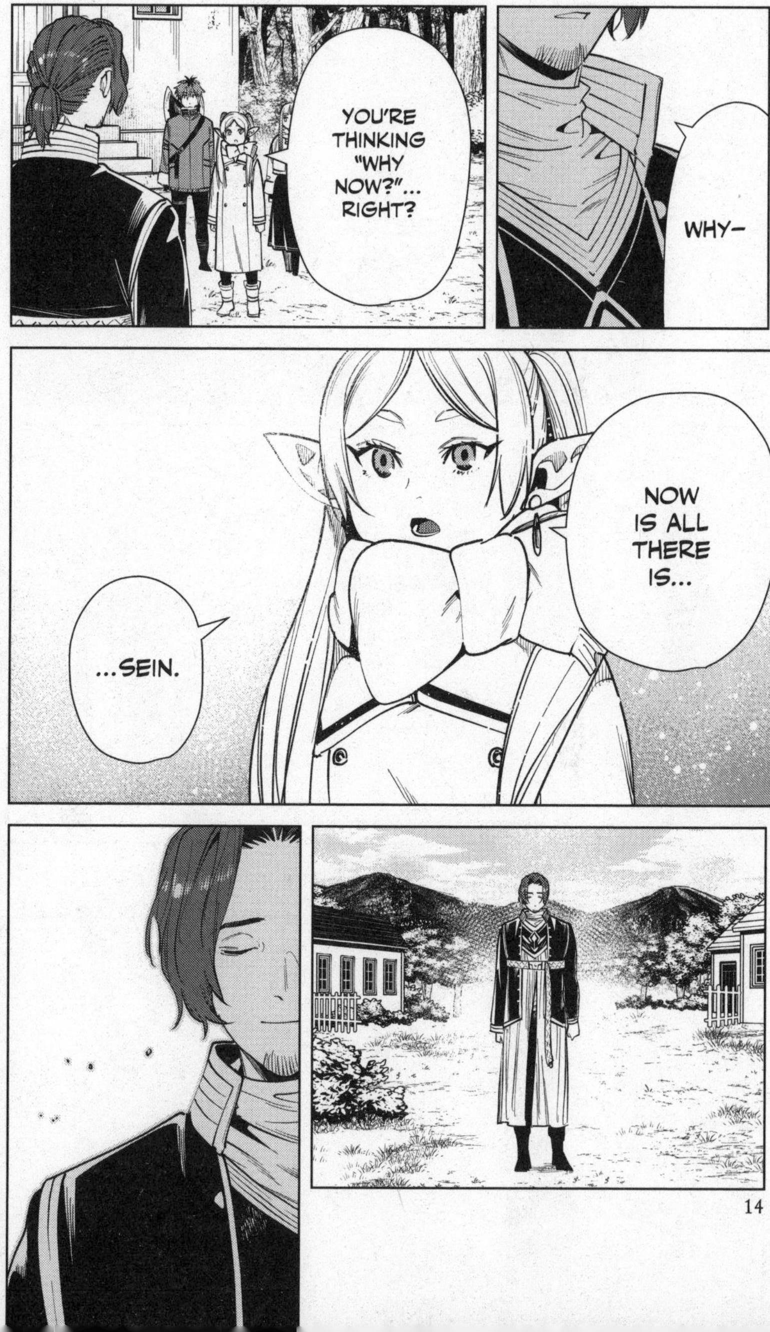
WHY—
YOU'RE THINKING "WHY NOW?"... RIGHT?
NOW IS ALL THERE IS...
...SEIN.

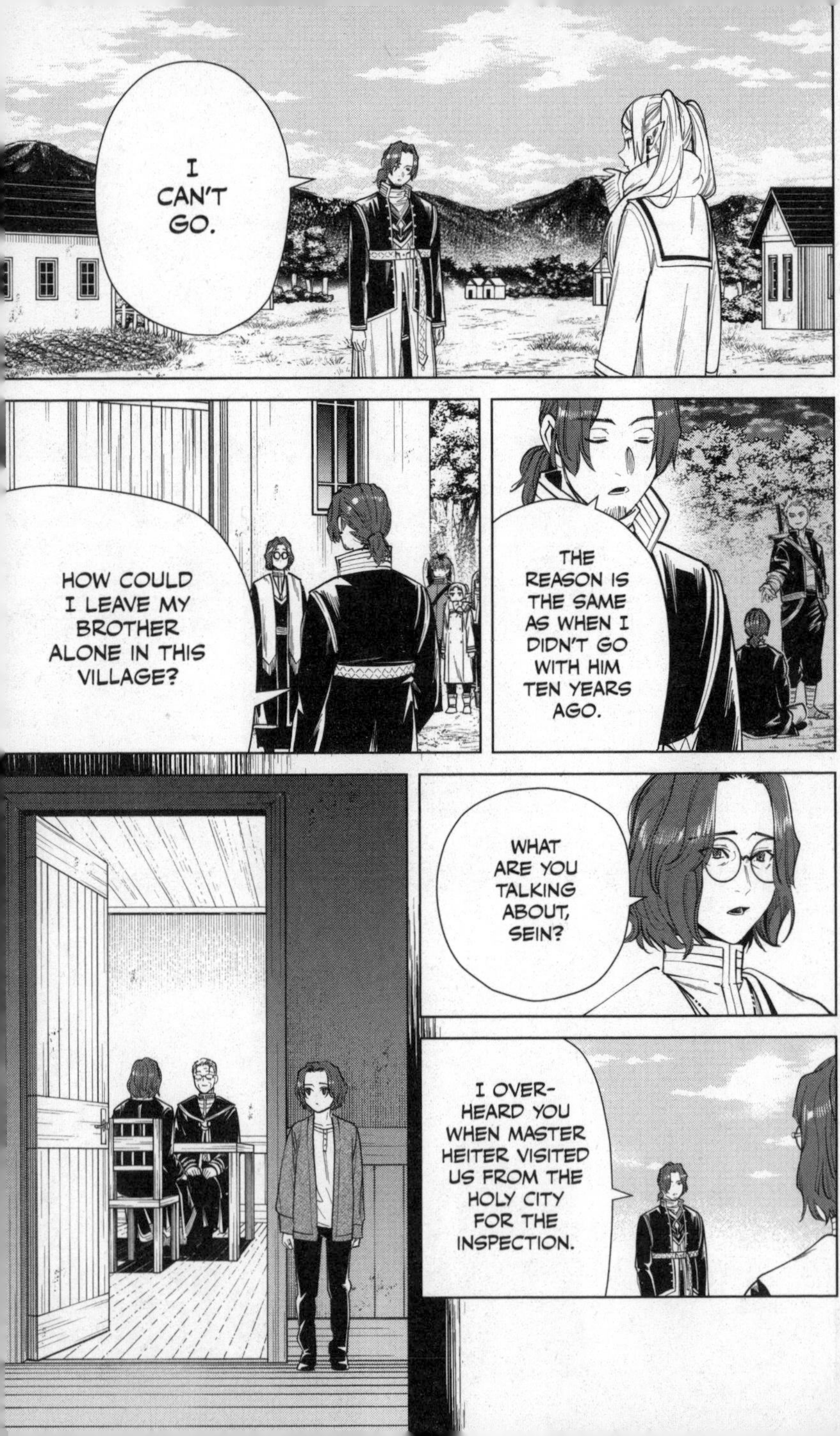
I CAN'T GO.
THE REASON IS THE SAME AS WHEN I DIDN'T GO WITH HIM TEN YEARS AGO.
HOW COULD I LEAVE MY BROTHER ALONE IN THIS VILLAGE?
WHAT ARE YOU TALKING ABOUT, SEIN?
I OVER-HEARD YOU WHEN MASTER HEITER VISITED US FROM THE HOLY CITY FOR THE INSPECTION.

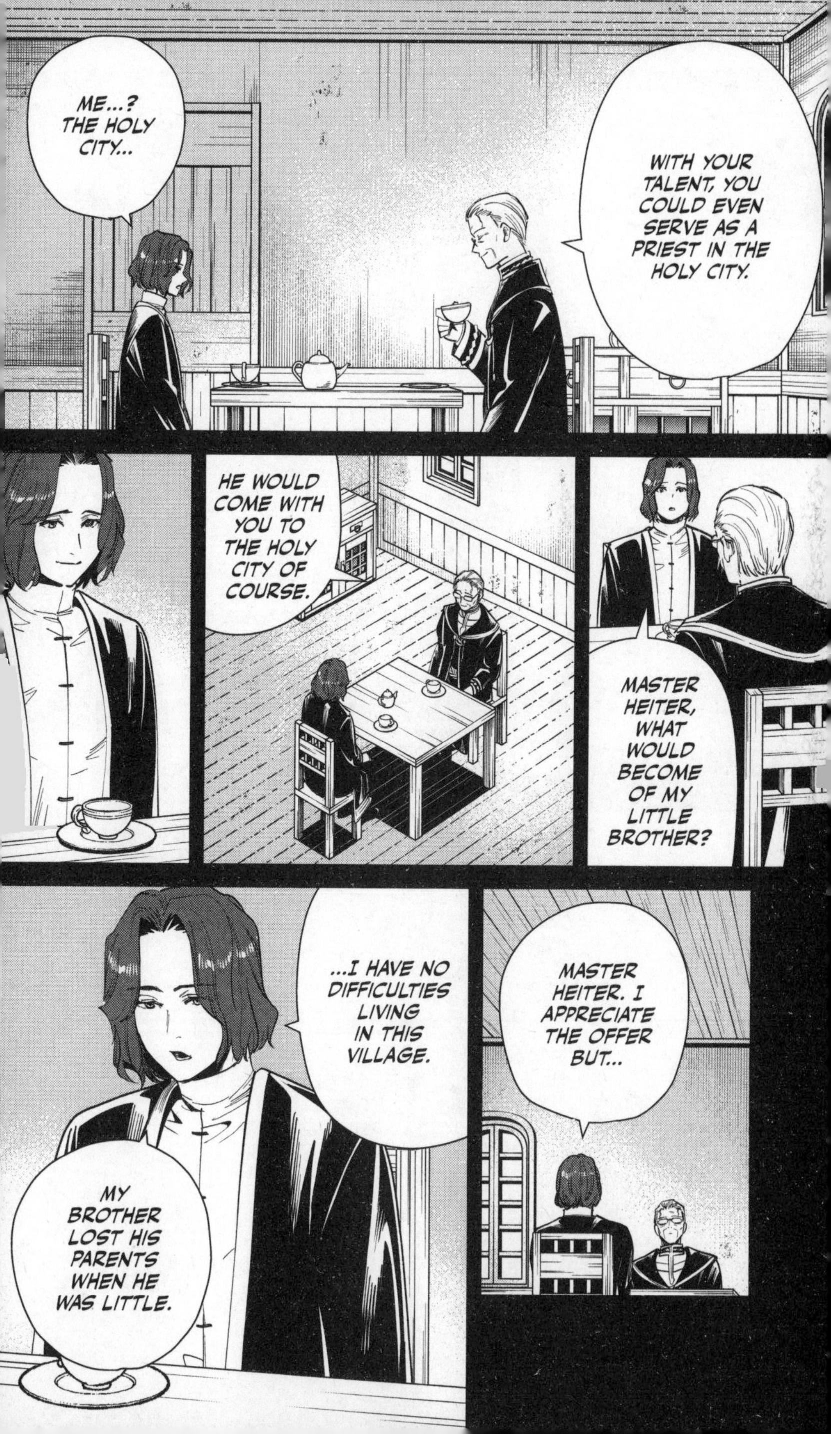
WITH YOUR TALENT, YOU COULD EVEN SERVE AS A PRIEST IN THE HOLY CITY.
ME...? THE HOLY CITY...
MASTER HEITER, WHAT WOULD BECOME OF MY LITTLE BROTHER?
HE WOULD COME WITH YOU TO THE HOLY CITY OF COURSE.
MASTER HEITER. I APPRECIATE THE OFFER BUT...
...I HAVE NO DIFFICULTIES LIVING IN THIS VILLAGE.
MY BROTHER LOST HIS PARENTS WHEN HE WAS LITTLE.

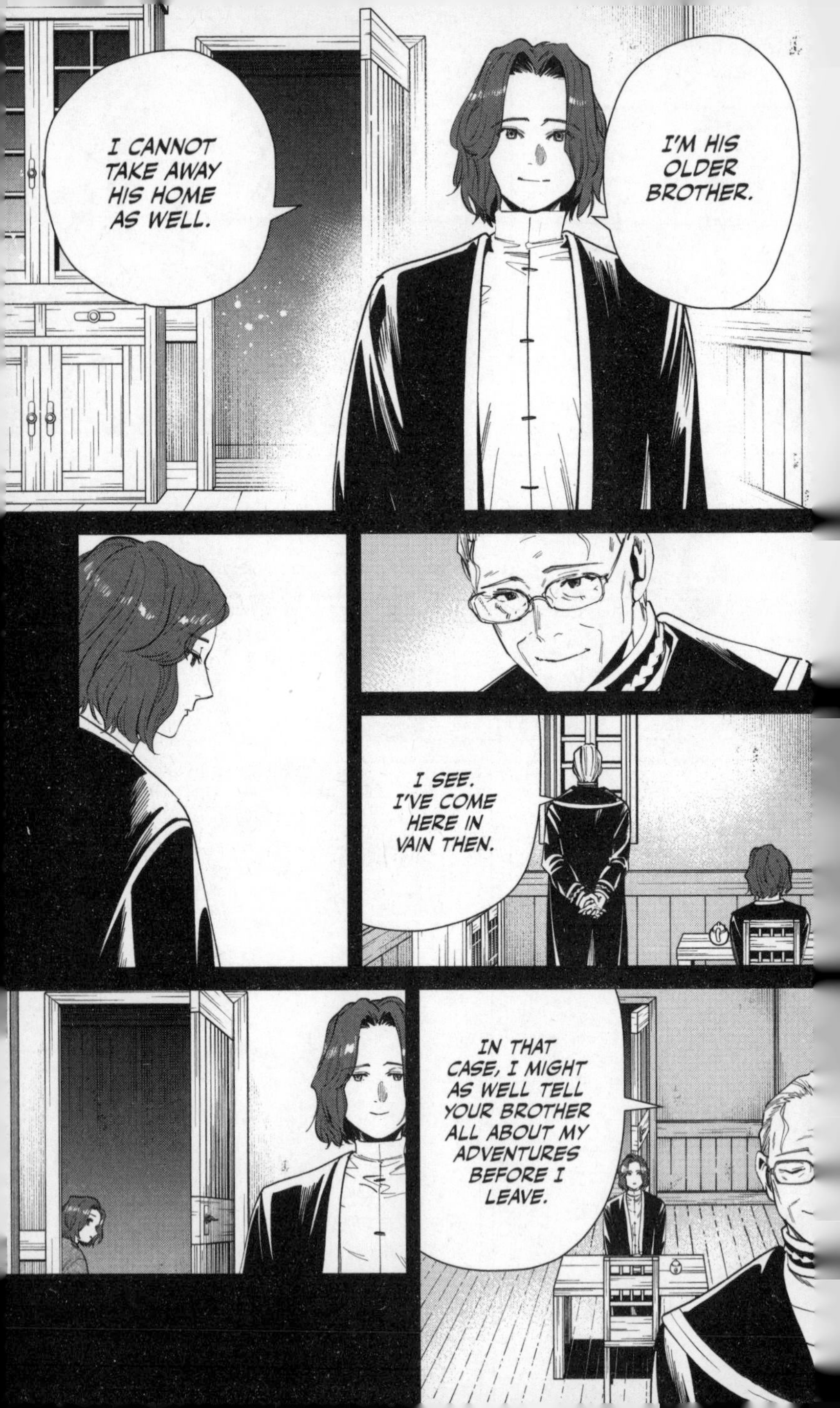
I'M HIS OLDER BROTHER.
I CANNOT TAKE AWAY HIS HOME AS WELL.
I SEE. I'VE COME HERE IN VAIN THEN.
IN THAT CASE, I MIGHT AS WELL TELL YOUR BROTHER ALL ABOUT MY ADVENTURES BEFORE I LEAVE.

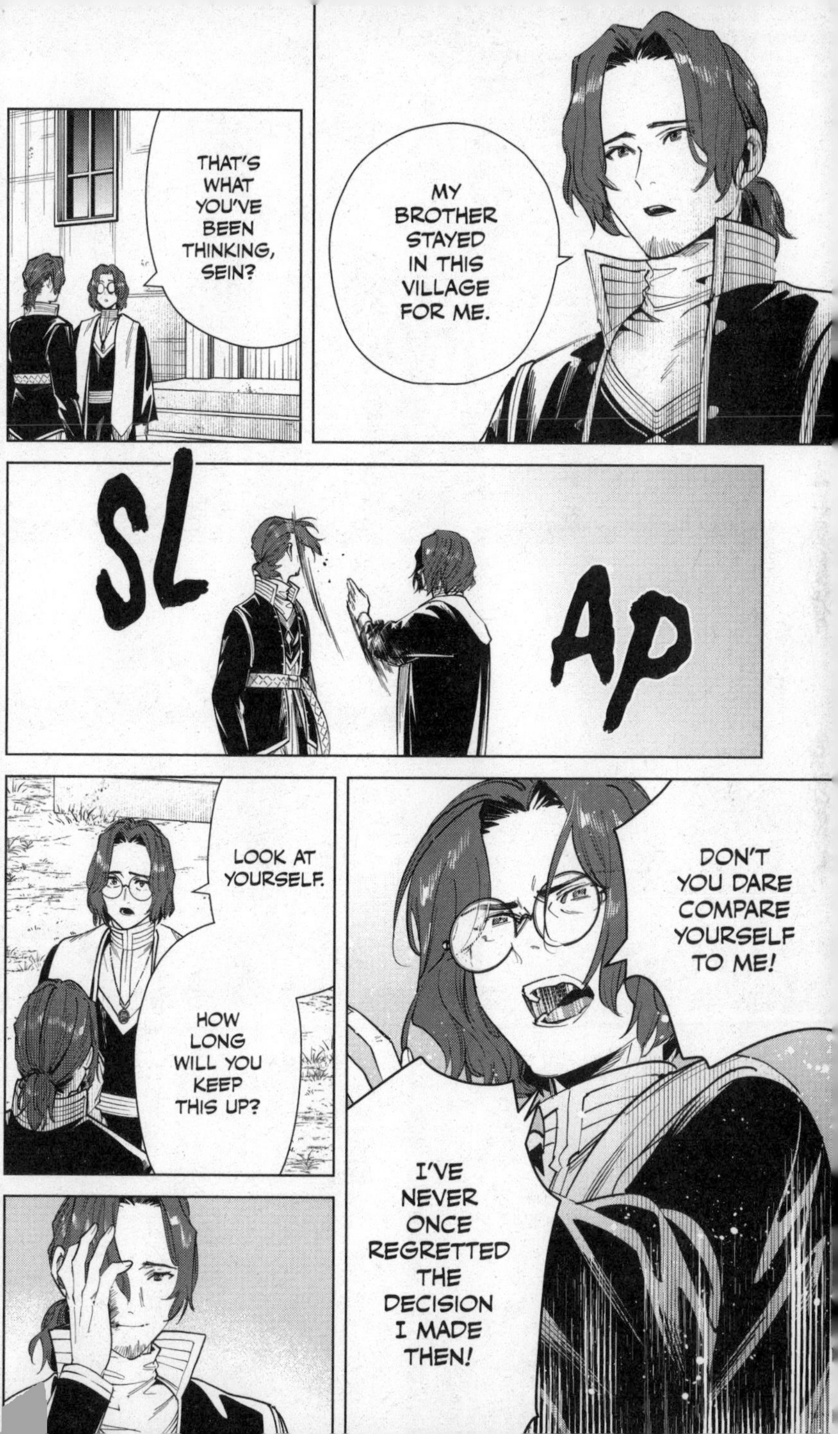
MY BROTHER STAYED IN THIS VILLAGE FOR ME.
THAT'S WHAT YOU'VE BEEN THINKING, SEIN?
SLAP
DON'T YOU DARE COMPARE YOURSELF TO ME!
I'VE NEVER ONCE REGRETTED THE DECISION I MADE THEN!
LOOK AT YOURSELF.
HOW LONG WILL YOU KEEP THIS UP?

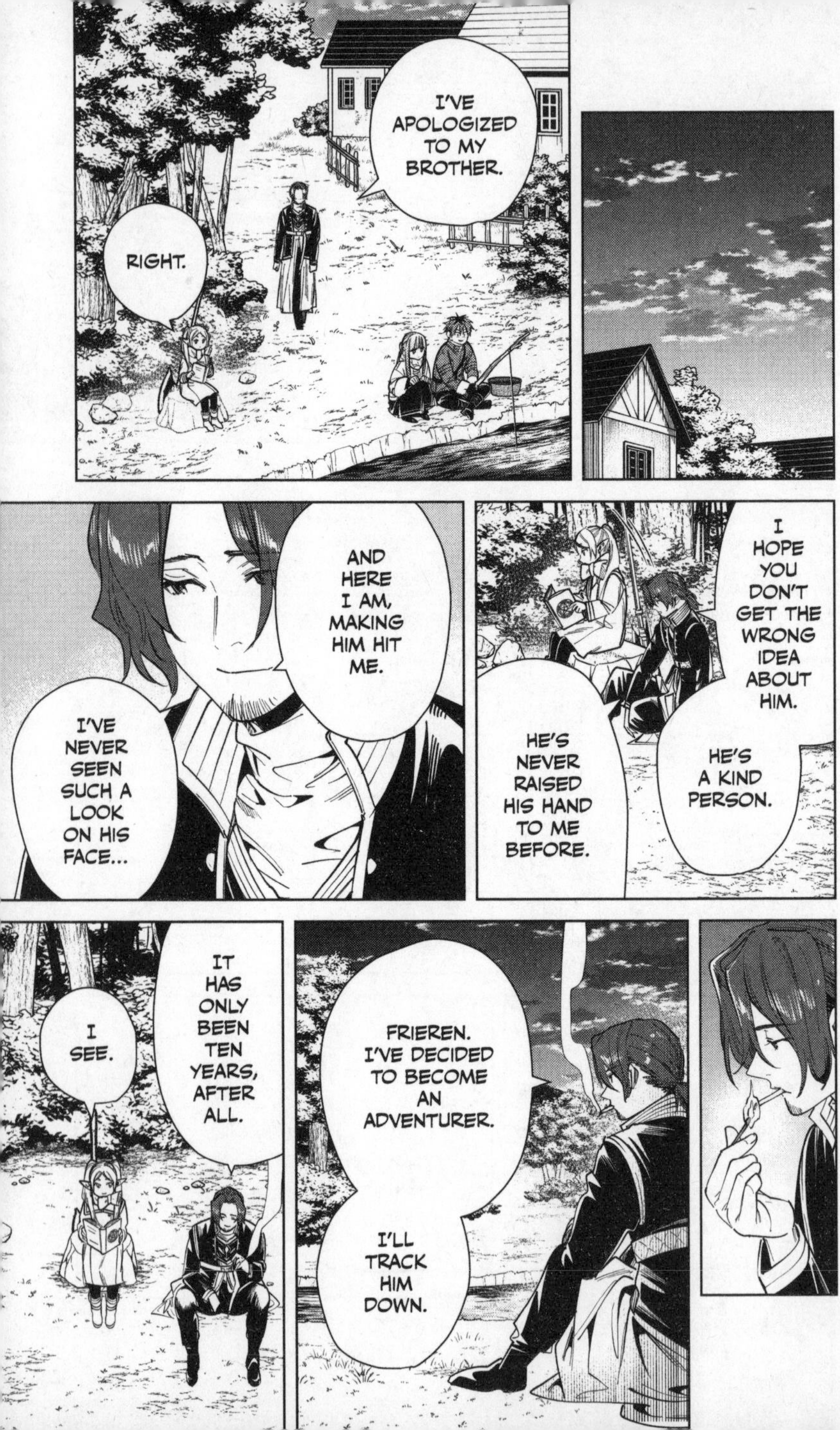
I'VE APOLOGIZED TO MY BROTHER.
RIGHT.
I HOPE YOU DON'T GET THE WRONG IDEA ABOUT HIM.
HE'S A KIND PERSON.
HE'S NEVER RAISED HIS HAND TO ME BEFORE.
AND HERE I AM, MAKING HIM HIT ME.
I'VE NEVER SEEN SUCH A LOOK ON HIS FACE...
FRIEREN. I'VE DECIDED TO BECOME AN ADVENTURER.
I'LL TRACK HIM DOWN.
IT HAS ONLY BEEN TEN YEARS, AFTER ALL.
I SEE.

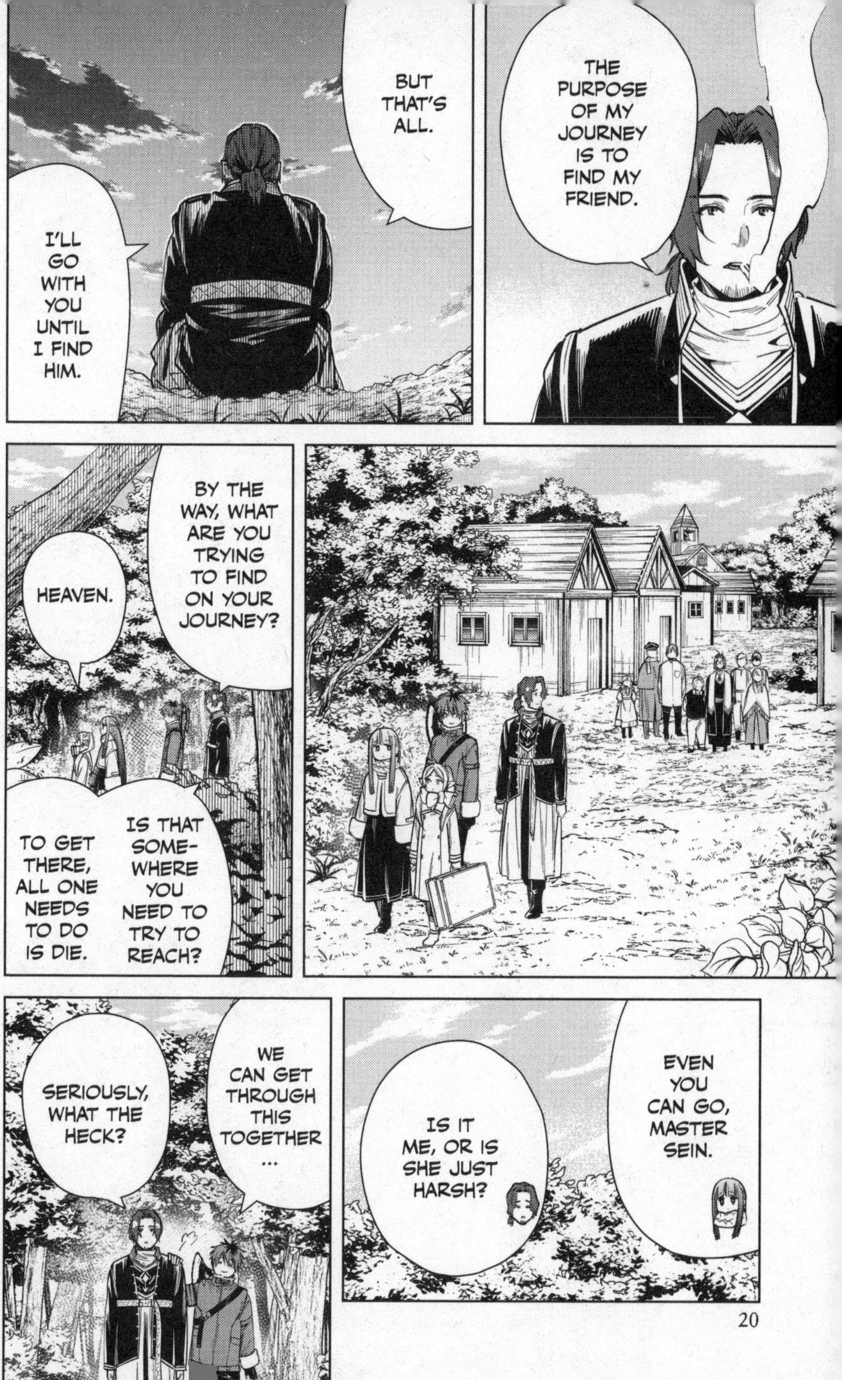
THE PURPOSE OF MY JOURNEY IS TO FIND MY FRIEND.
BUT THAT'S ALL.
I'LL GO WITH YOU UNTIL I FIND HIM.
BY THE WAY, WHAT ARE YOU TRYING TO FIND ON YOUR JOURNEY?
HEAVEN.
IS THAT SOMEWHERE YOU NEED TO TRY TO REACH?
TO GET THERE, ALL ONE NEEDS TO DO IS DIE.
EVEN YOU CAN GO, MASTER SEIN.
IS IT ME, OR IS SHE JUST HARSH?
WE CAN GET THROUGH THIS TOGETHER...
SERIOUSLY, WHAT THE HECK?

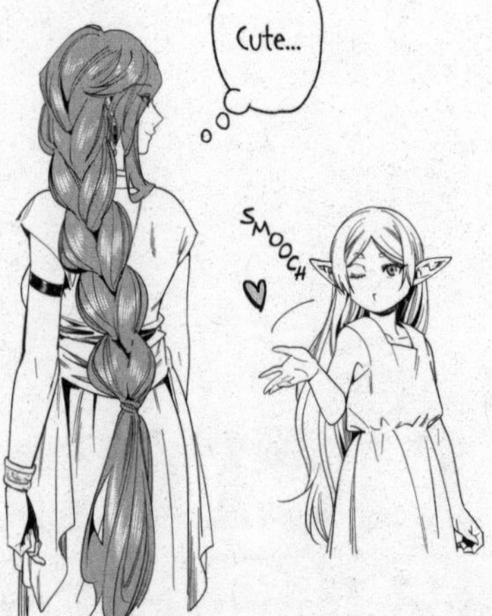
Cute...
SMOOCH

Frieren

Beyond Journey's End

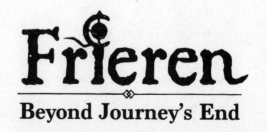

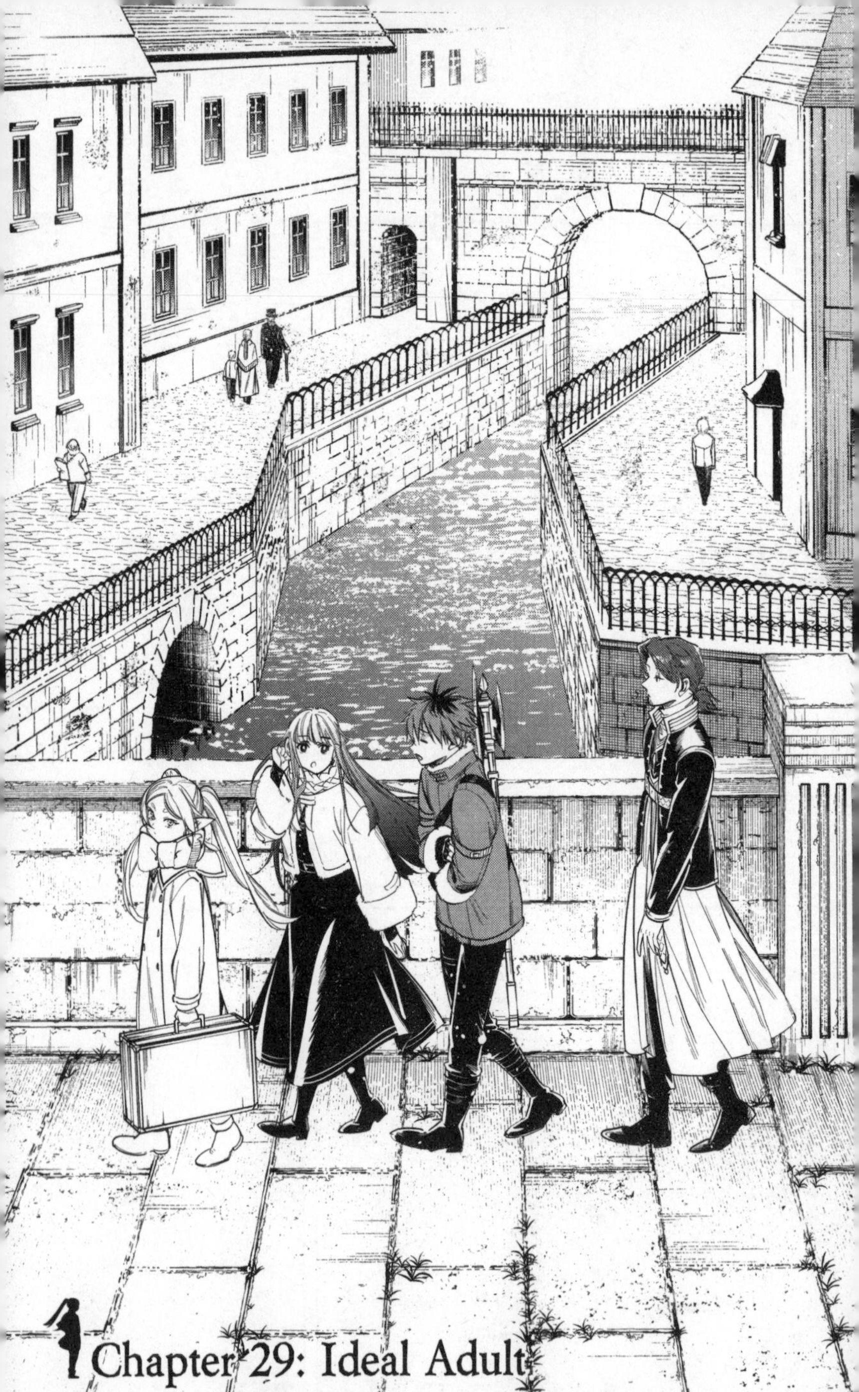

Chapter 29: Ideal Adult

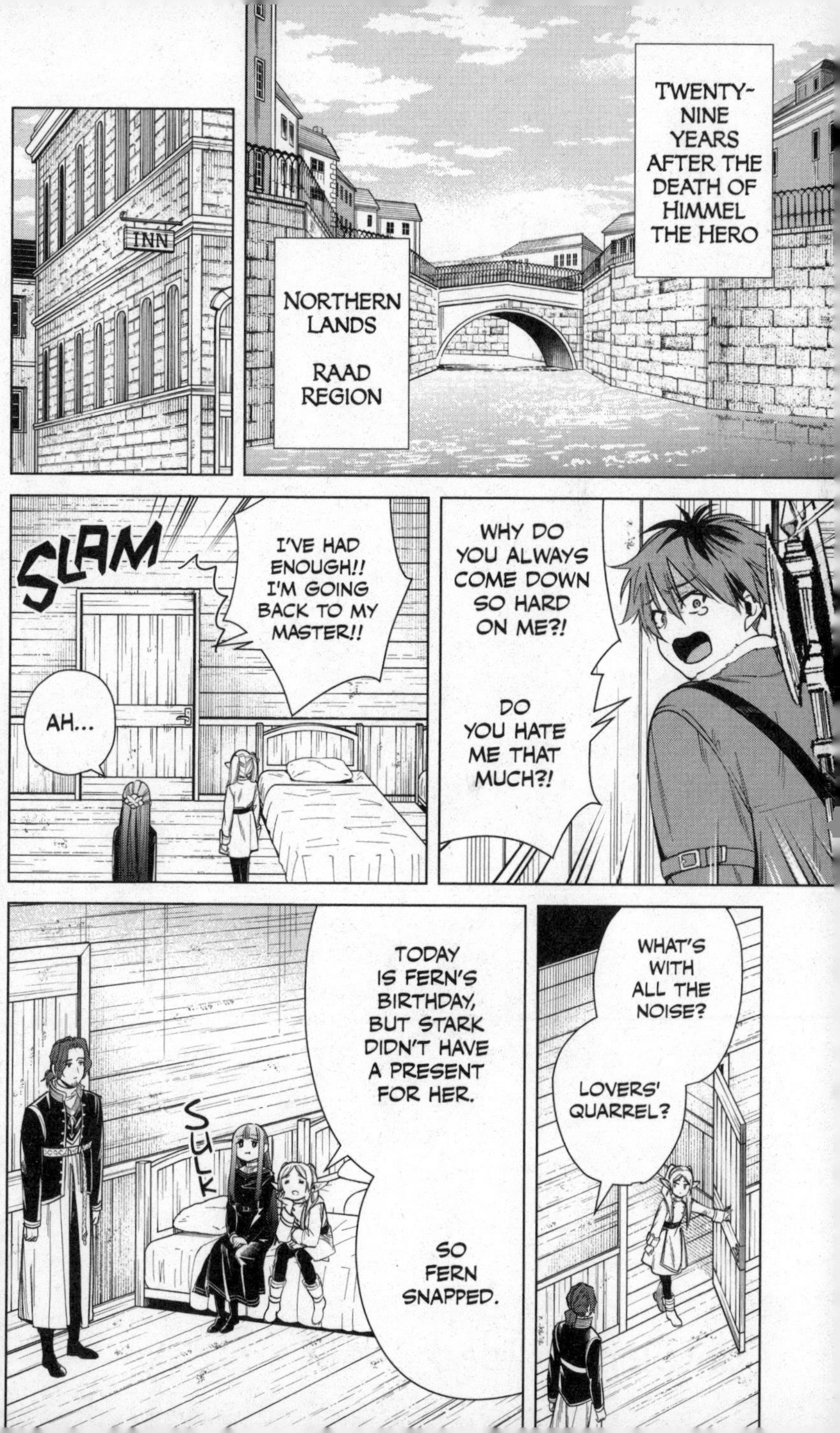
TWENTY-NINE YEARS AFTER THE DEATH OF HIMMEL THE HERO
NORTHERN LANDS
RAAD REGION
INN
WHY DO YOU ALWAYS COME DOWN SO HARD ON ME?!
DO YOU HATE ME THAT MUCH?!
I'VE HAD ENOUGH!! I'M GOING BACK TO MY MASTER!!
SLAM
AH...
WHAT'S WITH ALL THE NOISE?
LOVERS' QUARREL?
TODAY IS FERN'S BIRTHDAY, BUT STARK DIDN'T HAVE A PRESENT FOR HER.
SO FERN SNAPPED.
SULK

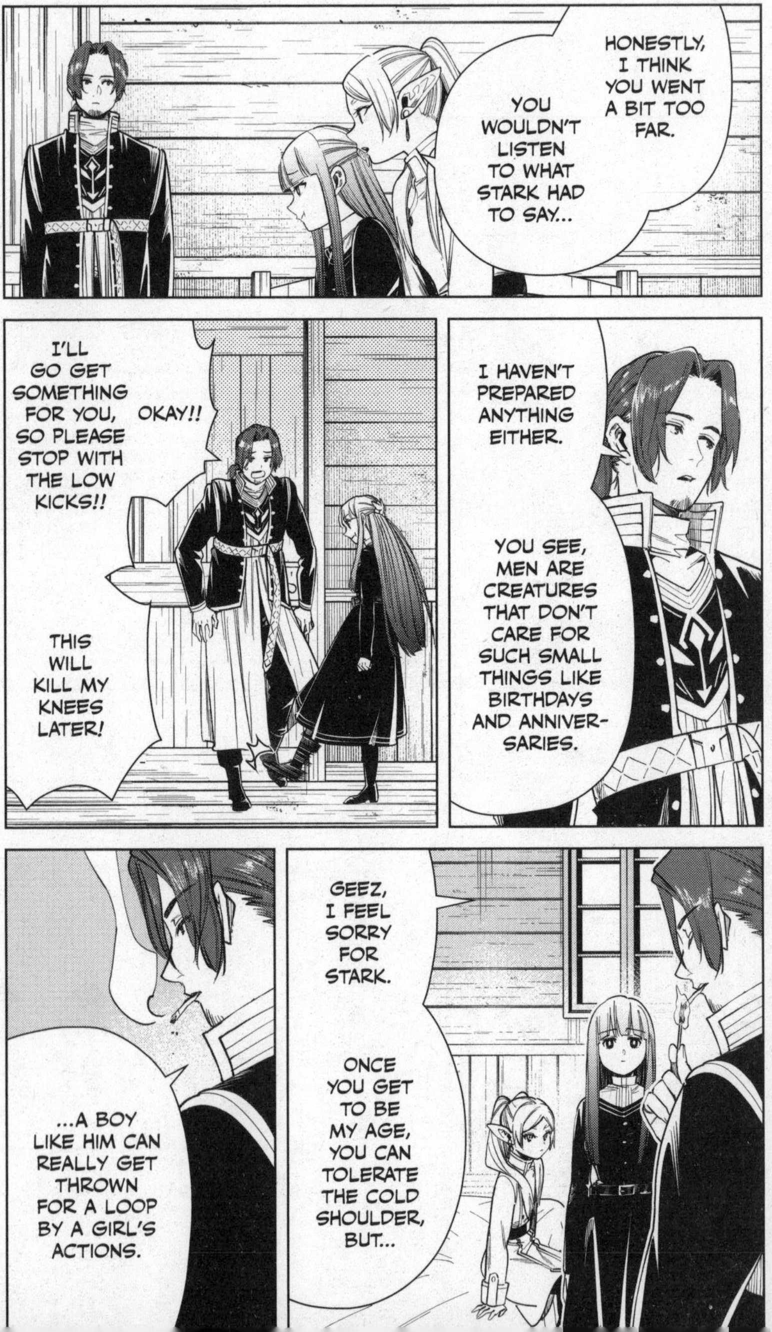
HONESTLY, I THINK YOU WENT A BIT TOO FAR.
YOU WOULDN'T LISTEN TO WHAT STARK HAD TO SAY...
I HAVEN'T PREPARED ANYTHING EITHER.
YOU SEE, MEN ARE CREATURES THAT DON'T CARE FOR SUCH SMALL THINGS LIKE BIRTHDAYS AND ANNIVER-SARIES.
OKAY!!
I'LL GO GET SOMETHING FOR YOU, SO PLEASE STOP WITH THE LOW KICKS!!
THIS WILL KILL MY KNEES LATER!
GEEZ, I FEEL SORRY FOR STARK.
ONCE YOU GET TO BE MY AGE, YOU CAN TOLERATE THE COLD SHOULDER, BUT...
...A BOY LIKE HIM CAN REALLY GET THROWN FOR A LOOP BY A GIRL'S ACTIONS.

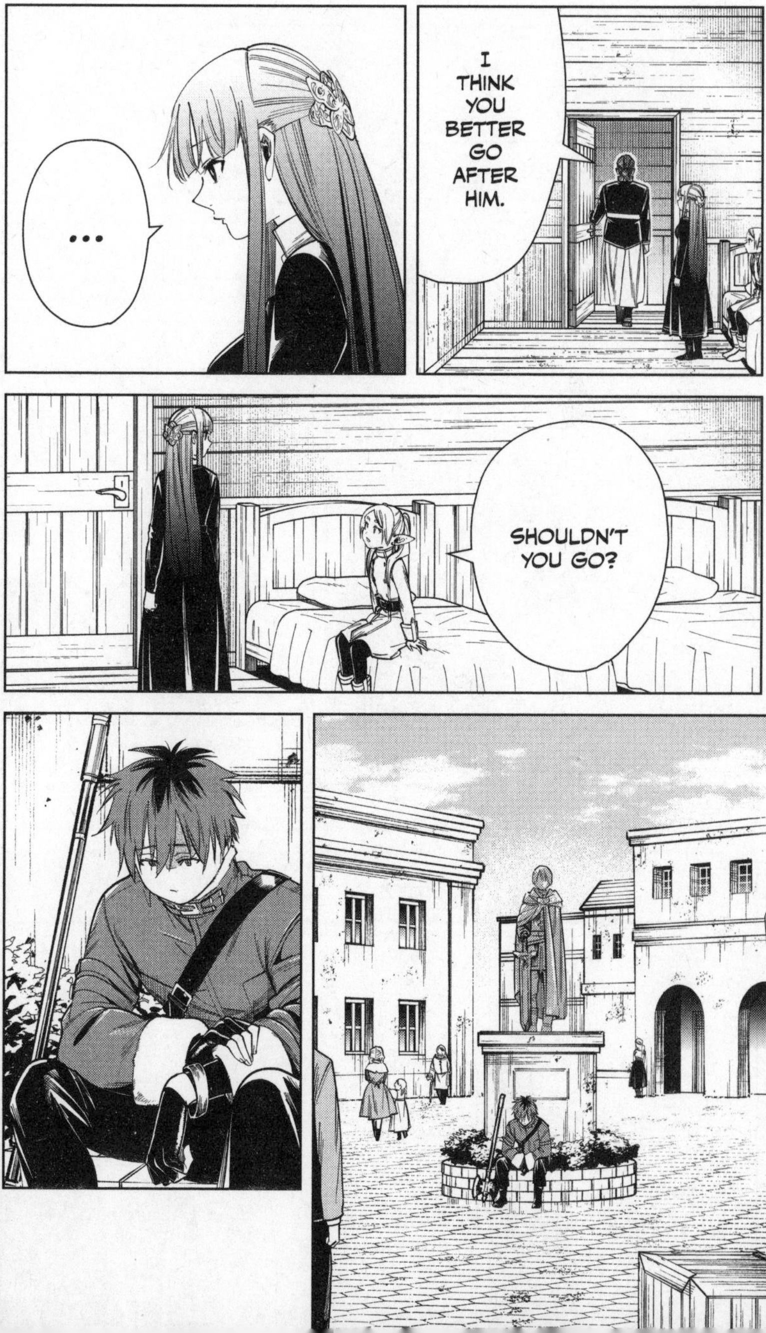
I THINK YOU BETTER GO AFTER HIM.
...
SHOULDN'T YOU GO?

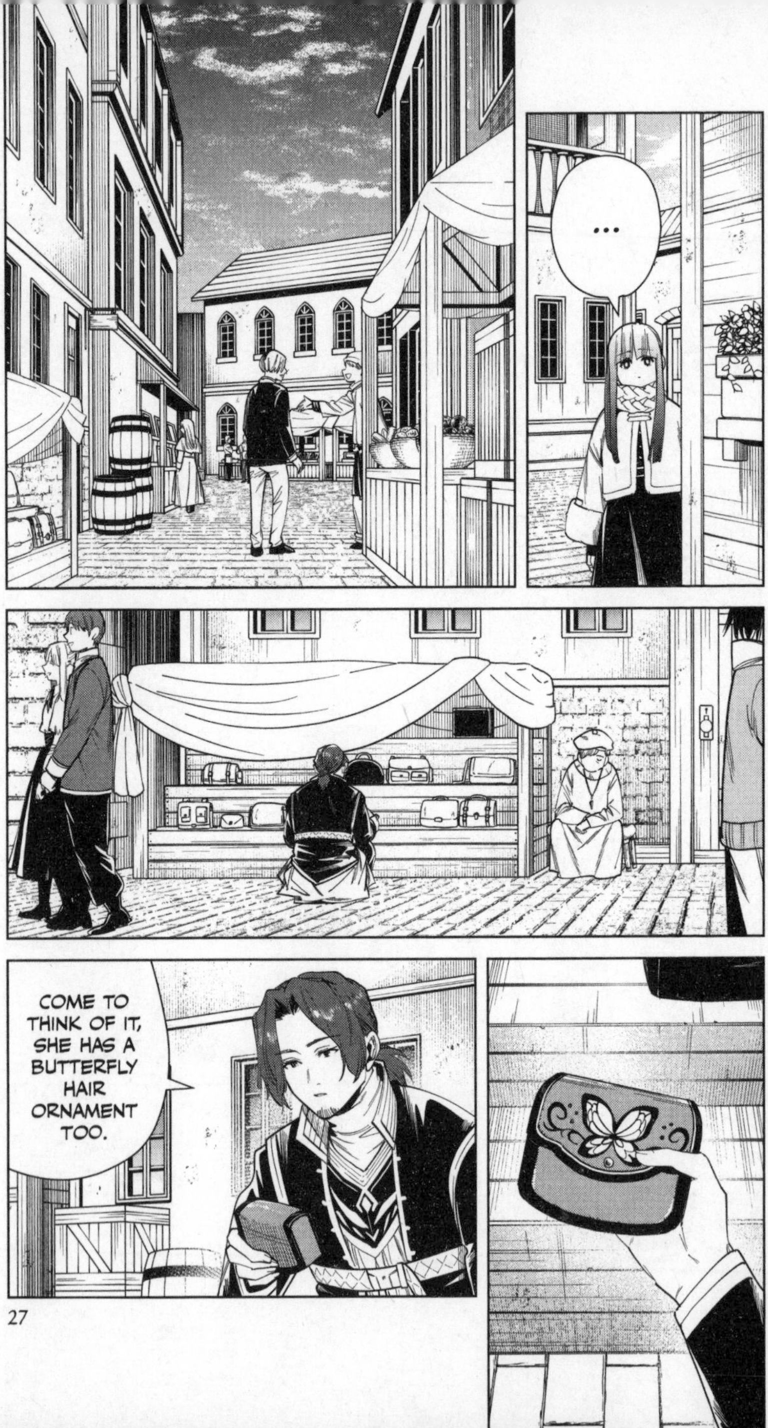
...
COME TO THINK OF IT, SHE HAS A BUTTERFLY HAIR ORNAMENT TOO.

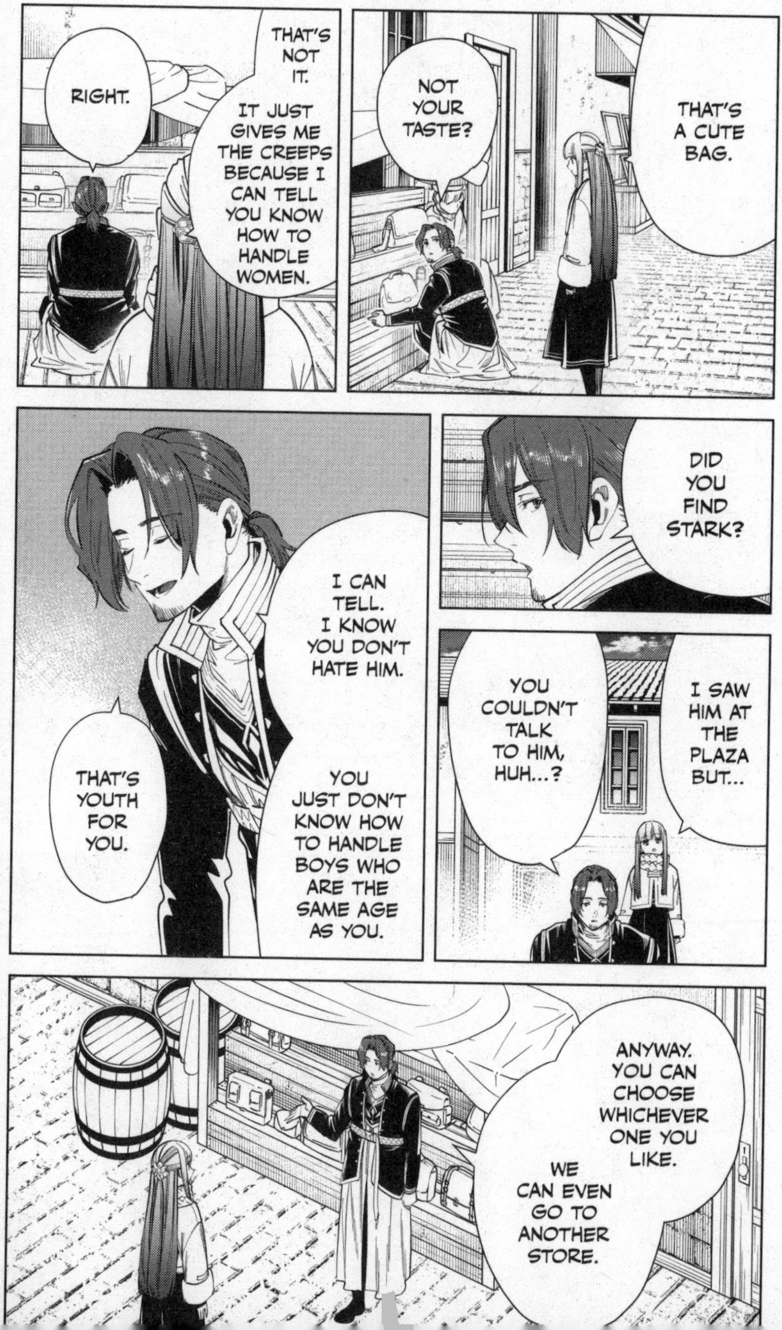
THAT'S A CUTE BAG.
NOT YOUR TASTE?
THAT'S NOT IT.
IT JUST GIVES ME THE CREEPS BECAUSE I CAN TELL YOU KNOW HOW TO HANDLE WOMEN.
RIGHT.
DID YOU FIND STARK?
I SAW HIM AT THE PLAZA BUT...
YOU COULDN'T TALK TO HIM, HUH...?
I CAN TELL. I KNOW YOU DON'T HATE HIM.
YOU JUST DON'T KNOW HOW TO HANDLE BOYS WHO ARE THE SAME AGE AS YOU.
THAT'S YOUTH FOR YOU.
ANYWAY. YOU CAN CHOOSE WHICHEVER ONE YOU LIKE.
WE CAN EVEN GO TO ANOTHER STORE.

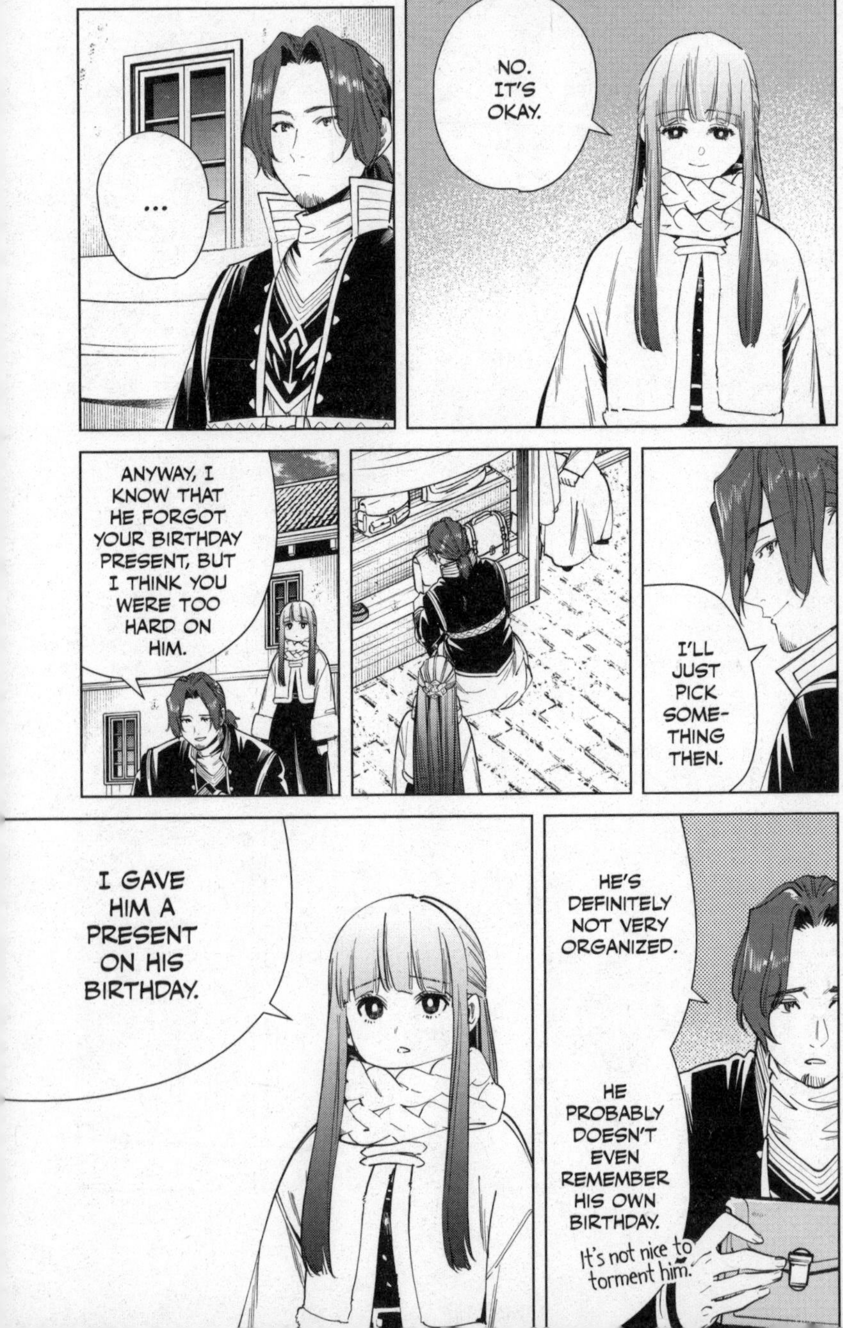
NO. IT'S OKAY.
...
I'LL JUST PICK SOME-THING THEN.
ANYWAY, I KNOW THAT HE FORGOT YOUR BIRTHDAY PRESENT, BUT I THINK YOU WERE TOO HARD ON HIM.
HE'S DEFINITELY NOT VERY ORGANIZED.
HE PROBABLY DOESN'T EVEN REMEMBER HIS OWN BIRTHDAY.
It's not nice to torment him.
I GAVE HIM A PRESENT ON HIS BIRTHDAY.

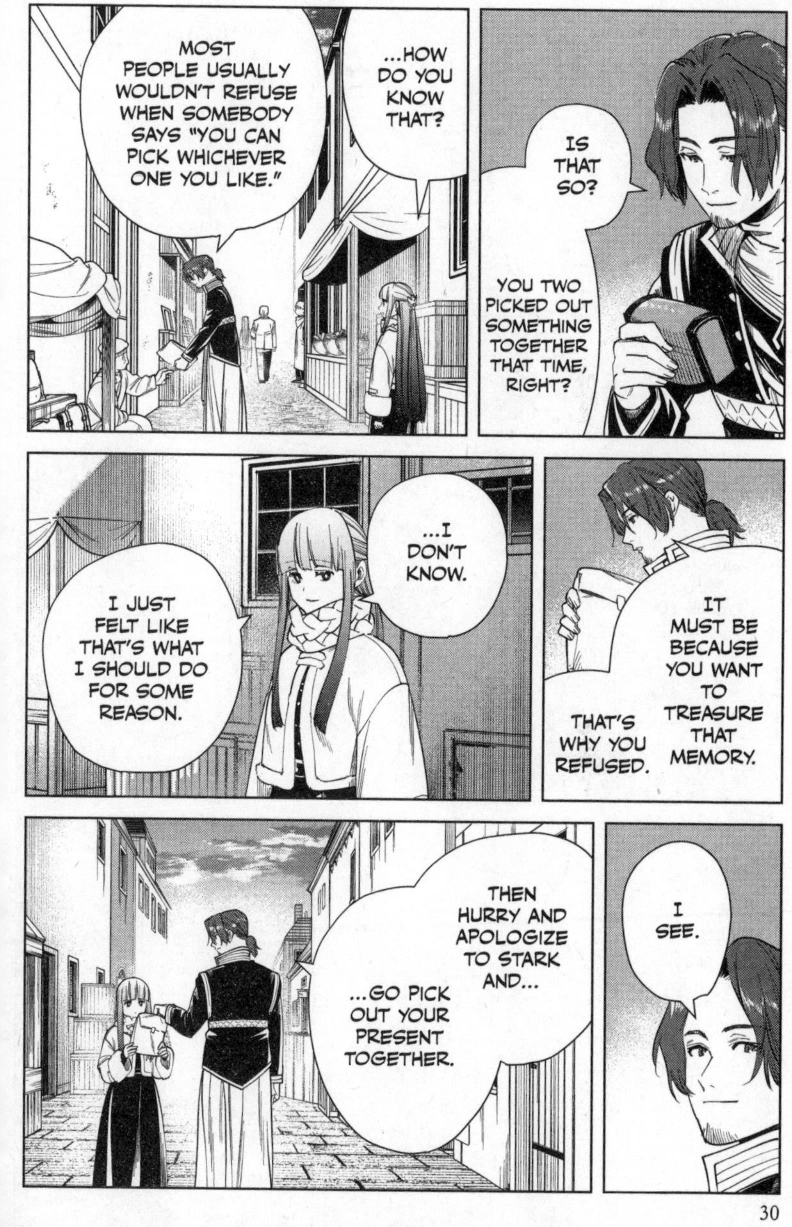
IS THAT SO?
YOU TWO PICKED OUT SOMETHING TOGETHER THAT TIME, RIGHT?
...HOW DO YOU KNOW THAT?
MOST PEOPLE USUALLY WOULDN'T REFUSE WHEN SOMEBODY SAYS "YOU CAN PICK WHICHEVER ONE YOU LIKE."
IT MUST BE BECAUSE YOU WANT TO TREASURE THAT MEMORY.
THAT'S WHY YOU REFUSED.
...I DON'T KNOW.
I JUST FELT LIKE THAT'S WHAT I SHOULD DO FOR SOME REASON.
I SEE.
THEN HURRY AND APOLOGIZE TO STARK AND...
...GO PICK OUT YOUR PRESENT TOGETHER.

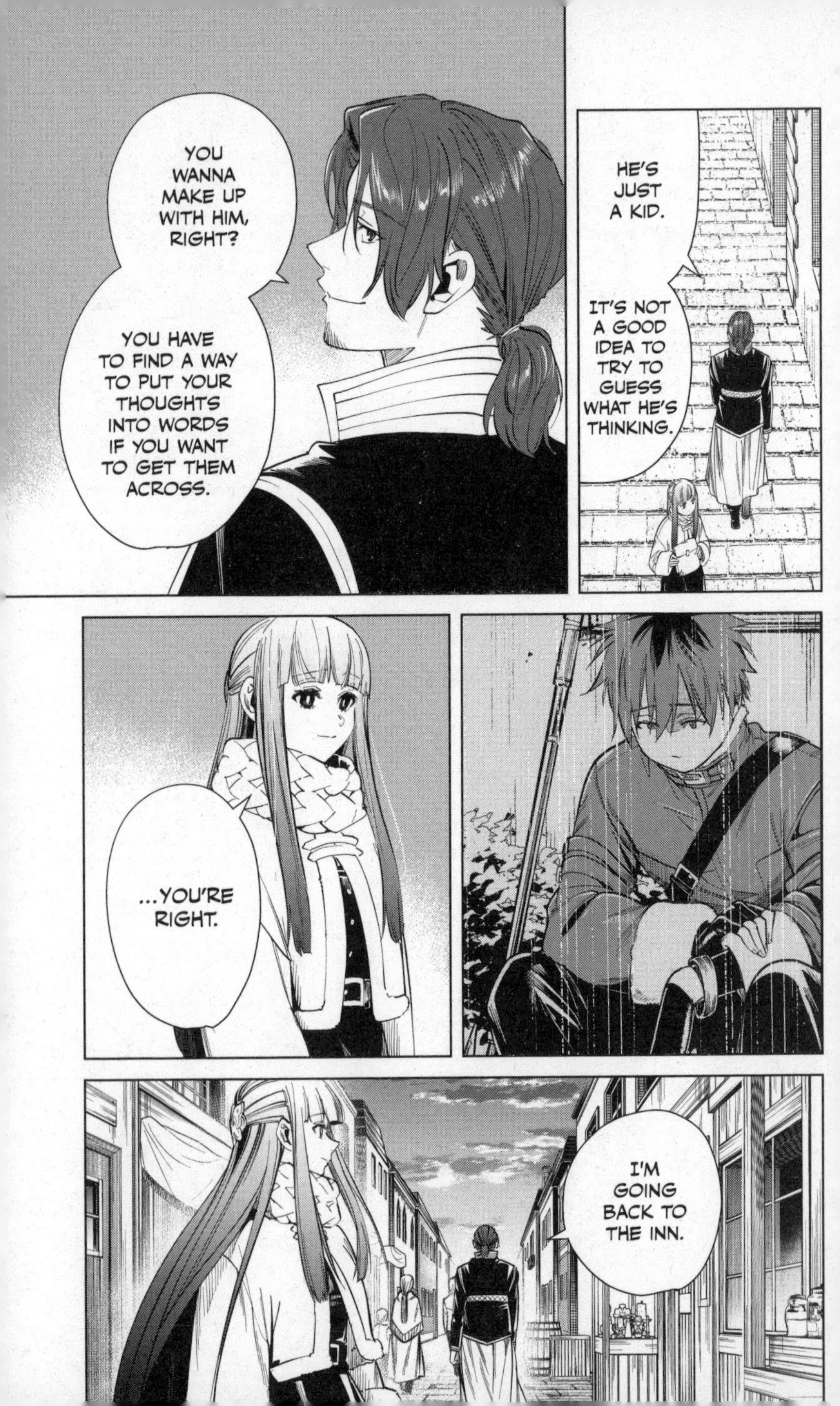
HE'S JUST A KID.
IT'S NOT A GOOD IDEA TO TRY TO GUESS WHAT HE'S THINKING.
YOU WANNA MAKE UP WITH HIM, RIGHT?
YOU HAVE TO FIND A WAY TO PUT YOUR THOUGHTS INTO WORDS IF YOU WANT TO GET THEM ACROSS.
...YOU'RE RIGHT.
I'M GOING BACK TO THE INN.

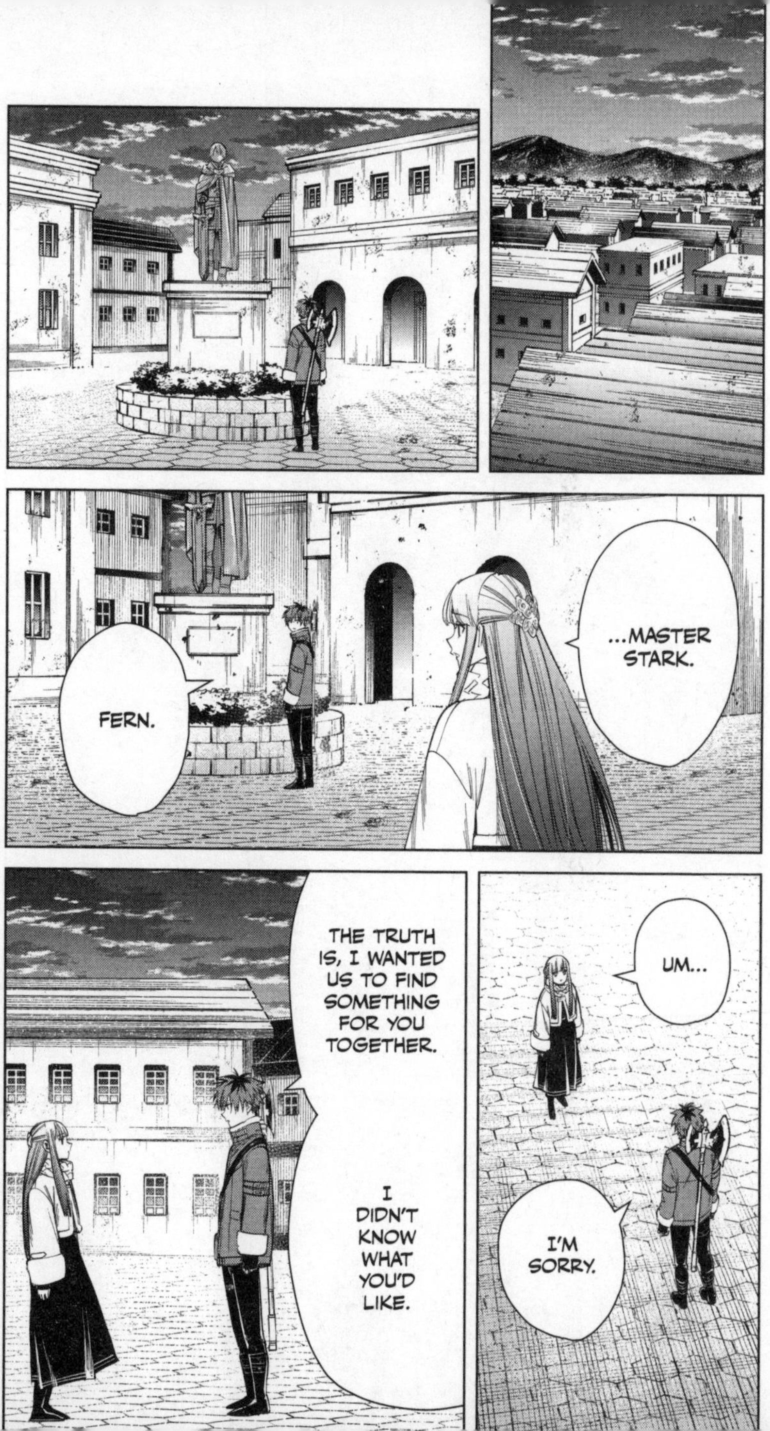
...MASTER STARK.
FERN.
UM...
I'M SORRY.
THE TRUTH IS, I WANTED US TO FIND SOMETHING FOR YOU TOGETHER.
I DIDN'T KNOW WHAT YOU'D LIKE.

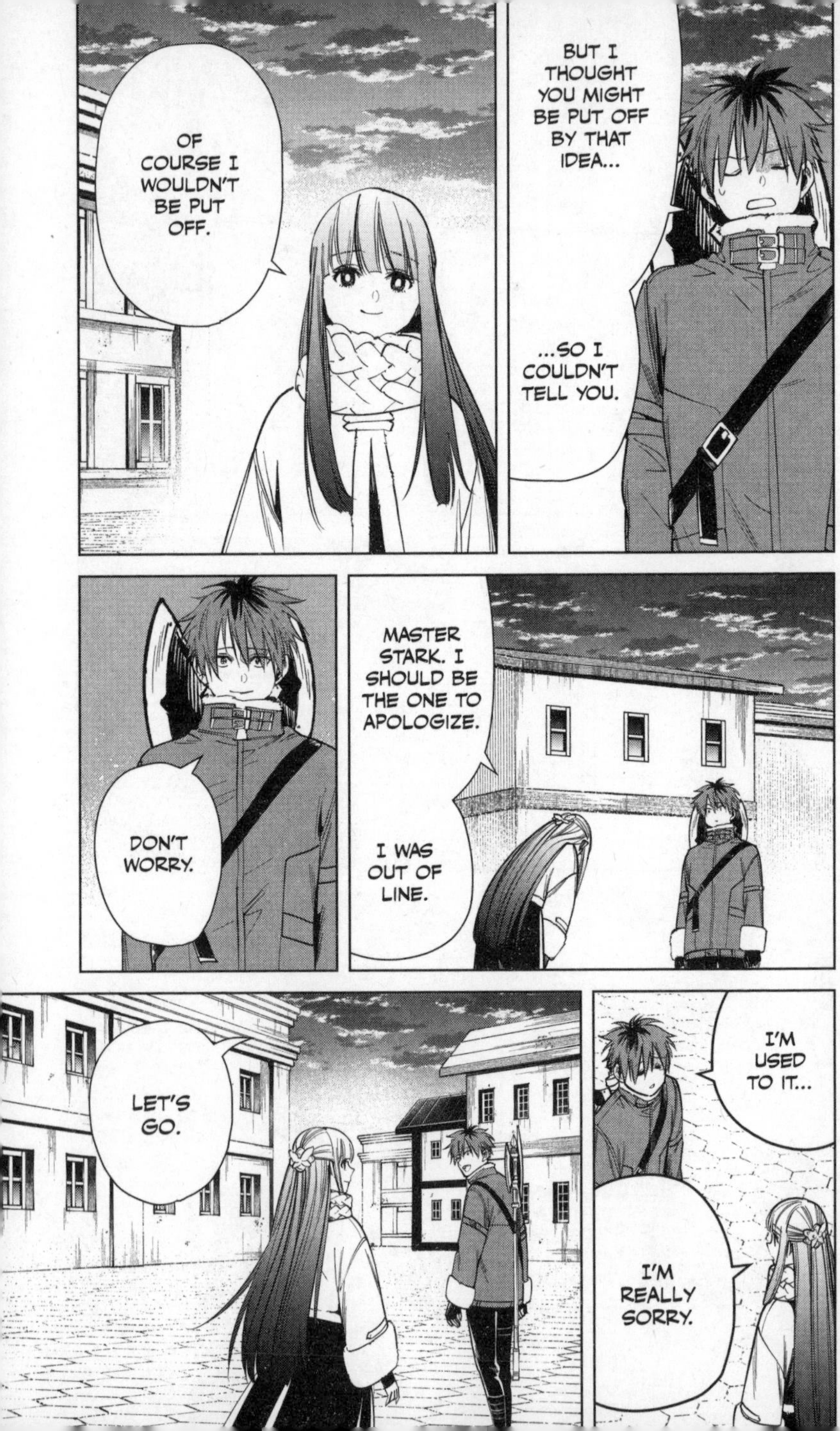
BUT I THOUGHT YOU MIGHT BE PUT OFF BY THAT IDEA...
...SO I COULDN'T TELL YOU.
OF COURSE I WOULDN'T BE PUT OFF.
MASTER STARK. I SHOULD BE THE ONE TO APOLOGIZE.
I WAS OUT OF LINE.
DON'T WORRY.
I'M USED TO IT...
I'M REALLY SORRY.
LET'S GO.

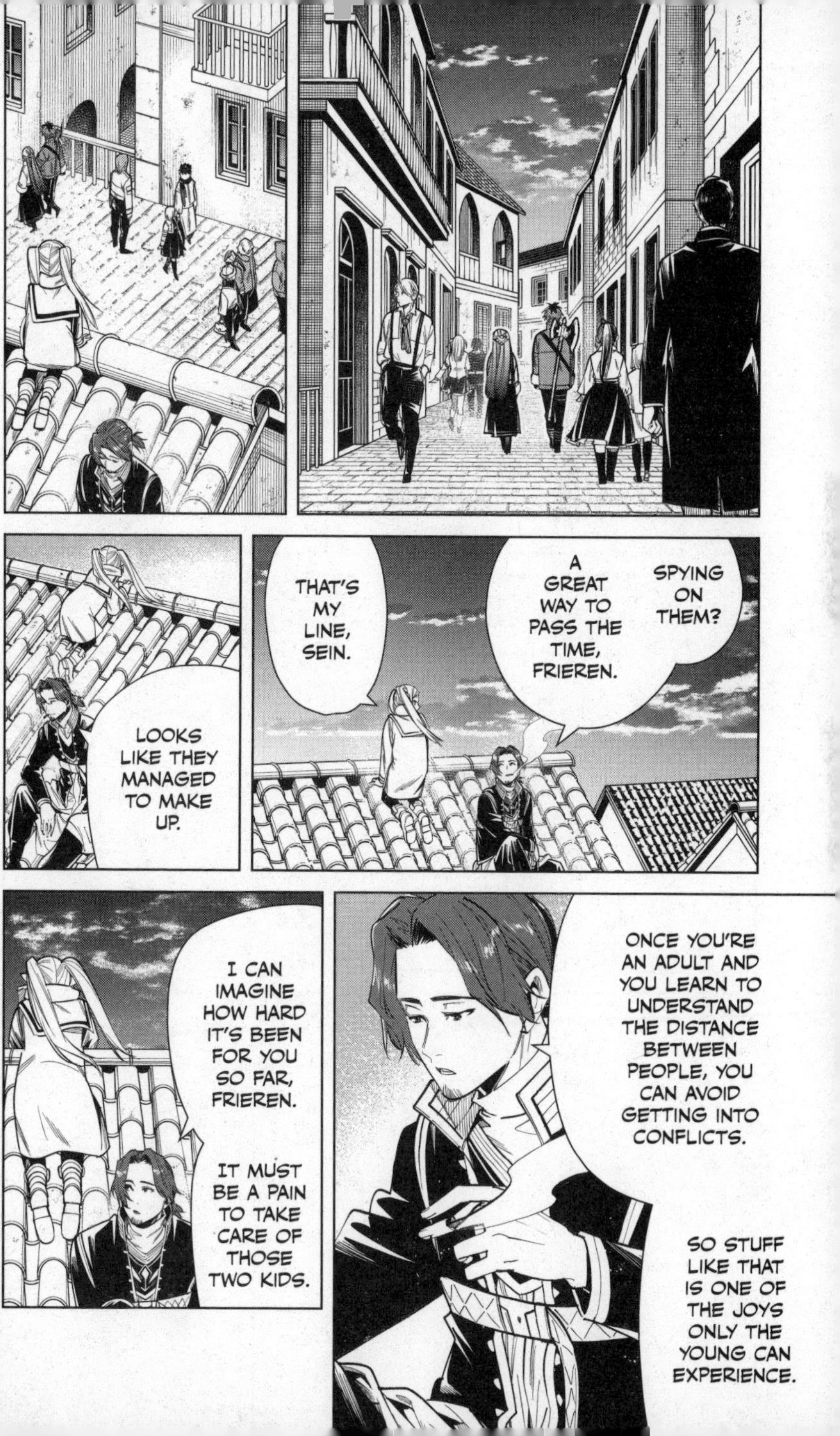
SPYING ON THEM?
A GREAT WAY TO PASS THE TIME, FRIEREN.
THAT'S MY LINE, SEIN.
LOOKS LIKE THEY MANAGED TO MAKE UP.
ONCE YOU'RE AN ADULT AND YOU LEARN TO UNDERSTAND THE DISTANCE BETWEEN PEOPLE, YOU CAN AVOID GETTING INTO CONFLICTS.
SO STUFF LIKE THAT IS ONE OF THE JOYS ONLY THE YOUNG CAN EXPERIENCE.
I CAN IMAGINE HOW HARD IT'S BEEN FOR YOU SO FAR, FRIEREN.
IT MUST BE A PAIN TO TAKE CARE OF THOSE TWO KIDS.

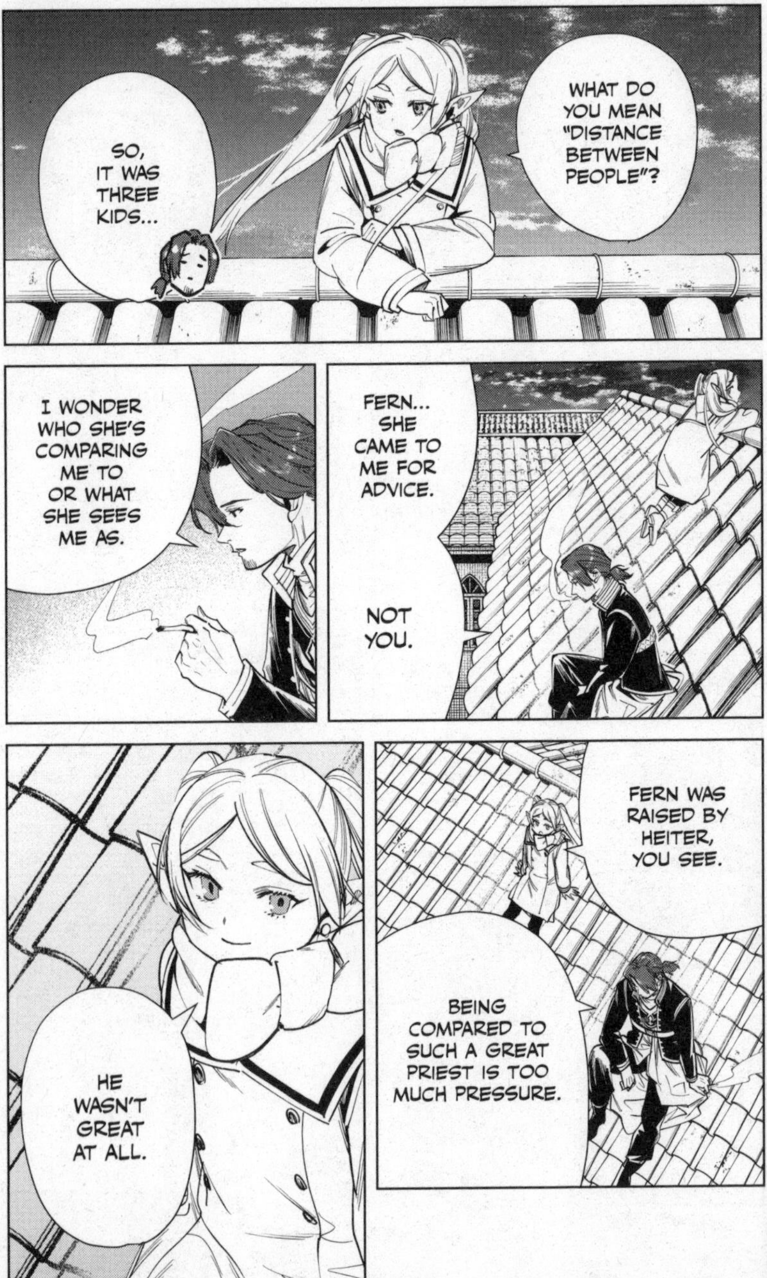
WHAT DO YOU MEAN "DISTANCE BETWEEN PEOPLE"?
SO, IT WAS THREE KIDS...
FERN... SHE CAME TO ME FOR ADVICE.
NOT YOU.
I WONDER WHO SHE'S COMPARING ME TO OR WHAT SHE SEES ME AS.
FERN WAS RAISED BY HEITER, YOU SEE.
BEING COMPARED TO SUCH A GREAT PRIEST IS TOO MUCH PRESSURE.
HE WASN'T GREAT AT ALL.

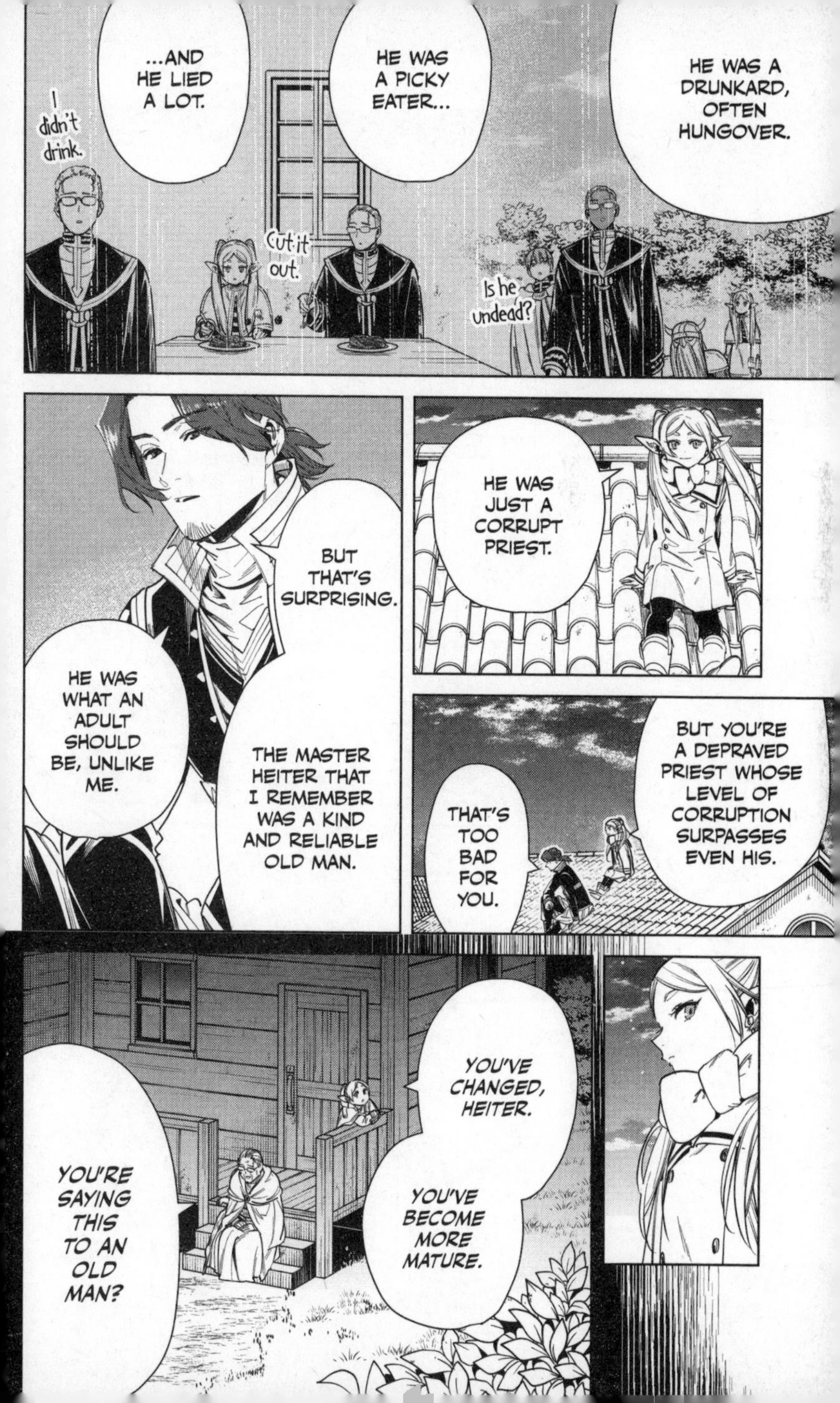
HE WAS A DRUNKARD, OFTEN HUNGOVER.
Is he undead?
HE WAS A PICKY EATER...
Cut it out.
...AND HE LIED A LOT.
I didn't drink.
HE WAS JUST A CORRUPT PRIEST.
BUT YOU'RE A DEPRAVED PRIEST WHOSE LEVEL OF CORRUPTION SURPASSES EVEN HIS.
THAT'S TOO BAD FOR YOU.
BUT THAT'S SURPRISING.
THE MASTER HEITER THAT I REMEMBER WAS A KIND AND RELIABLE OLD MAN.
HE WAS WHAT AN ADULT SHOULD BE, UNLIKE ME.
YOU'VE CHANGED, HEITER.
YOU'VE BECOME MORE MATURE.
YOU'RE SAYING THIS TO AN OLD MAN?

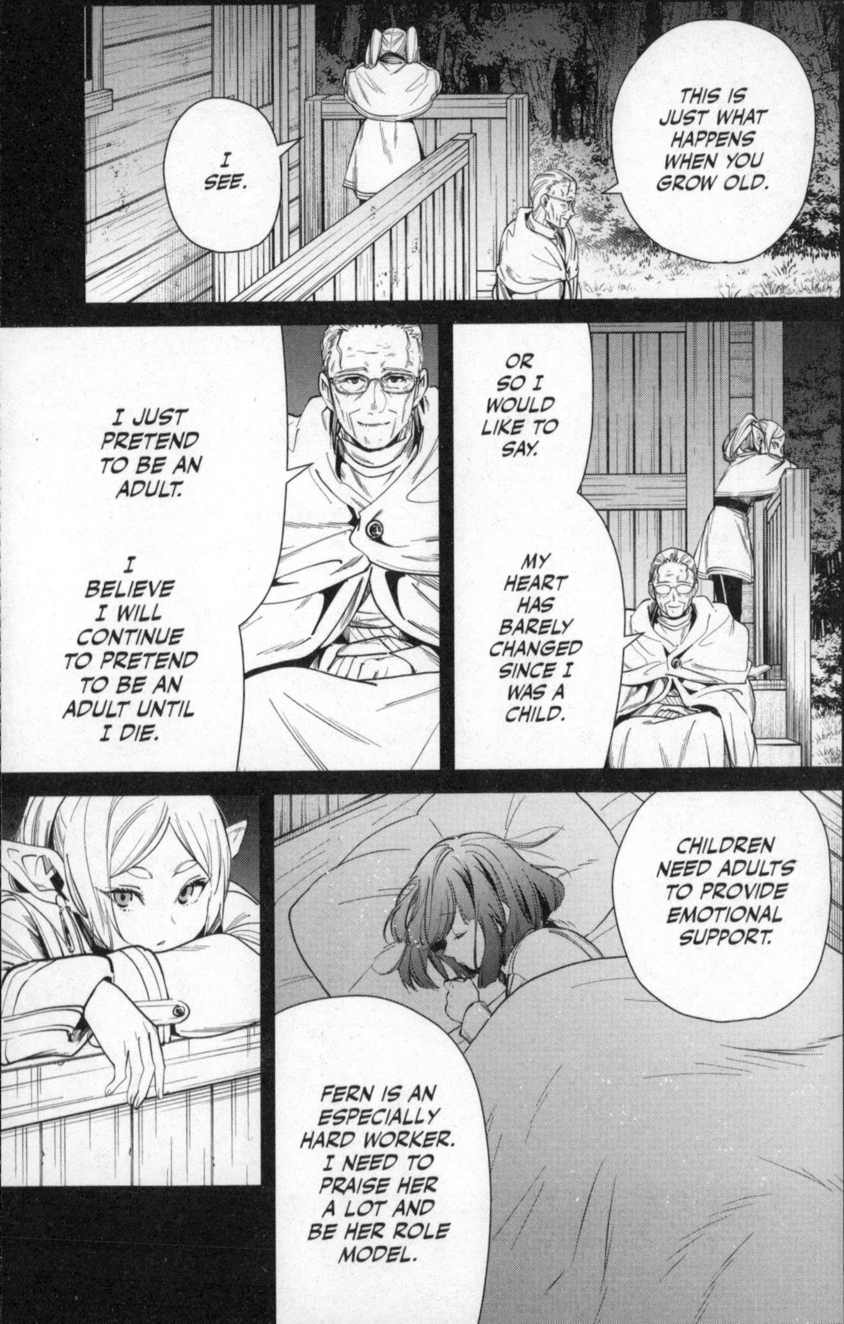
THIS IS JUST WHAT HAPPENS WHEN YOU GROW OLD.
I SEE.
OR SO I WOULD LIKE TO SAY.
MY HEART HAS BARELY CHANGED SINCE I WAS A CHILD.
I JUST PRETEND TO BE AN ADULT.
I BELIEVE I WILL CONTINUE TO PRETEND TO BE AN ADULT UNTIL I DIE.
CHILDREN NEED ADULTS TO PROVIDE EMOTIONAL SUPPORT.
FERN IS AN ESPECIALLY HARD WORKER. I NEED TO PRAISE HER A LOT AND BE HER ROLE MODEL.

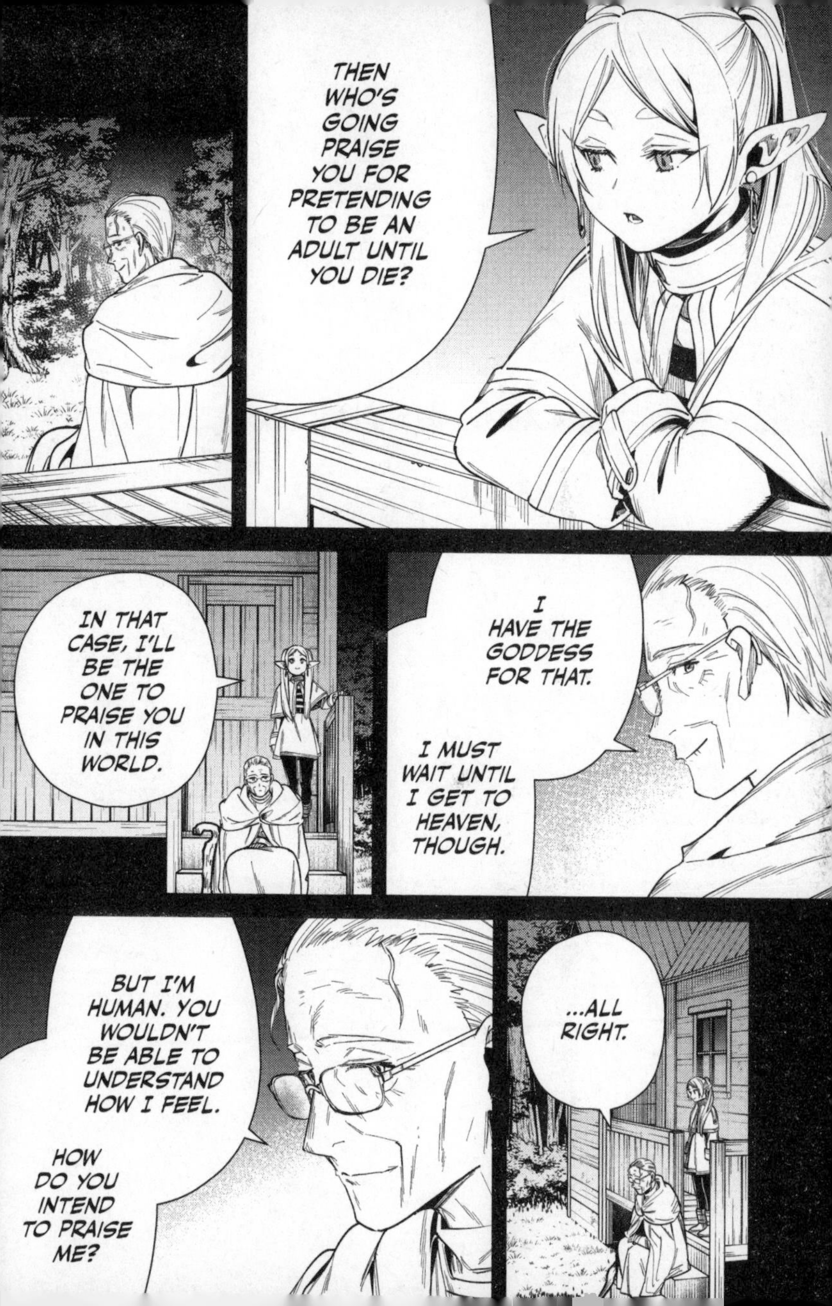
THEN WHO'S GOING PRAISE YOU FOR PRETENDING TO BE AN ADULT UNTIL YOU DIE?
I HAVE THE GODDESS FOR THAT.
I MUST WAIT UNTIL I GET TO HEAVEN, THOUGH.
IN THAT CASE, I'LL BE THE ONE TO PRAISE YOU IN THIS WORLD.
...ALL RIGHT.
BUT I'M HUMAN. YOU WOULDN'T BE ABLE TO UNDERSTAND HOW I FEEL.
HOW DO YOU INTEND TO PRAISE ME?

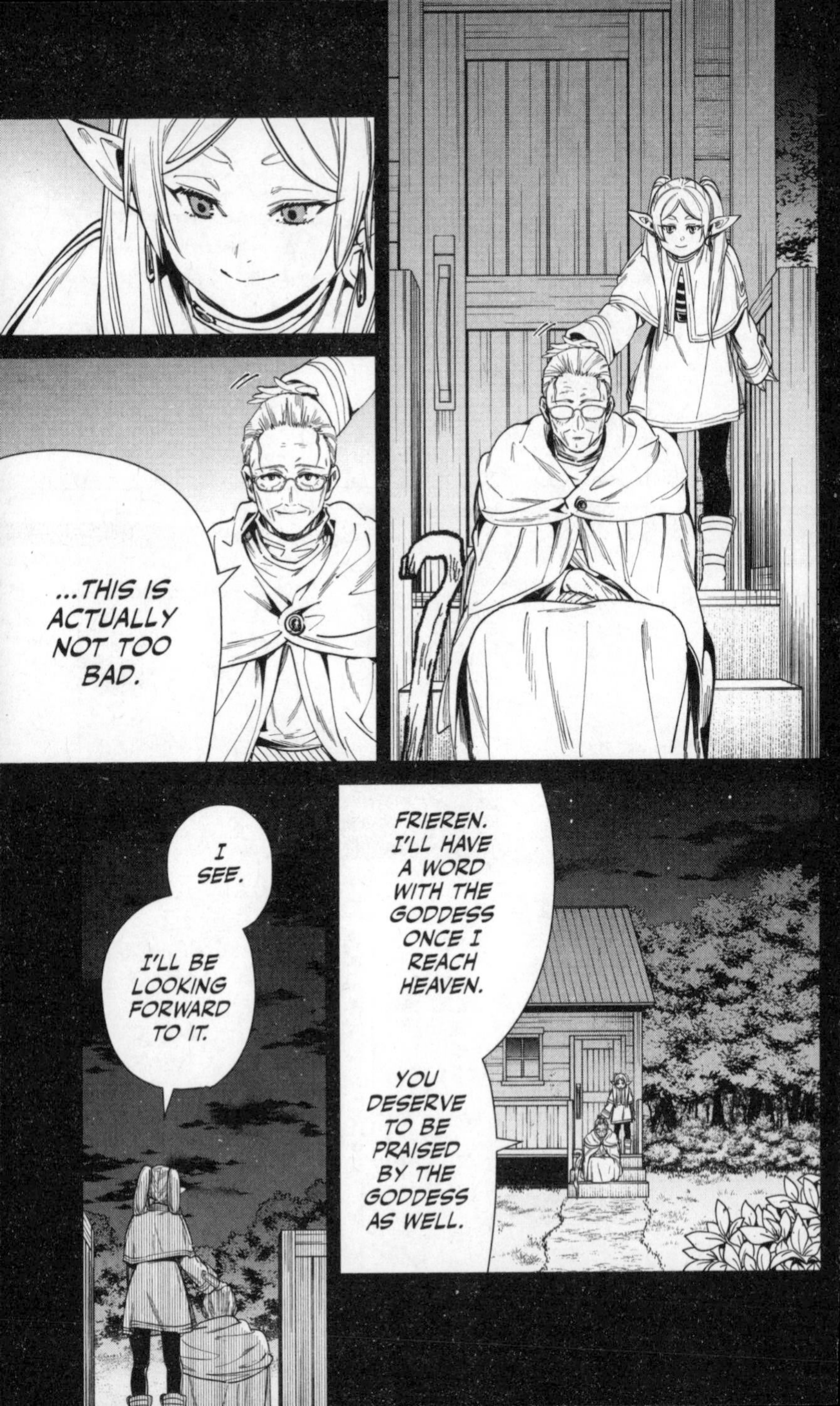
...THIS IS ACTUALLY NOT TOO BAD.
FRIEREN. I'LL HAVE A WORD WITH THE GODDESS ONCE I REACH HEAVEN.
YOU DESERVE TO BE PRAISED BY THE GODDESS AS WELL.
I SEE.
I'LL BE LOOKING FORWARD TO IT.

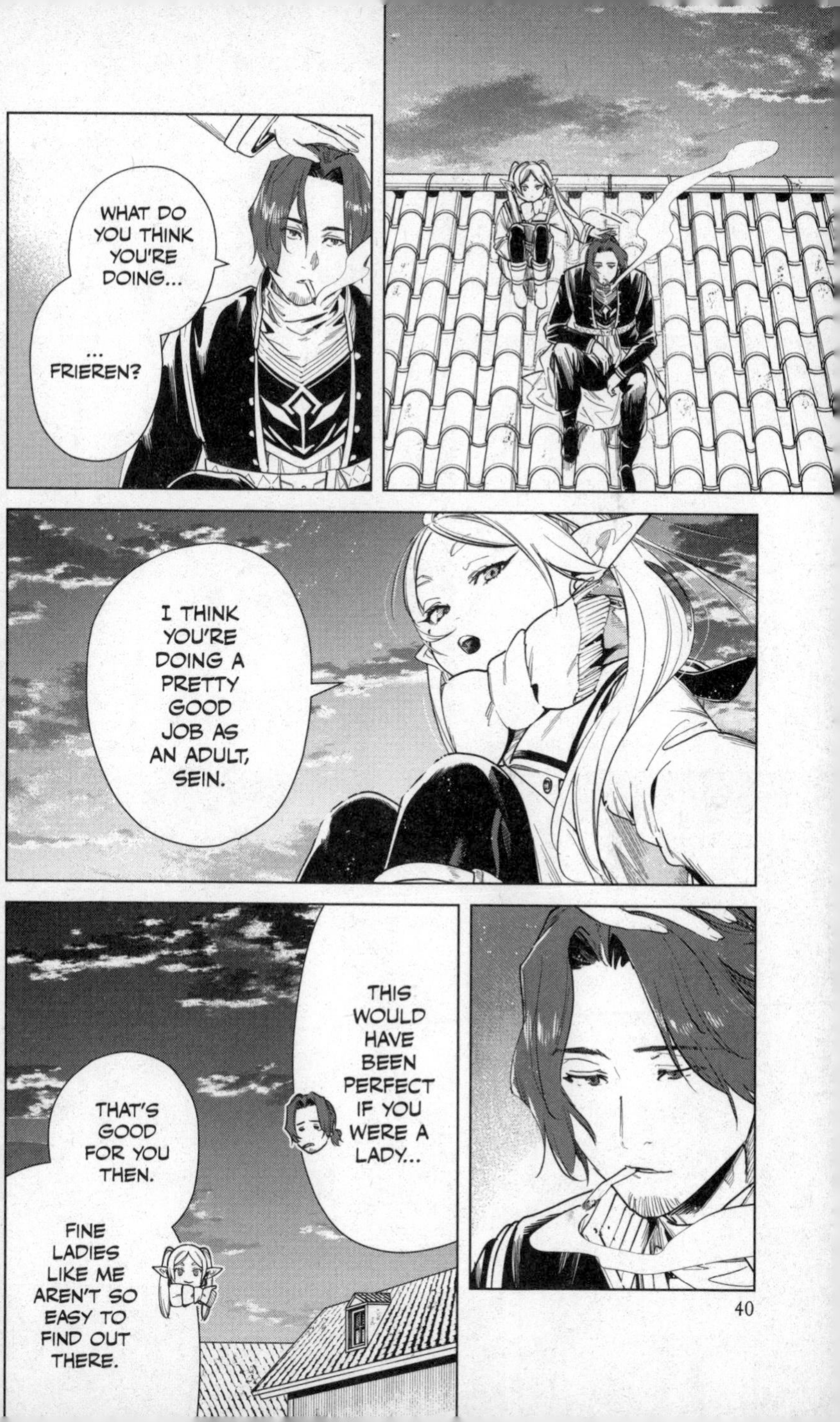
WHAT DO YOU THINK YOU'RE DOING...
... FRIEREN?
I THINK YOU'RE DOING A PRETTY GOOD JOB AS AN ADULT, SEIN.
THIS WOULD HAVE BEEN PERFECT IF YOU WERE A LADY...
THAT'S GOOD FOR YOU THEN.
FINE LADIES LIKE ME AREN'T SO EASY TO FIND OUT THERE.

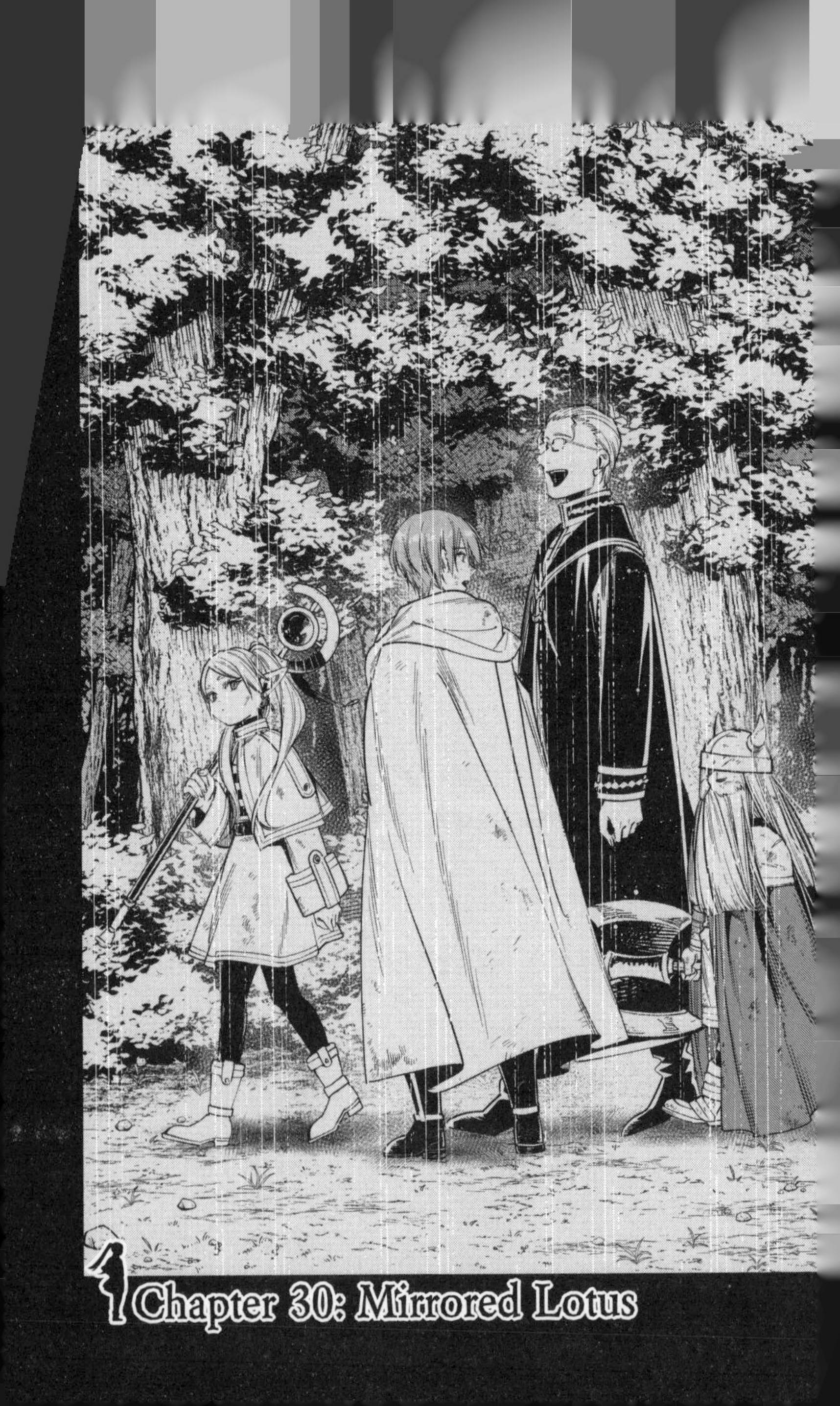

Chapter 30: Mirrored Lotus

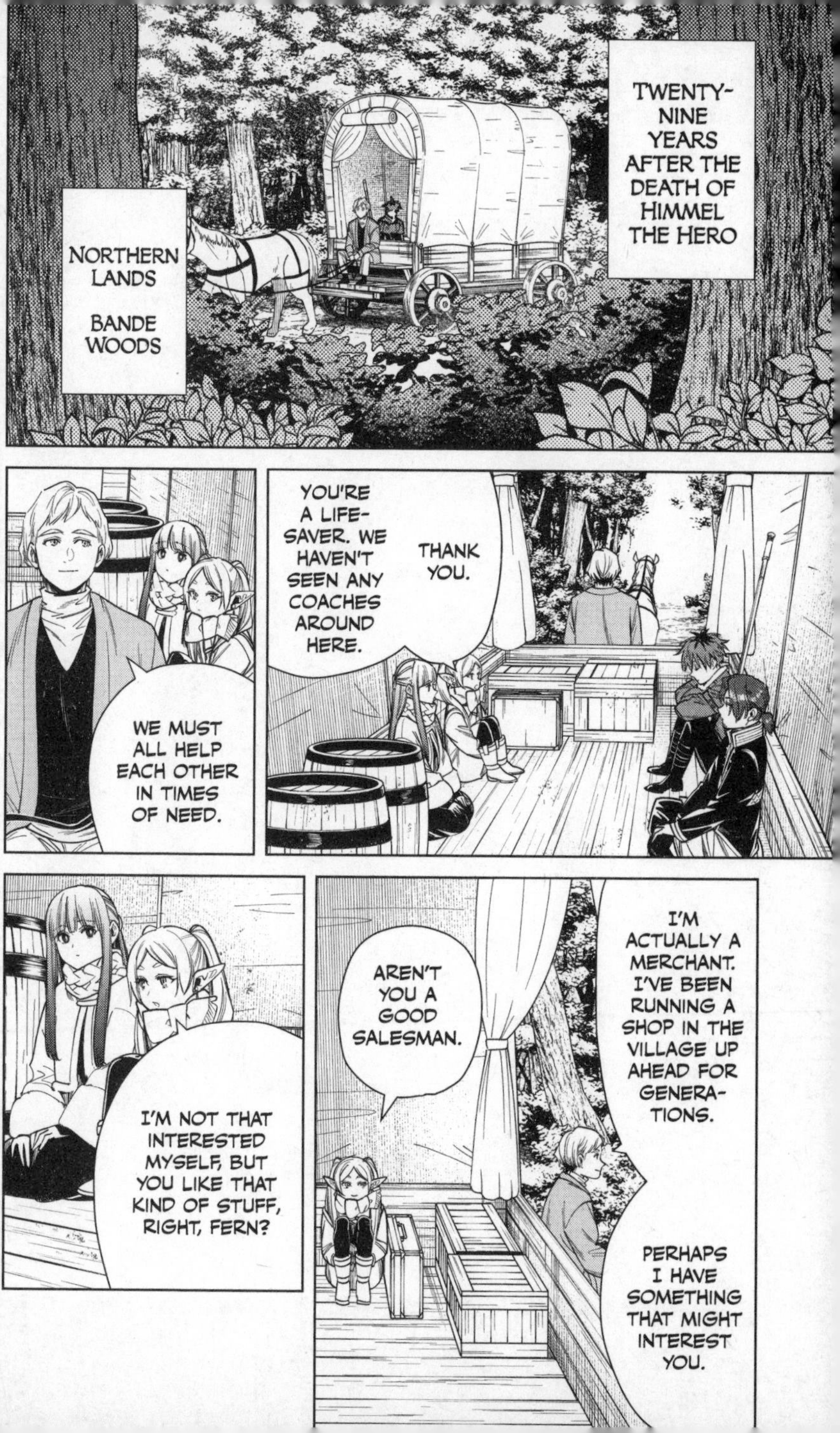

TWENTY-NINE YEARS AFTER THE DEATH OF HIMMEL THE HERO
NORTHERN LANDS
BANDE WOODS
THANK YOU.
YOU'RE A LIFE-SAVER. WE HAVEN'T SEEN ANY COACHES AROUND HERE.
WE MUST ALL HELP EACH OTHER IN TIMES OF NEED.
I'M ACTUALLY A MERCHANT. I'VE BEEN RUNNING A SHOP IN THE VILLAGE UP AHEAD FOR GENERA-TIONS.
PERHAPS I HAVE SOMETHING THAT MIGHT INTEREST YOU.
AREN'T YOU A GOOD SALESMAN.
I'M NOT THAT INTERESTED MYSELF, BUT YOU LIKE THAT KIND OF STUFF, RIGHT, FERN?

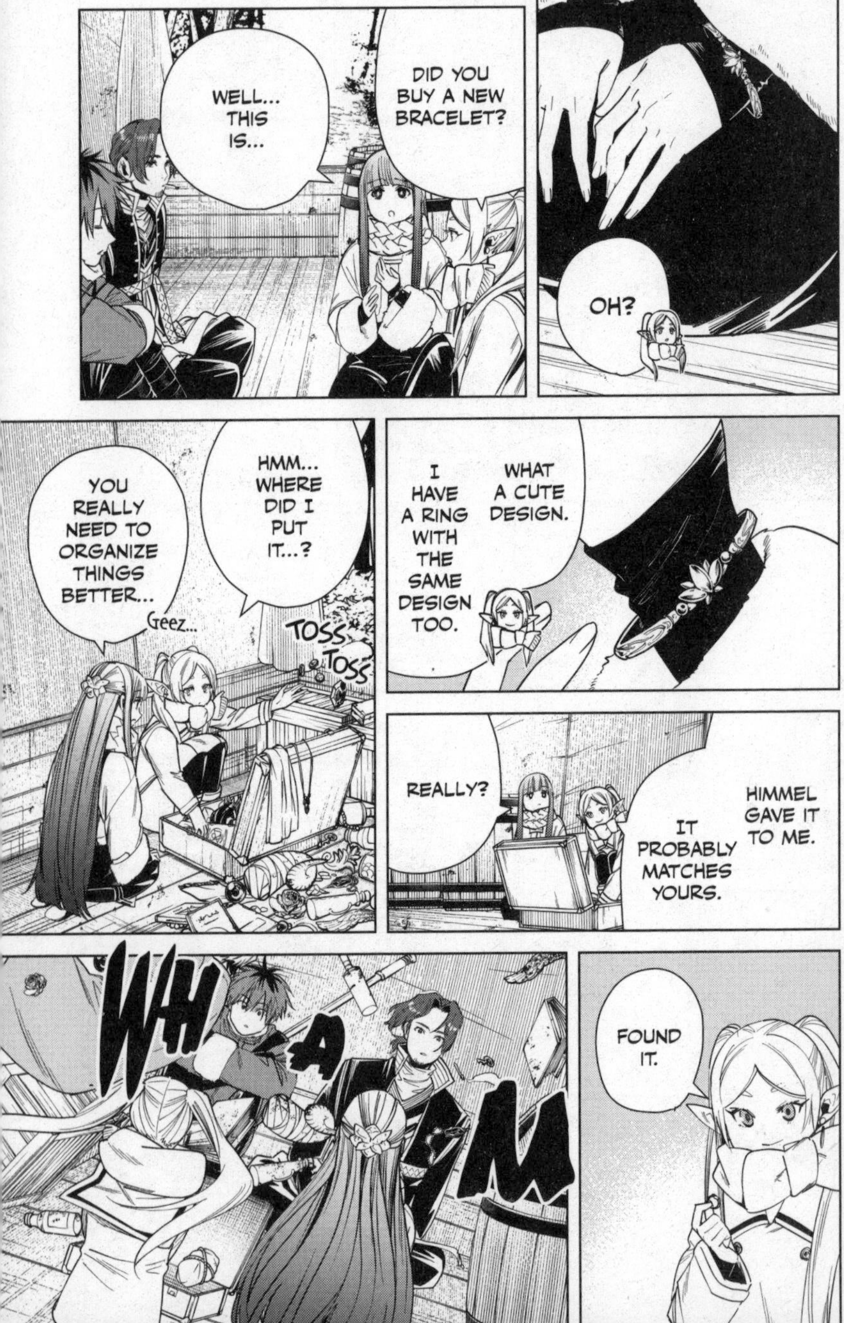
OH?
DID YOU BUY A NEW BRACELET?
WELL... THIS IS...
WHAT A CUTE DESIGN.
I HAVE A RING WITH THE SAME DESIGN TOO.
HIMMEL GAVE IT TO ME.
IT PROBABLY MATCHES YOURS.
REALLY?
HMM... WHERE DID I PUT IT...?
TOSS TOSS
YOU REALLY NEED TO ORGANIZE THINGS BETTER...
Geez...
FOUND IT.
WHAM

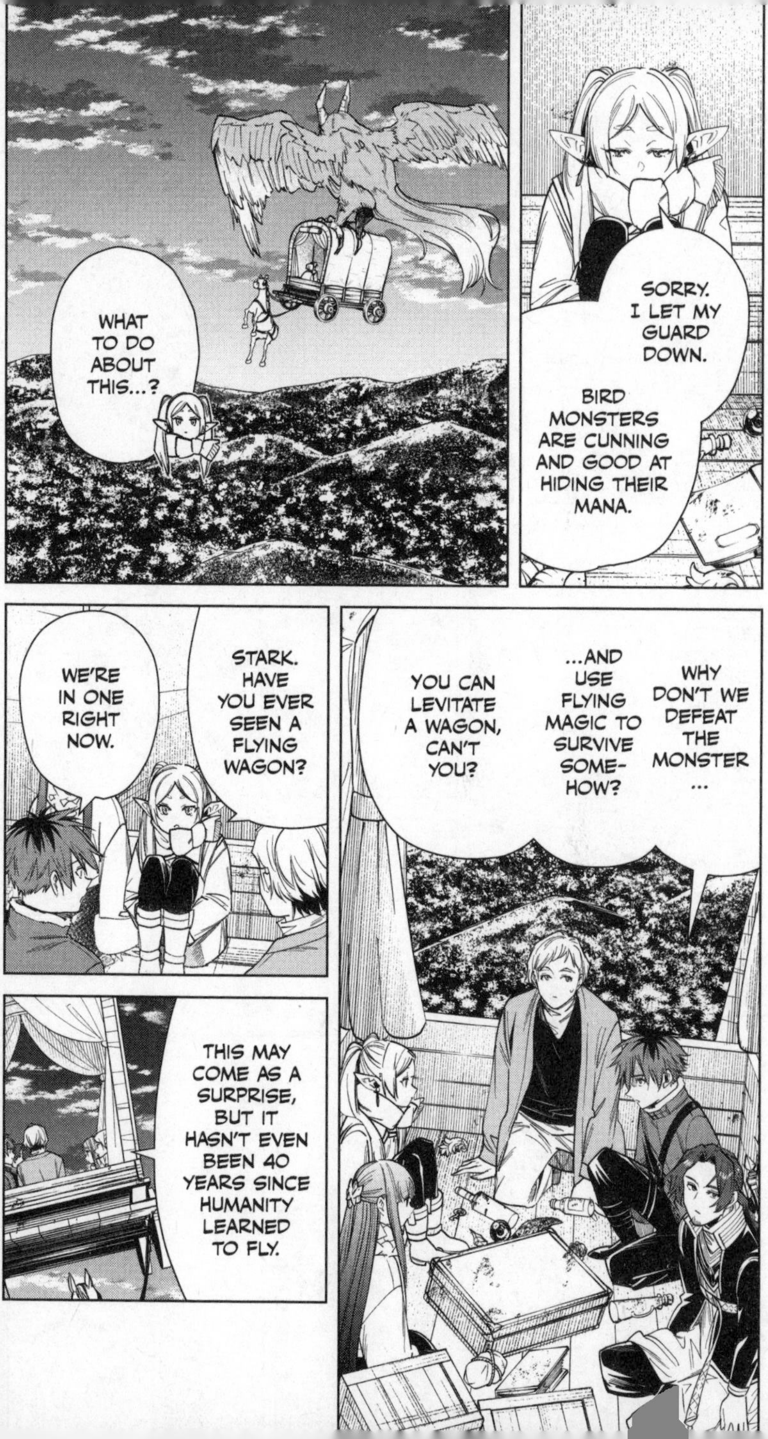
SORRY. I LET MY GUARD DOWN.
BIRD MONSTERS ARE CUNNING AND GOOD AT HIDING THEIR MANA.
WHAT TO DO ABOUT THIS...?
WHY DON'T WE DEFEAT THE MONSTER...
...AND USE FLYING MAGIC TO SURVIVE SOME-HOW?
YOU CAN LEVITATE A WAGON, CAN'T YOU?
STARK. HAVE YOU EVER SEEN A FLYING WAGON?
WE'RE IN ONE RIGHT NOW.
THIS MAY COME AS A SURPRISE, BUT IT HASN'T EVEN BEEN 40 YEARS SINCE HUMANITY LEARNED TO FLY.

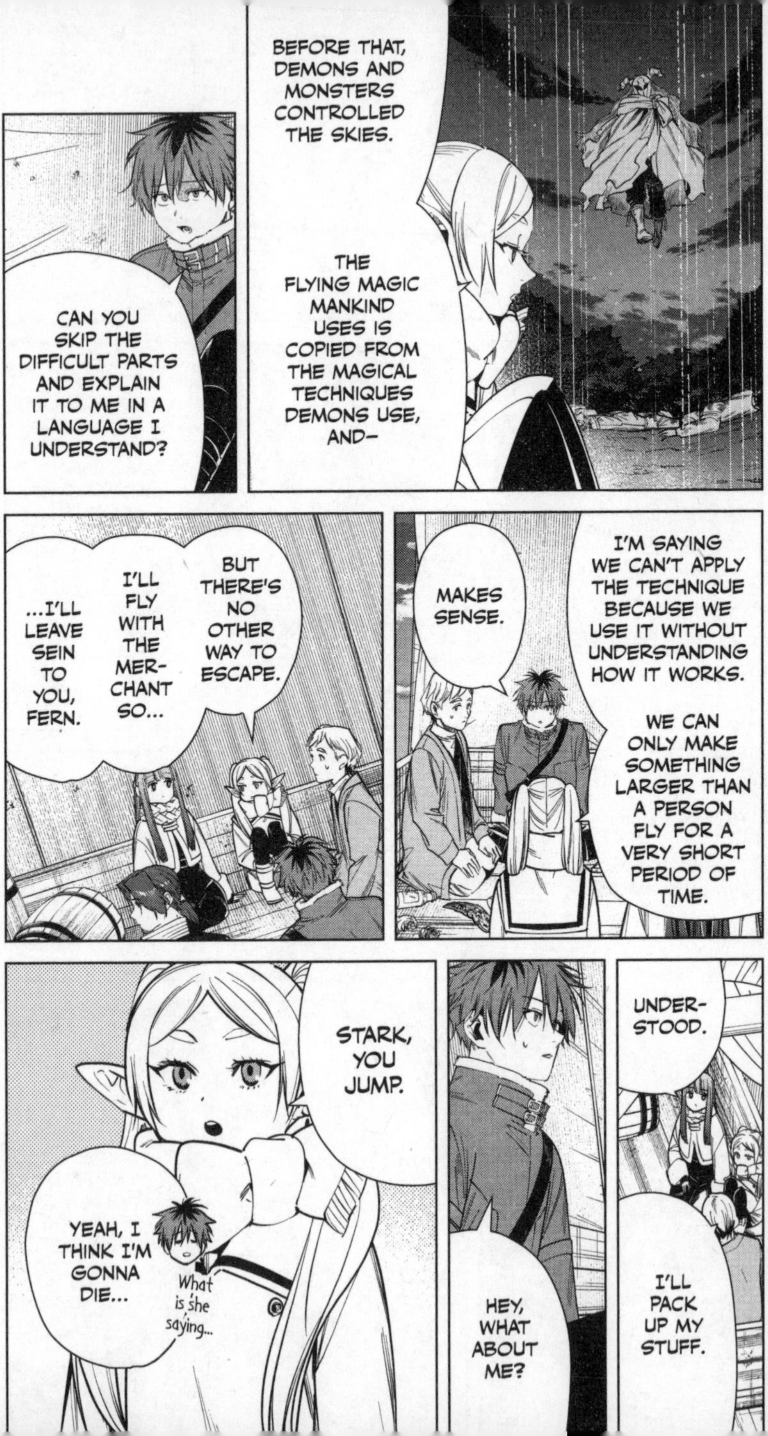
BEFORE THAT, DEMONS AND MONSTERS CONTROLLED THE SKIES.
THE FLYING MAGIC MANKIND USES IS COPIED FROM THE MAGICAL TECHNIQUES DEMONS USE, AND—
CAN YOU SKIP THE DIFFICULT PARTS AND EXPLAIN IT TO ME IN A LANGUAGE I UNDERSTAND?
I'M SAYING WE CAN'T APPLY THE TECHNIQUE BECAUSE WE USE IT WITHOUT UNDERSTANDING HOW IT WORKS.
WE CAN ONLY MAKE SOMETHING LARGER THAN A PERSON FLY FOR A VERY SHORT PERIOD OF TIME.
MAKES SENSE.
BUT THERE'S NO OTHER WAY TO ESCAPE.
I'LL FLY WITH THE MER-CHANT SO...
...I'LL LEAVE SEIN TO YOU, FERN.
UNDER-STOOD.
I'LL PACK UP MY STUFF.
HEY, WHAT ABOUT ME?
STARK, YOU JUMP.
YEAH, I THINK I'M GONNA DIE...
What is she saying...

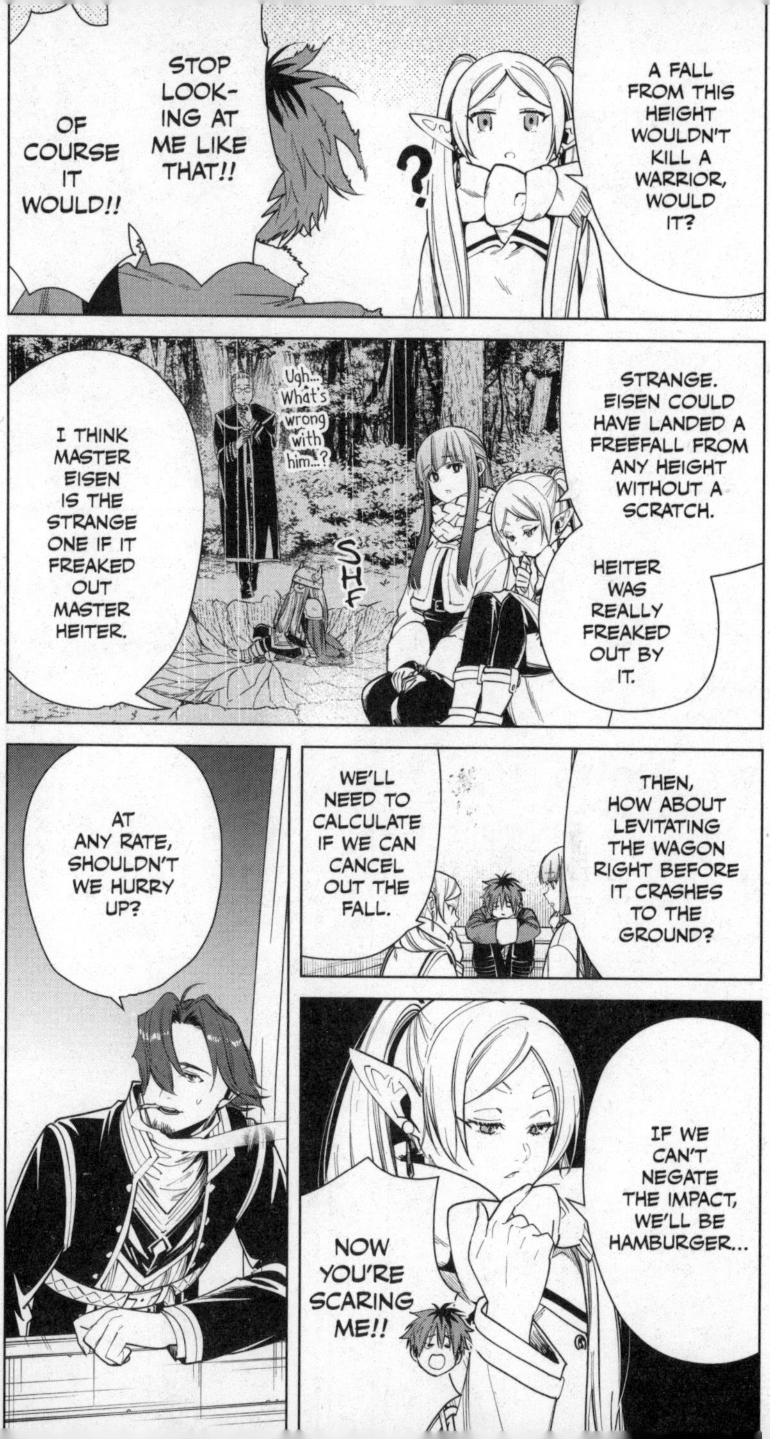
A FALL FROM THIS HEIGHT WOULDN'T KILL A WARRIOR, WOULD IT?
?
STOP LOOKING AT ME LIKE THAT!!
OF COURSE IT WOULD!!
STRANGE. EISEN COULD HAVE LANDED A FREEFALL FROM ANY HEIGHT WITHOUT A SCRATCH.
HEITER WAS REALLY FREAKED OUT BY IT.
SHF
Ugh... What's wrong with him...?
I THINK MASTER EISEN IS THE STRANGE ONE IF IT FREAKED OUT MASTER HEITER.
THEN, HOW ABOUT LEVITATING THE WAGON RIGHT BEFORE IT CRASHES TO THE GROUND?
WE'LL NEED TO CALCULATE IF WE CAN CANCEL OUT THE FALL.
IF WE CAN'T NEGATE THE IMPACT, WE'LL BE HAMBURGER...
NOW YOU'RE SCARING ME!!
AT ANY RATE, SHOULDN'T WE HURRY UP?

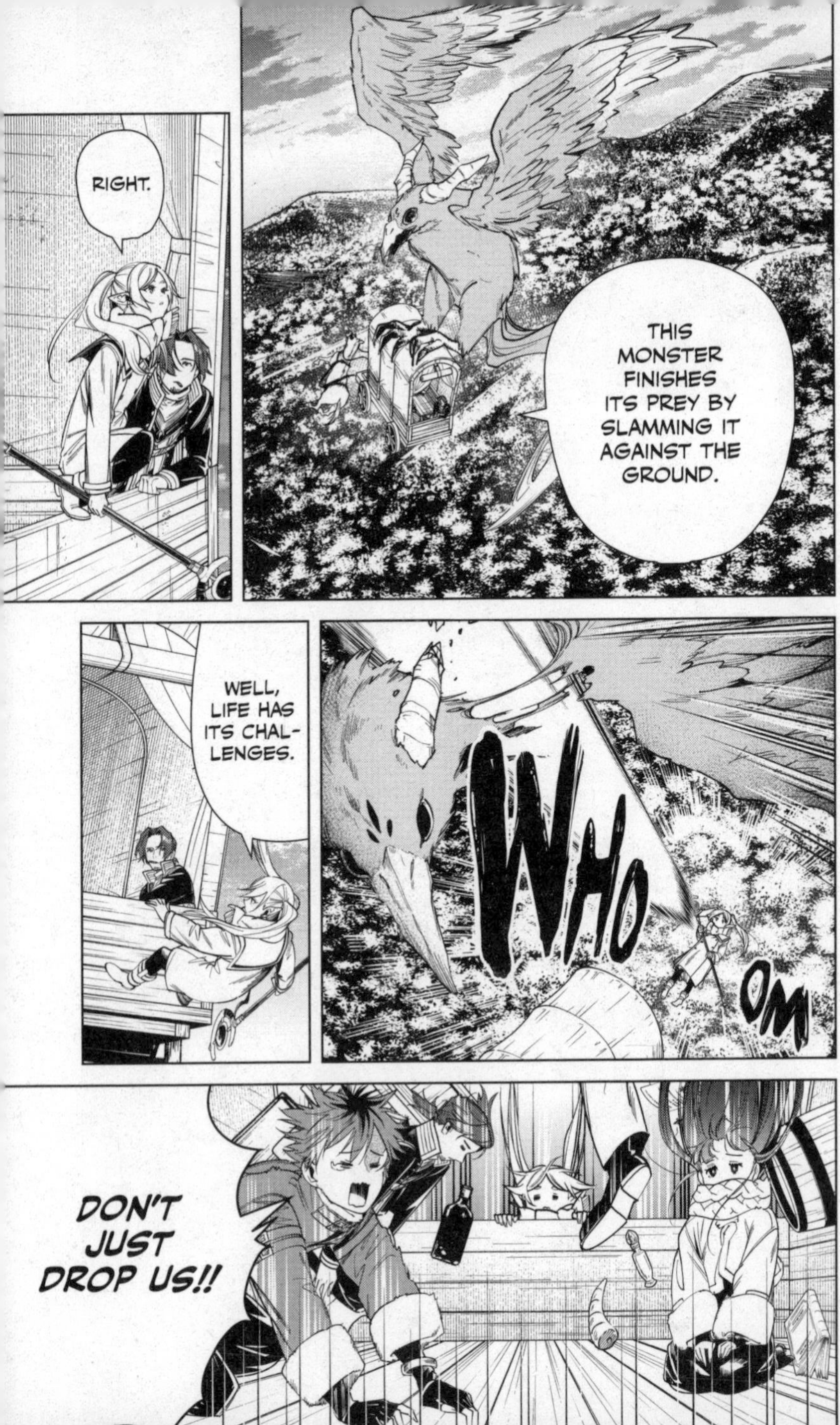
THIS MONSTER FINISHES ITS PREY BY SLAMMING IT AGAINST THE GROUND.
RIGHT.
WHOOM
WELL, LIFE HAS ITS CHAL-LENGES.
DON'T JUST DROP US!!

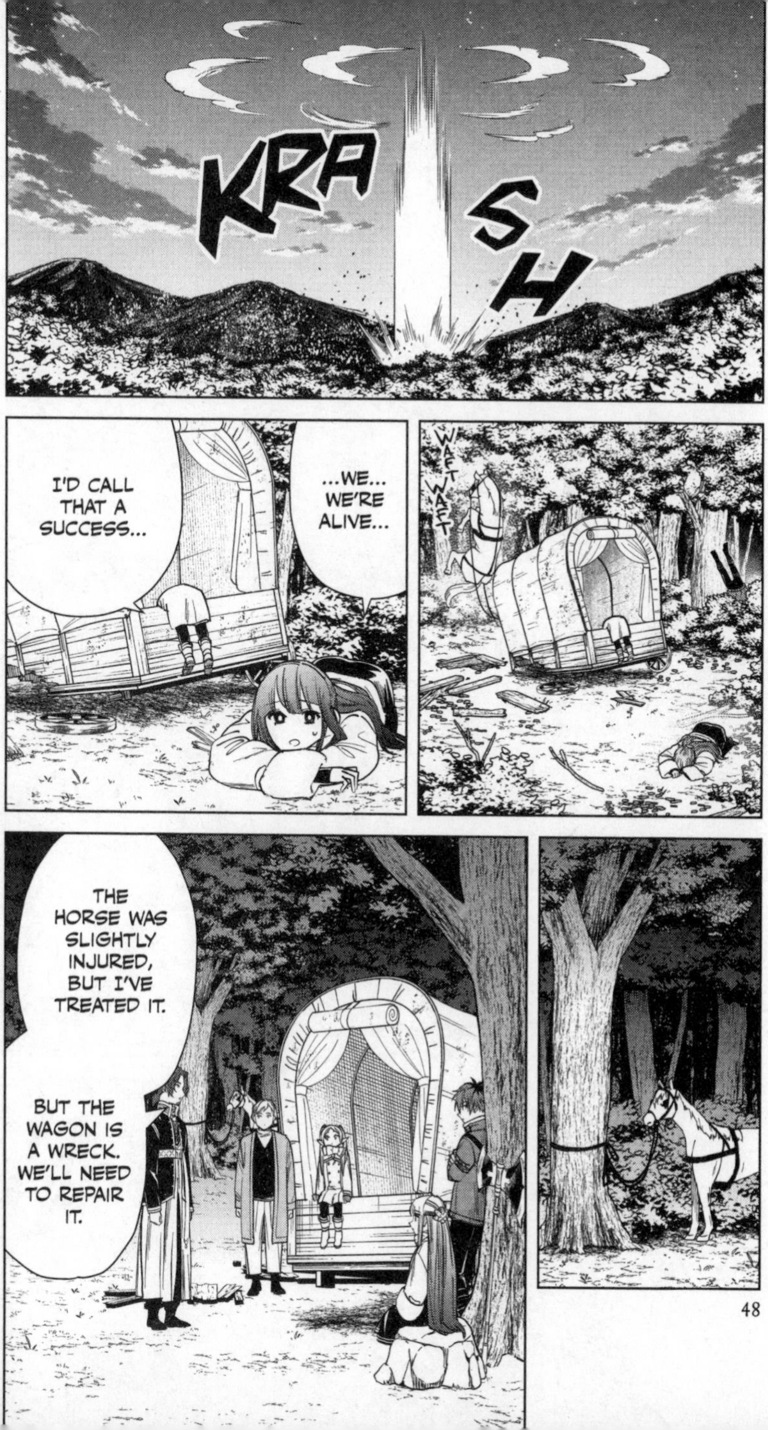
KRASH
WAFT WAFT
...WE... WE'RE ALIVE...
I'D CALL THAT A SUCCESS...
THE HORSE WAS SLIGHTLY INJURED, BUT I'VE TREATED IT.
BUT THE WAGON IS A WRECK. WE'LL NEED TO REPAIR IT.

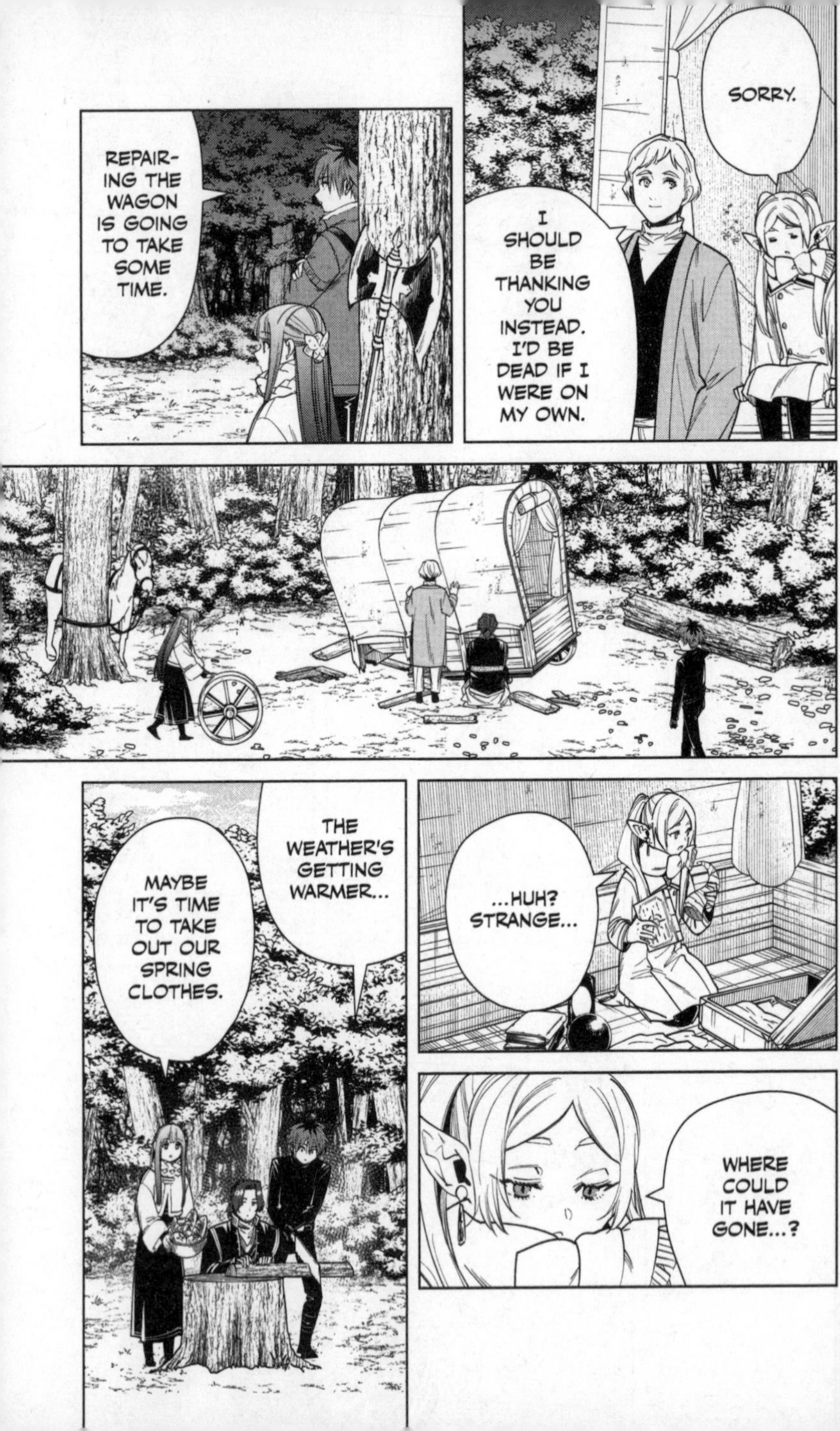
SORRY.
I SHOULD BE THANKING YOU INSTEAD. I'D BE DEAD IF I WERE ON MY OWN.
REPAIR-ING THE WAGON IS GOING TO TAKE SOME TIME.
THE WEATHER'S GETTING WARMER...
MAYBE IT'S TIME TO TAKE OUT OUR SPRING CLOTHES.
...HUH? STRANGE...
WHERE COULD IT HAVE GONE...?

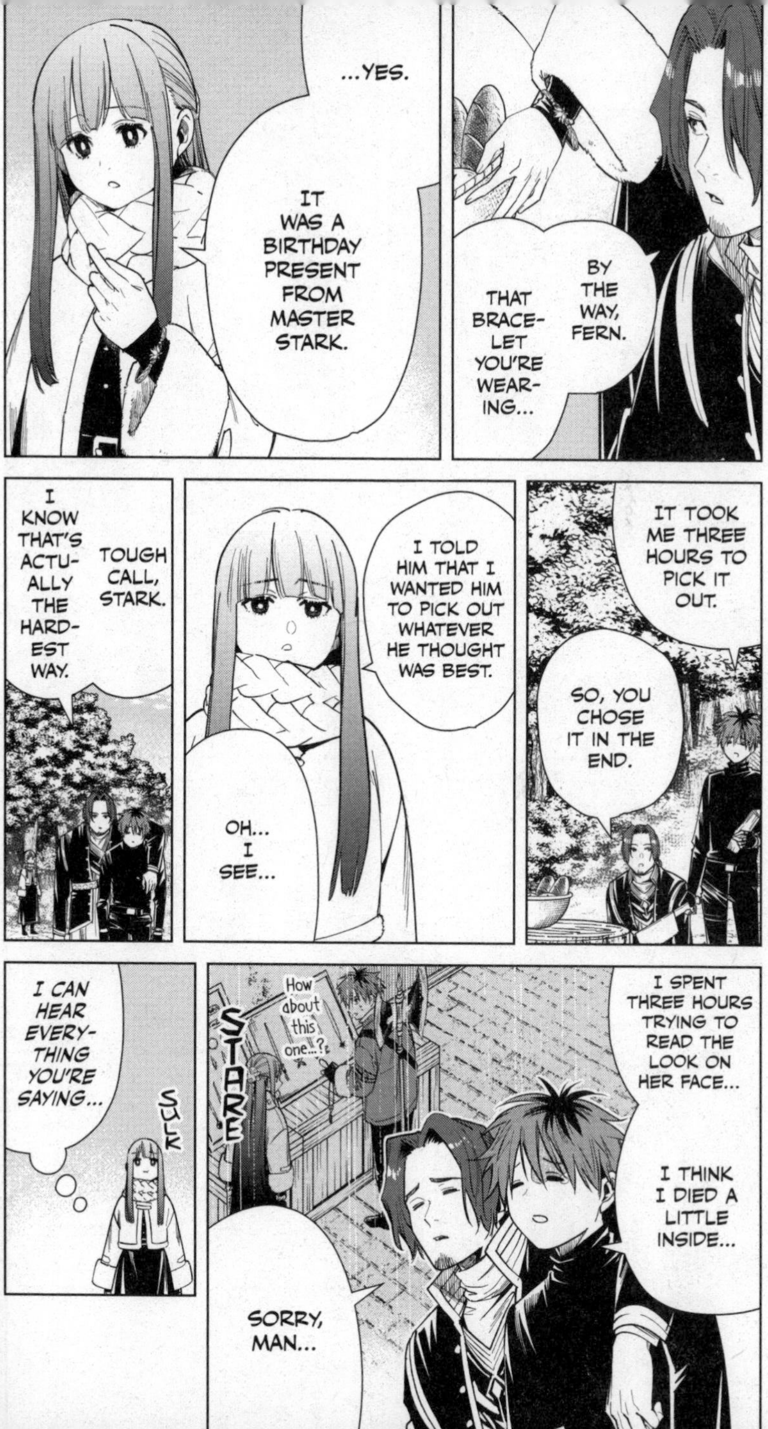
BY THE WAY, FERN.
THAT BRACELET YOU'RE WEARING...
...YES.
IT WAS A BIRTHDAY PRESENT FROM MASTER STARK.
IT TOOK ME THREE HOURS TO PICK IT OUT.
SO, YOU CHOSE IT IN THE END.
I TOLD HIM THAT I WANTED HIM TO PICK OUT WHATEVER HE THOUGHT WAS BEST.
OH... I SEE...
TOUGH CALL, STARK.
I KNOW THAT'S ACTUALLY THE HARDEST WAY.
I SPENT THREE HOURS TRYING TO READ THE LOOK ON HER FACE...
STARE
How about this one...?
I THINK I DIED A LITTLE INSIDE...
SORRY, MAN...
I CAN HEAR EVERYTHING YOU'RE SAYING...
SULK

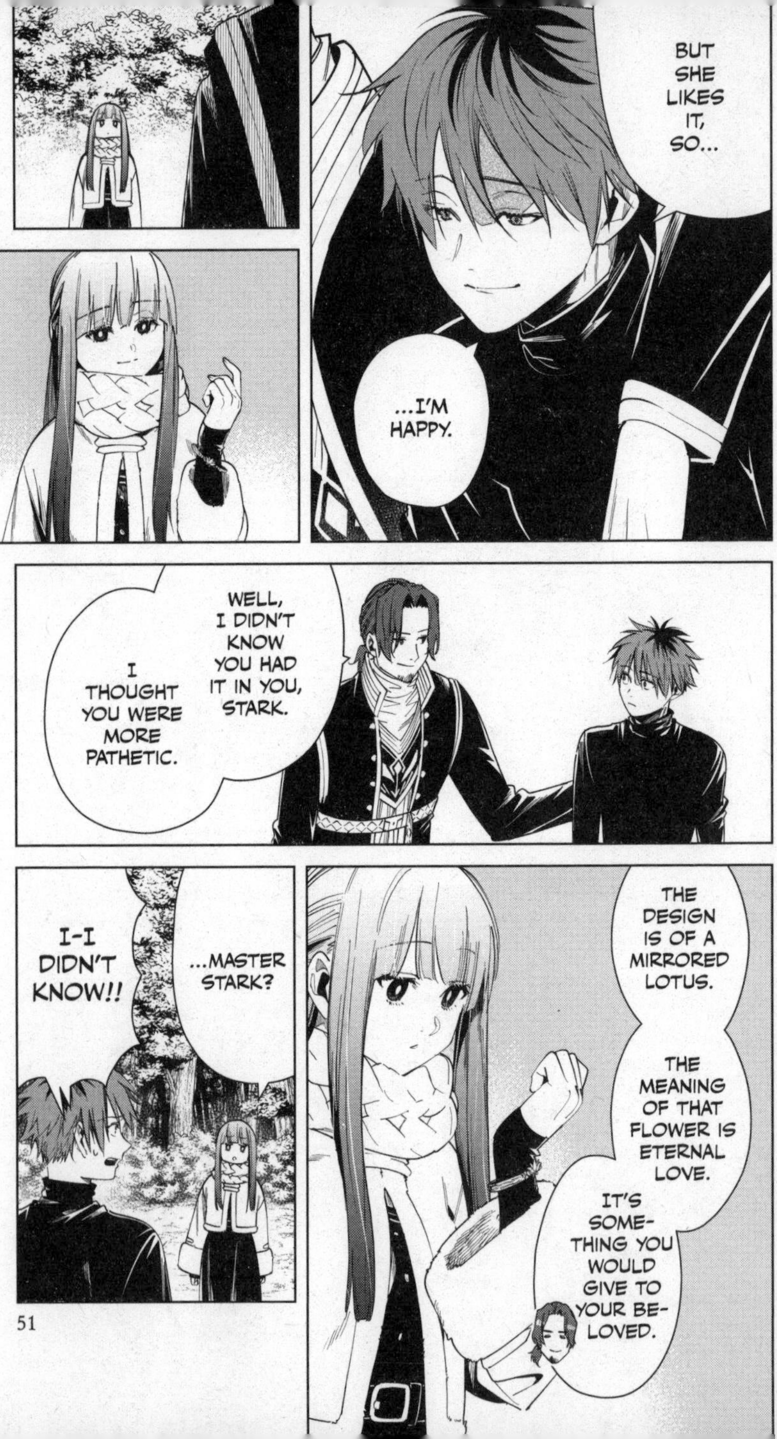

BUT SHE LIKES IT, SO...
...I'M HAPPY.
WELL, I DIDN'T KNOW YOU HAD IT IN YOU, STARK.
I THOUGHT YOU WERE MORE PATHETIC.
THE DESIGN IS OF A MIRRORED LOTUS.
THE MEANING OF THAT FLOWER IS ETERNAL LOVE.
IT'S SOME-THING YOU WOULD GIVE TO YOUR BE-LOVED.
...MASTER STARK?
I-I DIDN'T KNOW!!

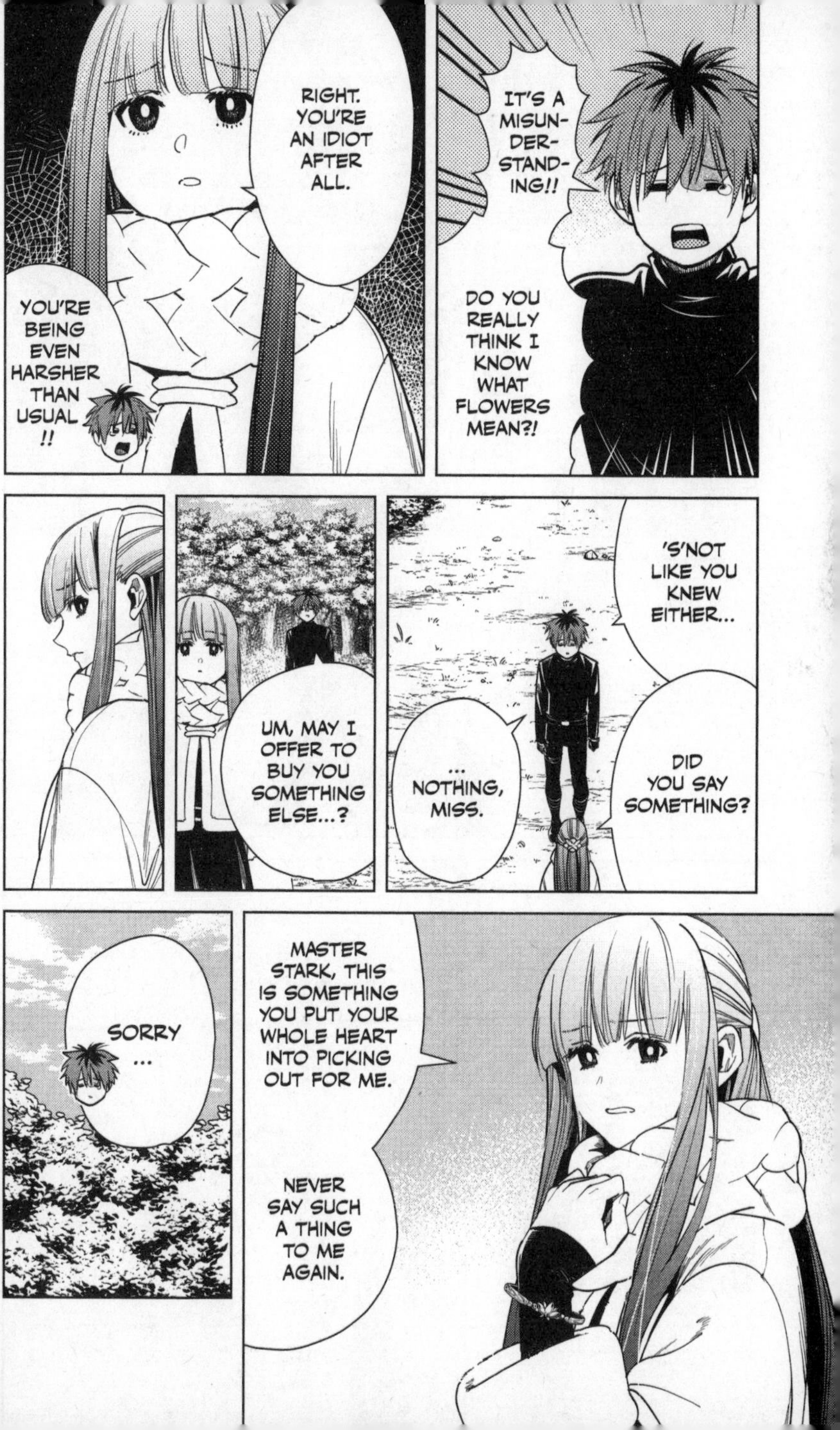
IT'S A MISUNDERSTANDING!!
DO YOU REALLY THINK I KNOW WHAT FLOWERS MEAN?!
RIGHT. YOU'RE AN IDIOT AFTER ALL.
YOU'RE BEING EVEN HARSHER THAN USUAL!!
'S'NOT LIKE YOU KNEW EITHER...
DID YOU SAY SOMETHING?
... NOTHING, MISS.
UM, MAY I OFFER TO BUY YOU SOMETHING ELSE...?
MASTER STARK, THIS IS SOMETHING YOU PUT YOUR WHOLE HEART INTO PICKING OUT FOR ME.
NEVER SAY SUCH A THING TO ME AGAIN.
SORRY ...

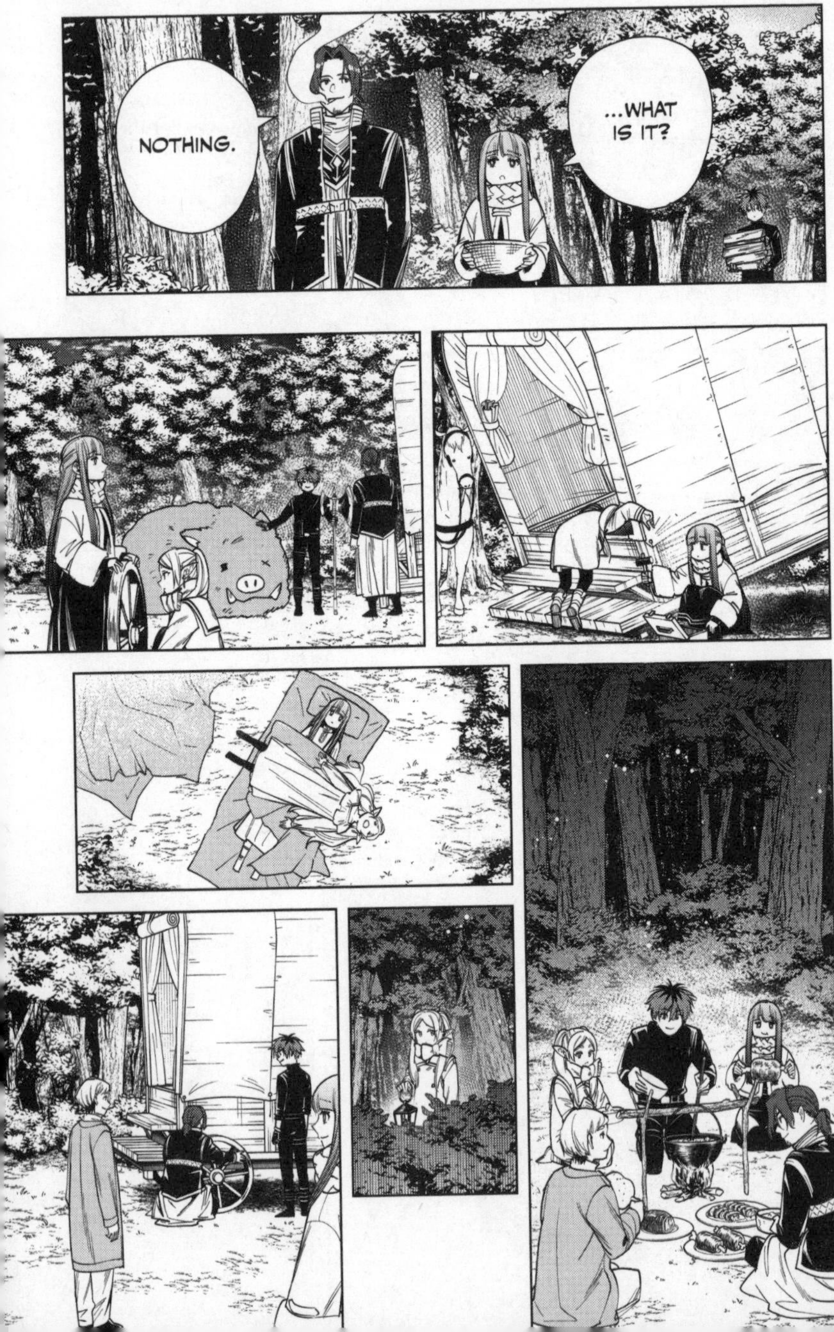
...WHAT IS IT?
NOTHING.

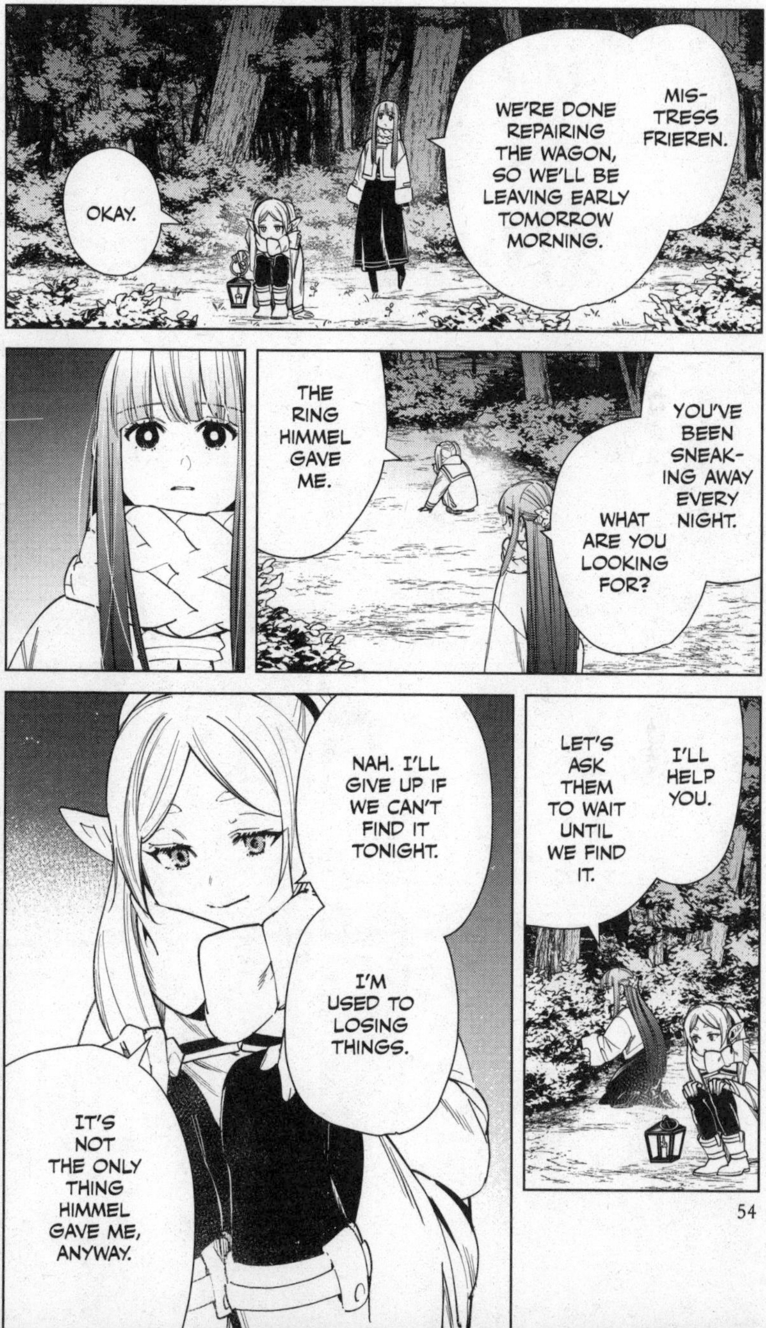
MISTRESS FRIEREN.
WE'RE DONE REPAIRING THE WAGON, SO WE'LL BE LEAVING EARLY TOMORROW MORNING.
OKAY.
YOU'VE BEEN SNEAKING AWAY EVERY NIGHT.
WHAT ARE YOU LOOKING FOR?
THE RING HIMMEL GAVE ME.
I'LL HELP YOU.
LET'S ASK THEM TO WAIT UNTIL WE FIND IT.
NAH. I'LL GIVE UP IF WE CAN'T FIND IT TONIGHT.
I'M USED TO LOSING THINGS.
IT'S NOT THE ONLY THING HIMMEL GAVE ME, ANYWAY.

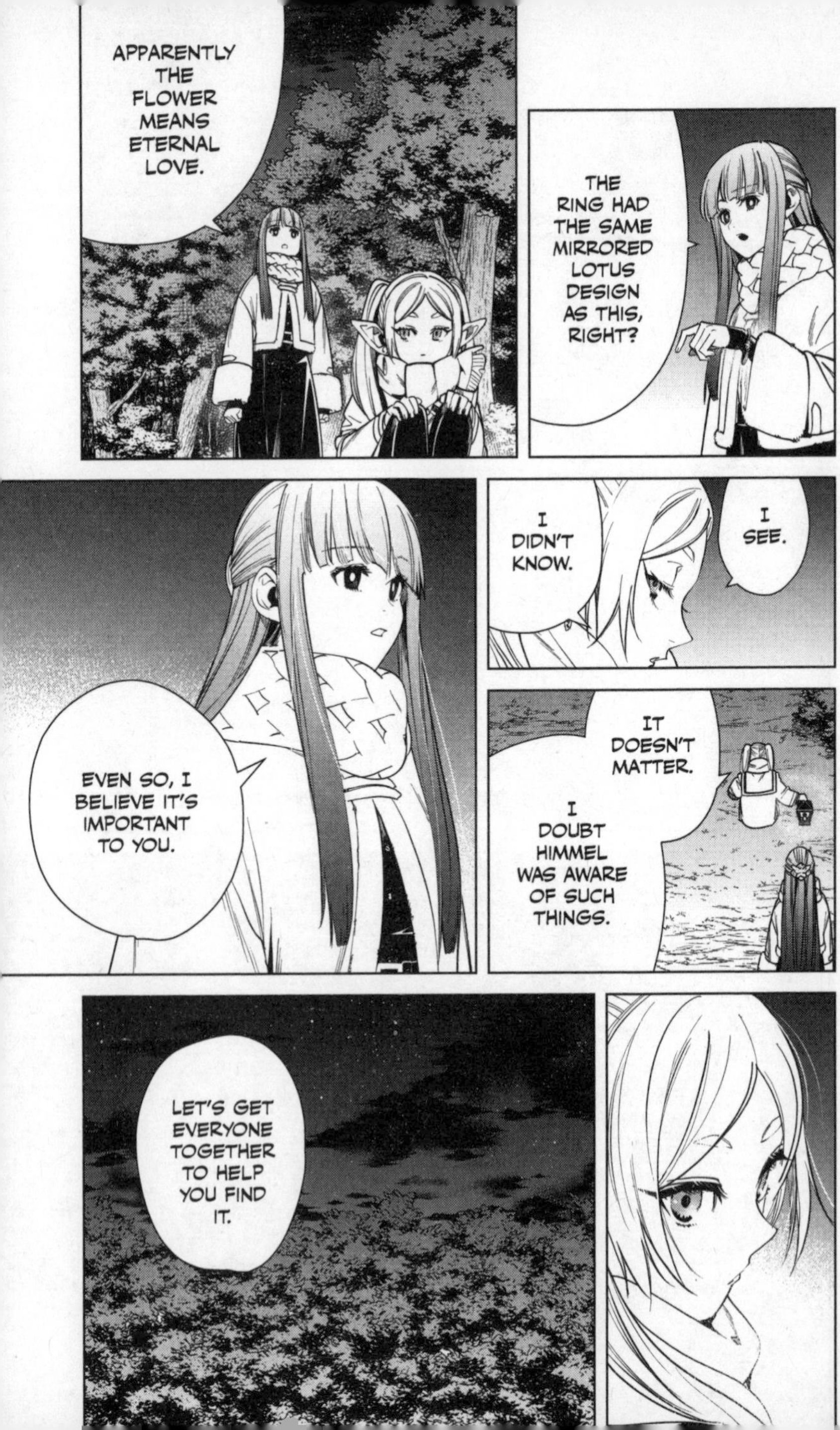
THE RING HAD THE SAME MIRRORED LOTUS DESIGN AS THIS, RIGHT?
APPARENTLY THE FLOWER MEANS ETERNAL LOVE.
I SEE.
I DIDN'T KNOW.
IT DOESN'T MATTER.
I DOUBT HIMMEL WAS AWARE OF SUCH THINGS.
EVEN SO, I BELIEVE IT'S IMPORTANT TO YOU.
LET'S GET EVERYONE TOGETHER TO HELP YOU FIND IT.

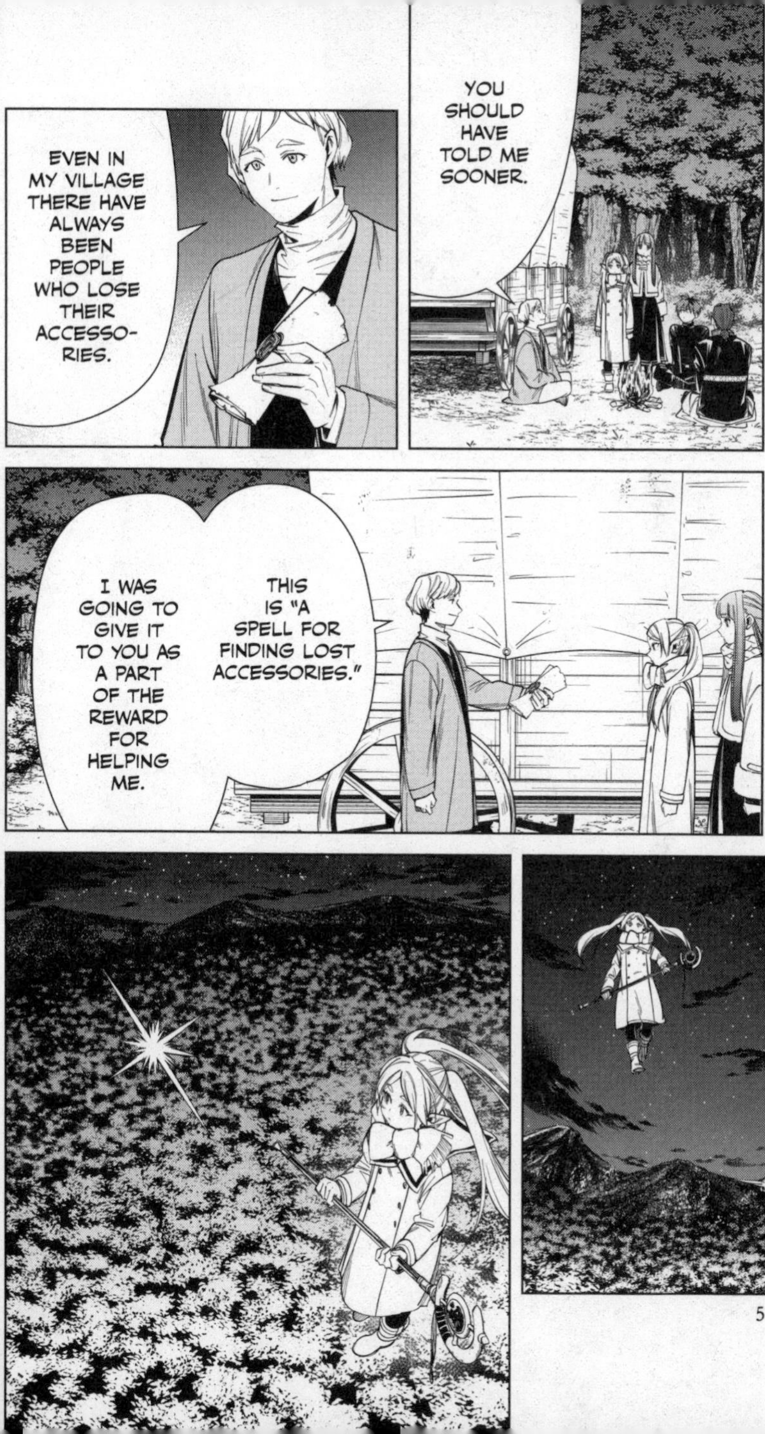
YOU SHOULD HAVE TOLD ME SOONER.
EVEN IN MY VILLAGE THERE HAVE ALWAYS BEEN PEOPLE WHO LOSE THEIR ACCESSO-RIES.
THIS IS "A SPELL FOR FINDING LOST ACCESSORIES."
I WAS GOING TO GIVE IT TO YOU AS A PART OF THE REWARD FOR HELPING ME.

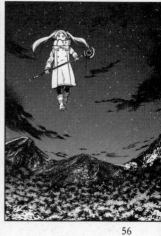

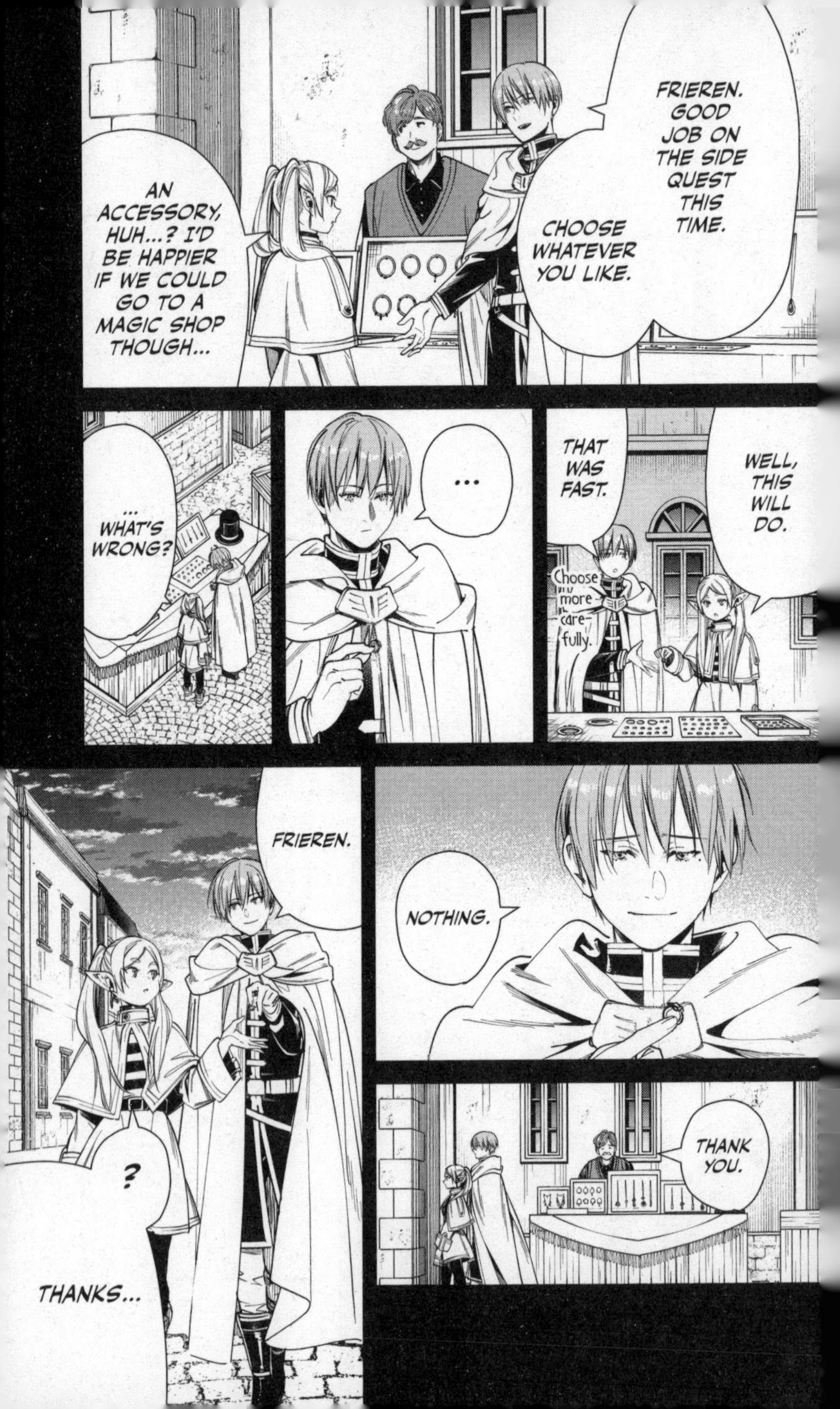
FRIEREN. GOOD JOB ON THE SIDE QUEST THIS TIME.
CHOOSE WHATEVER YOU LIKE.
AN ACCESSORY, HUH...? I'D BE HAPPIER IF WE COULD GO TO A MAGIC SHOP THOUGH...
WELL, THIS WILL DO.
THAT WAS FAST.
Choose more carefully.
...
... WHAT'S WRONG?
NOTHING.
THANK YOU.
FRIEREN.
?
THANKS...

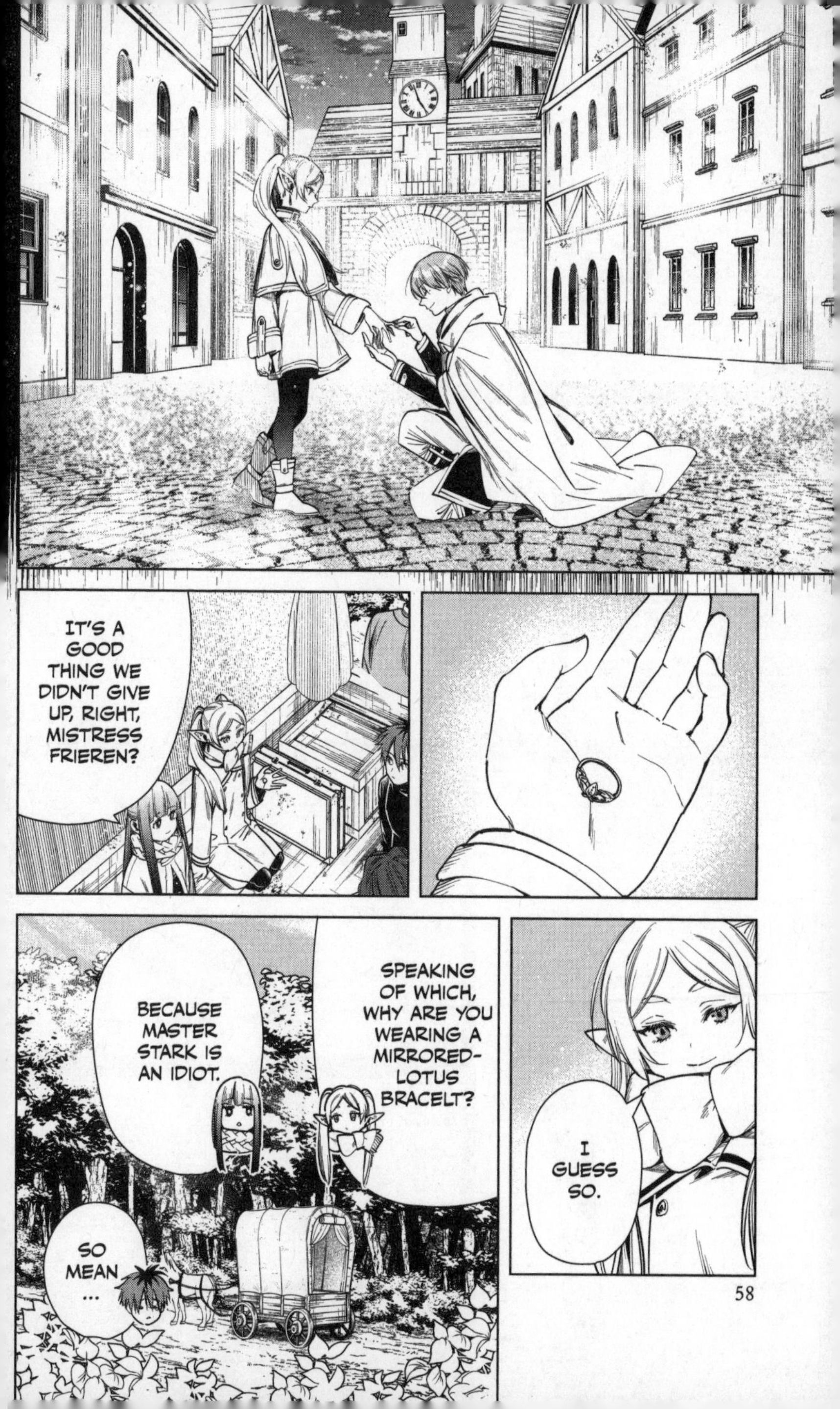
IT'S A GOOD THING WE DIDN'T GIVE UP, RIGHT, MISTRESS FRIEREN?
I GUESS SO.
SPEAKING OF WHICH, WHY ARE YOU WEARING A MIRRORED-LOTUS BRACELT?
BECAUSE MASTER STARK IS AN IDIOT.
SO MEAN ...

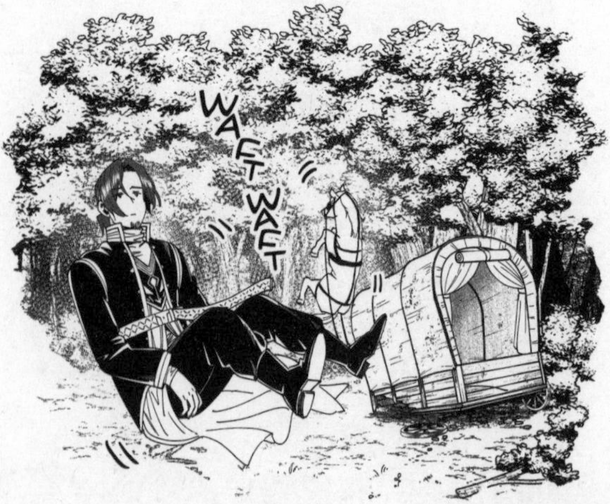
WAFT WAFT

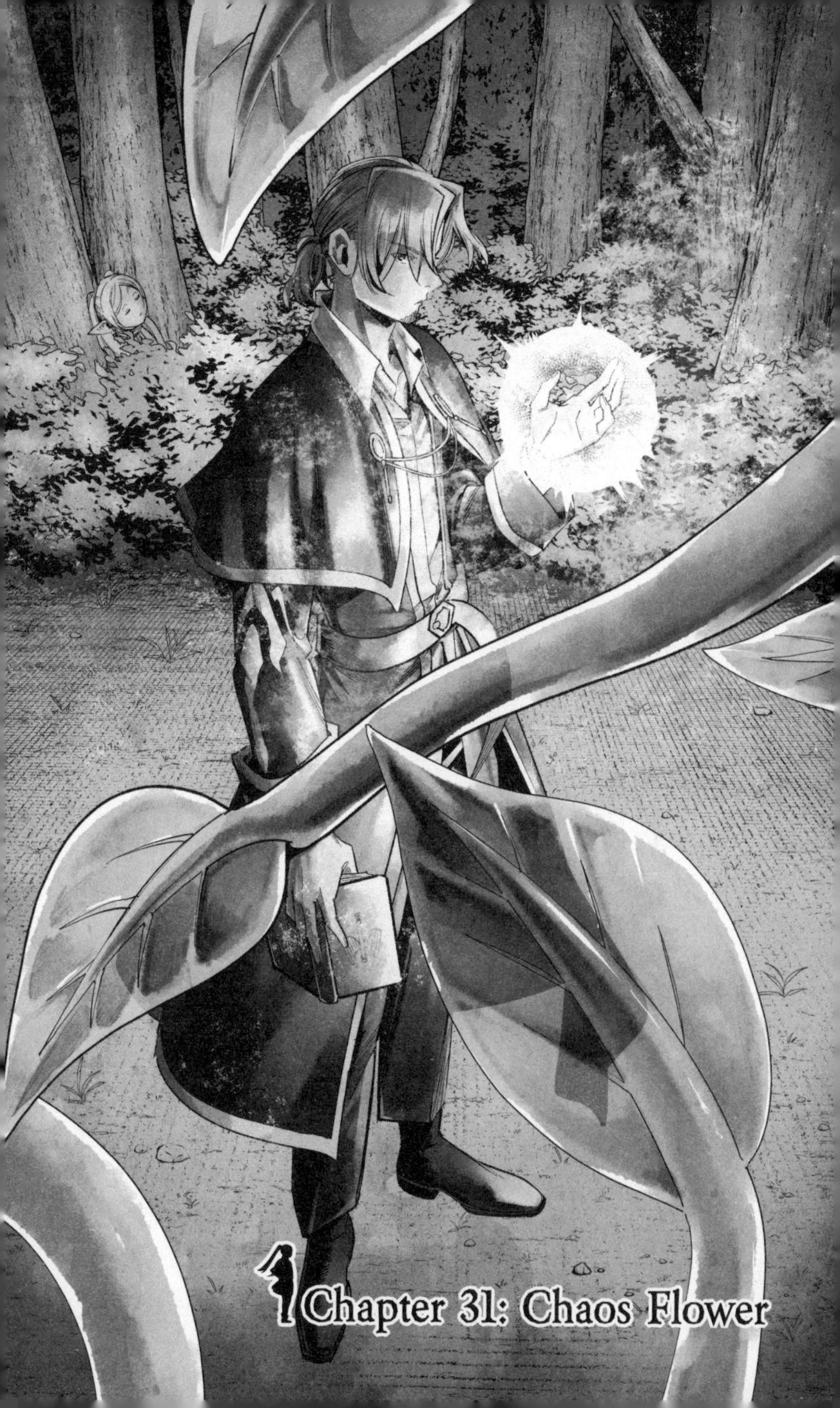
Chapter 31: Chaos Flower

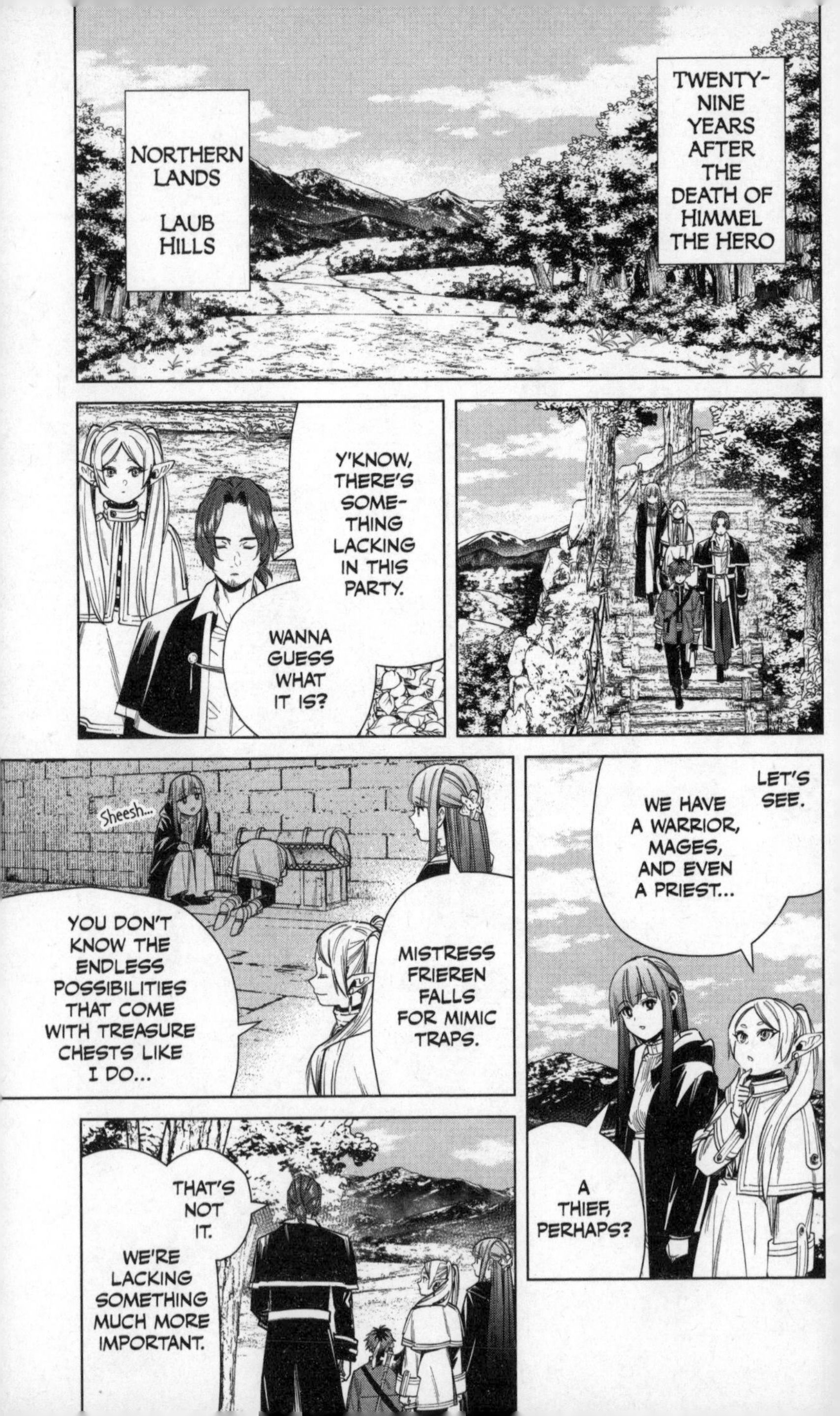
TWENTY-NINE YEARS AFTER THE DEATH OF HIMMEL THE HERO
NORTHERN LANDS
LAUB HILLS
Y'KNOW, THERE'S SOME-THING LACKING IN THIS PARTY.
WANNA GUESS WHAT IT IS?
LET'S SEE.
WE HAVE A WARRIOR, MAGES, AND EVEN A PRIEST...
A THIEF, PERHAPS?
Sheesh...
MISTRESS FRIEREN FALLS FOR MIMIC TRAPS.
YOU DON'T KNOW THE ENDLESS POSSIBILITIES THAT COME WITH TREASURE CHESTS LIKE I DO...
THAT'S NOT IT.
WE'RE LACKING SOMETHING MUCH MORE IMPORTANT.

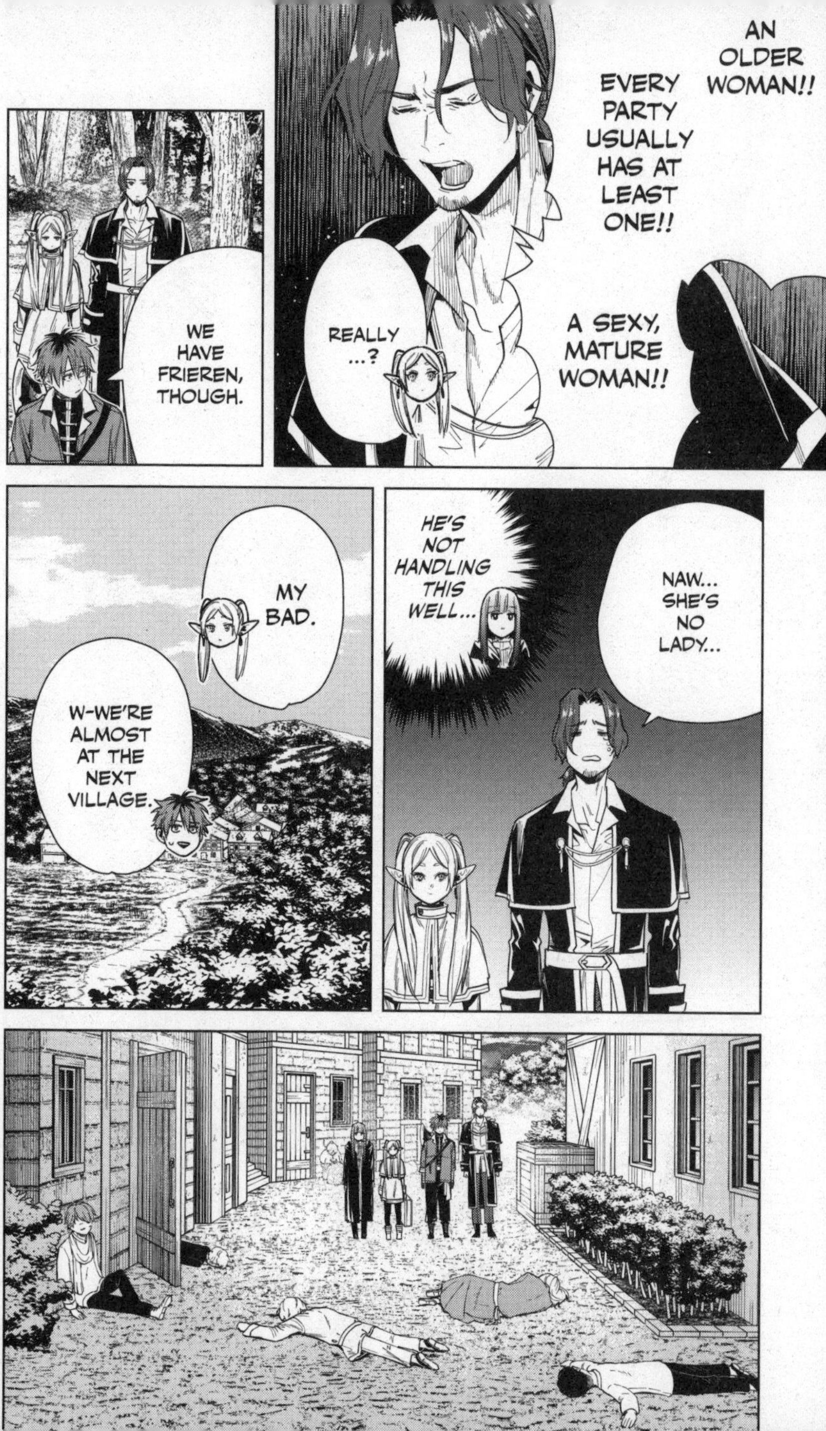
AN OLDER WOMAN!!
EVERY PARTY USUALLY HAS AT LEAST ONE!!
A SEXY, MATURE WOMAN!!
REALLY ...?
WE HAVE FRIEREN, THOUGH.
NAW... SHE'S NO LADY...
HE'S NOT HANDLING THIS WELL...
MY BAD.
W-WE'RE ALMOST AT THE NEXT VILLAGE.

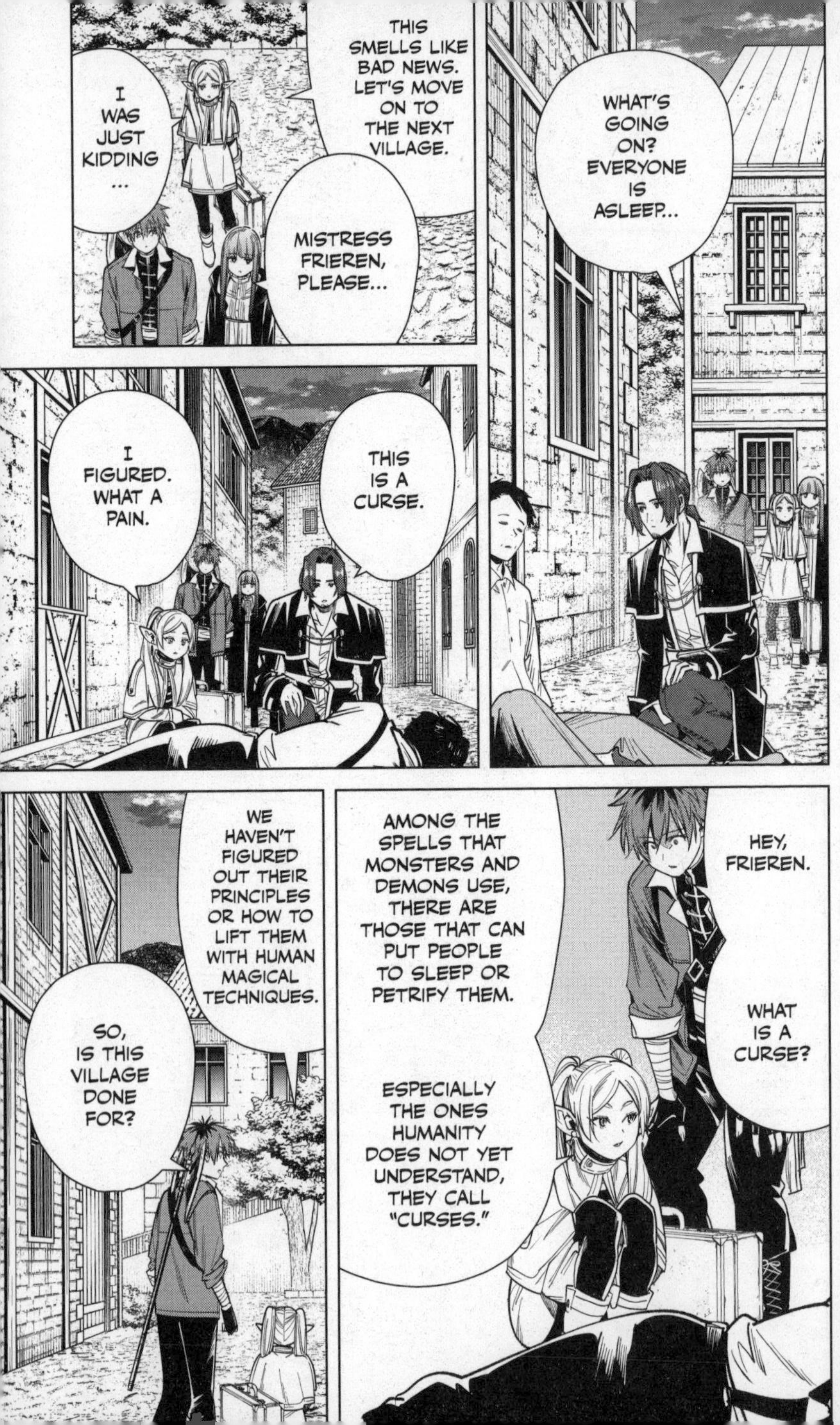
WHAT'S GOING ON? EVERYONE IS ASLEEP...
THIS SMELLS LIKE BAD NEWS. LET'S MOVE ON TO THE NEXT VILLAGE.
MISTRESS FRIEREN, PLEASE...
I WAS JUST KIDDING ...
THIS IS A CURSE.
I FIGURED. WHAT A PAIN.
HEY, FRIEREN.
WHAT IS A CURSE?
AMONG THE SPELLS THAT MONSTERS AND DEMONS USE, THERE ARE THOSE THAT CAN PUT PEOPLE TO SLEEP OR PETRIFY THEM.
ESPECIALLY THE ONES HUMANITY DOES NOT YET UNDERSTAND, THEY CALL "CURSES."
WE HAVEN'T FIGURED OUT THEIR PRINCIPLES OR HOW TO LIFT THEM WITH HUMAN MAGICAL TECHNIQUES.
SO, IS THIS VILLAGE DONE FOR?

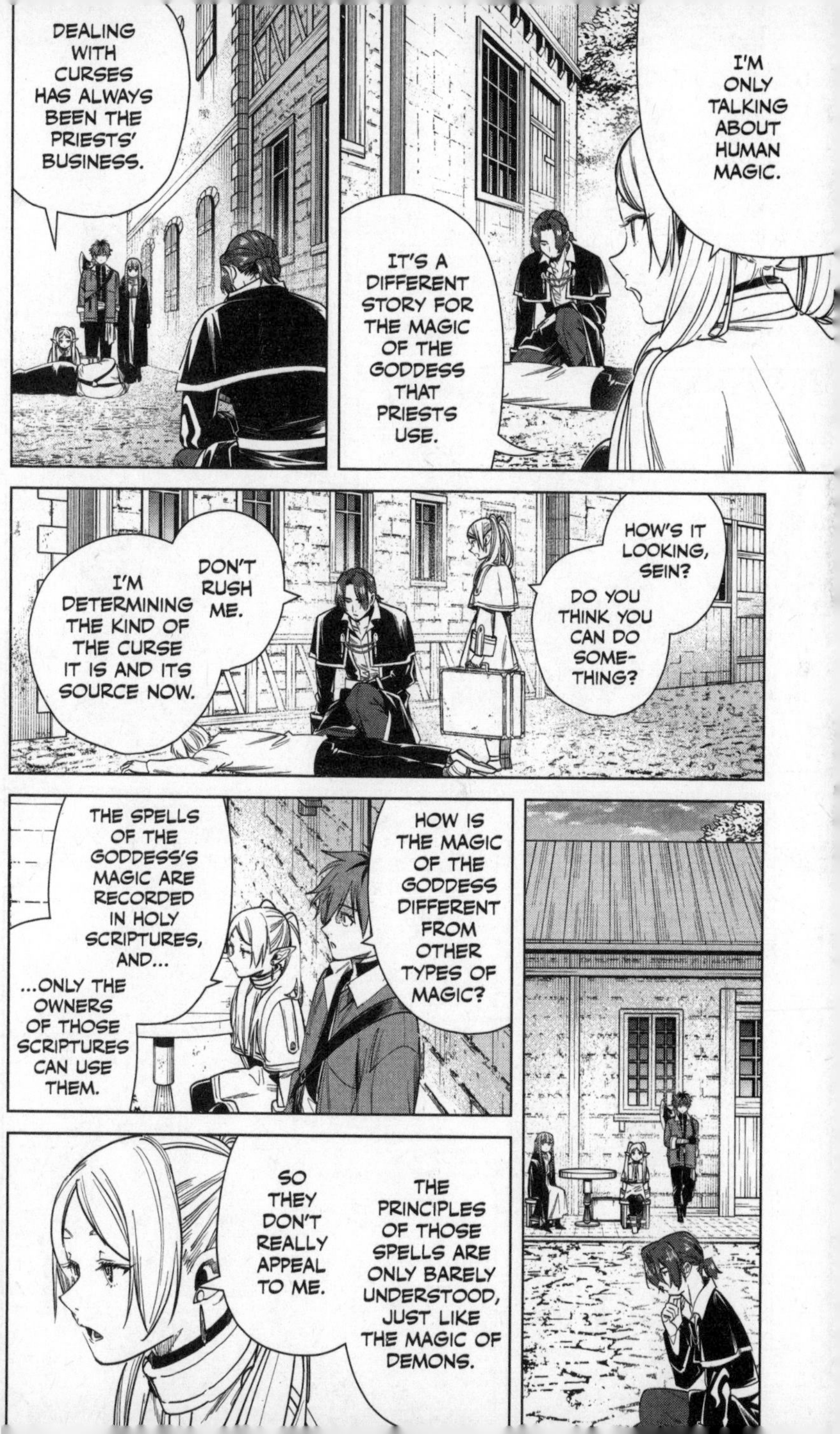
I'M ONLY TALKING ABOUT HUMAN MAGIC.
IT'S A DIFFERENT STORY FOR THE MAGIC OF THE GODDESS THAT PRIESTS USE.
DEALING WITH CURSES HAS ALWAYS BEEN THE PRIESTS' BUSINESS.
HOW'S IT LOOKING, SEIN?
DO YOU THINK YOU CAN DO SOME-THING?
DON'T RUSH ME.
I'M DETERMINING THE KIND OF THE CURSE IT IS AND ITS SOURCE NOW.
HOW IS THE MAGIC OF THE GODDESS DIFFERENT FROM OTHER TYPES OF MAGIC?
THE SPELLS OF THE GODDESS'S MAGIC ARE RECORDED IN HOLY SCRIPTURES, AND...
...ONLY THE OWNERS OF THOSE SCRIPTURES CAN USE THEM.
THE PRINCIPLES OF THOSE SPELLS ARE ONLY BARELY UNDERSTOOD, JUST LIKE THE MAGIC OF DEMONS.
SO THEY DON'T REALLY APPEAL TO ME.

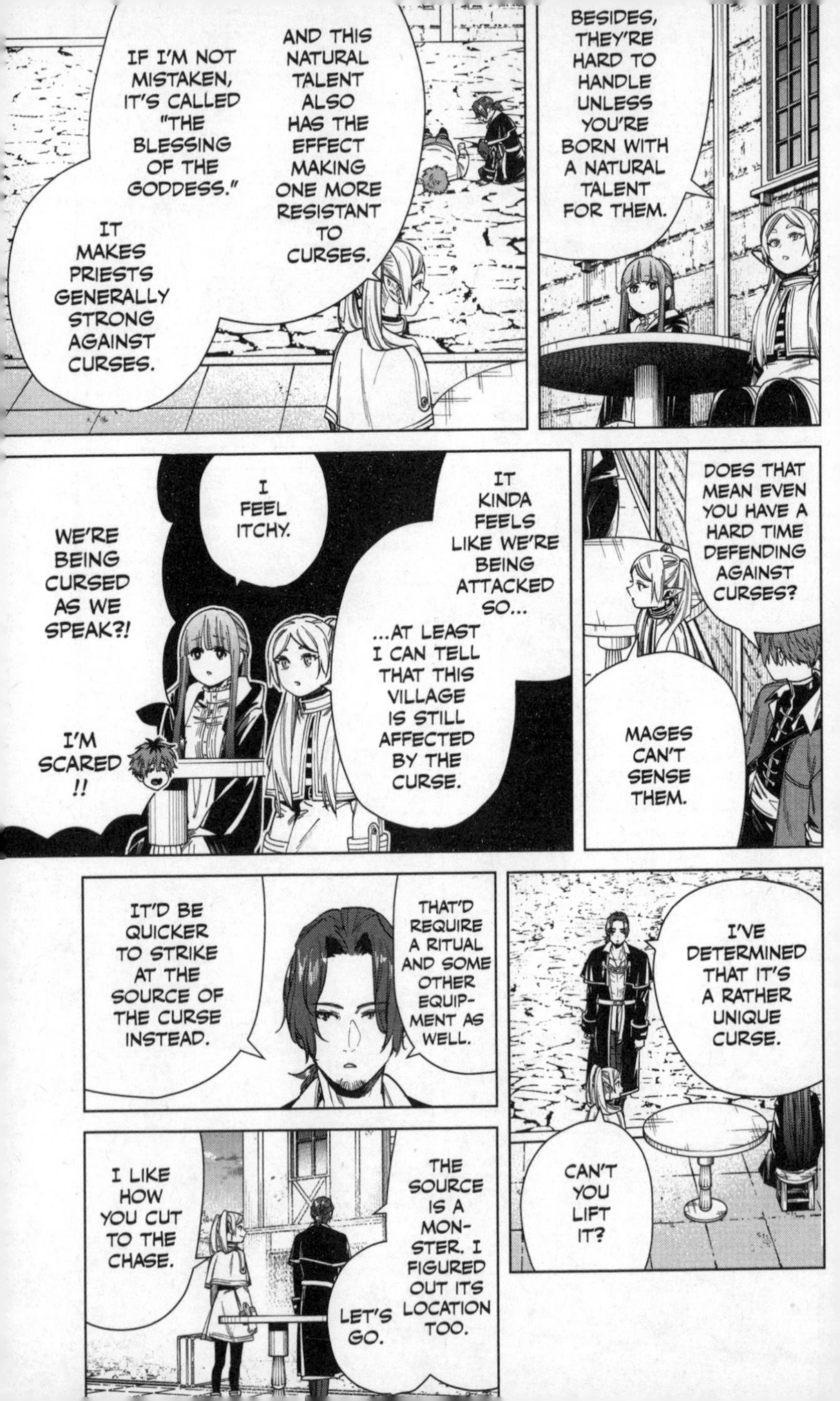
BESIDES, THEY'RE HARD TO HANDLE UNLESS YOU'RE BORN WITH A NATURAL TALENT FOR THEM.
AND THIS NATURAL TALENT ALSO HAS THE EFFECT MAKING ONE MORE RESISTANT TO CURSES.
IF I'M NOT MISTAKEN, IT'S CALLED "THE BLESSING OF THE GODDESS."
IT MAKES PRIESTS GENERALLY STRONG AGAINST CURSES.
DOES THAT MEAN EVEN YOU HAVE A HARD TIME DEFENDING AGAINST CURSES?
MAGES CAN'T SENSE THEM.
IT KINDA FEELS LIKE WE'RE BEING ATTACKED SO...
...AT LEAST I CAN TELL THAT THIS VILLAGE IS STILL AFFECTED BY THE CURSE.
I FEEL ITCHY.
WE'RE BEING CURSED AS WE SPEAK?!
I'M SCARED !!
I'VE DETERMINED THAT IT'S A RATHER UNIQUE CURSE.
CAN'T YOU LIFT IT?
THAT'D REQUIRE A RITUAL AND SOME OTHER EQUIP-MENT AS WELL.
IT'D BE QUICKER TO STRIKE AT THE SOURCE OF THE CURSE INSTEAD.
THE SOURCE IS A MON-STER. I FIGURED OUT ITS LOCATION TOO.
LET'S GO.
I LIKE HOW YOU CUT TO THE CHASE.

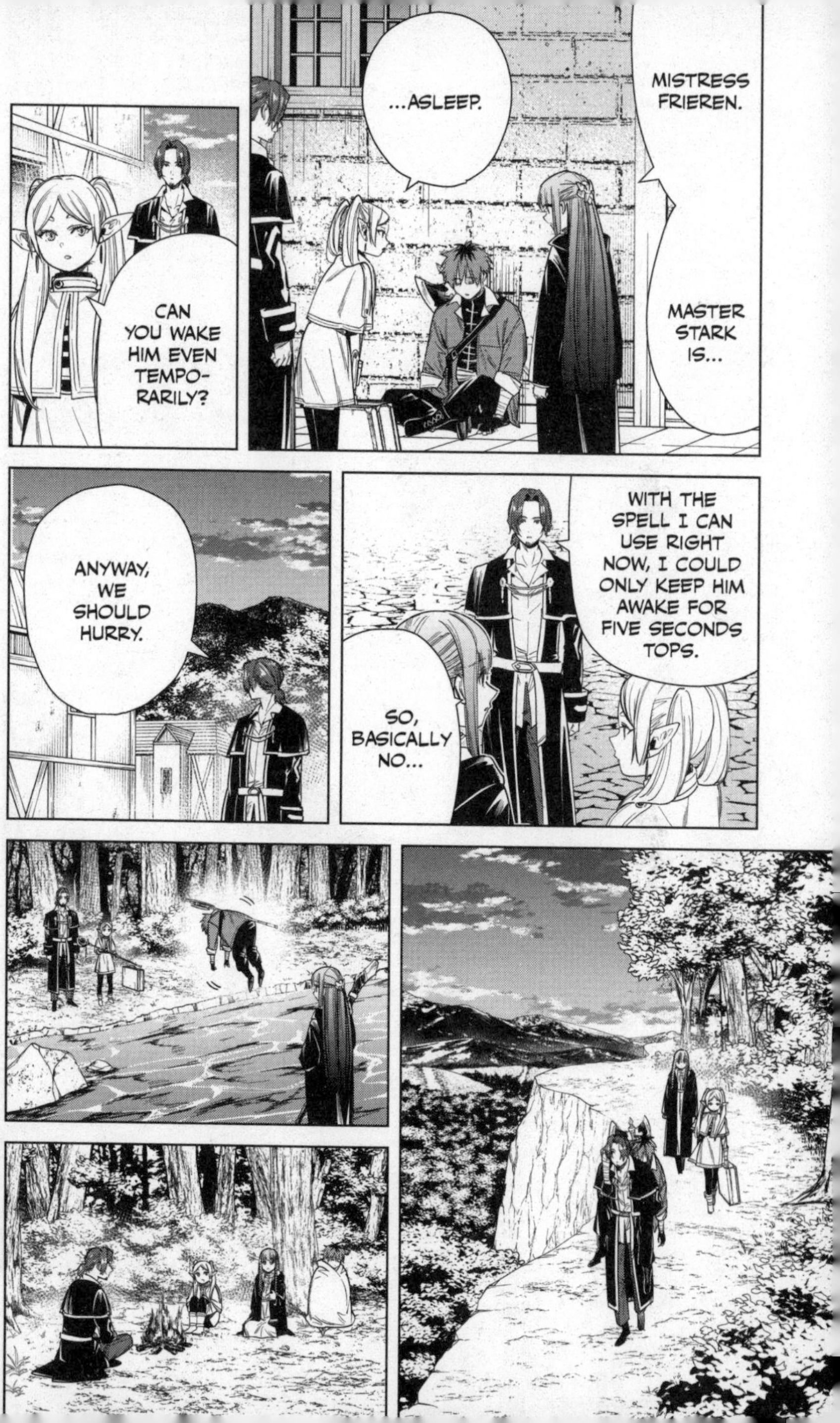
MISTRESS FRIEREN.
MASTER STARK IS...
...ASLEEP.
CAN YOU WAKE HIM EVEN TEMPO-RARILY?
WITH THE SPELL I CAN USE RIGHT NOW, I COULD ONLY KEEP HIM AWAKE FOR FIVE SECONDS TOPS.
SO, BASICALLY NO...
ANYWAY, WE SHOULD HURRY.

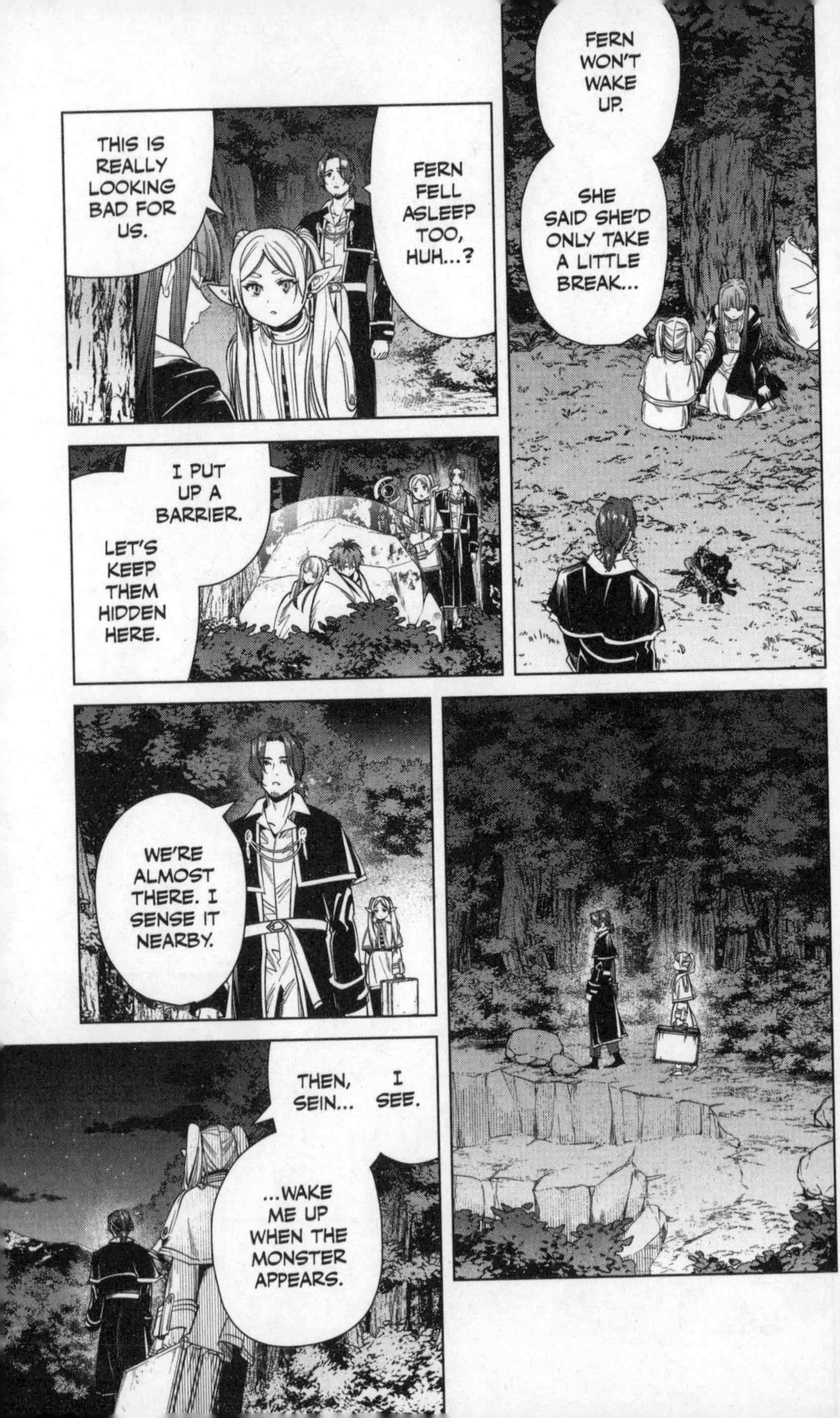
FERN WON'T WAKE UP.
SHE SAID SHE'D ONLY TAKE A LITTLE BREAK...
FERN FELL ASLEEP TOO, HUH...?
THIS IS REALLY LOOKING BAD FOR US.
I PUT UP A BARRIER.
LET'S KEEP THEM HIDDEN HERE.
WE'RE ALMOST THERE. I SENSE IT NEARBY.
I SEE.
THEN, SEIN...
...WAKE ME UP WHEN THE MONSTER APPEARS.

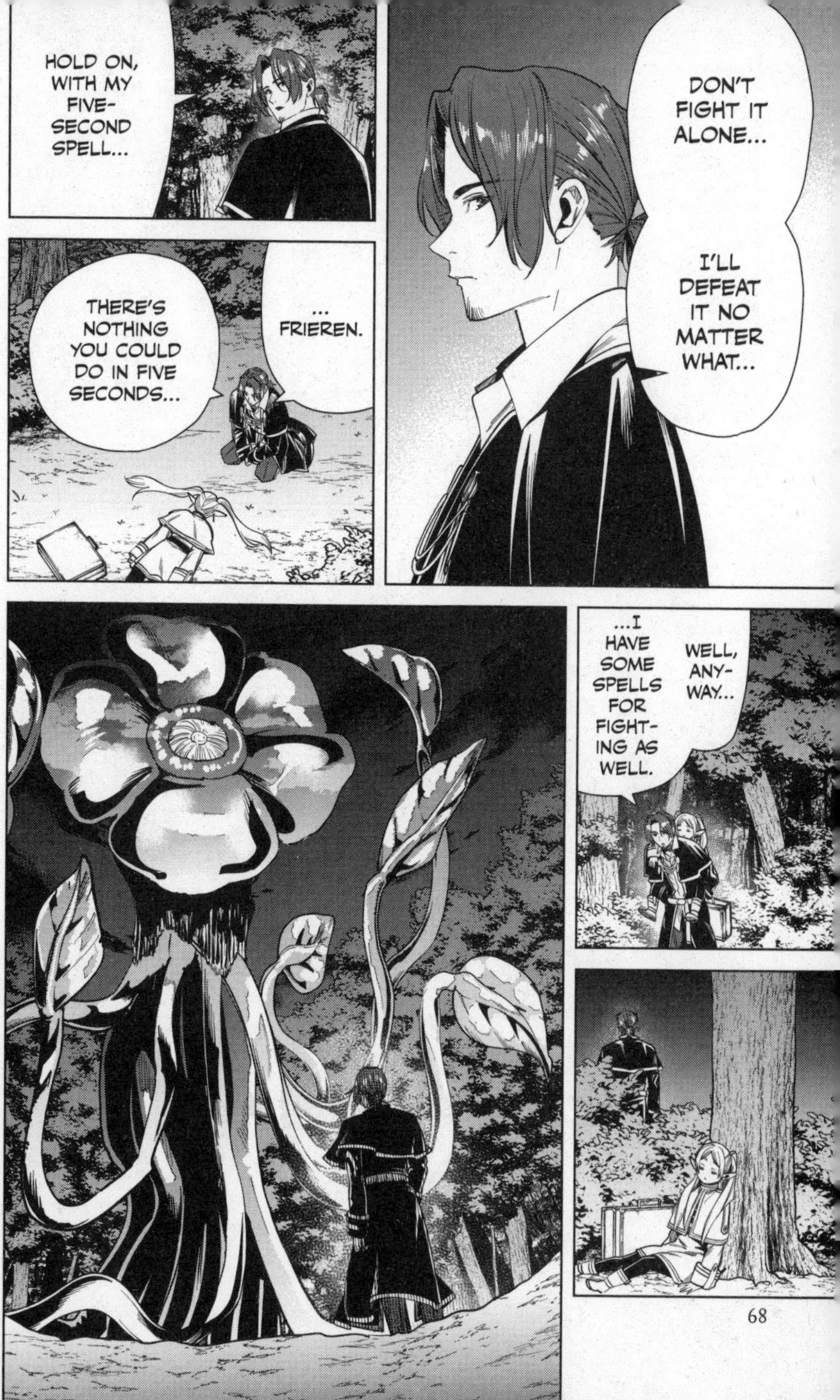
DON'T FIGHT IT ALONE...
I'LL DEFEAT IT NO MATTER WHAT...
HOLD ON, WITH MY FIVE-SECOND SPELL...
...FRIEREN.
THERE'S NOTHING YOU COULD DO IN FIVE SECONDS...
WELL, ANY-WAY...
...I HAVE SOME SPELLS FOR FIGHT-ING AS WELL.

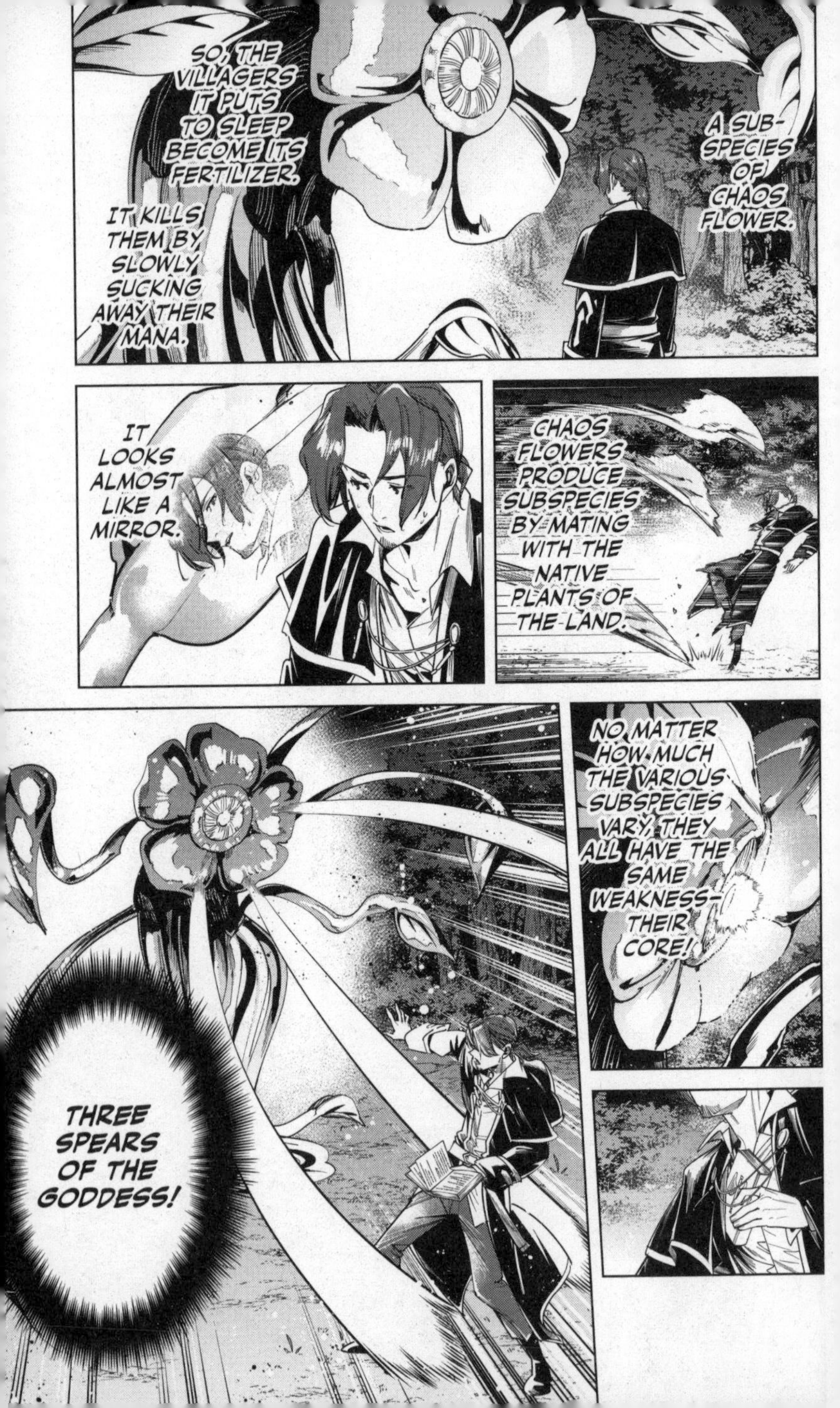
A SUB-SPECIES OF CHAOS FLOWER.
SO, THE VILLAGERS IT PUTS TO SLEEP BECOME ITS FERTILIZER.
IT KILLS THEM BY SLOWLY SUCKING AWAY THEIR MANA.
CHAOS FLOWERS PRODUCE SUBSPECIES BY MATING WITH THE NATIVE PLANTS OF THE LAND.
IT LOOKS ALMOST LIKE A MIRROR.
NO MATTER HOW MUCH THE VARIOUS SUBSPECIES VARY, THEY ALL HAVE THE SAME WEAKNESS-THEIR CORE!
THREE SPEARS OF THE GODDESS!

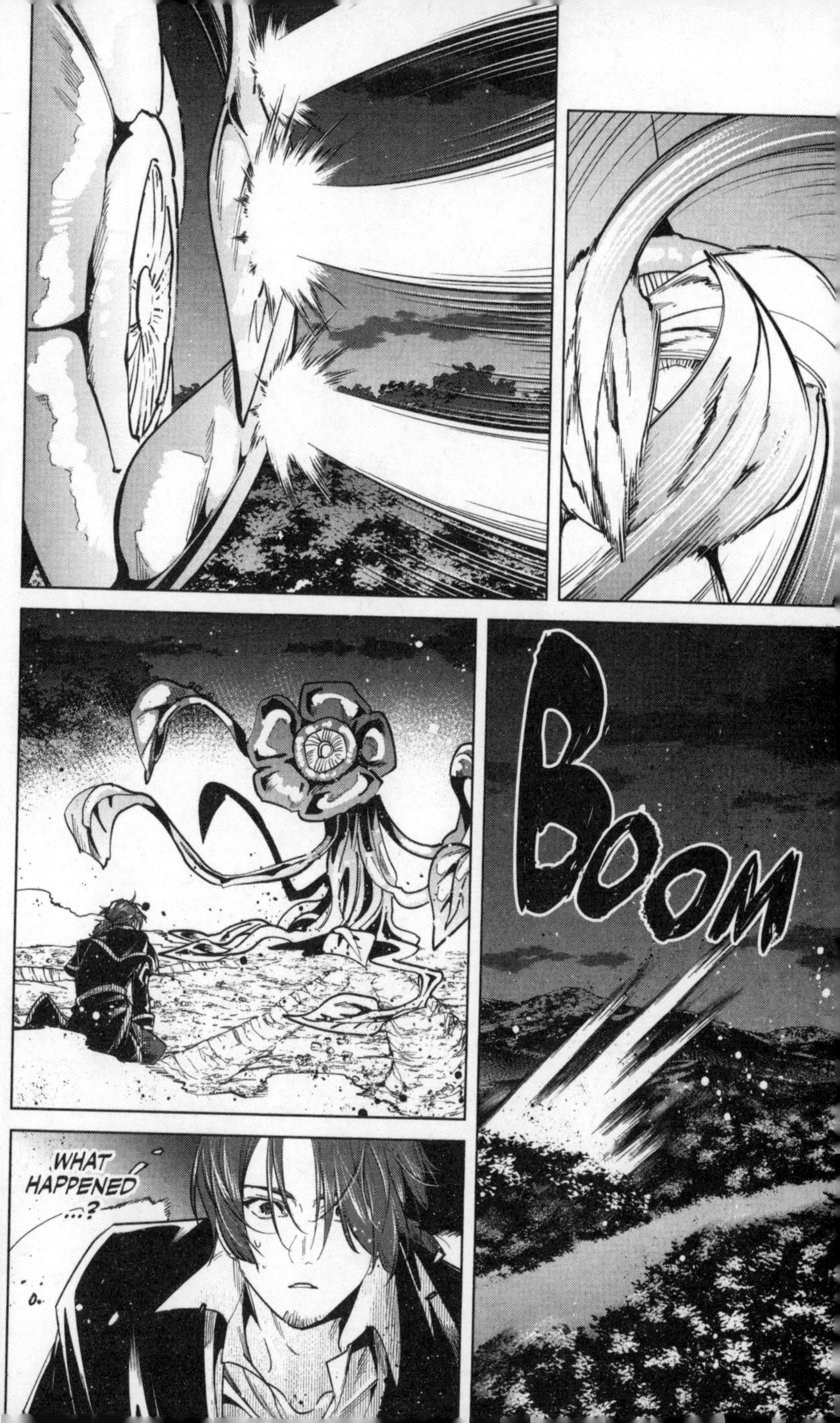
BOOM
WHAT HAPPENED ...?
O..

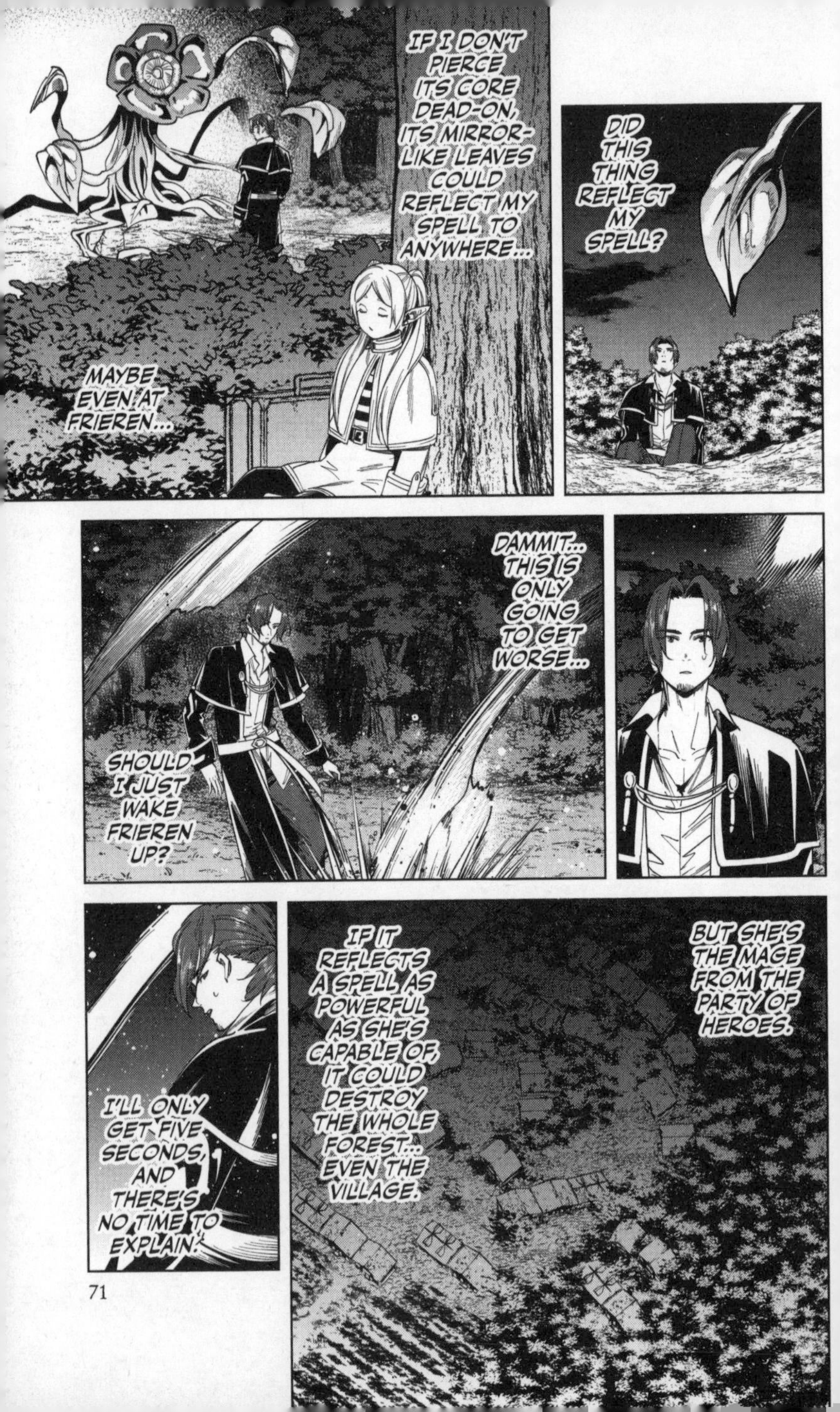
DID THIS THING REFLECT MY SPELL?
IF I DON'T PIERCE ITS CORE DEAD-ON, ITS MIRROR-LIKE LEAVES COULD REFLECT MY SPELL TO ANYWHERE...
MAYBE EVEN AT FRIEREN...
DAMMIT... THIS IS ONLY GOING TO GET WORSE...
SHOULD I JUST WAKE FRIEREN UP?
BUT SHE'S THE MAGE FROM THE PARTY OF HEROES.
IF IT REFLECTS A SPELL AS POWERFUL AS SHE'S CAPABLE OF, IT COULD DESTROY THE WHOLE FOREST... EVEN THE VILLAGE.
I'LL ONLY GET FIVE SECONDS, AND THERE'S NO TIME TO EXPLAIN.

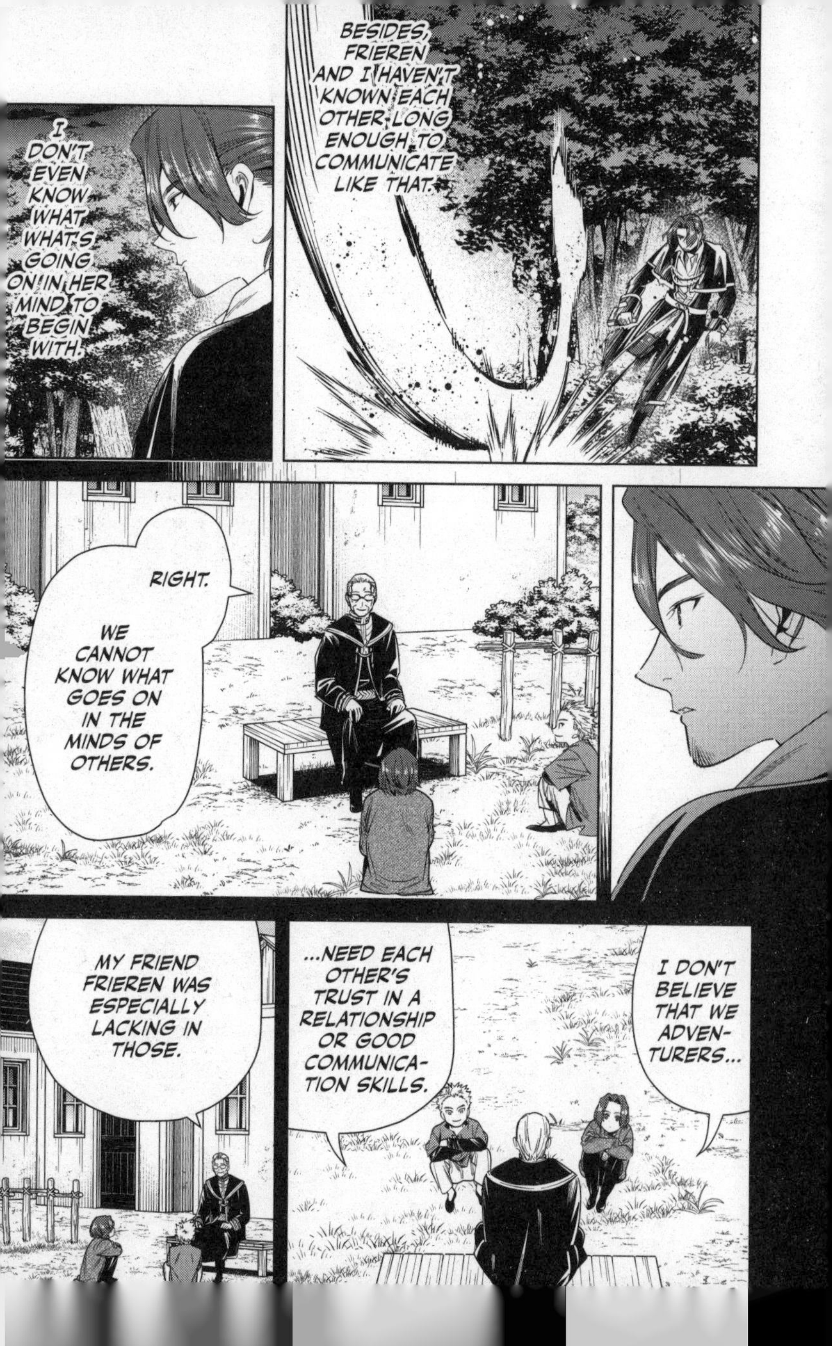
BESIDES, FRIEREN AND I HAVEN'T KNOWN EACH OTHER LONG ENOUGH TO COMMUNICATE LIKE THAT.
I DON'T EVEN KNOW WHAT WHAT'S GOING ON IN HER MIND TO BEGIN WITH.
RIGHT.
WE CANNOT KNOW WHAT GOES ON IN THE MINDS OF OTHERS.
I DON'T BELIEVE THAT WE ADVENTURERS...
...NEED EACH OTHER'S TRUST IN A RELATIONSHIP OR GOOD COMMUNICATION SKILLS.
MY FRIEND FRIEREN WAS ESPECIALLY LACKING IN THOSE.

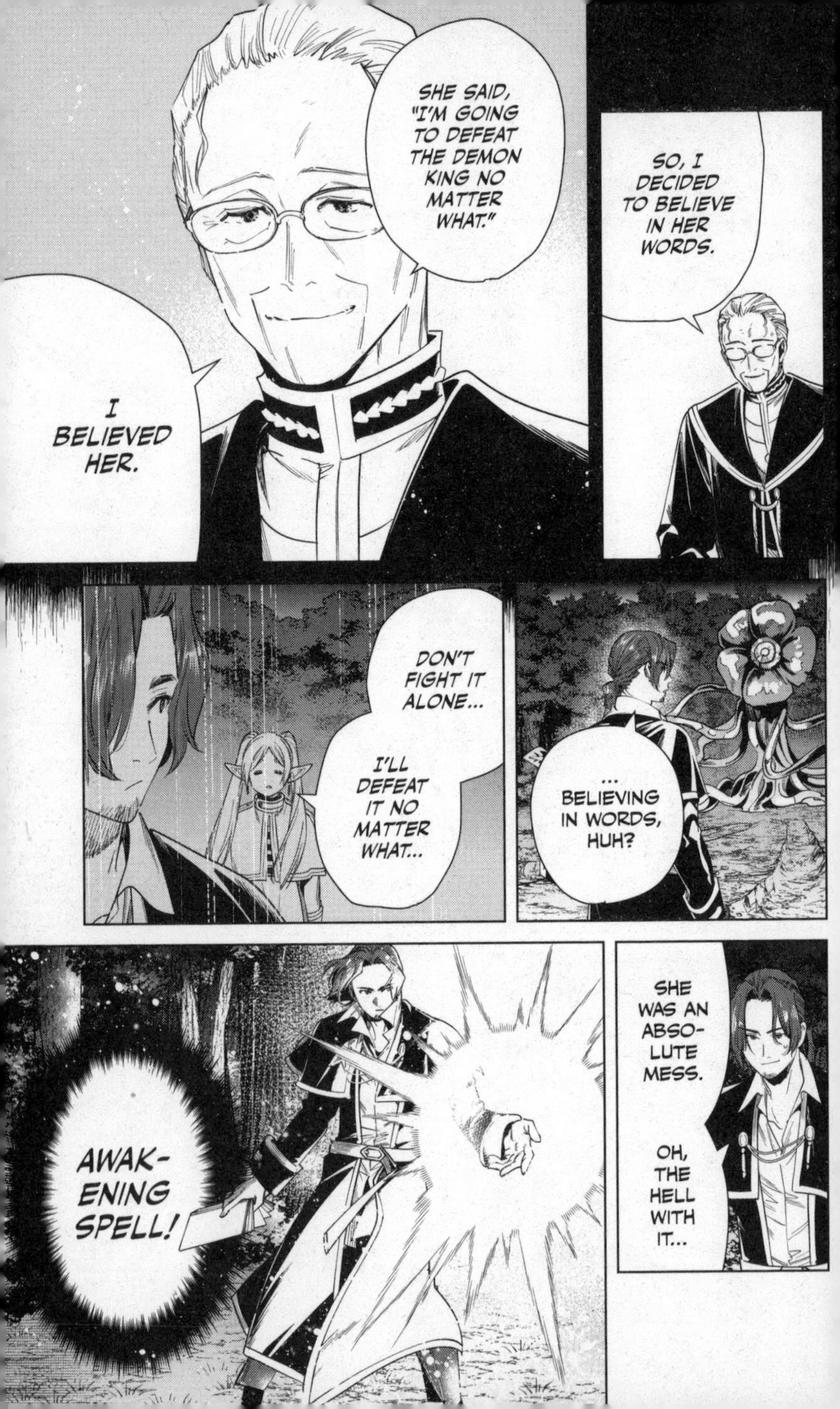
SO, I DECIDED TO BELIEVE IN HER WORDS.
SHE SAID, "I'M GOING TO DEFEAT THE DEMON KING NO MATTER WHAT."
I BELIEVED HER.
...BELIEVING IN WORDS, HUH?
DON'T FIGHT IT ALONE...
I'LL DEFEAT IT NO MATTER WHAT...
SHE WAS AN ABSO-LUTE MESS.
OH, THE HELL WITH IT...
AWAK-ENING SPELL!

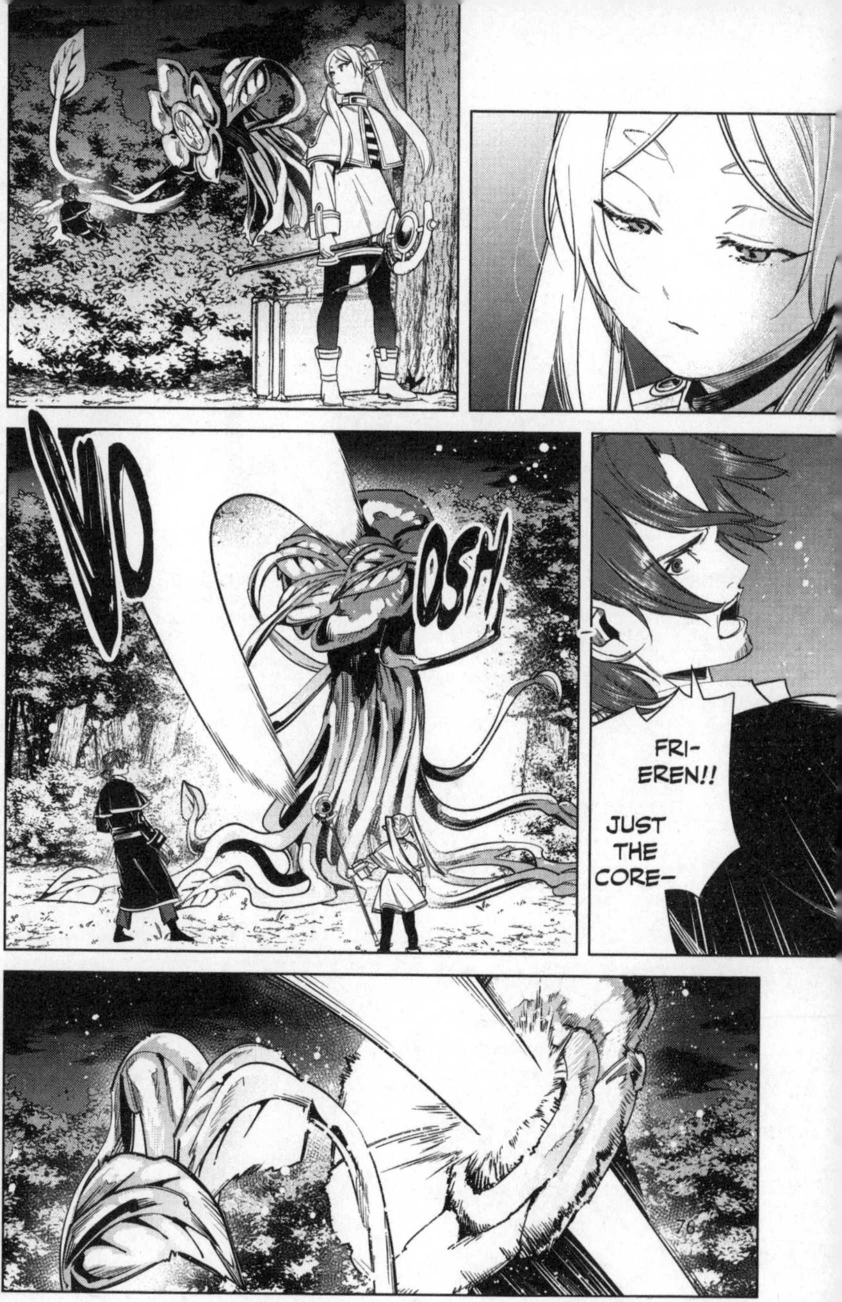
FRI-
EREN!!
JUST
THE
CORE-
VO
OSH

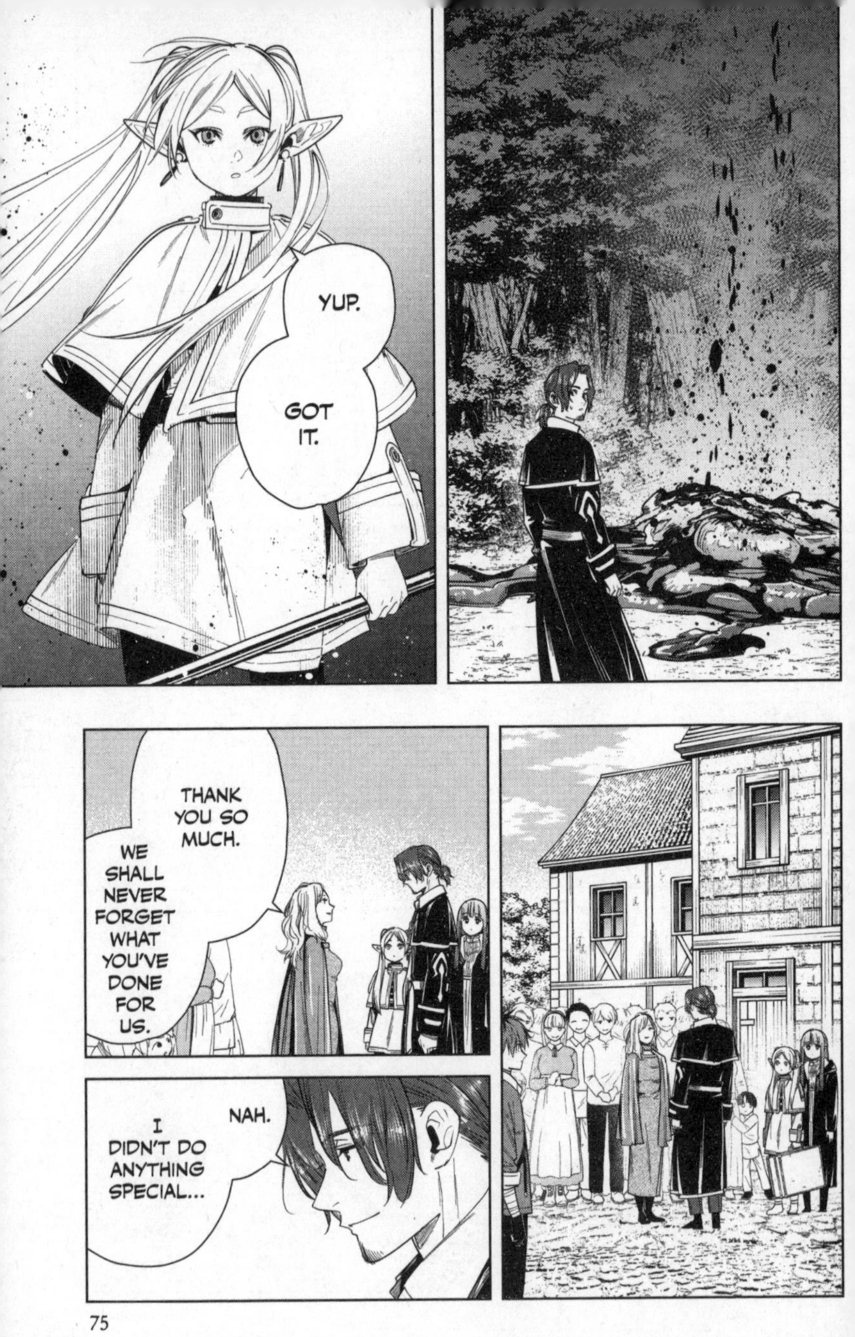
YUP.
GOT IT.
THANK YOU SO MUCH.
WE SHALL NEVER FORGET WHAT YOU'VE DONE FOR US.
NAH.
I DIDN'T DO ANYTHING SPECIAL...

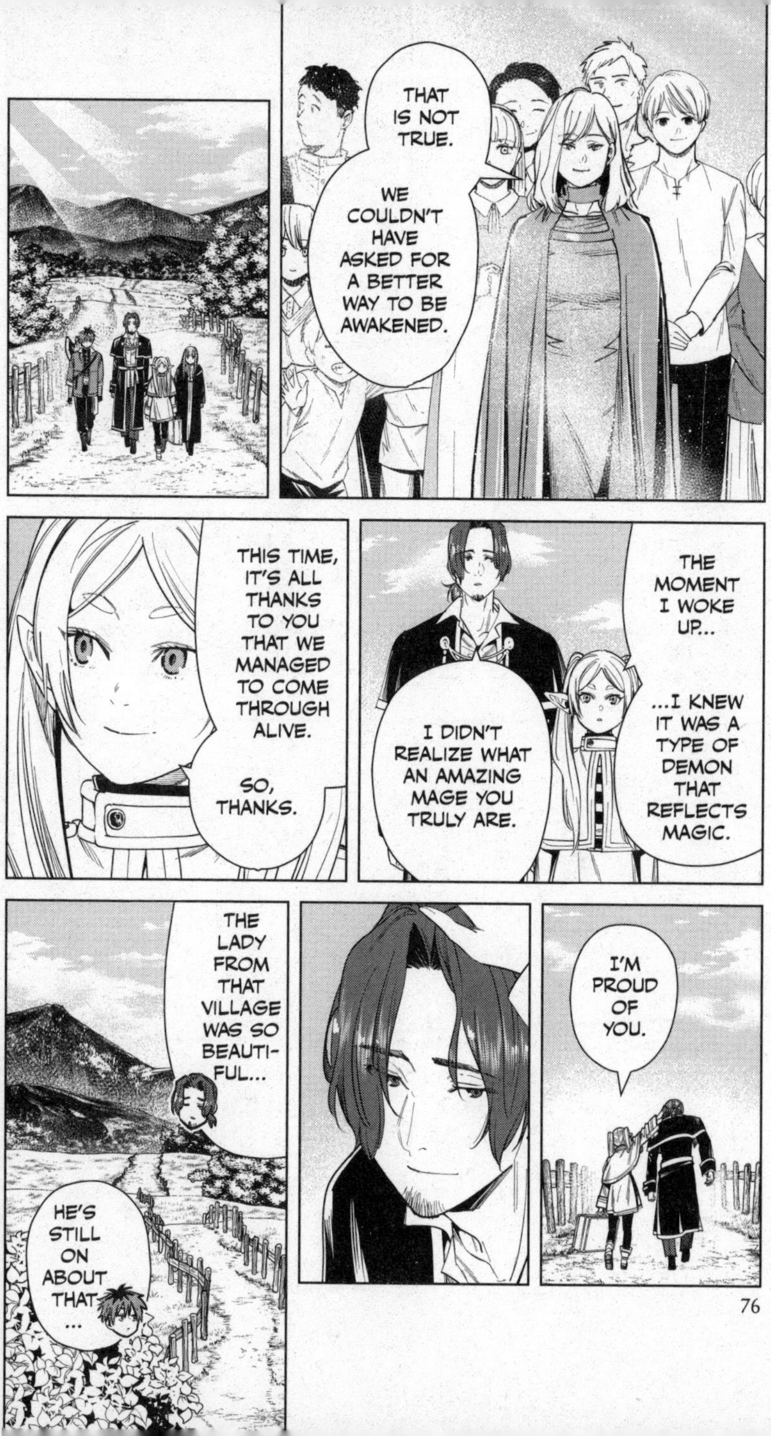
THAT IS NOT TRUE.
WE COULDN'T HAVE ASKED FOR A BETTER WAY TO BE AWAKENED.
THE MOMENT I WOKE UP...
...I KNEW IT WAS A TYPE OF DEMON THAT REFLECTS MAGIC.
I DIDN'T REALIZE WHAT AN AMAZING MAGE YOU TRULY ARE.
THIS TIME, IT'S ALL THANKS TO YOU THAT WE MANAGED TO COME THROUGH ALIVE.
SO, THANKS.
I'M PROUD OF YOU.
THE LADY FROM THAT VILLAGE WAS SO BEAUTI-FUL...
HE'S STILL ON ABOUT THAT...

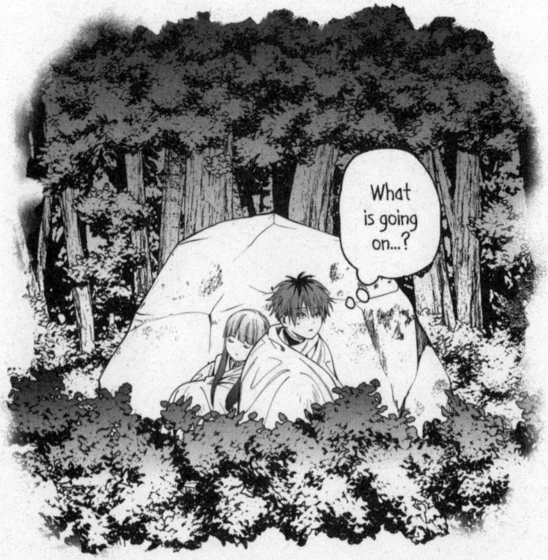
What is going on...?

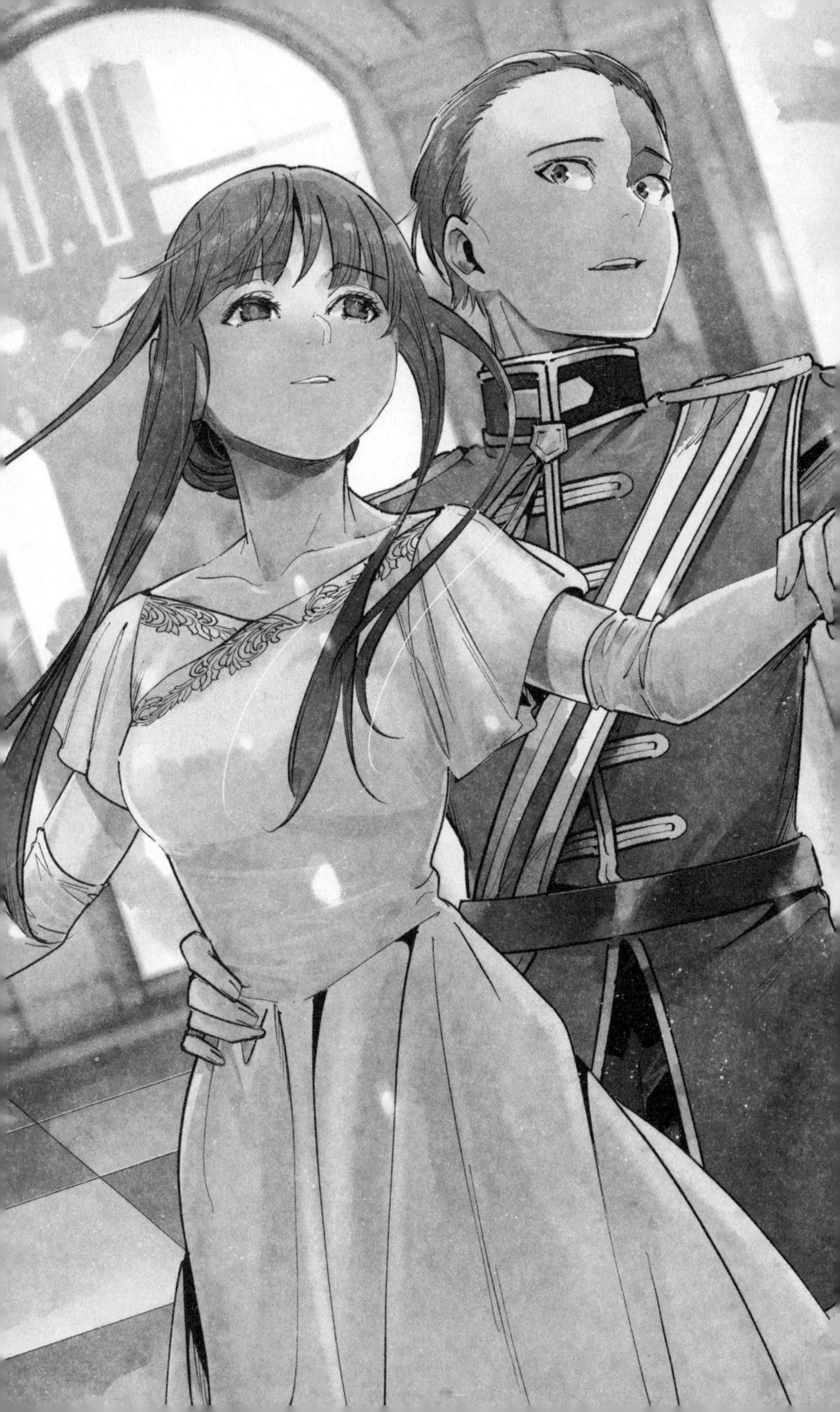

Chapter 32: The Orden Family

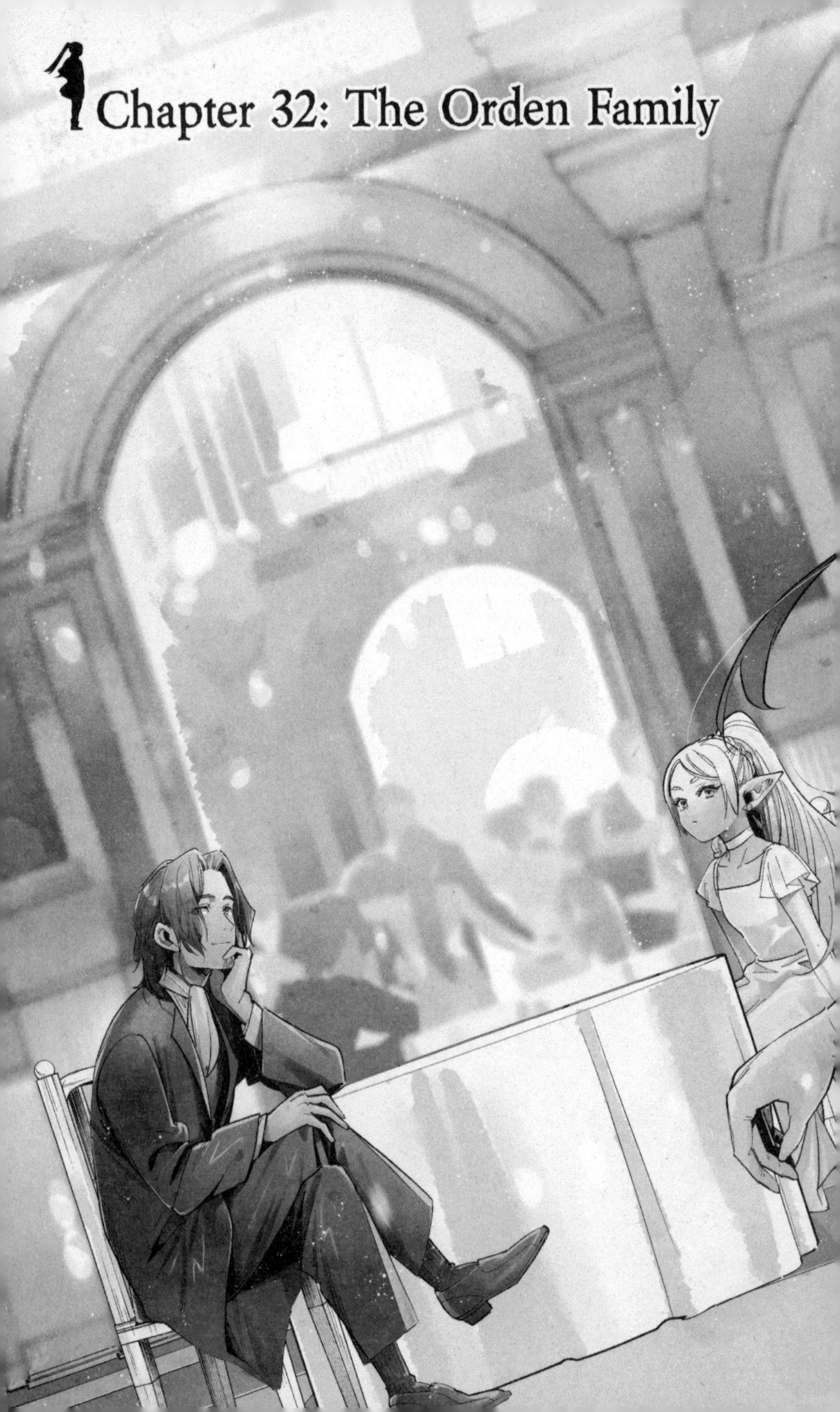

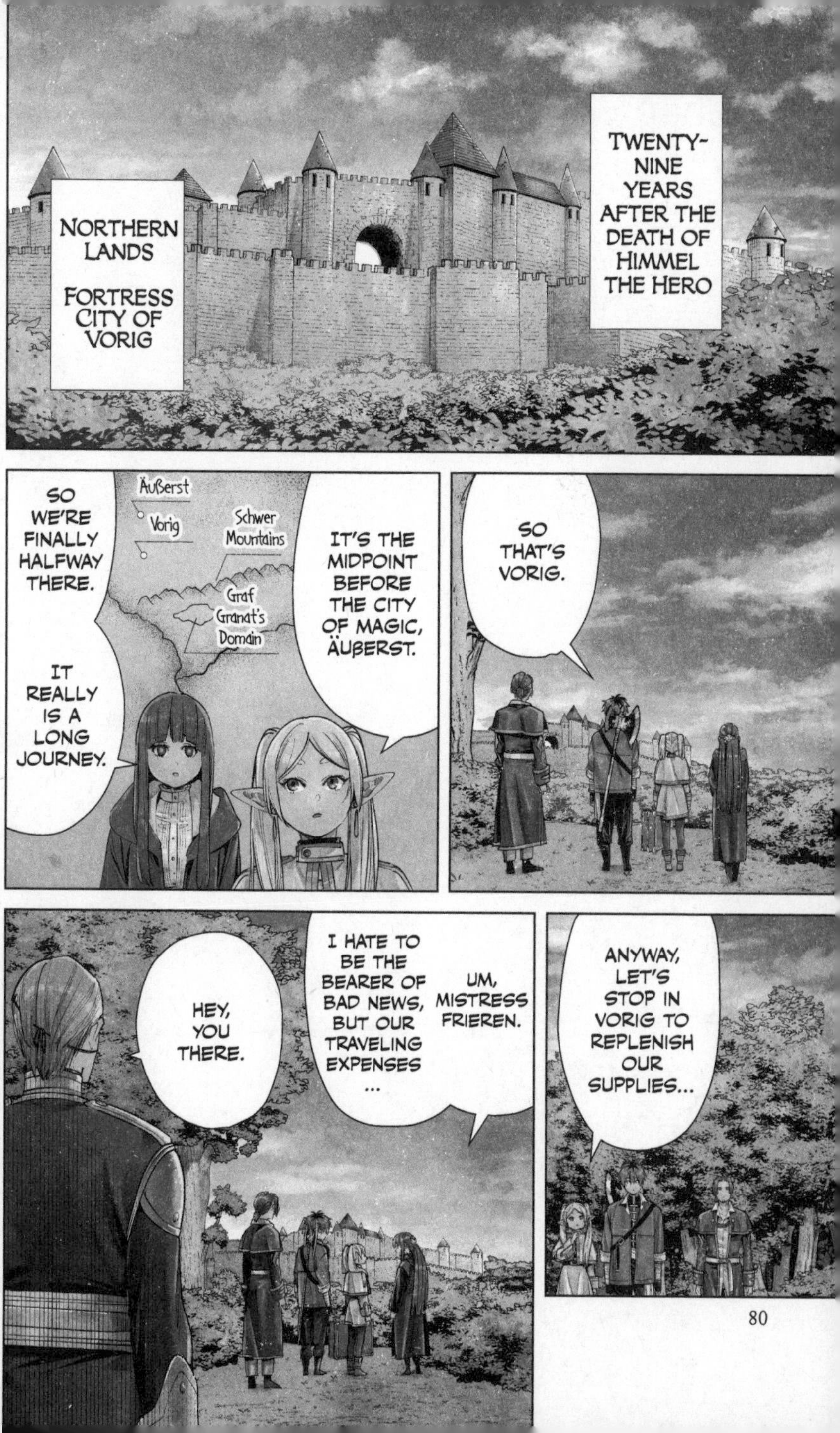
TWENTY-NINE YEARS AFTER THE DEATH OF HIMMEL THE HERO
NORTHERN LANDS
FORTRESS CITY OF VORIG
SO THAT'S VORIG.
IT'S THE MIDPOINT BEFORE THE CITY OF MAGIC, ÄUßERST.
SO WE'RE FINALLY HALFWAY THERE.
Äußerst
Vorig
Schwer Mountains
Graf Granat's Domain
IT REALLY IS A LONG JOURNEY.
ANYWAY, LET'S STOP IN VORIG TO REPLENISH OUR SUPPLIES...
UM, MISTRESS FRIEREN.
I HATE TO BE THE BEARER OF BAD NEWS, BUT OUR TRAVELING EXPENSES ...
HEY, YOU THERE.

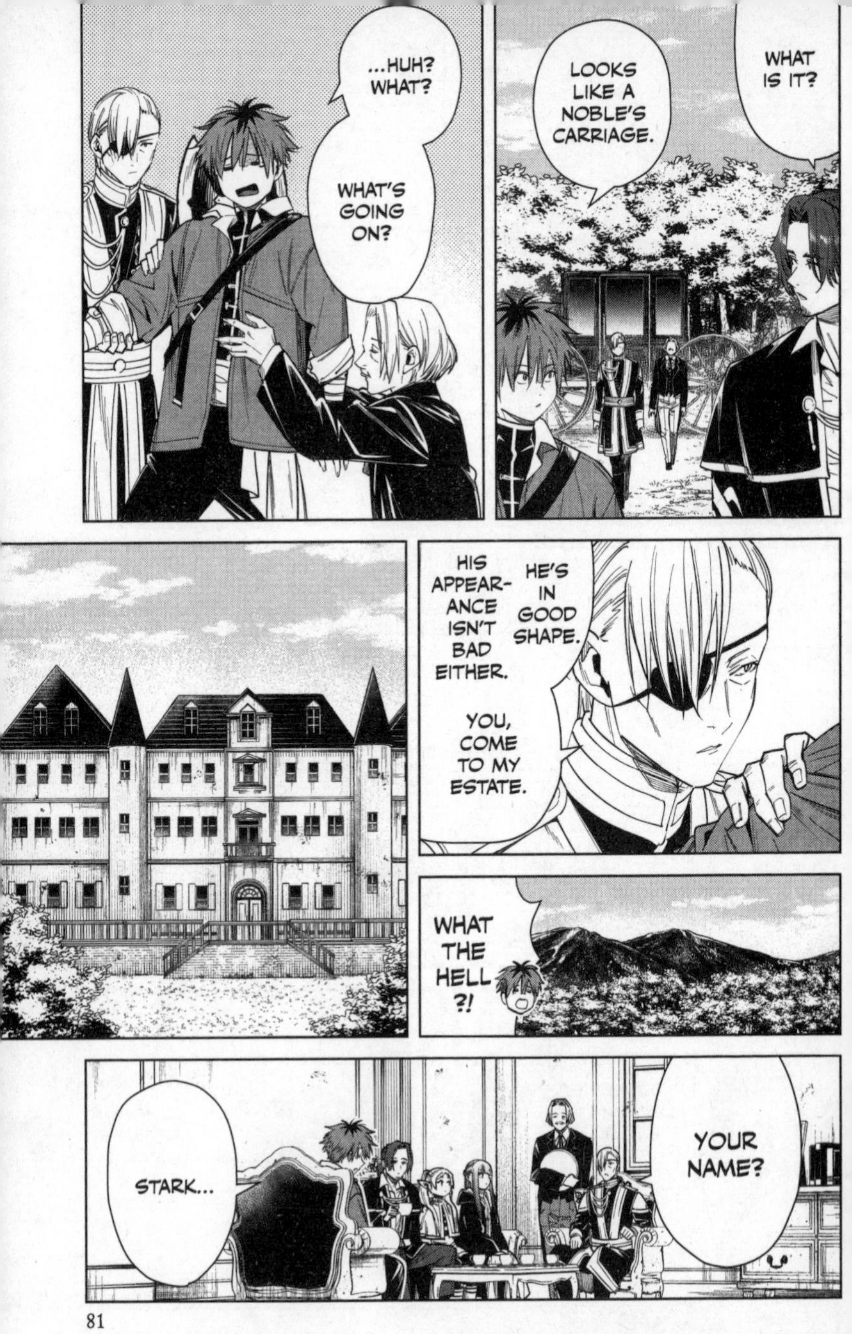
WHAT IS IT?
LOOKS LIKE A NOBLE'S CARRIAGE.
...HUH? WHAT?
WHAT'S GOING ON?
HE'S IN GOOD SHAPE.
HIS APPEARANCE ISN'T BAD EITHER.
YOU, COME TO MY ESTATE.
WHAT THE HELL?!
YOUR NAME?
STARK...

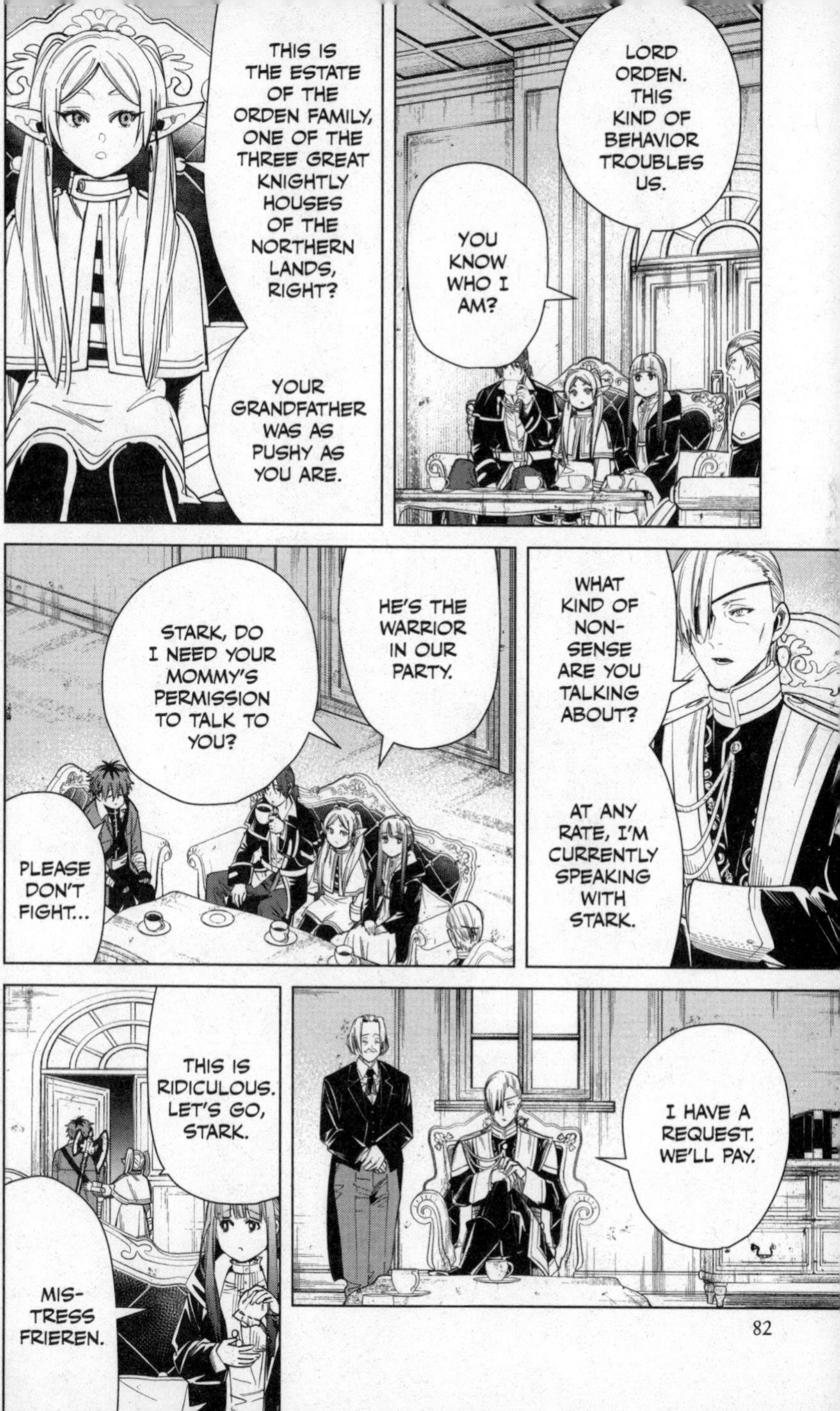
LORD ORDEN. THIS KIND OF BEHAVIOR TROUBLES US.
YOU KNOW WHO I AM?
THIS IS THE ESTATE OF THE ORDEN FAMILY, ONE OF THE THREE GREAT KNIGHTLY HOUSES OF THE NORTHERN LANDS, RIGHT?
YOUR GRANDFATHER WAS AS PUSHY AS YOU ARE.
WHAT KIND OF NON-SENSE ARE YOU TALKING ABOUT?
AT ANY RATE, I'M CURRENTLY SPEAKING WITH STARK.
HE'S THE WARRIOR IN OUR PARTY.
STARK, DO I NEED YOUR MOMMY'S PERMISSION TO TALK TO YOU?
PLEASE DON'T FIGHT...
I HAVE A REQUEST. WE'LL PAY.
THIS IS RIDICULOUS. LET'S GO, STARK.
MIS-TRESS FRIEREN.

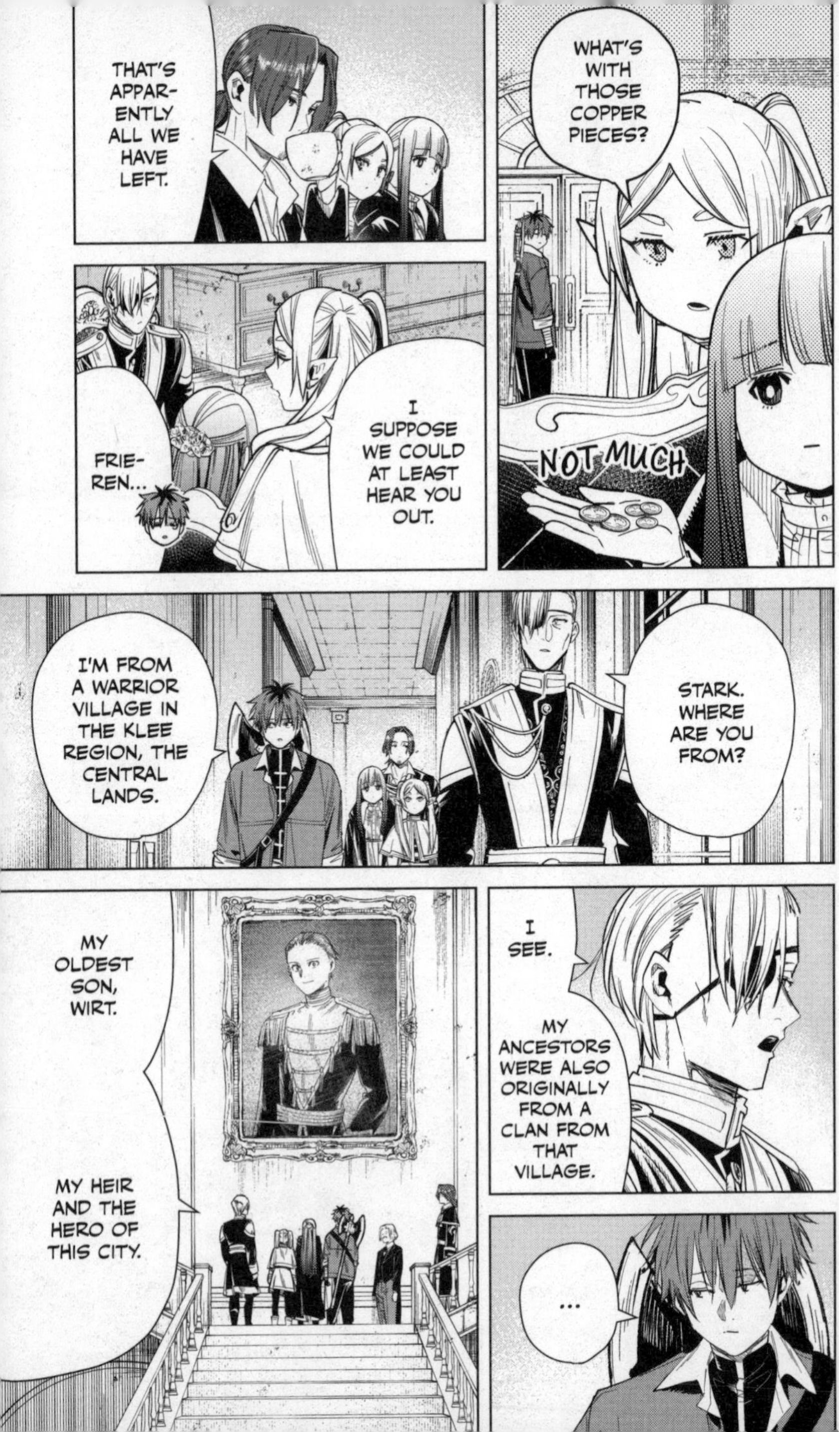
WHAT'S WITH THOSE COPPER PIECES?
NOT MUCH
THAT'S APPARENTLY ALL WE HAVE LEFT.
I SUPPOSE WE COULD AT LEAST HEAR YOU OUT.
FRIEREN...
STARK. WHERE ARE YOU FROM?
I'M FROM A WARRIOR VILLAGE IN THE KLEE REGION, THE CENTRAL LANDS.
I SEE.
MY ANCESTORS WERE ALSO ORIGINALLY FROM A CLAN FROM THAT VILLAGE.
...
MY OLDEST SON, WIRT.
MY HEIR AND THE HERO OF THIS CITY.

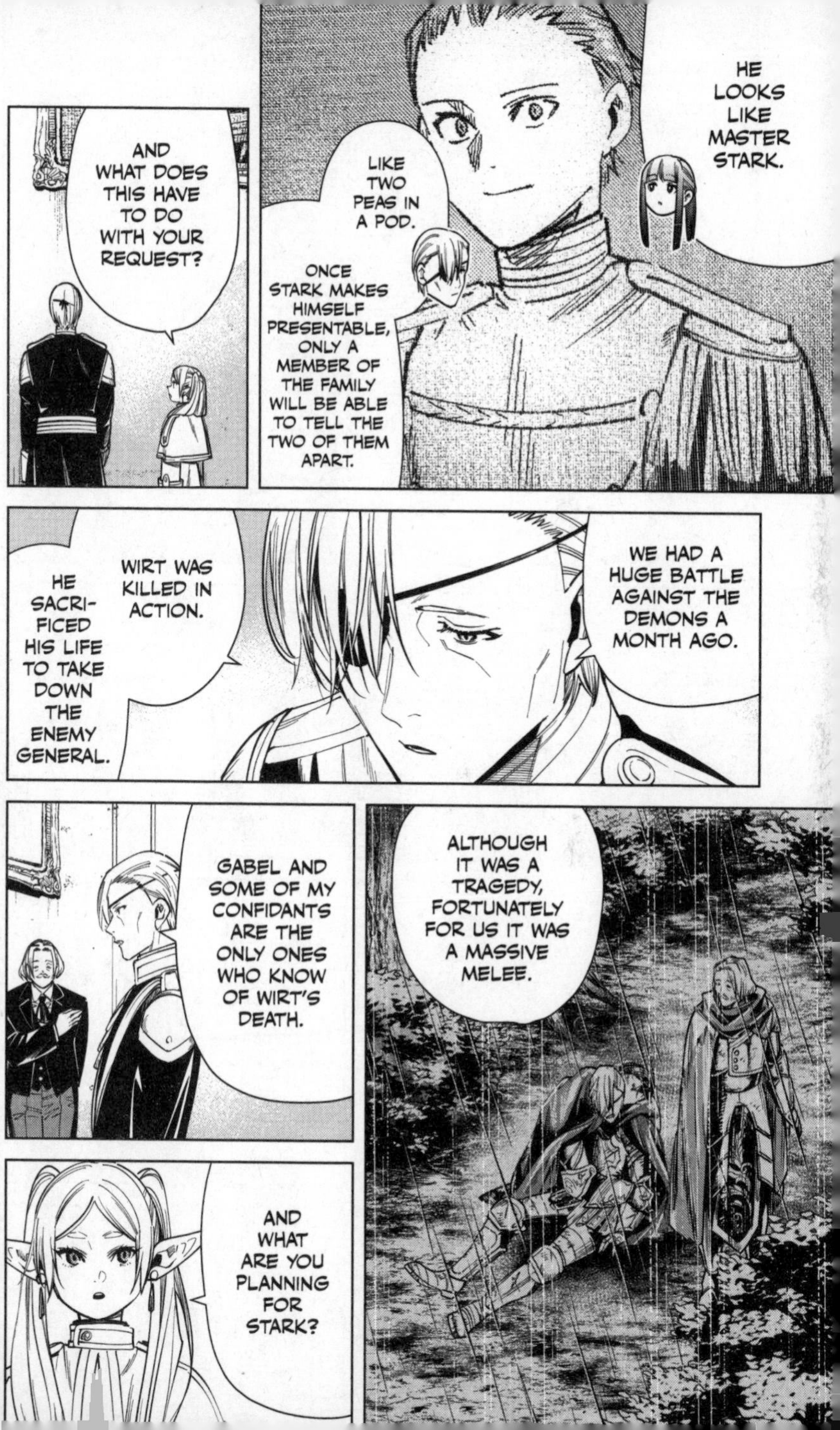
HE LOOKS LIKE MASTER STARK.
LIKE TWO PEAS IN A POD.
ONCE STARK MAKES HIMSELF PRESENTABLE, ONLY A MEMBER OF THE FAMILY WILL BE ABLE TO TELL THE TWO OF THEM APART.
AND WHAT DOES THIS HAVE TO DO WITH YOUR REQUEST?
WE HAD A HUGE BATTLE AGAINST THE DEMONS A MONTH AGO.
WIRT WAS KILLED IN ACTION.
HE SACRI-FICED HIS LIFE TO TAKE DOWN THE ENEMY GENERAL.
ALTHOUGH IT WAS A TRAGEDY, FORTUNATELY FOR US IT WAS A MASSIVE MELEE.
GABEL AND SOME OF MY CONFIDANTS ARE THE ONLY ONES WHO KNOW OF WIRT'S DEATH.
AND WHAT ARE YOU PLANNING FOR STARK?

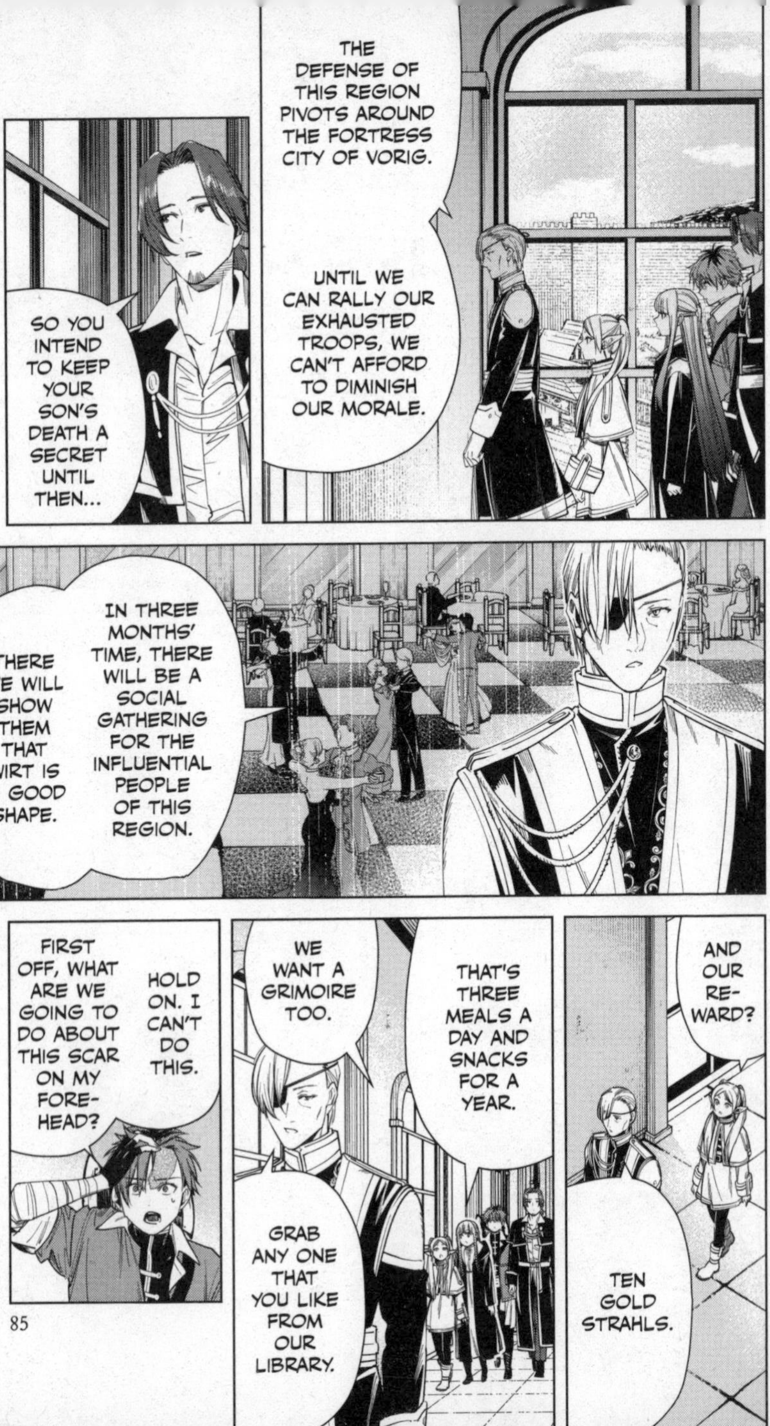
THE DEFENSE OF THIS REGION PIVOTS AROUND THE FORTRESS CITY OF VORIG.
UNTIL WE CAN RALLY OUR EXHAUSTED TROOPS, WE CAN'T AFFORD TO DIMINISH OUR MORALE.
SO YOU INTEND TO KEEP YOUR SON'S DEATH A SECRET UNTIL THEN...
IN THREE MONTHS' TIME, THERE WILL BE A SOCIAL GATHERING FOR THE INFLUENTIAL PEOPLE OF THIS REGION.
THERE WE WILL SHOW THEM THAT WIRT IS IN GOOD SHAPE.
AND OUR RE-WARD?
TEN GOLD STRAHLS.
THAT'S THREE MEALS A DAY AND SNACKS FOR A YEAR.
WE WANT A GRIMOIRE TOO.
GRAB ANY ONE THAT YOU LIKE FROM OUR LIBRARY.
HOLD ON. I CAN'T DO THIS.
FIRST OFF, WHAT ARE WE GOING TO DO ABOUT THIS SCAR ON MY FORE-HEAD?

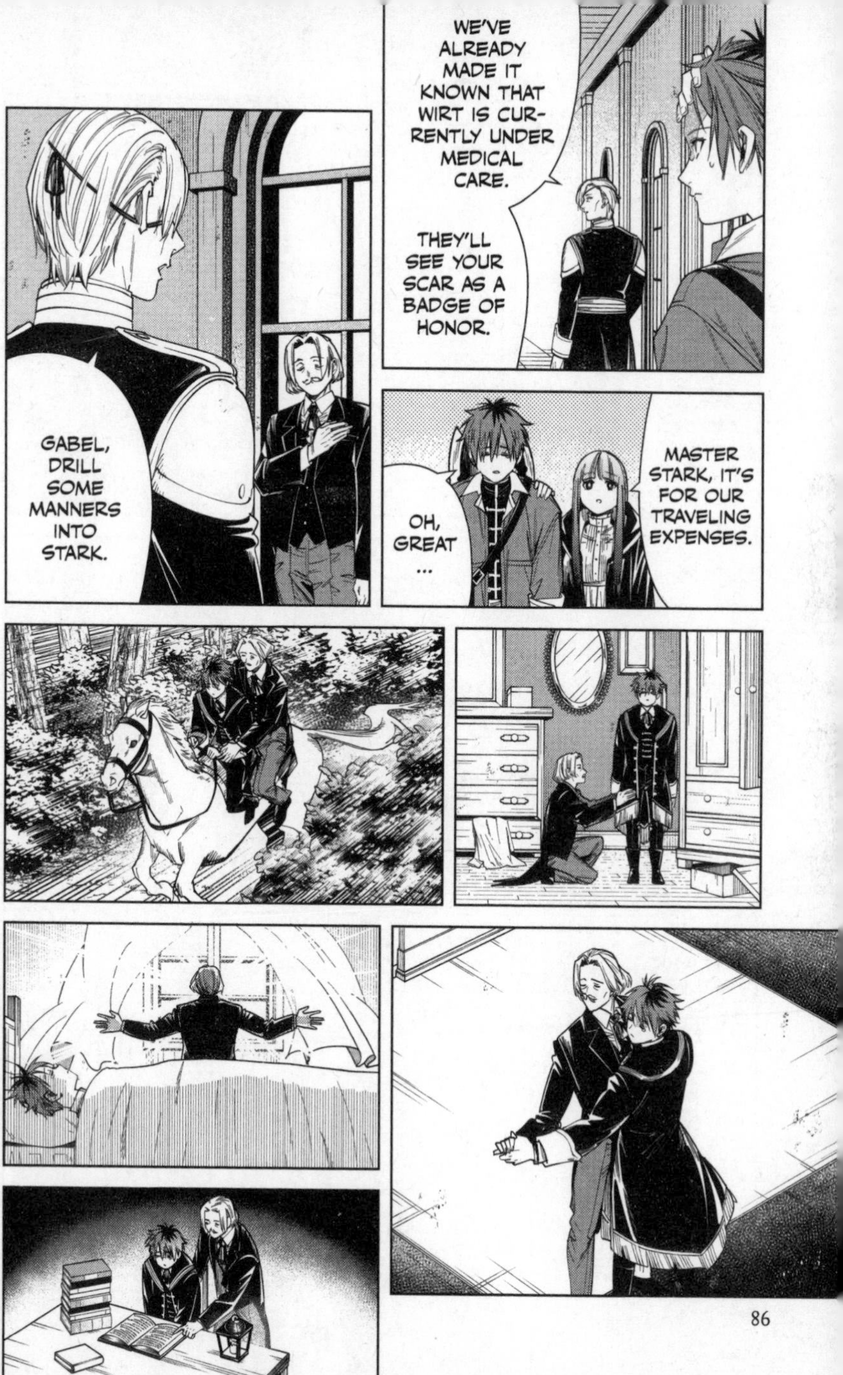
WE'VE ALREADY MADE IT KNOWN THAT WIRT IS CUR-RENTLY UNDER MEDICAL CARE.
THEY'LL SEE YOUR SCAR AS A BADGE OF HONOR.
MASTER STARK, IT'S FOR OUR TRAVELING EXPENSES.
OH, GREAT ...
GABEL, DRILL SOME MANNERS INTO STARK.

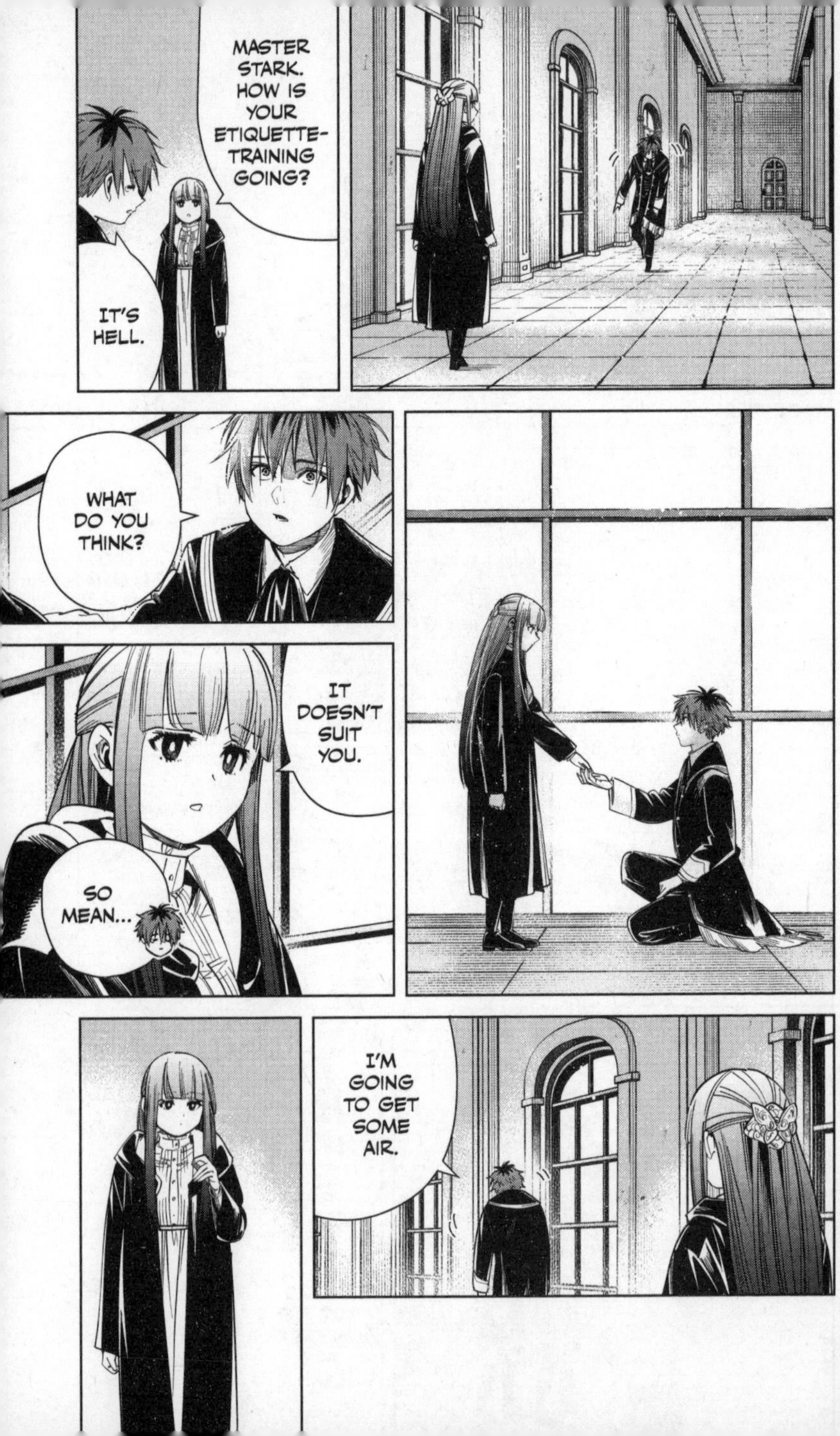
MASTER STARK. HOW IS YOUR ETIQUETTE-TRAINING GOING?
IT'S HELL.
WHAT DO YOU THINK?
IT DOESN'T SUIT YOU.
SO MEAN...
I'M GOING TO GET SOME AIR.

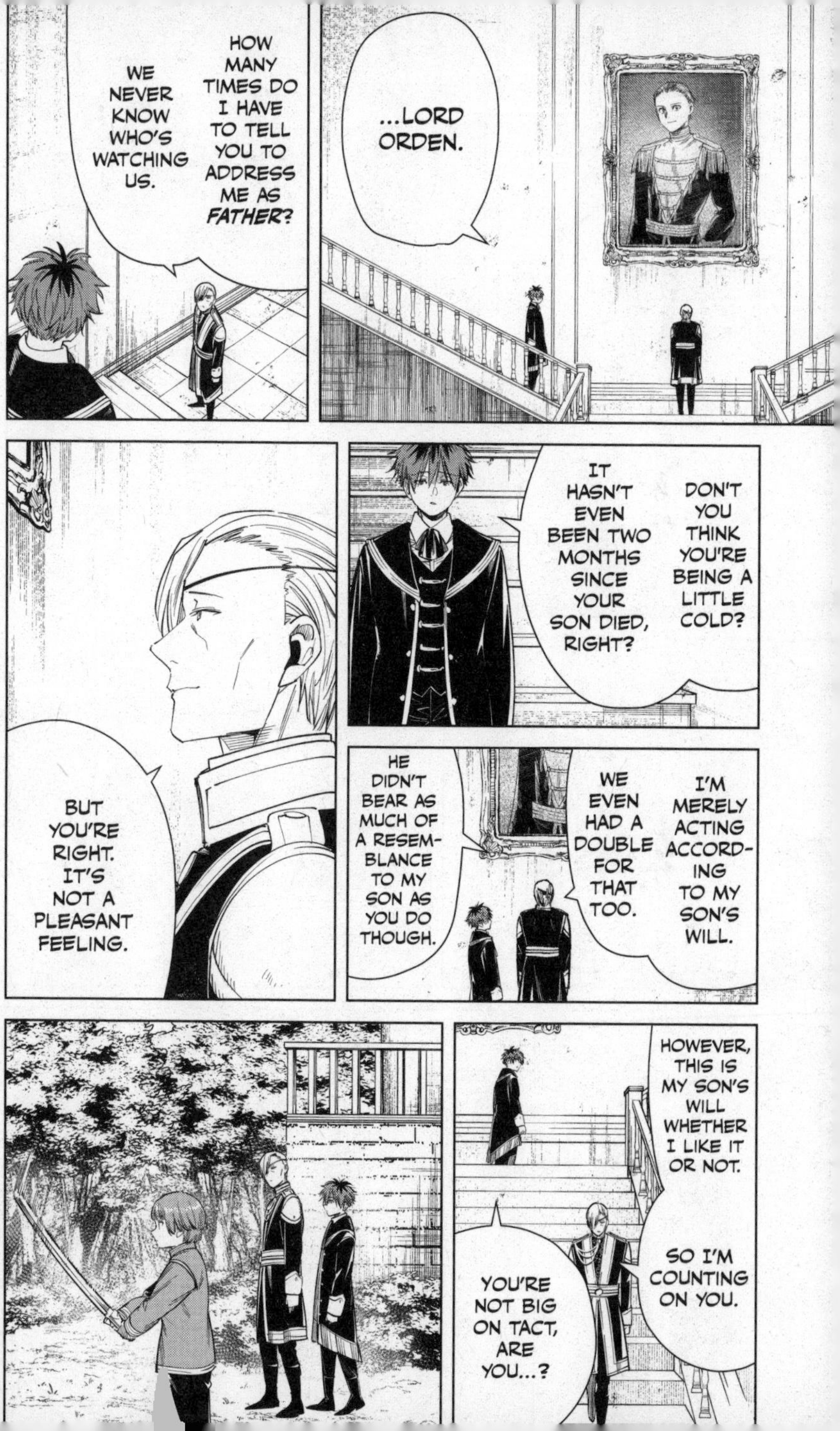
...LORD ORDEN.
HOW MANY TIMES DO I HAVE TO TELL YOU TO ADDRESS ME AS *FATHER*?
WE NEVER KNOW WHO'S WATCHING US.
DON'T YOU THINK YOU'RE BEING A LITTLE COLD?
IT HASN'T EVEN BEEN TWO MONTHS SINCE YOUR SON DIED, RIGHT?
I'M MERELY ACTING ACCORDING TO MY SON'S WILL.
WE EVEN HAD A DOUBLE FOR THAT TOO.
HE DIDN'T BEAR AS MUCH OF A RESEMBLANCE TO MY SON AS YOU DO THOUGH.
BUT YOU'RE RIGHT. IT'S NOT A PLEASANT FEELING.
HOWEVER, THIS IS MY SON'S WILL WHETHER I LIKE IT OR NOT.
SO I'M COUNTING ON YOU.
YOU'RE NOT BIG ON TACT, ARE YOU...?

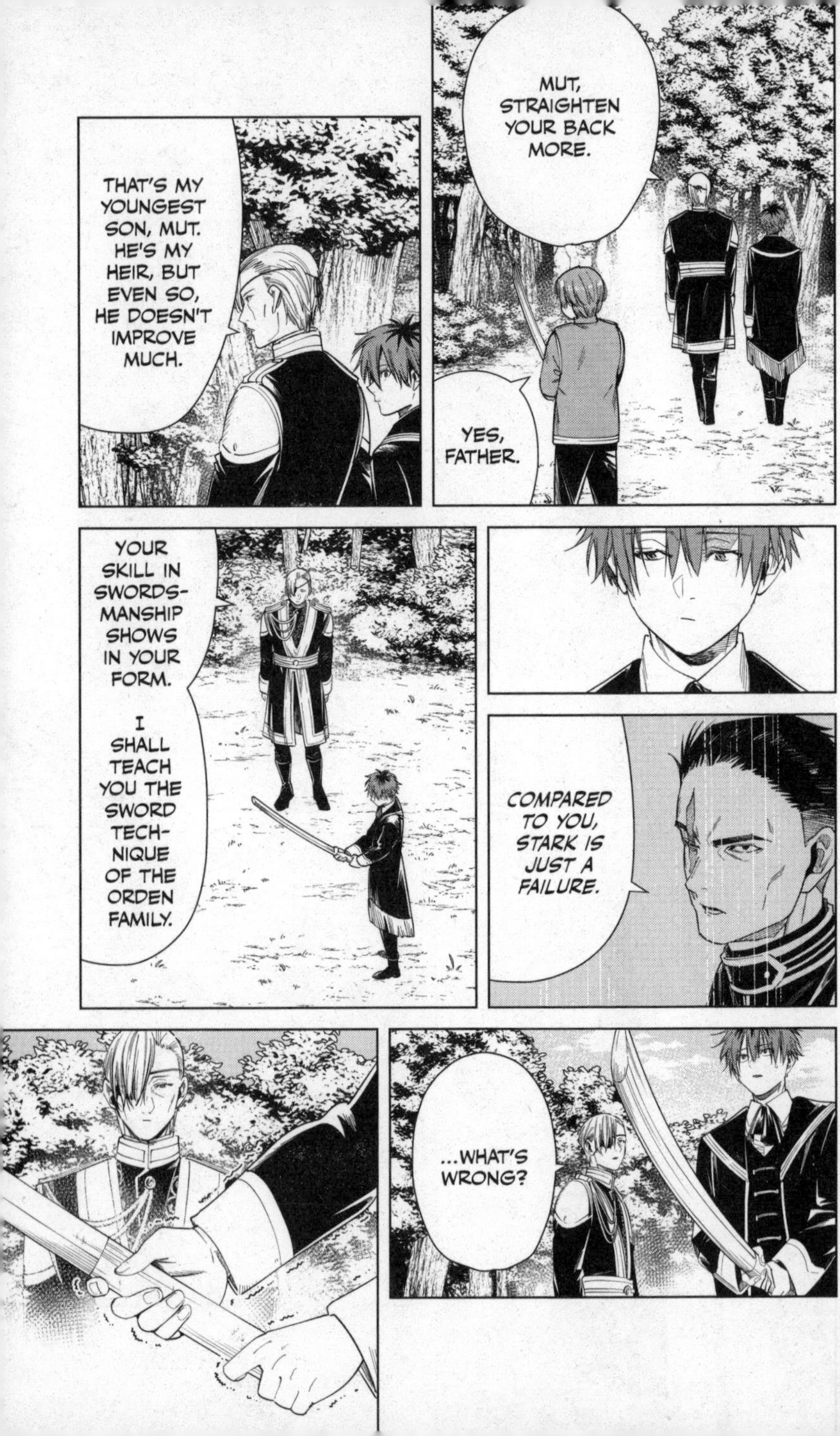
MUT, STRAIGHTEN YOUR BACK MORE.
YES, FATHER.
THAT'S MY YOUNGEST SON, MUT. HE'S MY HEIR, BUT EVEN SO, HE DOESN'T IMPROVE MUCH.
COMPARED TO YOU, STARK IS JUST A FAILURE.
YOUR SKILL IN SWORDS-MANSHIP SHOWS IN YOUR FORM.
I SHALL TEACH YOU THE SWORD TECH-NIQUE OF THE ORDEN FAMILY.
...WHAT'S WRONG?

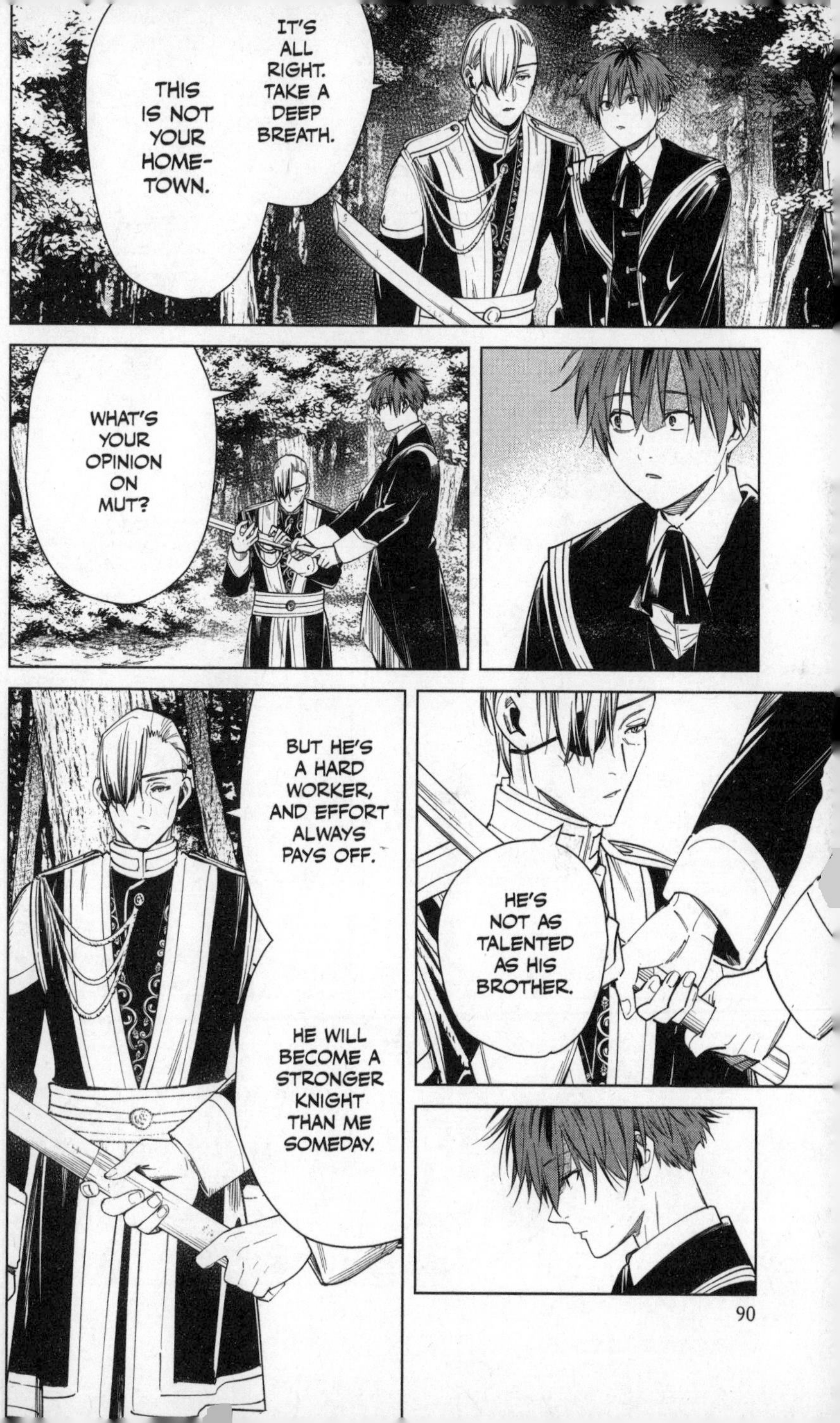
IT'S ALL RIGHT. TAKE A DEEP BREATH.
THIS IS NOT YOUR HOME-TOWN.
WHAT'S YOUR OPINION ON MUT?
HE'S NOT AS TALENTED AS HIS BROTHER.
BUT HE'S A HARD WORKER, AND EFFORT ALWAYS PAYS OFF.
HE WILL BECOME A STRONGER KNIGHT THAN ME SOMEDAY.

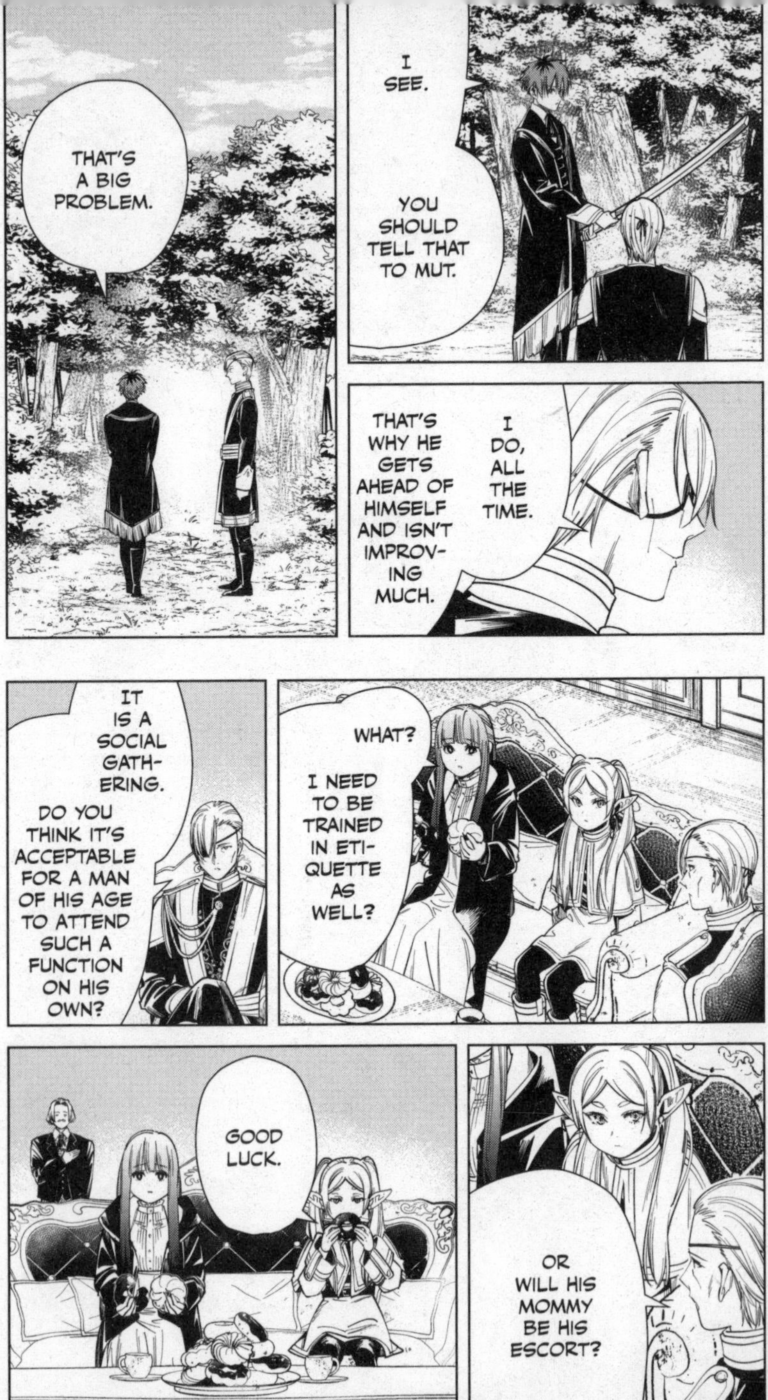
I SEE.
YOU SHOULD TELL THAT TO MUT.
I DO, ALL THE TIME.
THAT'S WHY HE GETS AHEAD OF HIMSELF AND ISN'T IMPROV-ING MUCH.
THAT'S A BIG PROBLEM.
WHAT?
I NEED TO BE TRAINED IN ETI-QUETTE AS WELL?
IT IS A SOCIAL GATH-ERING.
DO YOU THINK IT'S ACCEPTABLE FOR A MAN OF HIS AGE TO ATTEND SUCH A FUNCTION ON HIS OWN?
OR WILL HIS MOMMY BE HIS ESCORT?
GOOD LUCK.

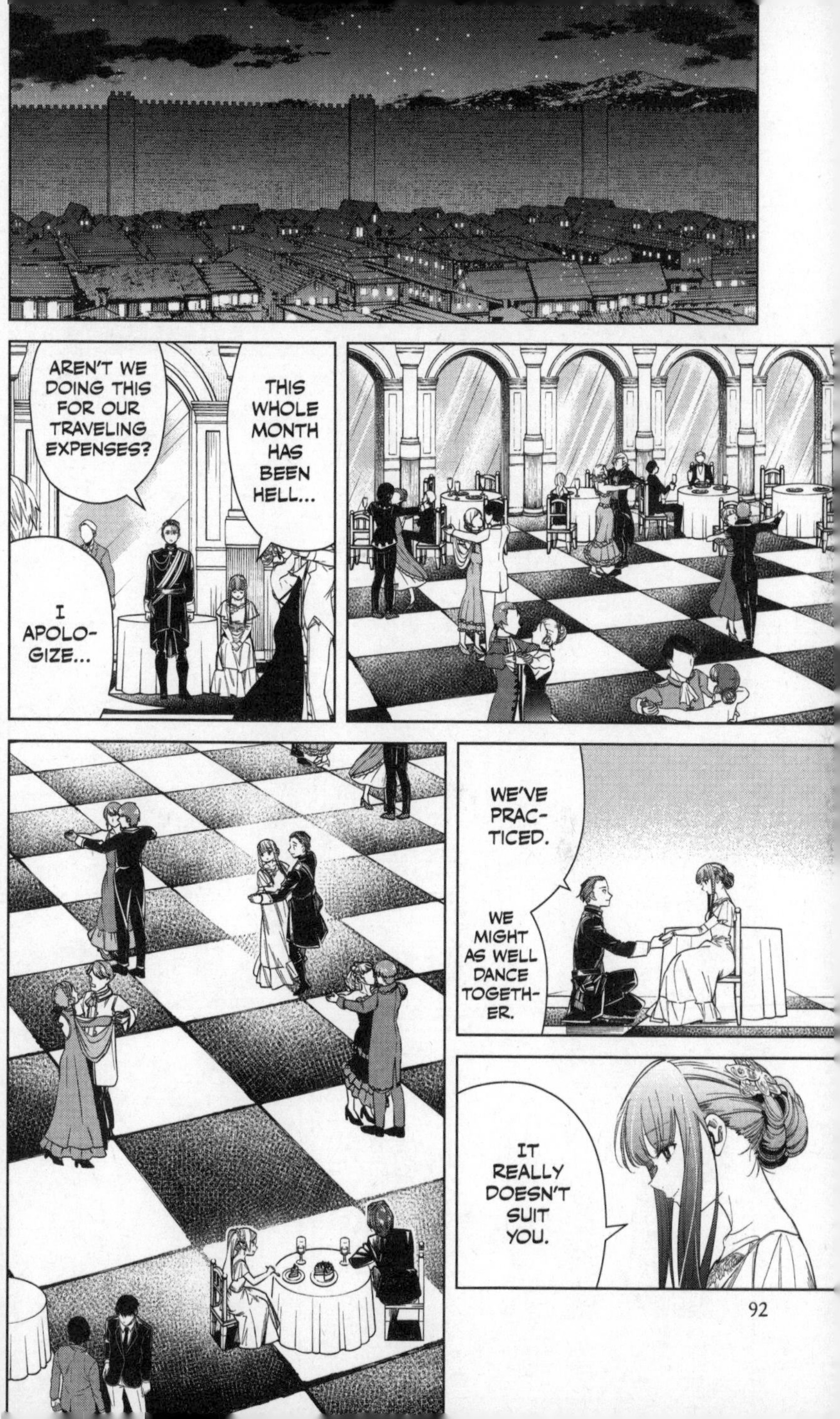
THIS WHOLE MONTH HAS BEEN HELL...
AREN'T WE DOING THIS FOR OUR TRAVELING EXPENSES?
I APOLOGIZE...
WE'VE PRACTICED.
WE MIGHT AS WELL DANCE TOGETHER.
IT REALLY DOESN'T SUIT YOU.

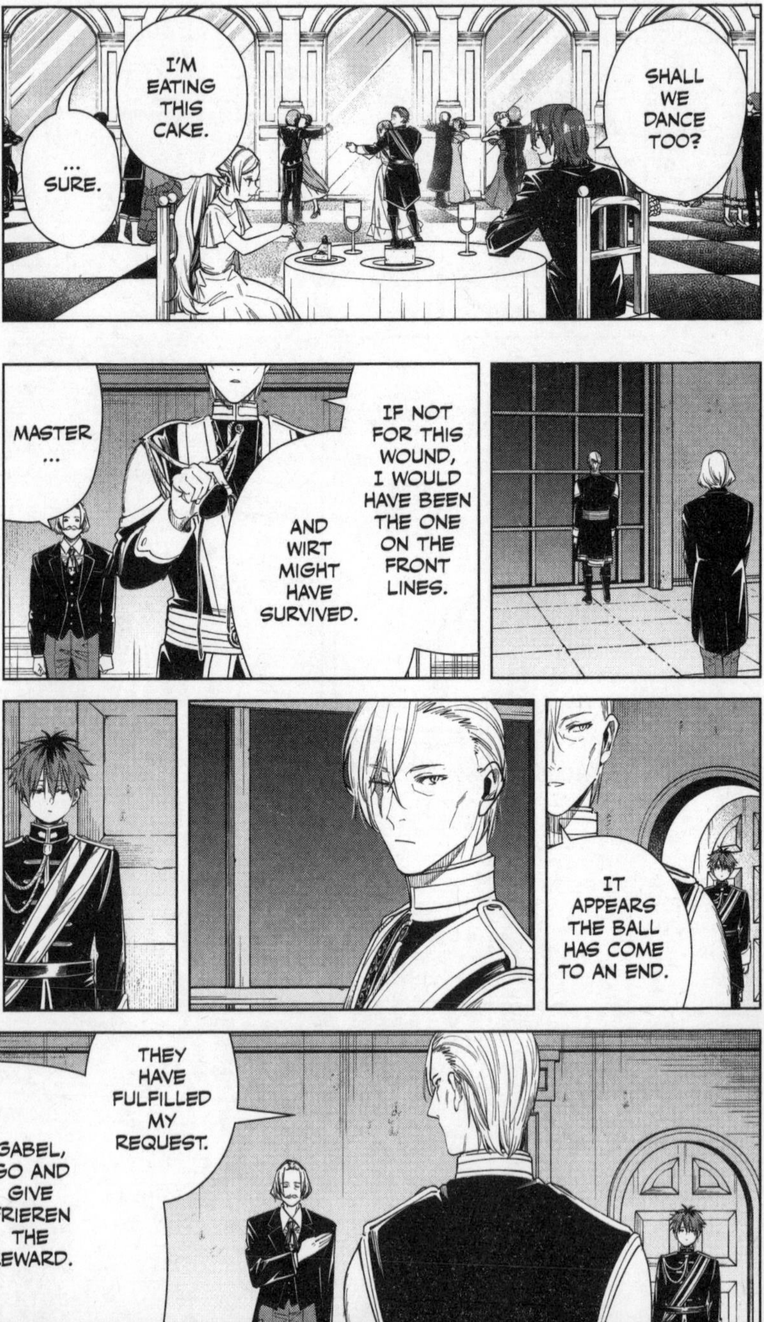
SHALL WE DANCE TOO?
I'M EATING THIS CAKE.
... SURE.
IF NOT FOR THIS WOUND, I WOULD HAVE BEEN THE ONE ON THE FRONT LINES.
AND WIRT MIGHT HAVE SURVIVED.
MASTER ...
IT APPEARS THE BALL HAS COME TO AN END.
THEY HAVE FULFILLED MY REQUEST.
GABEL, GO AND GIVE FRIEREN THE REWARD.

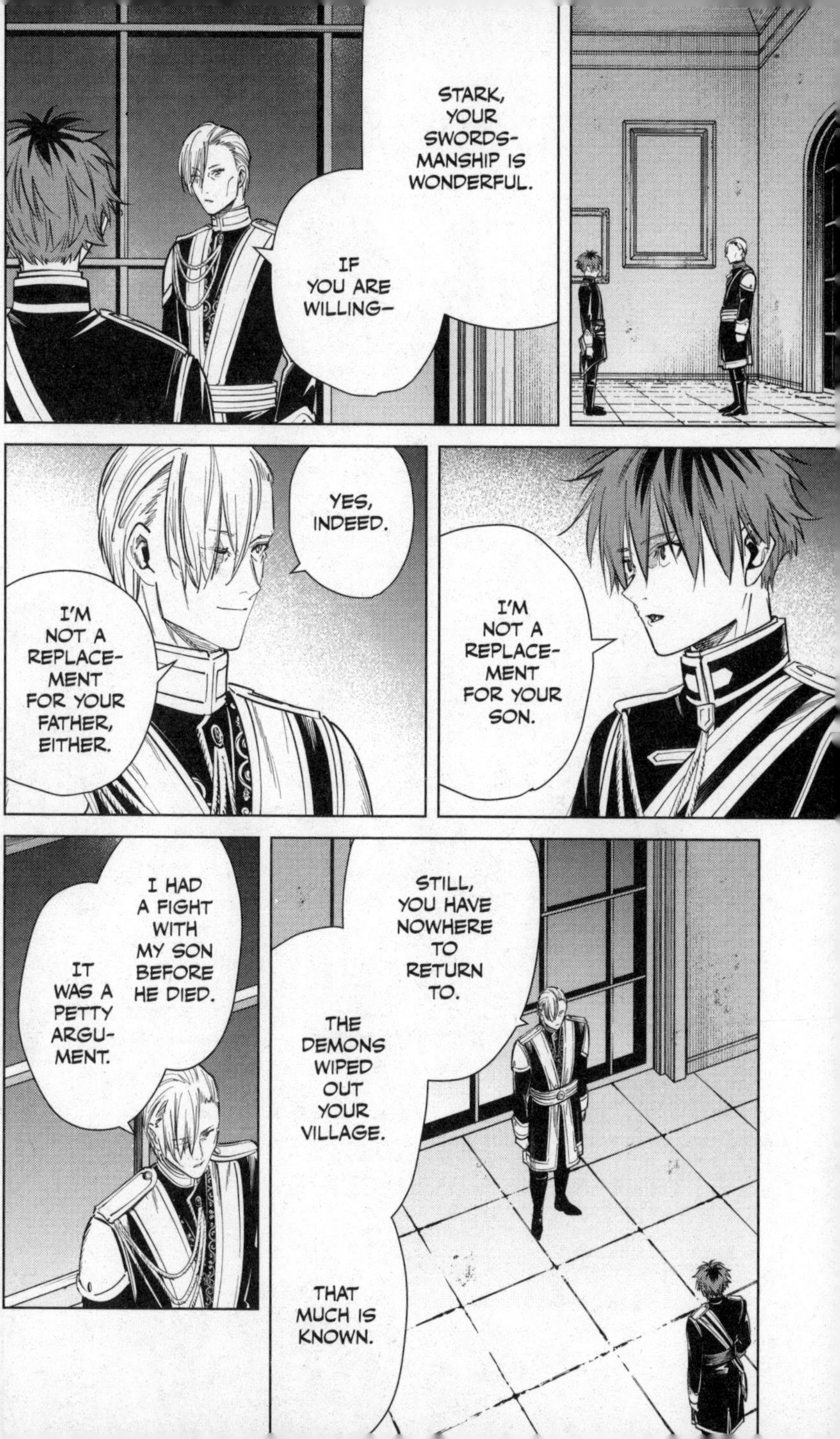
STARK, YOUR SWORDS-MANSHIP IS WONDERFUL.
IF YOU ARE WILLING—
I'M NOT A REPLACE-MENT FOR YOUR SON.
YES, INDEED.
I'M NOT A REPLACE-MENT FOR YOUR FATHER, EITHER.
STILL, YOU HAVE NOWHERE TO RETURN TO.
THE DEMONS WIPED OUT YOUR VILLAGE.
THAT MUCH IS KNOWN.
I HAD A FIGHT WITH MY SON BEFORE HE DIED.
IT WAS A PETTY ARGU-MENT.

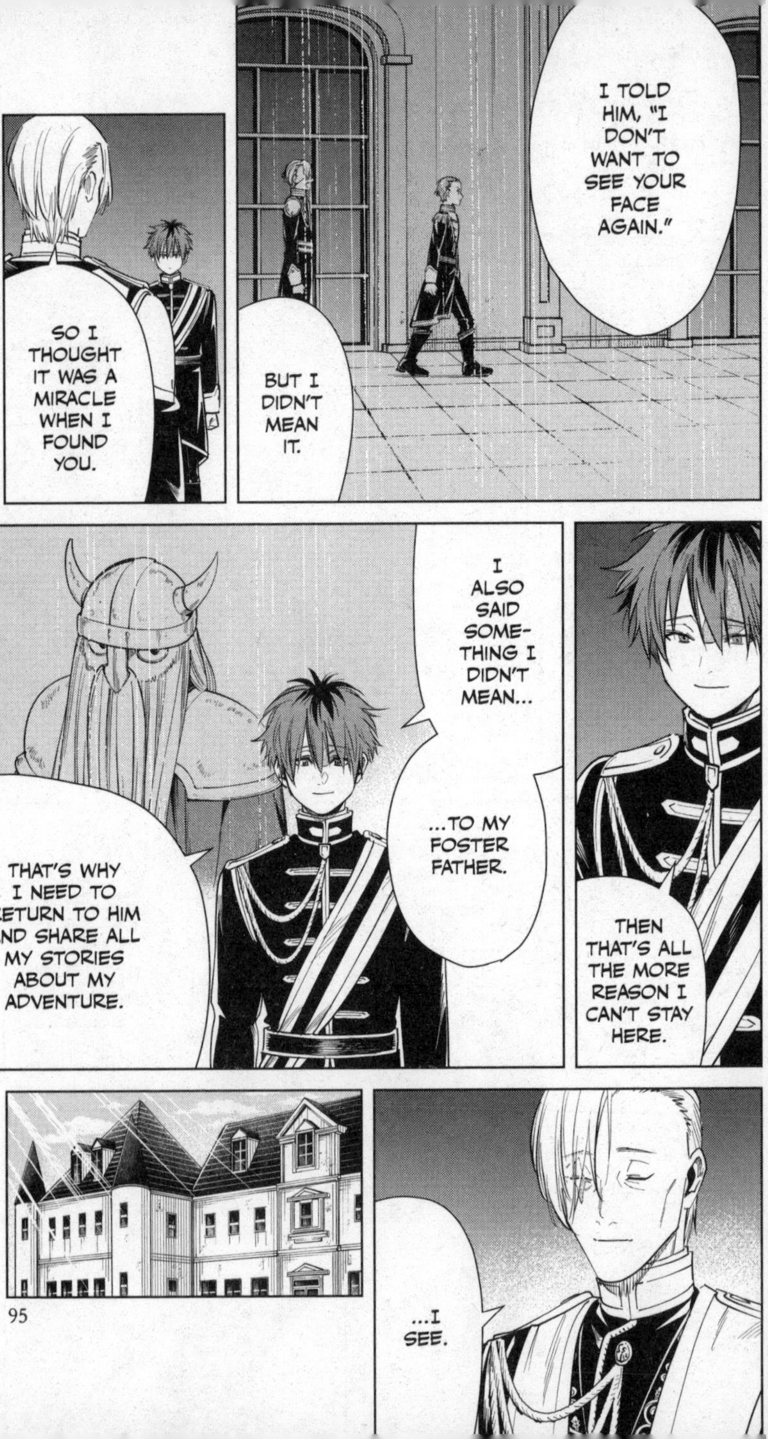
I TOLD HIM, "I DON'T WANT TO SEE YOUR FACE AGAIN."
BUT I DIDN'T MEAN IT.
SO I THOUGHT IT WAS A MIRACLE WHEN I FOUND YOU.
THEN THAT'S ALL THE MORE REASON I CAN'T STAY HERE.
I ALSO SAID SOME-THING I DIDN'T MEAN...
...TO MY FOSTER FATHER.
THAT'S WHY I NEED TO RETURN TO HIM AND SHARE ALL MY STORIES ABOUT MY ADVENTURE.
...I SEE.

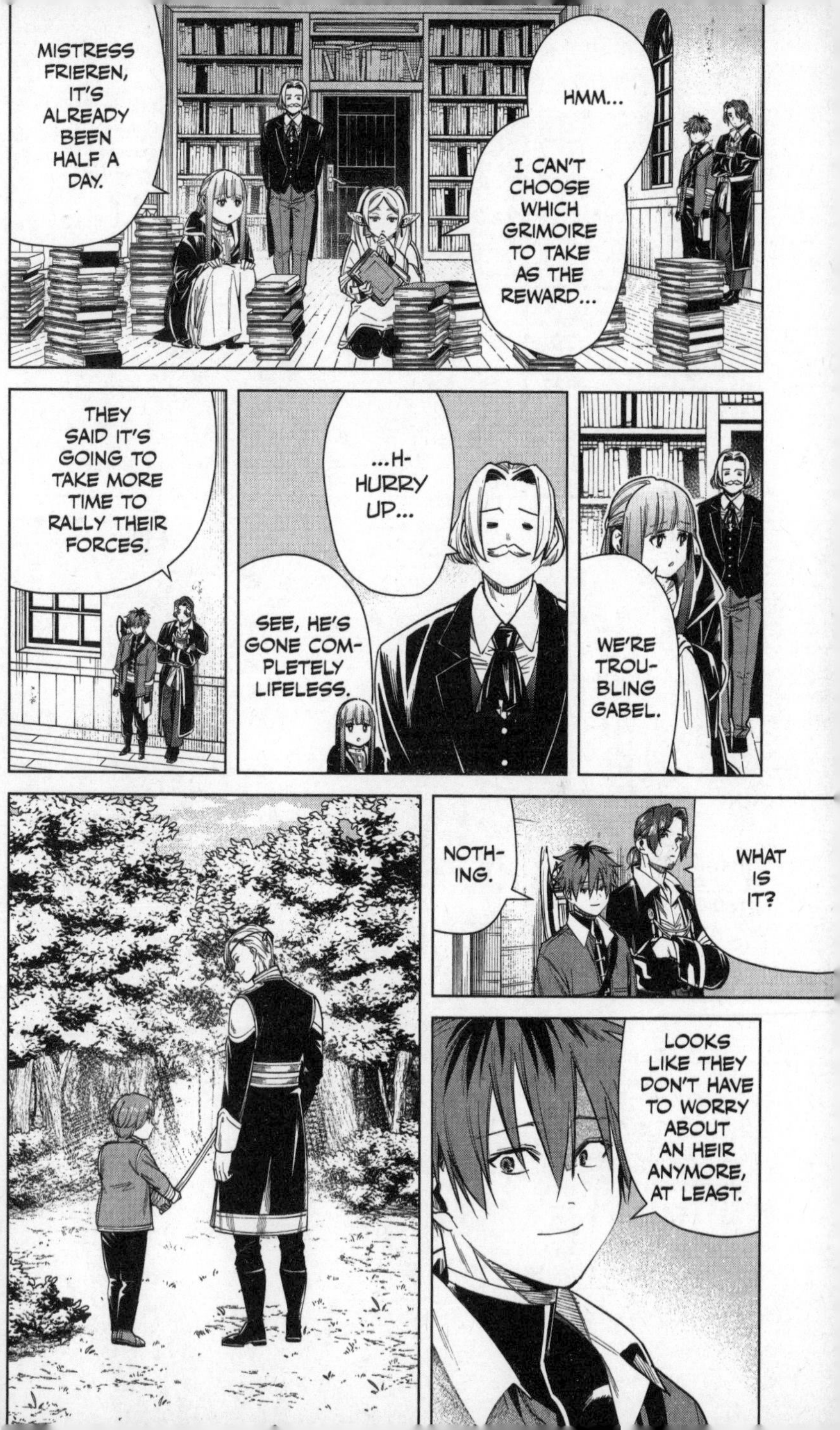
HMM...
I CAN'T CHOOSE WHICH GRIMOIRE TO TAKE AS THE REWARD...
MISTRESS FRIEREN, IT'S ALREADY BEEN HALF A DAY.
WE'RE TROUBLING GABEL.
...H-HURRY UP...
SEE, HE'S GONE COMPLETELY LIFELESS.
THEY SAID IT'S GOING TO TAKE MORE TIME TO RALLY THEIR FORCES.
WHAT IS IT?
NOTHING.
LOOKS LIKE THEY DON'T HAVE TO WORRY ABOUT AN HEIR ANYMORE, AT LEAST.

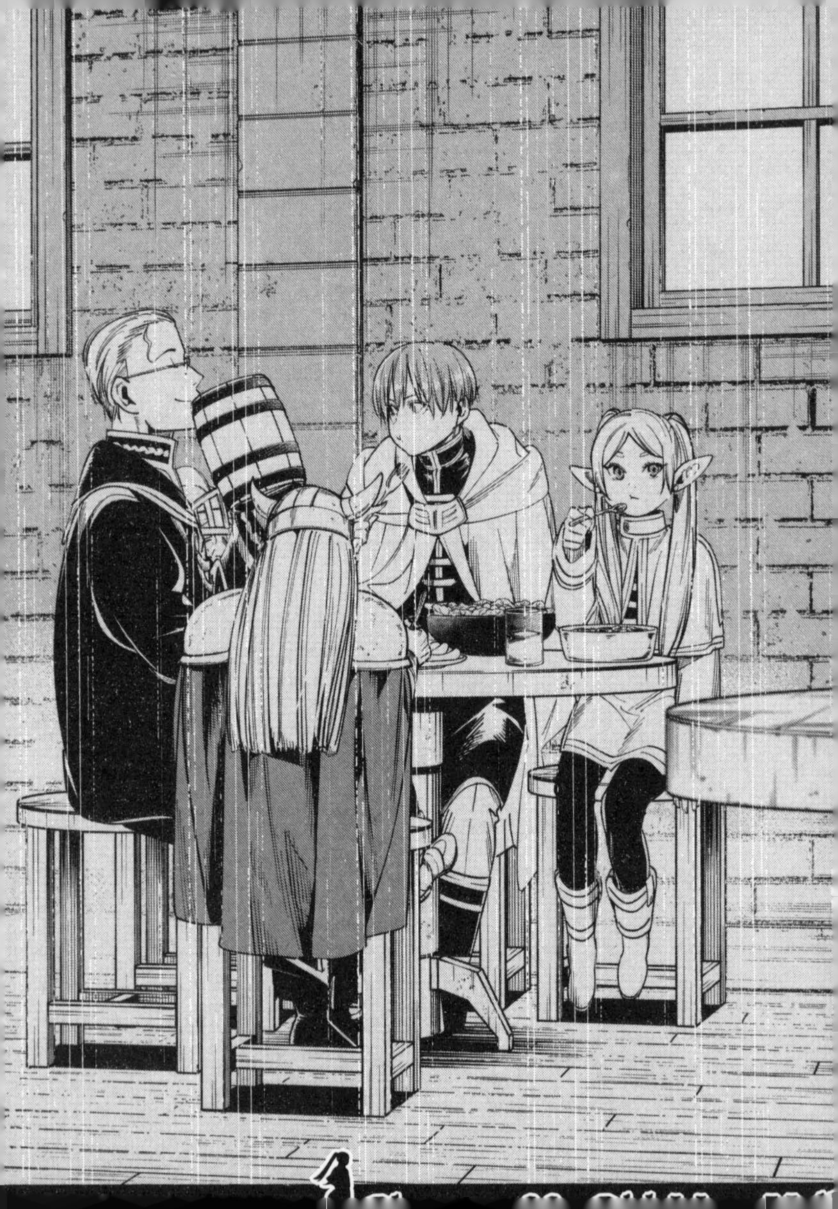

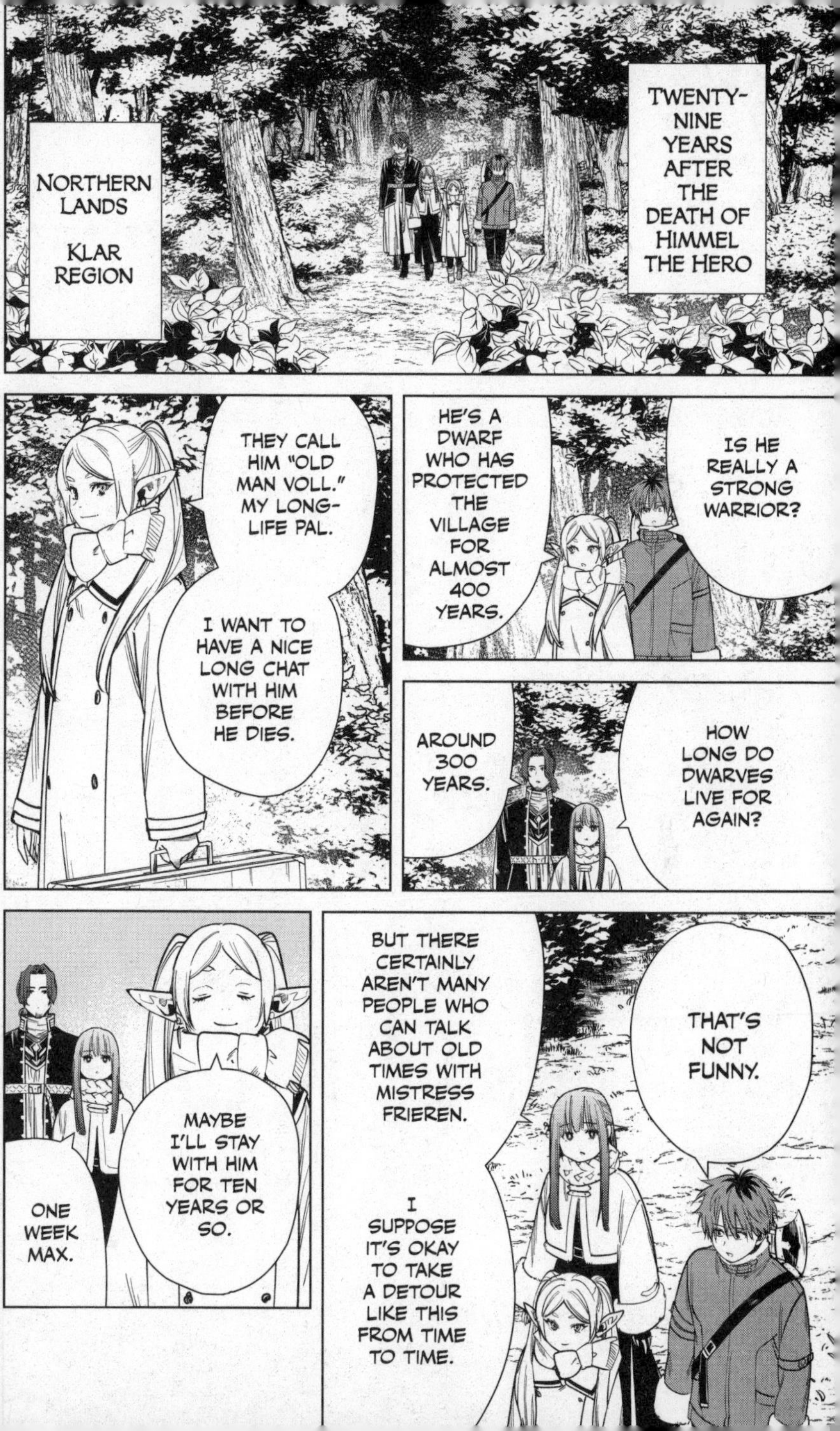

TWENTY-NINE YEARS AFTER THE DEATH OF HIMMEL THE HERO
NORTHERN LANDS
KLAR REGION
IS HE REALLY A STRONG WARRIOR?
HE'S A DWARF WHO HAS PROTECTED THE VILLAGE FOR ALMOST 400 YEARS.
HOW LONG DO DWARVES LIVE FOR AGAIN?
AROUND 300 YEARS.
THEY CALL HIM "OLD MAN VOLL." MY LONG-LIFE PAL.
I WANT TO HAVE A NICE LONG CHAT WITH HIM BEFORE HE DIES.
THAT'S NOT FUNNY.
BUT THERE CERTAINLY AREN'T MANY PEOPLE WHO CAN TALK ABOUT OLD TIMES WITH MISTRESS FRIEREN.
I SUPPOSE IT'S OKAY TO TAKE A DETOUR LIKE THIS FROM TIME TO TIME.
MAYBE I'LL STAY WITH HIM FOR TEN YEARS OR SO.
ONE WEEK MAX.

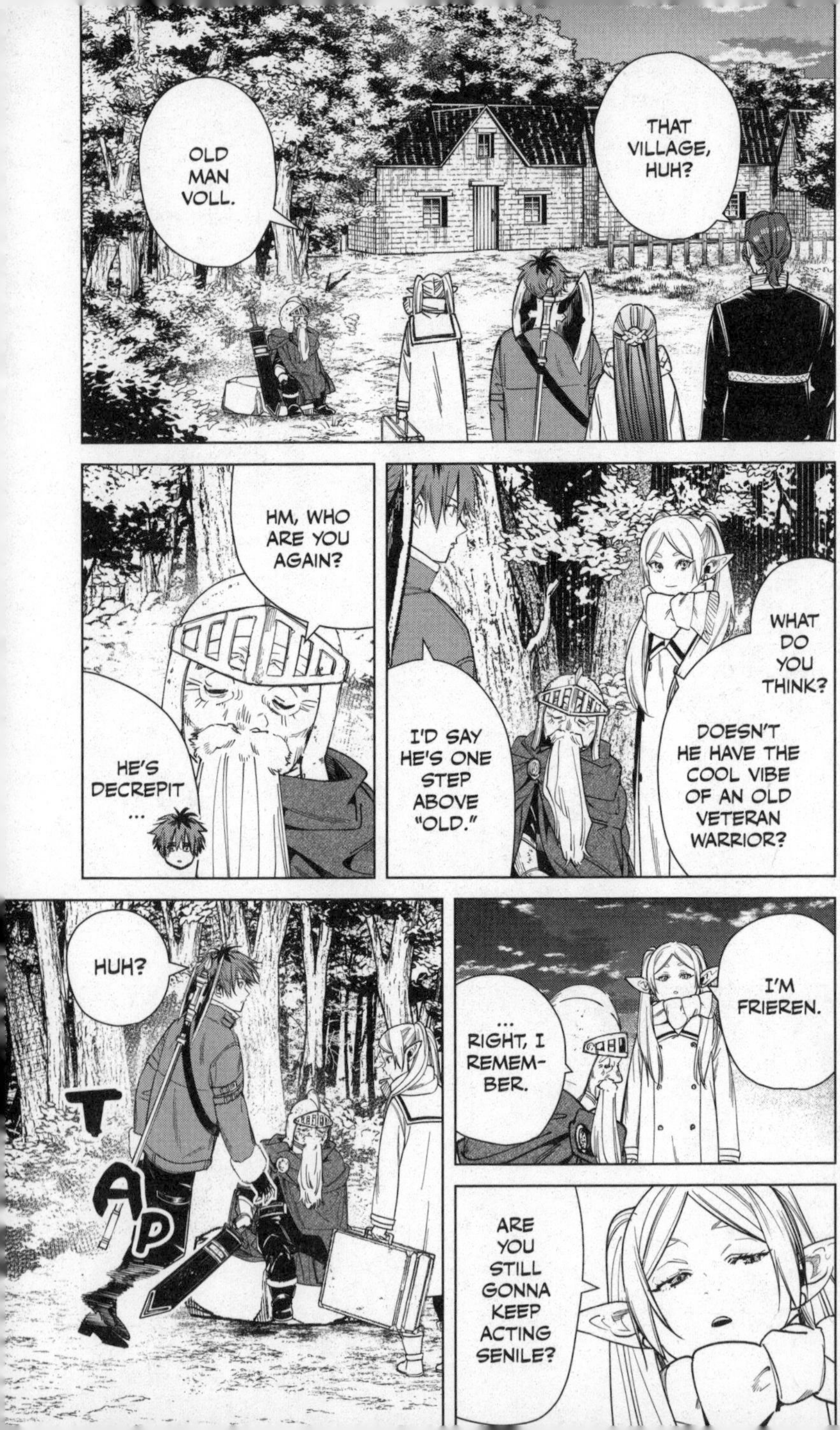
THAT VILLAGE, HUH?
OLD MAN VOLL.
WHAT DO YOU THINK?
DOESN'T HE HAVE THE COOL VIBE OF AN OLD VETERAN WARRIOR?
I'D SAY HE'S ONE STEP ABOVE "OLD."
HM, WHO ARE YOU AGAIN?
HE'S DECREPIT …
I'M FRIEREN.
… RIGHT, I REMEM-BER.
ARE YOU STILL GONNA KEEP ACTING SENILE?
HUH?
TAP

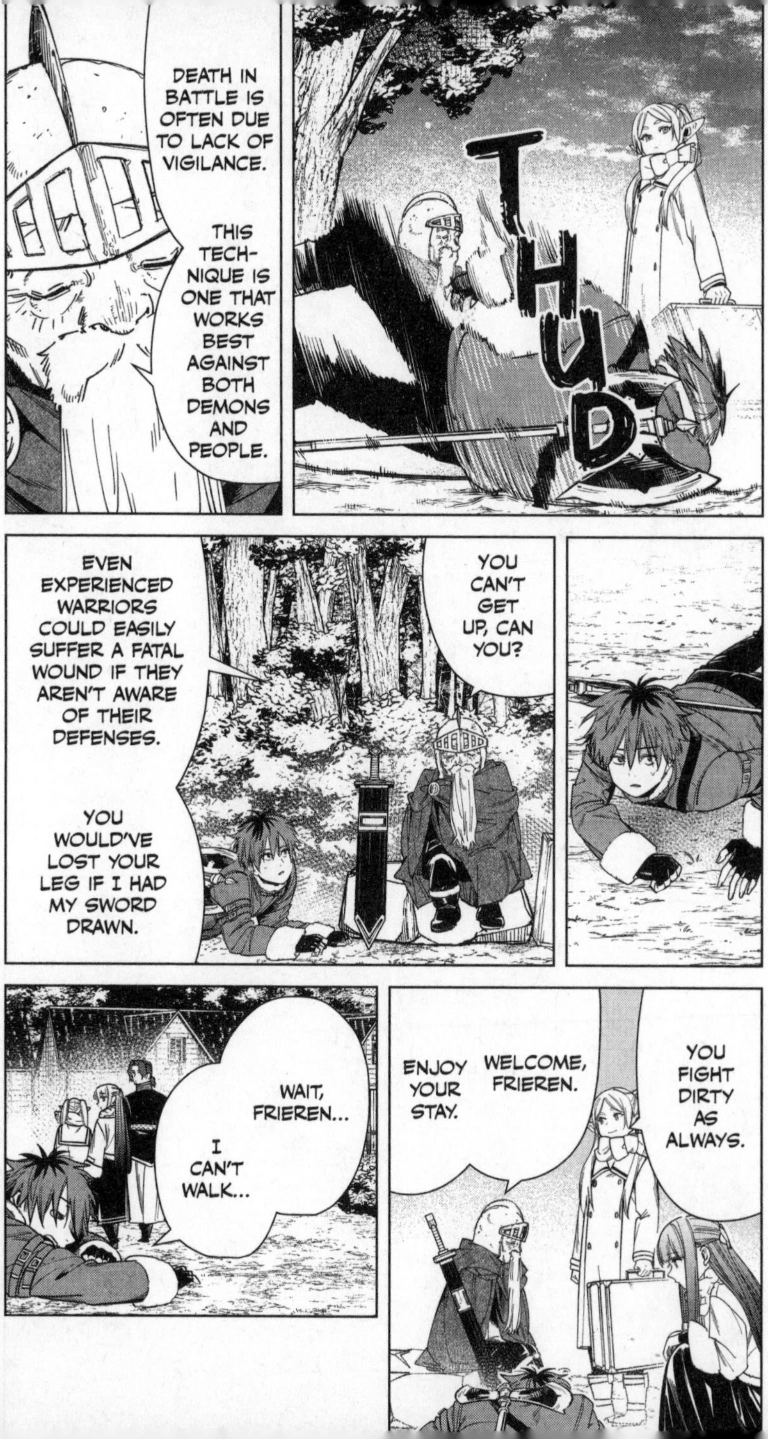
THUD
DEATH IN BATTLE IS OFTEN DUE TO LACK OF VIGILANCE.
THIS TECHNIQUE IS ONE THAT WORKS BEST AGAINST BOTH DEMONS AND PEOPLE.
YOU CAN'T GET UP, CAN YOU?
EVEN EXPERIENCED WARRIORS COULD EASILY SUFFER A FATAL WOUND IF THEY AREN'T AWARE OF THEIR DEFENSES.
YOU WOULD'VE LOST YOUR LEG IF I HAD MY SWORD DRAWN.
YOU FIGHT DIRTY AS ALWAYS.
WELCOME, FRIEREN.
ENJOY YOUR STAY.
WAIT, FRIEREN...
I CAN'T WALK...

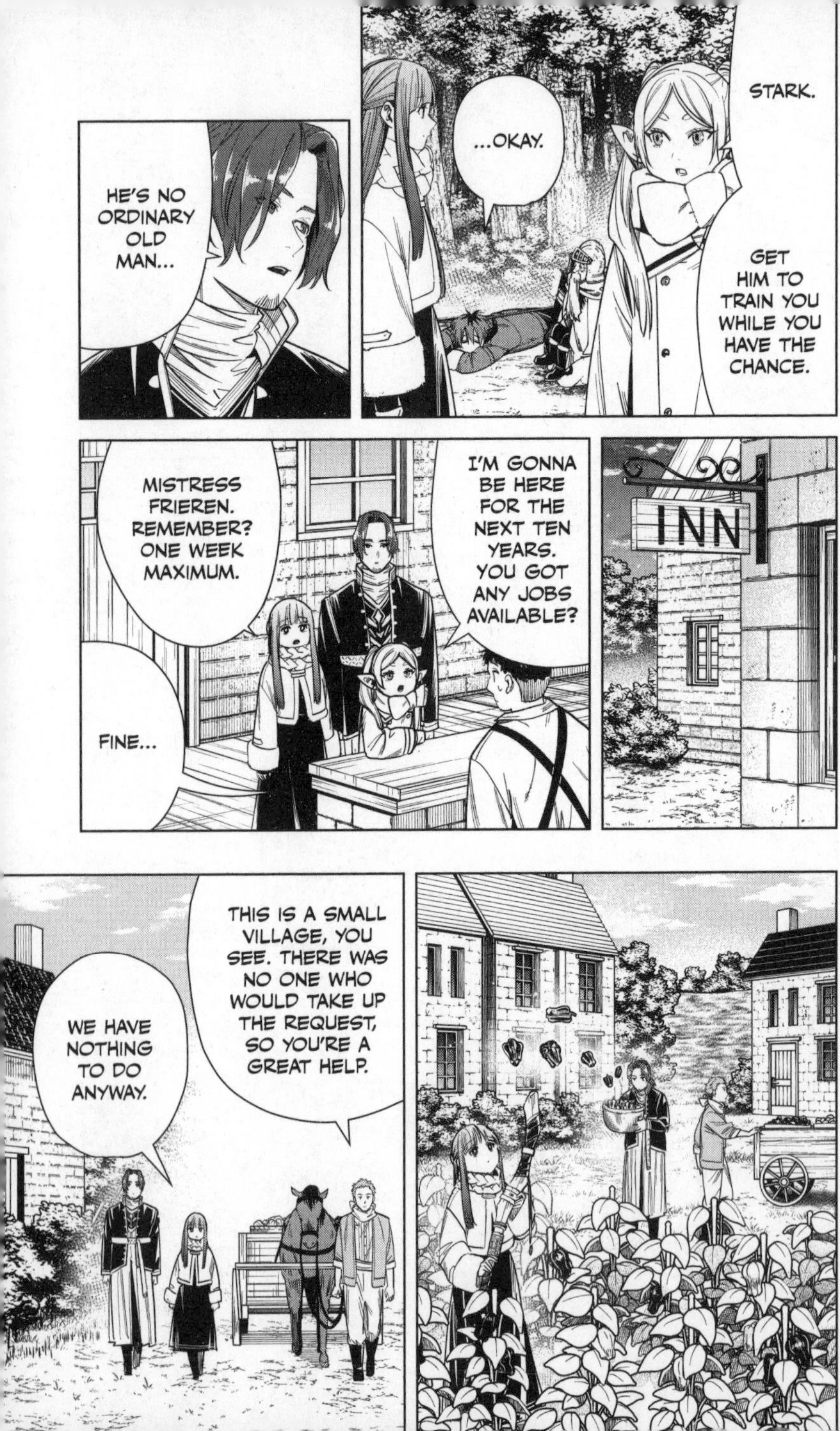
STARK.
GET HIM TO TRAIN YOU WHILE YOU HAVE THE CHANCE.
...OKAY.
HE'S NO ORDINARY OLD MAN...
INN
I'M GONNA BE HERE FOR THE NEXT TEN YEARS. YOU GOT ANY JOBS AVAILABLE?
MISTRESS FRIEREN. REMEMBER? ONE WEEK MAXIMUM.
FINE...
THIS IS A SMALL VILLAGE, YOU SEE. THERE WAS NO ONE WHO WOULD TAKE UP THE REQUEST, SO YOU'RE A GREAT HELP.
WE HAVE NOTHING TO DO ANYWAY.

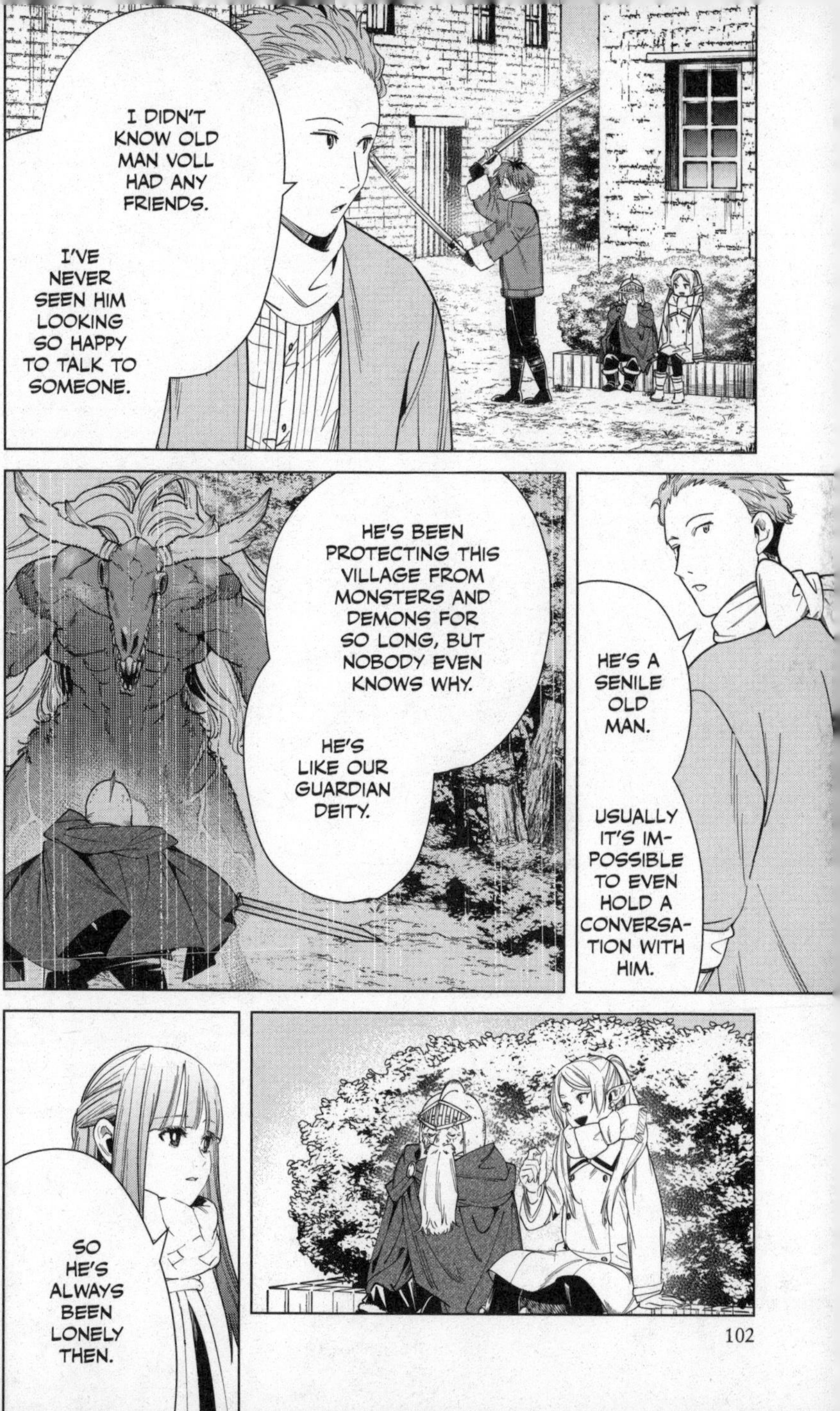
I DIDN'T KNOW OLD MAN VOLL HAD ANY FRIENDS.
I'VE NEVER SEEN HIM LOOKING SO HAPPY TO TALK TO SOMEONE.
HE'S A SENILE OLD MAN.
USUALLY IT'S IMPOSSIBLE TO EVEN HOLD A CONVERSATION WITH HIM.
HE'S BEEN PROTECTING THIS VILLAGE FROM MONSTERS AND DEMONS FOR SO LONG, BUT NOBODY EVEN KNOWS WHY.
HE'S LIKE OUR GUARDIAN DEITY.
SO HE'S ALWAYS BEEN LONELY THEN.

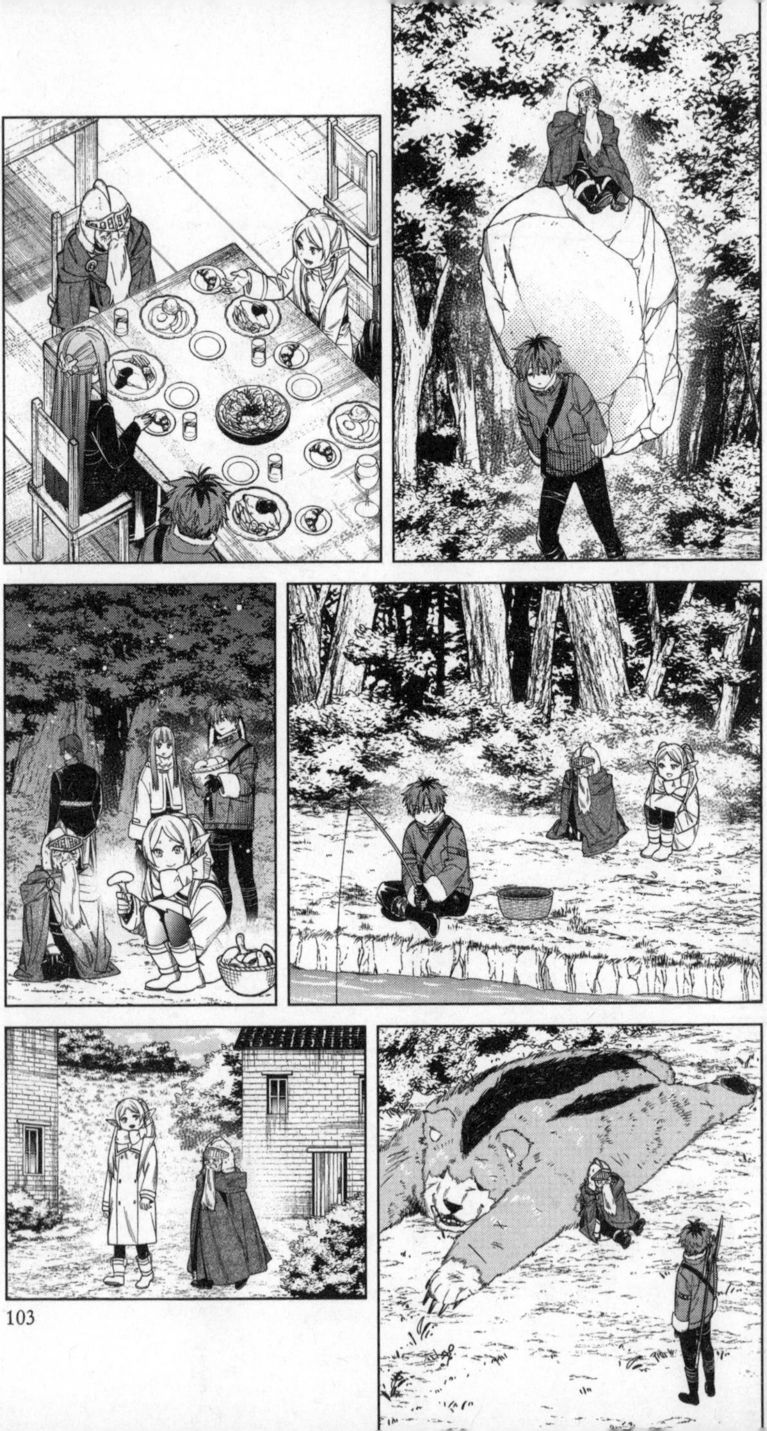

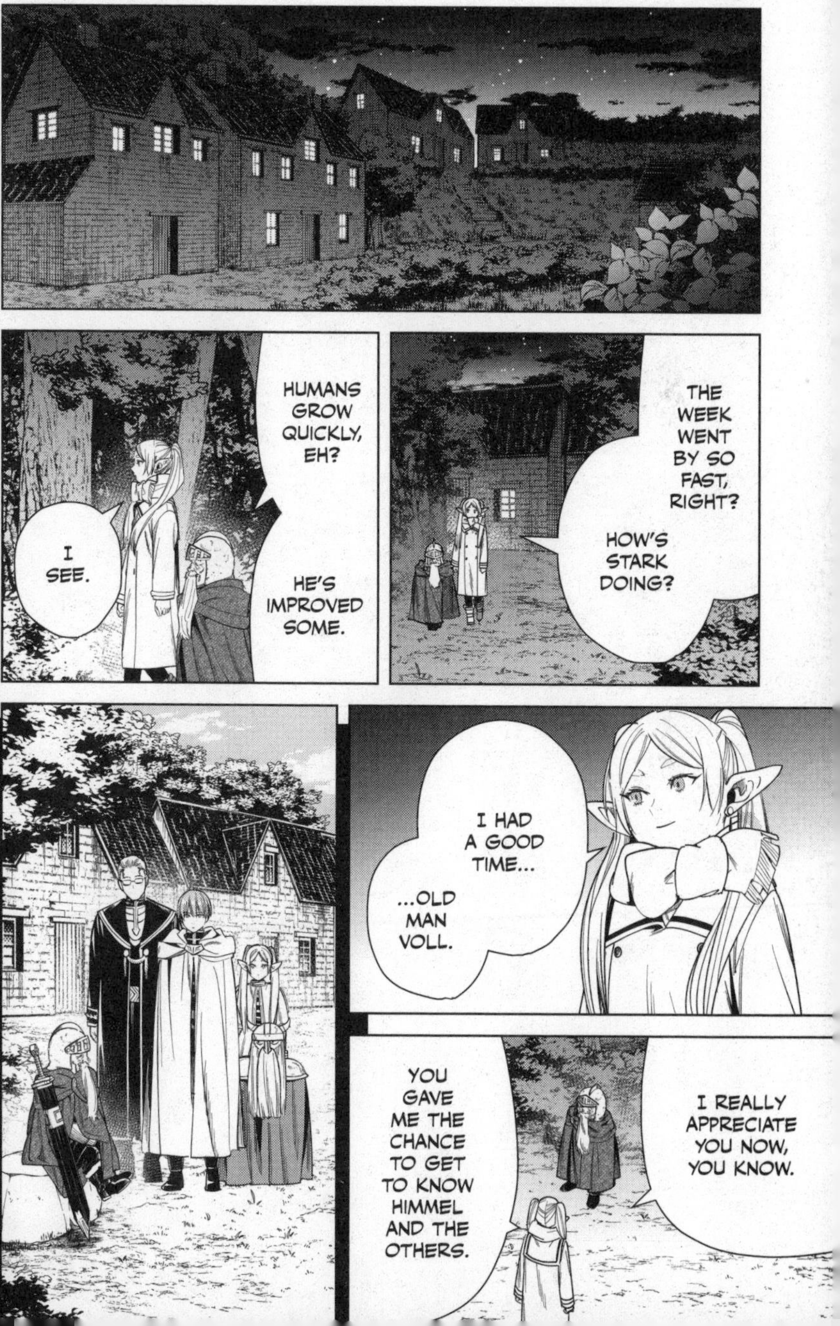
THE WEEK WENT BY SO FAST, RIGHT?
HOW'S STARK DOING?
HUMANS GROW QUICKLY, EH?
HE'S IMPROVED SOME.
I SEE.
I HAD A GOOD TIME...
...OLD MAN VOLL.
I REALLY APPRECIATE YOU NOW, YOU KNOW.
YOU GAVE ME THE CHANCE TO GET TO KNOW HIMMEL AND THE OTHERS.

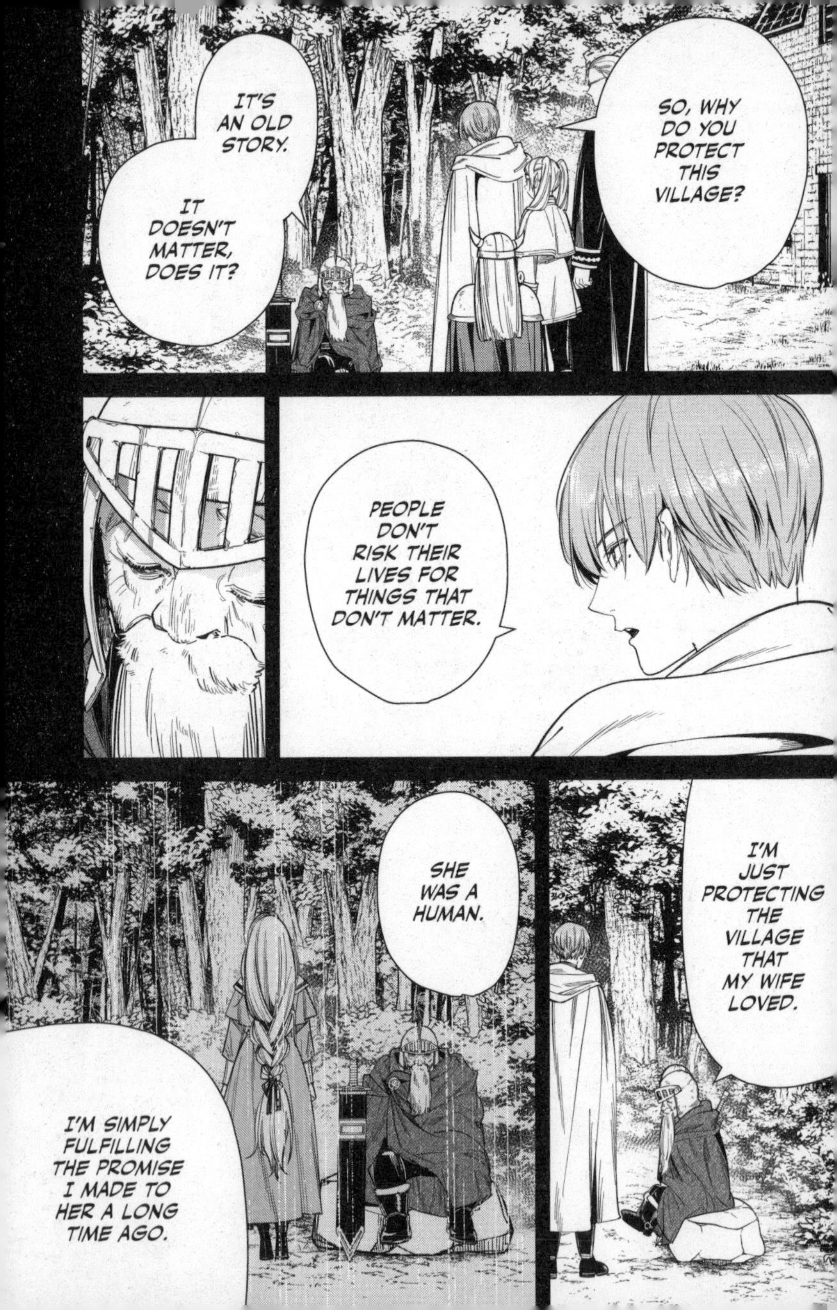

SO, WHY DO YOU PROTECT THIS VILLAGE?
IT'S AN OLD STORY.
IT DOESN'T MATTER, DOES IT?
PEOPLE DON'T RISK THEIR LIVES FOR THINGS THAT DON'T MATTER.
I'M JUST PROTECTING THE VILLAGE THAT MY WIFE LOVED.
SHE WAS A HUMAN.
I'M SIMPLY FULFILLING THE PROMISE I MADE TO HER A LONG TIME AGO.

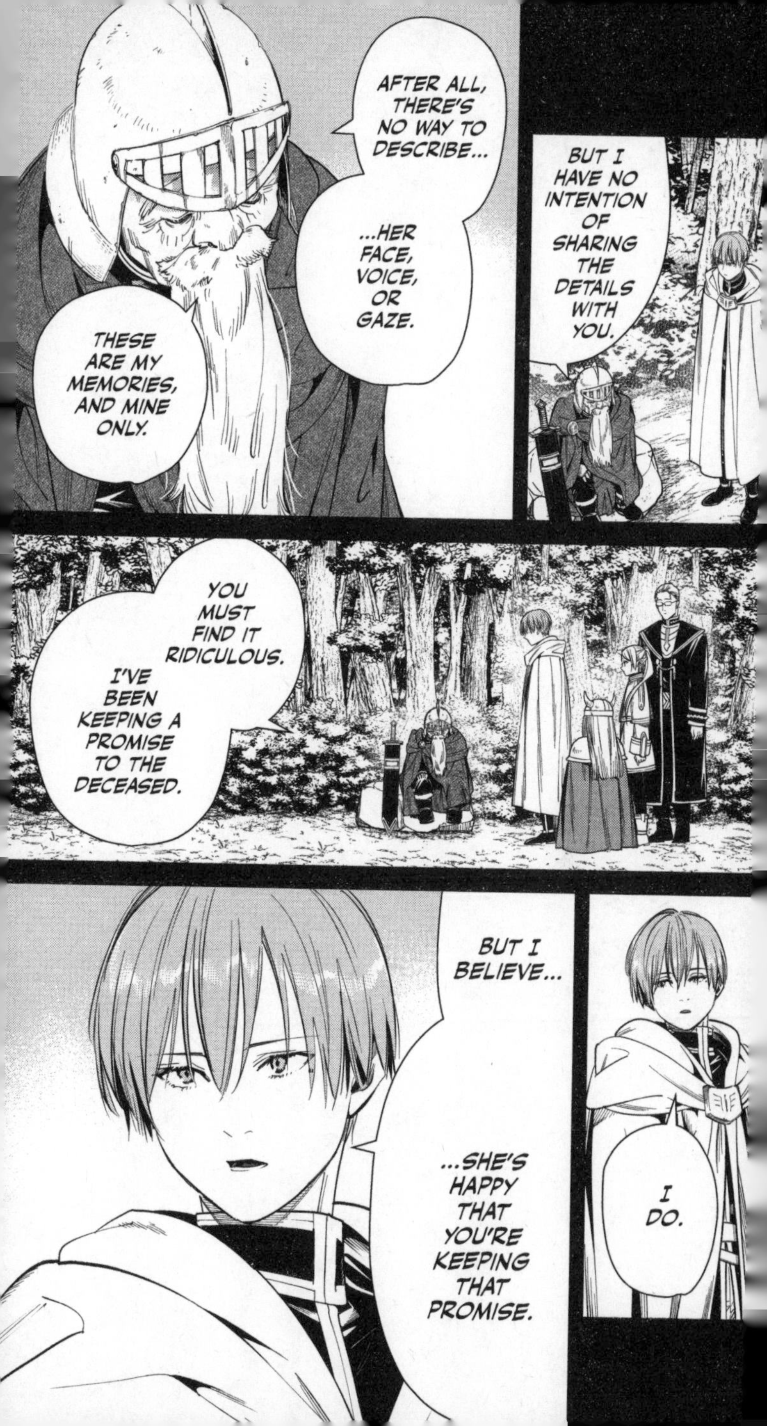
BUT I HAVE NO INTENTION OF SHARING THE DETAILS WITH YOU.
AFTER ALL, THERE'S NO WAY TO DESCRIBE...
...HER FACE, VOICE, OR GAZE.
THESE ARE MY MEMORIES, AND MINE ONLY.
YOU MUST FIND IT RIDICULOUS.
I'VE BEEN KEEPING A PROMISE TO THE DECEASED.
I DO.
BUT I BELIEVE...
...SHE'S HAPPY THAT YOU'RE KEEPING THAT PROMISE.

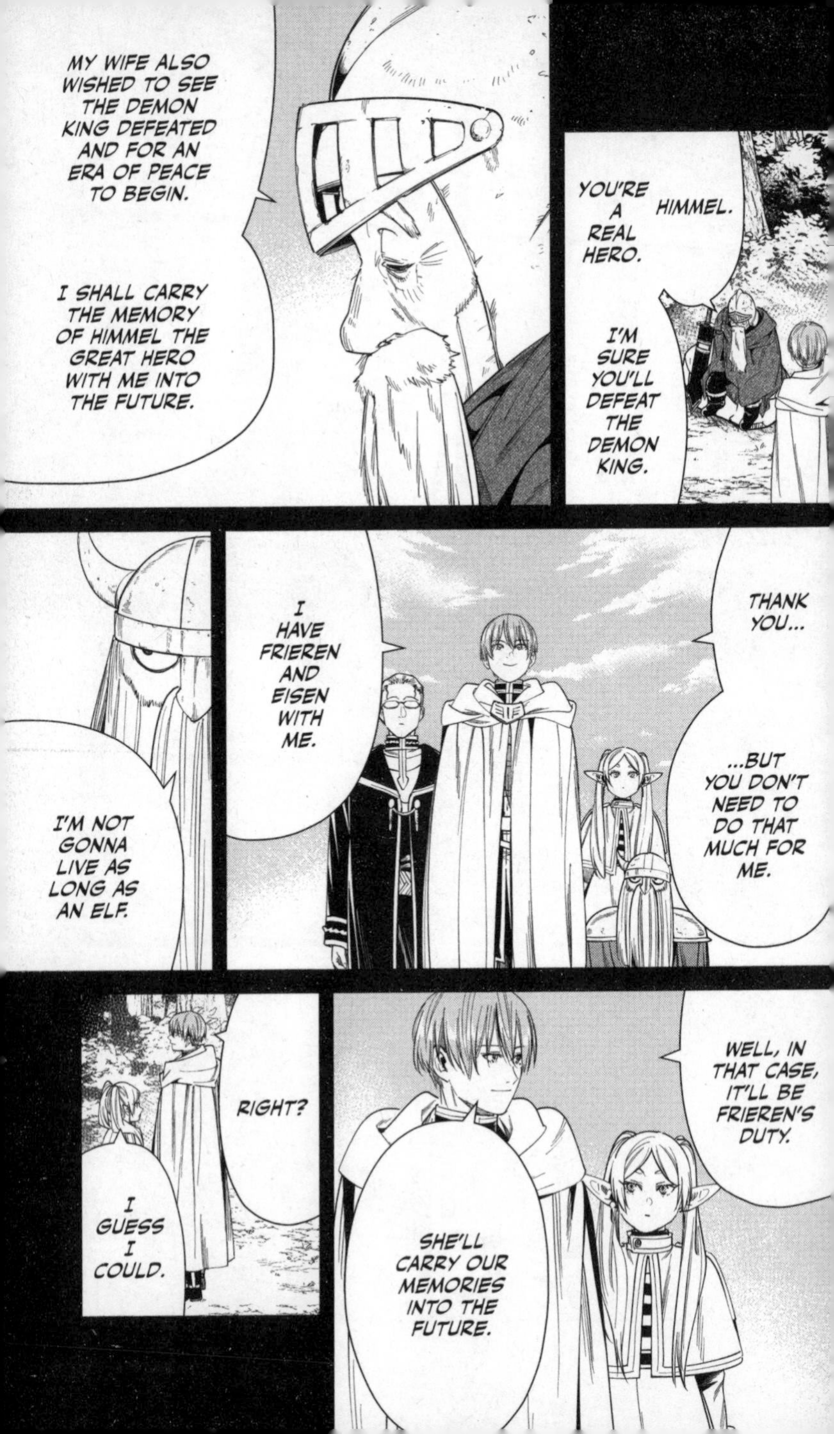
HIMMEL.
YOU'RE A REAL HERO.
I'M SURE YOU'LL DEFEAT THE DEMON KING.
MY WIFE ALSO WISHED TO SEE THE DEMON KING DEFEATED AND FOR AN ERA OF PEACE TO BEGIN.
I SHALL CARRY THE MEMORY OF HIMMEL THE GREAT HERO WITH ME INTO THE FUTURE.
THANK YOU...
...BUT YOU DON'T NEED TO DO THAT MUCH FOR ME.
I HAVE FRIEREN AND EISEN WITH ME.
I'M NOT GONNA LIVE AS LONG AS AN ELF.
WELL, IN THAT CASE, IT'LL BE FRIEREN'S DUTY.
SHE'LL CARRY OUR MEMORIES INTO THE FUTURE.
RIGHT?
I GUESS I COULD.

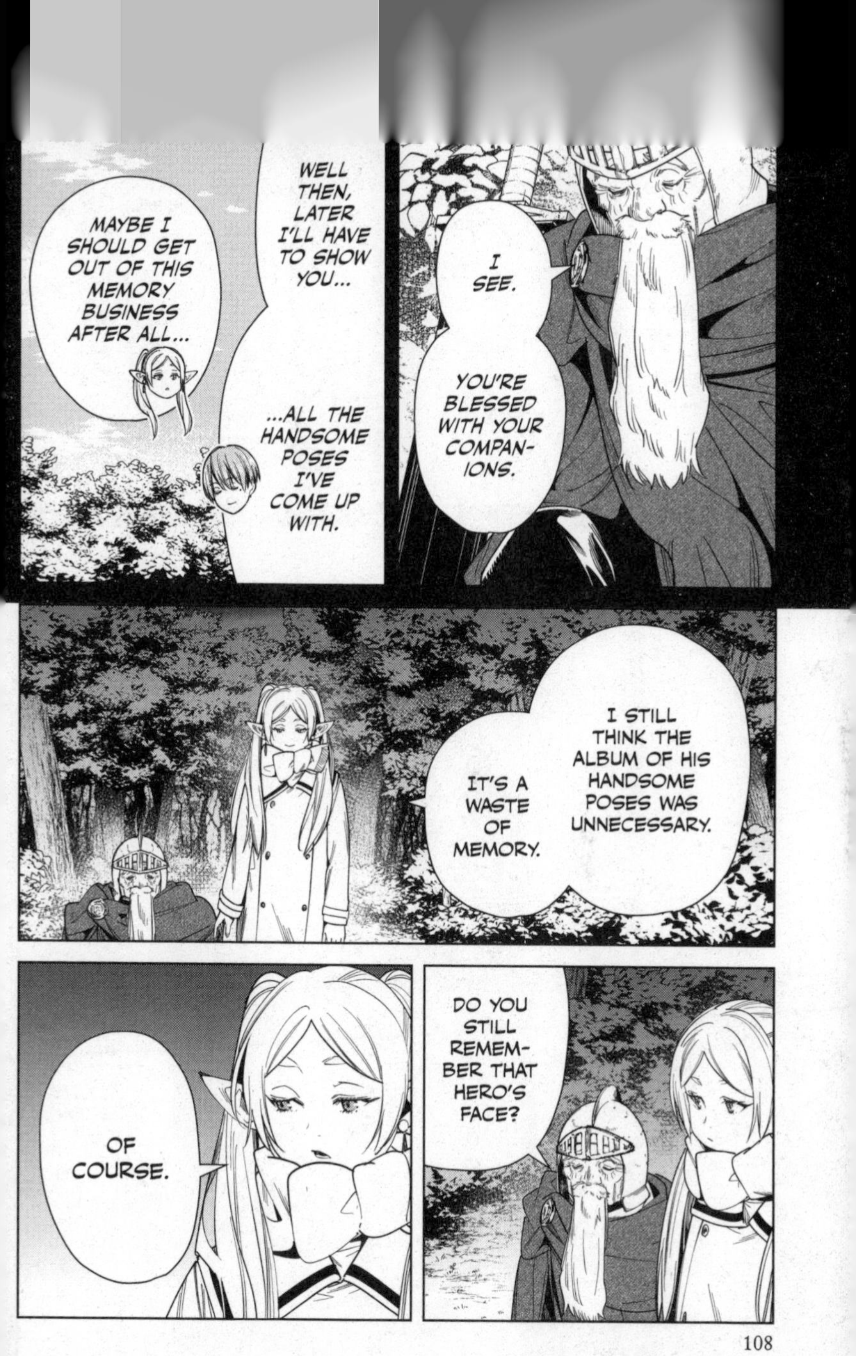
I SEE.
YOU'RE BLESSED WITH YOUR COMPAN-IONS.
WELL THEN, LATER I'LL HAVE TO SHOW YOU...
...ALL THE HANDSOME POSES I'VE COME UP WITH.
MAYBE I SHOULD GET OUT OF THIS MEMORY BUSINESS AFTER ALL...
I STILL THINK THE ALBUM OF HIS HANDSOME POSES WAS UNNECESSARY.
IT'S A WASTE OF MEMORY.
DO YOU STILL REMEMBER THAT HERO'S FACE?
OF COURSE.

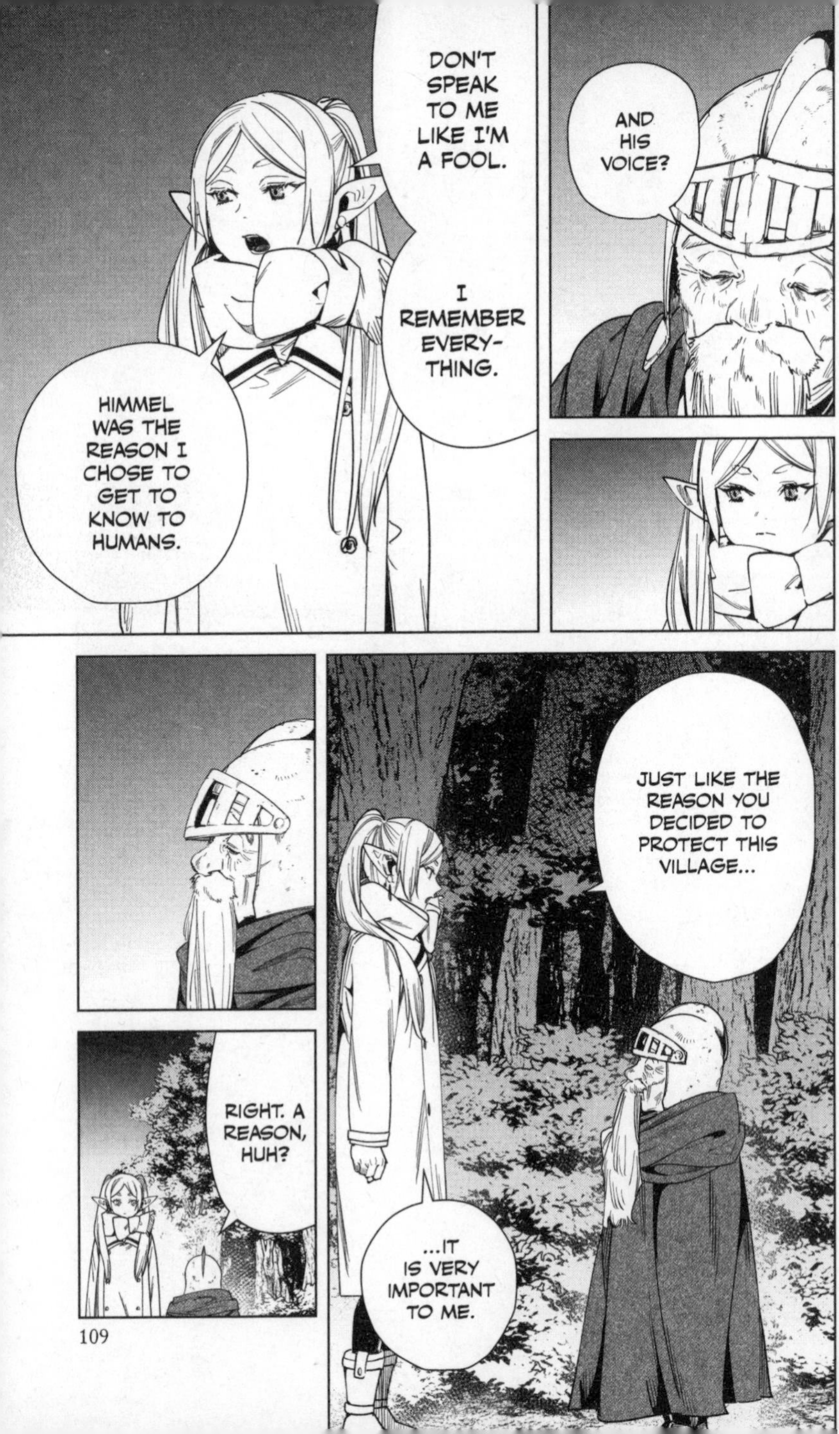
AND HIS VOICE?
DON'T SPEAK TO ME LIKE I'M A FOOL.
I REMEMBER EVERY-THING.
HIMMEL WAS THE REASON I CHOSE TO GET TO KNOW TO HUMANS.
JUST LIKE THE REASON YOU DECIDED TO PROTECT THIS VILLAGE...
...IT IS VERY IMPORTANT TO ME.
RIGHT. A REASON, HUH?

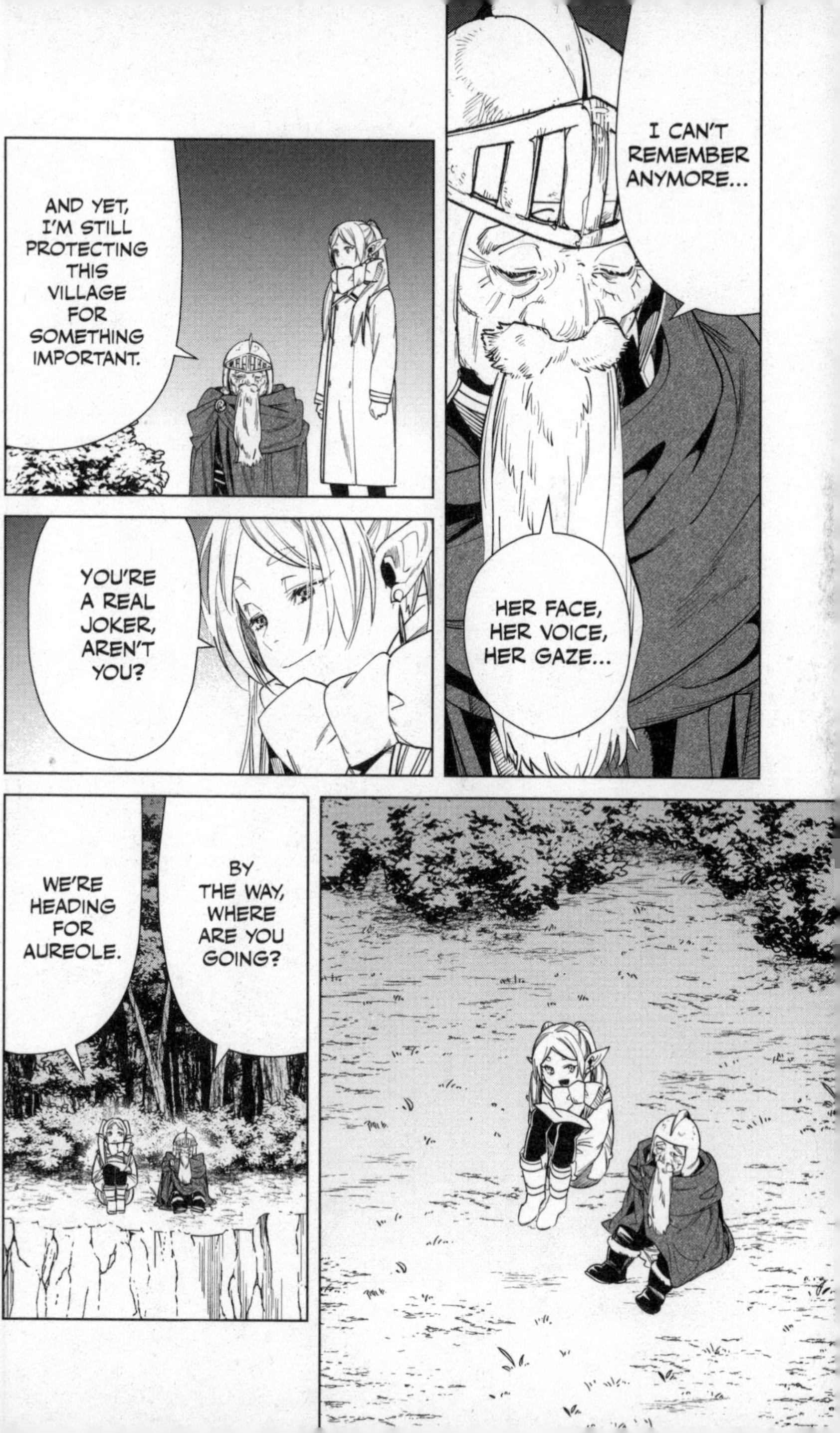
I CAN'T REMEMBER ANYMORE...
HER FACE, HER VOICE, HER GAZE...
AND YET, I'M STILL PROTECTING THIS VILLAGE FOR SOMETHING IMPORTANT.
YOU'RE A REAL JOKER, AREN'T YOU?
BY THE WAY, WHERE ARE YOU GOING?
WE'RE HEADING FOR AUREOLE.

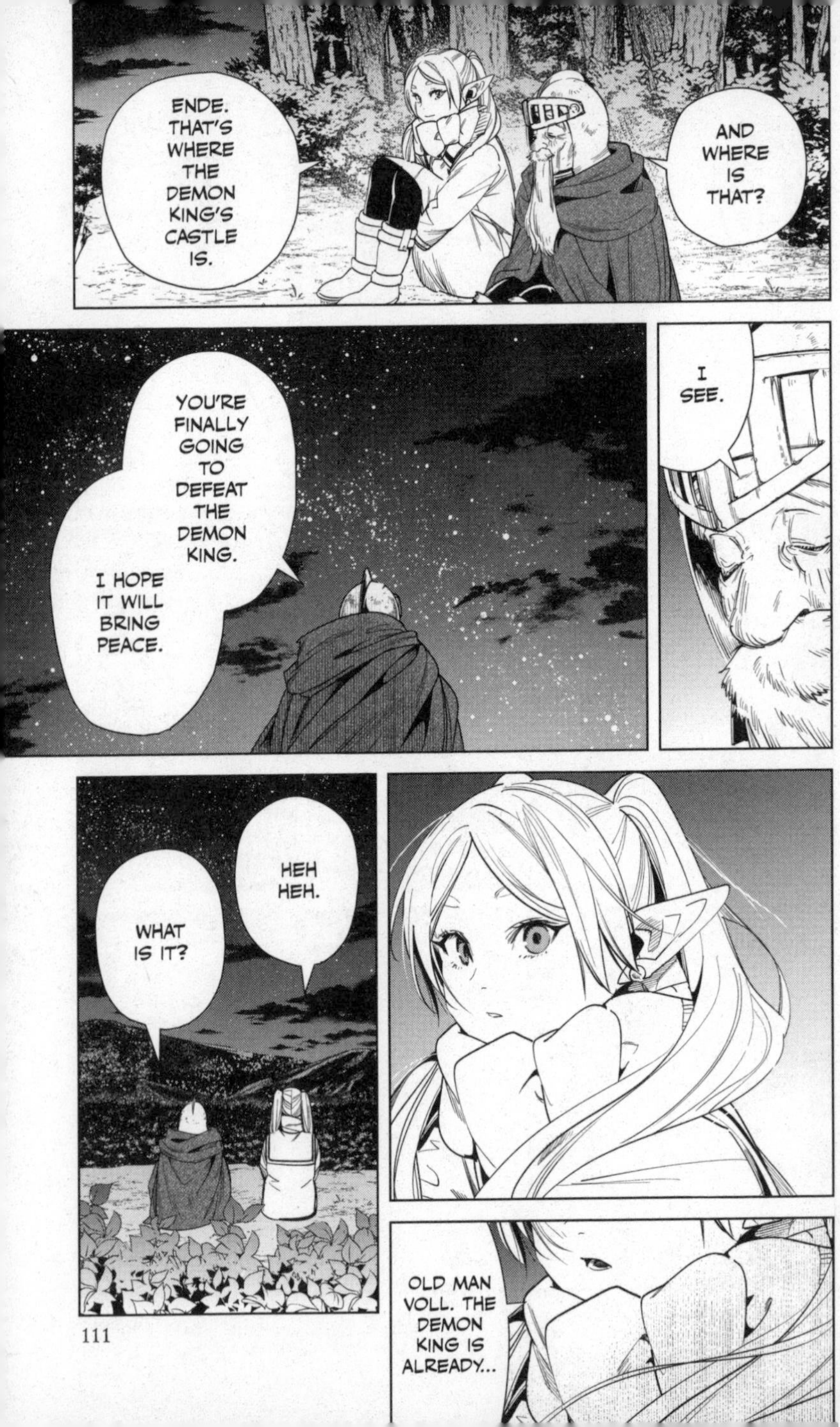
AND WHERE IS THAT?
ENDE. THAT'S WHERE THE DEMON KING'S CASTLE IS.
I SEE.
YOU'RE FINALLY GOING TO DEFEAT THE DEMON KING.
I HOPE IT WILL BRING PEACE.
OLD MAN VOLL. THE DEMON KING IS ALREADY...
HEH HEH.
WHAT IS IT?

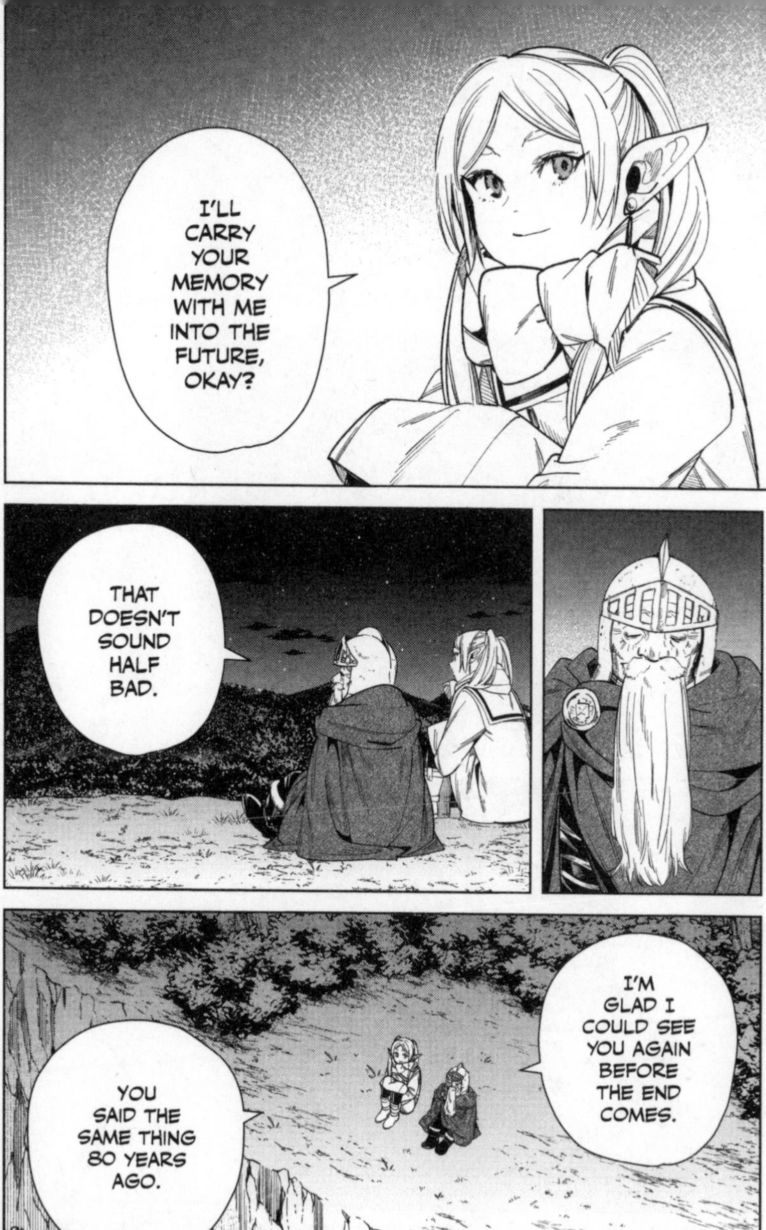
I'LL CARRY YOUR MEMORY WITH ME INTO THE FUTURE, OKAY?
THAT DOESN'T SOUND HALF BAD.
I'M GLAD I COULD SEE YOU AGAIN BEFORE THE END COMES.
YOU SAID THE SAME THING 80 YEARS AGO.

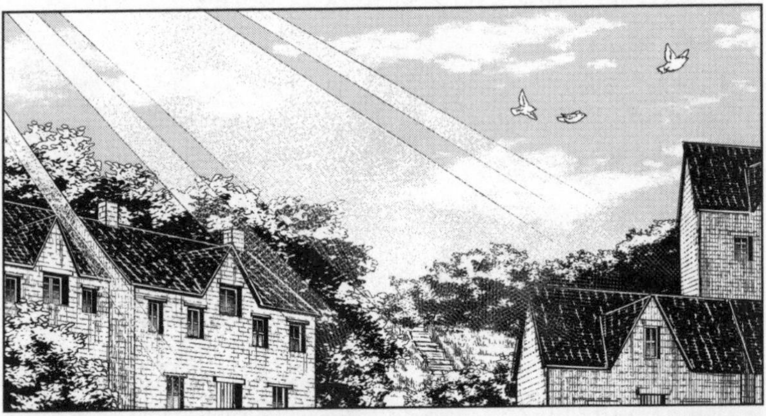

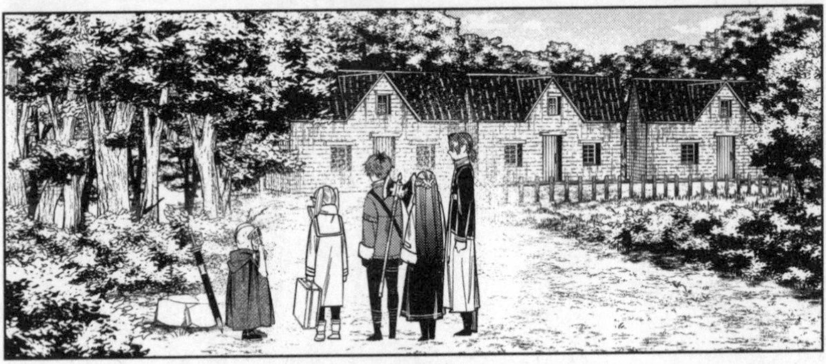

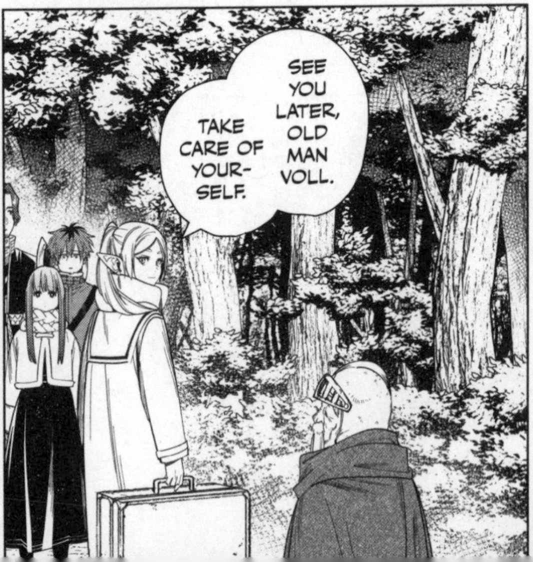
SEE YOU LATER, OLD MAN VOLL.
TAKE CARE OF YOUR-SELF.

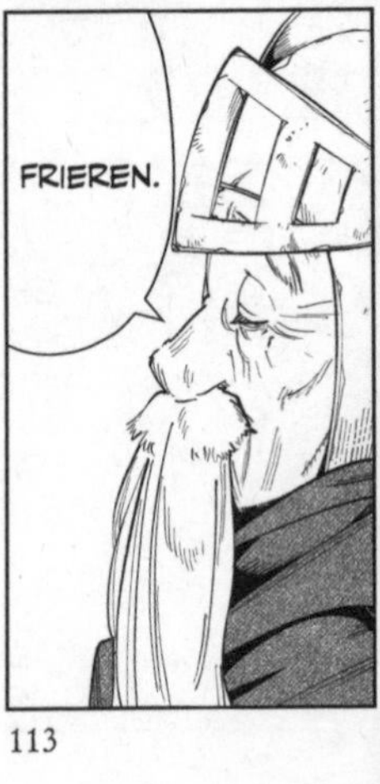
FRIEREN.

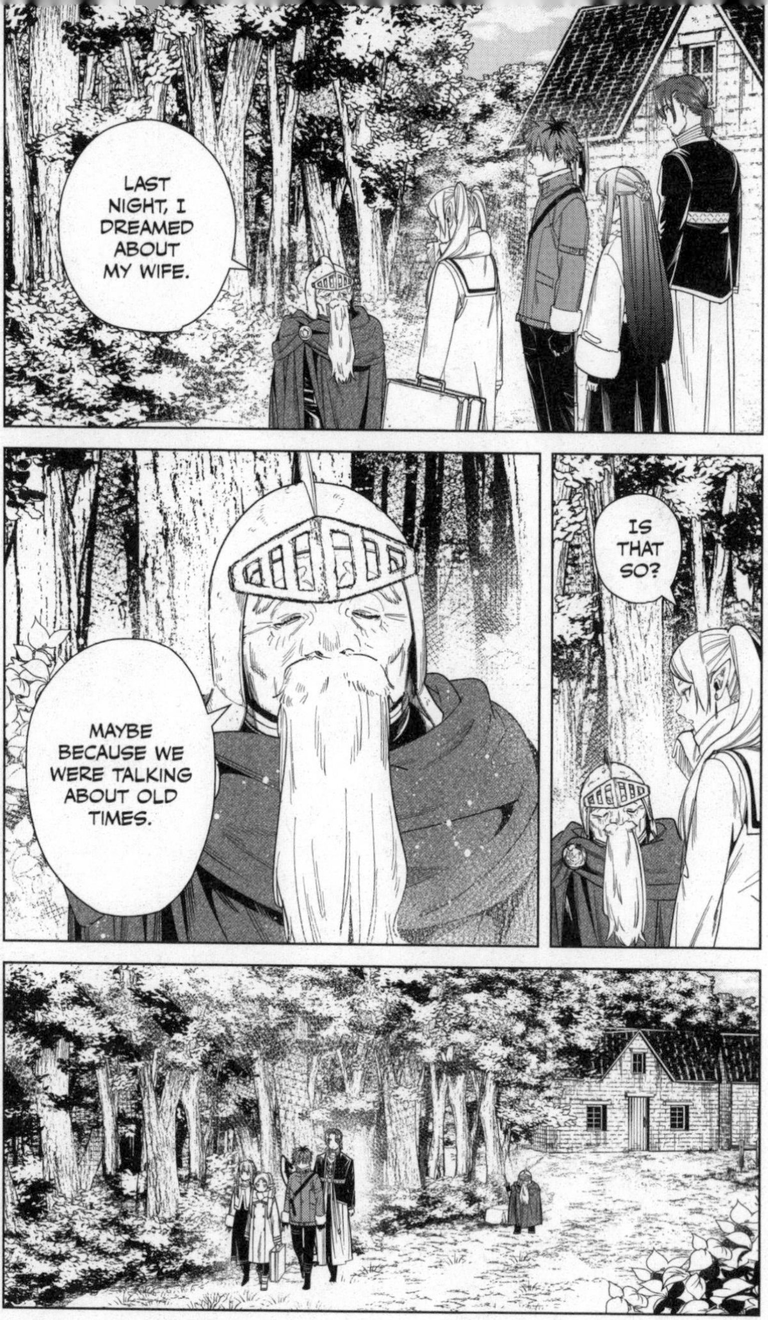
LAST NIGHT, I DREAMED ABOUT MY WIFE.
IS THAT SO?
MAYBE BECAUSE WE WERE TALKING ABOUT OLD TIMES.

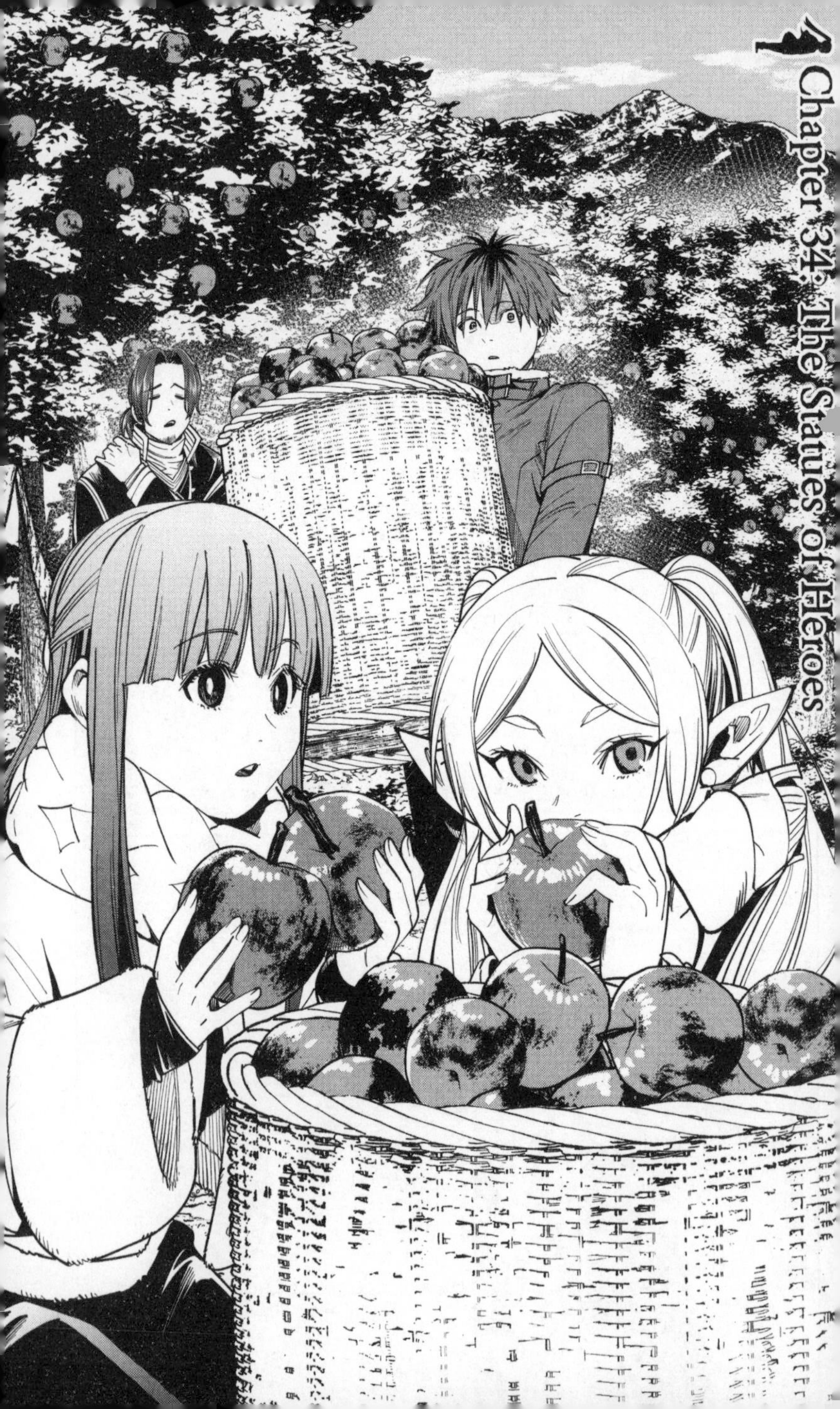
Chapter 34: The Statues of Heroes

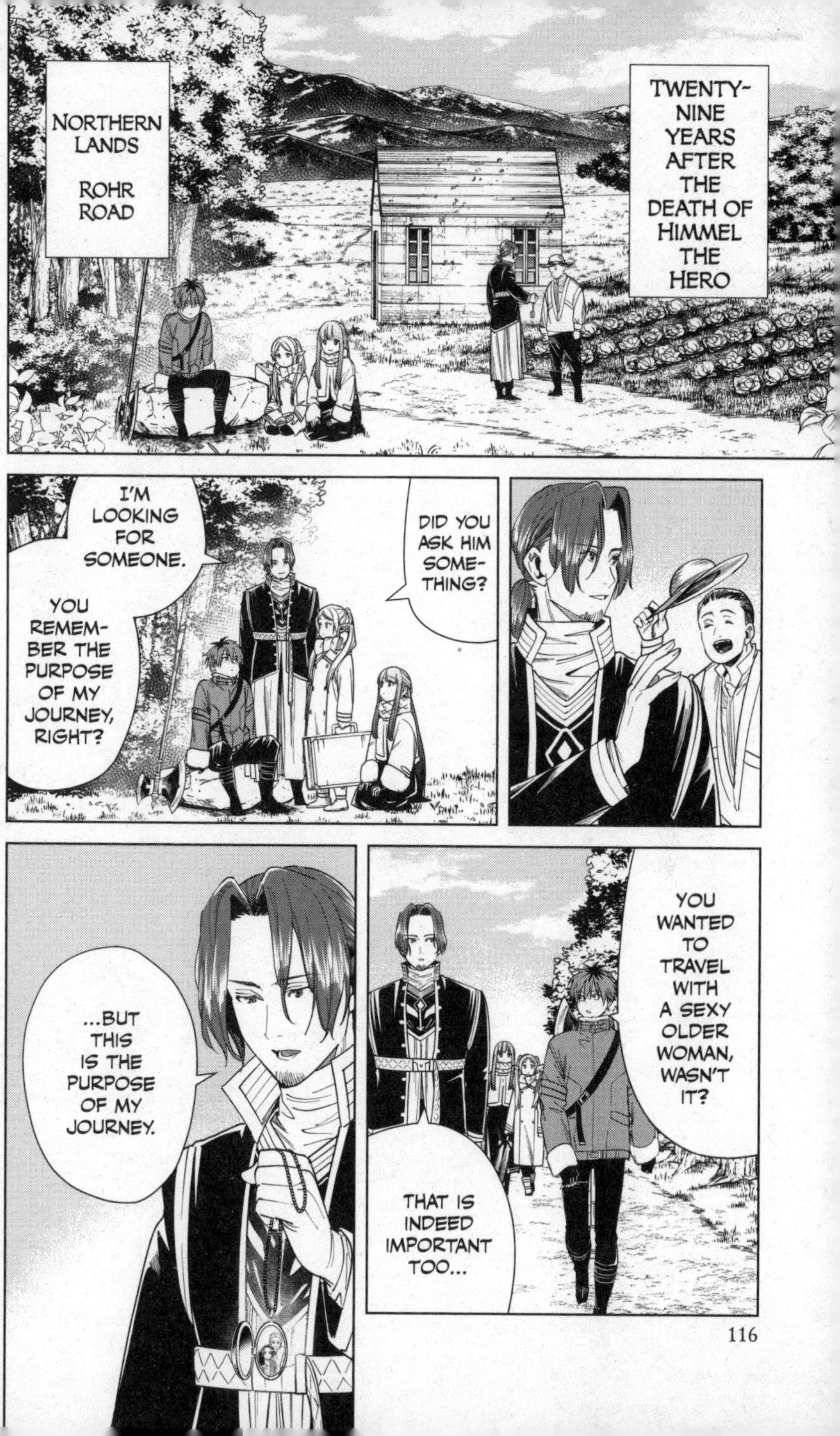
TWENTY-NINE YEARS AFTER THE DEATH OF HIMMEL THE HERO
NORTHERN LANDS
ROHR ROAD
DID YOU ASK HIM SOMETHING?
I'M LOOKING FOR SOMEONE.
YOU REMEMBER THE PURPOSE OF MY JOURNEY, RIGHT?
YOU WANTED TO TRAVEL WITH A SEXY OLDER WOMAN, WASN'T IT?
THAT IS INDEED IMPORTANT TOO...
...BUT THIS IS THE PURPOSE OF MY JOURNEY.

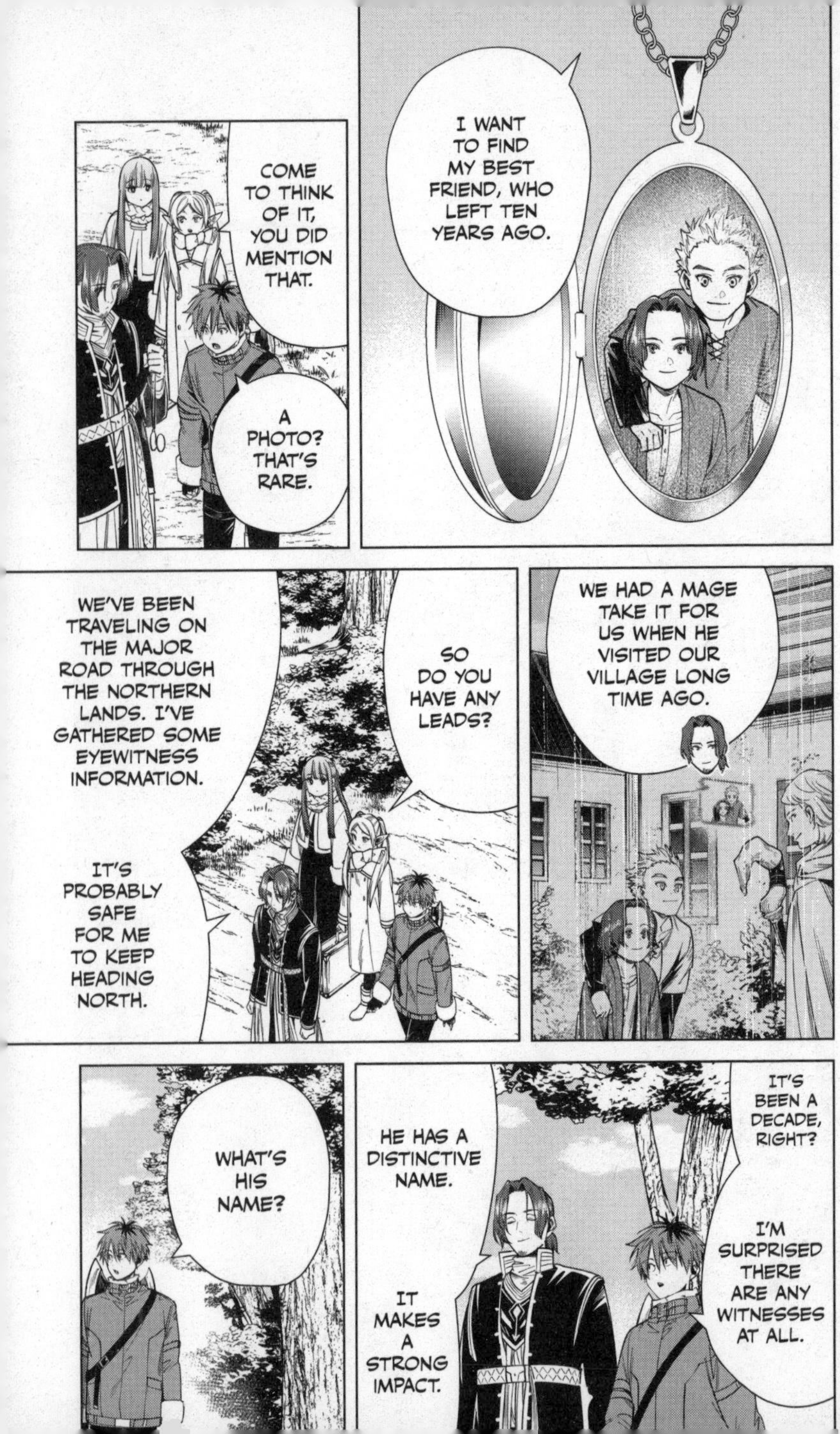
I WANT TO FIND MY BEST FRIEND, WHO LEFT TEN YEARS AGO.
COME TO THINK OF IT, YOU DID MENTION THAT.
A PHOTO? THAT'S RARE.
WE HAD A MAGE TAKE IT FOR US WHEN HE VISITED OUR VILLAGE LONG TIME AGO.
SO DO YOU HAVE ANY LEADS?
WE'VE BEEN TRAVELING ON THE MAJOR ROAD THROUGH THE NORTHERN LANDS. I'VE GATHERED SOME EYEWITNESS INFORMATION.
IT'S PROBABLY SAFE FOR ME TO KEEP HEADING NORTH.
IT'S BEEN A DECADE, RIGHT?
I'M SURPRISED THERE ARE ANY WITNESSES AT ALL.
HE HAS A DISTINCTIVE NAME.
IT MAKES A STRONG IMPACT.
WHAT'S HIS NAME?

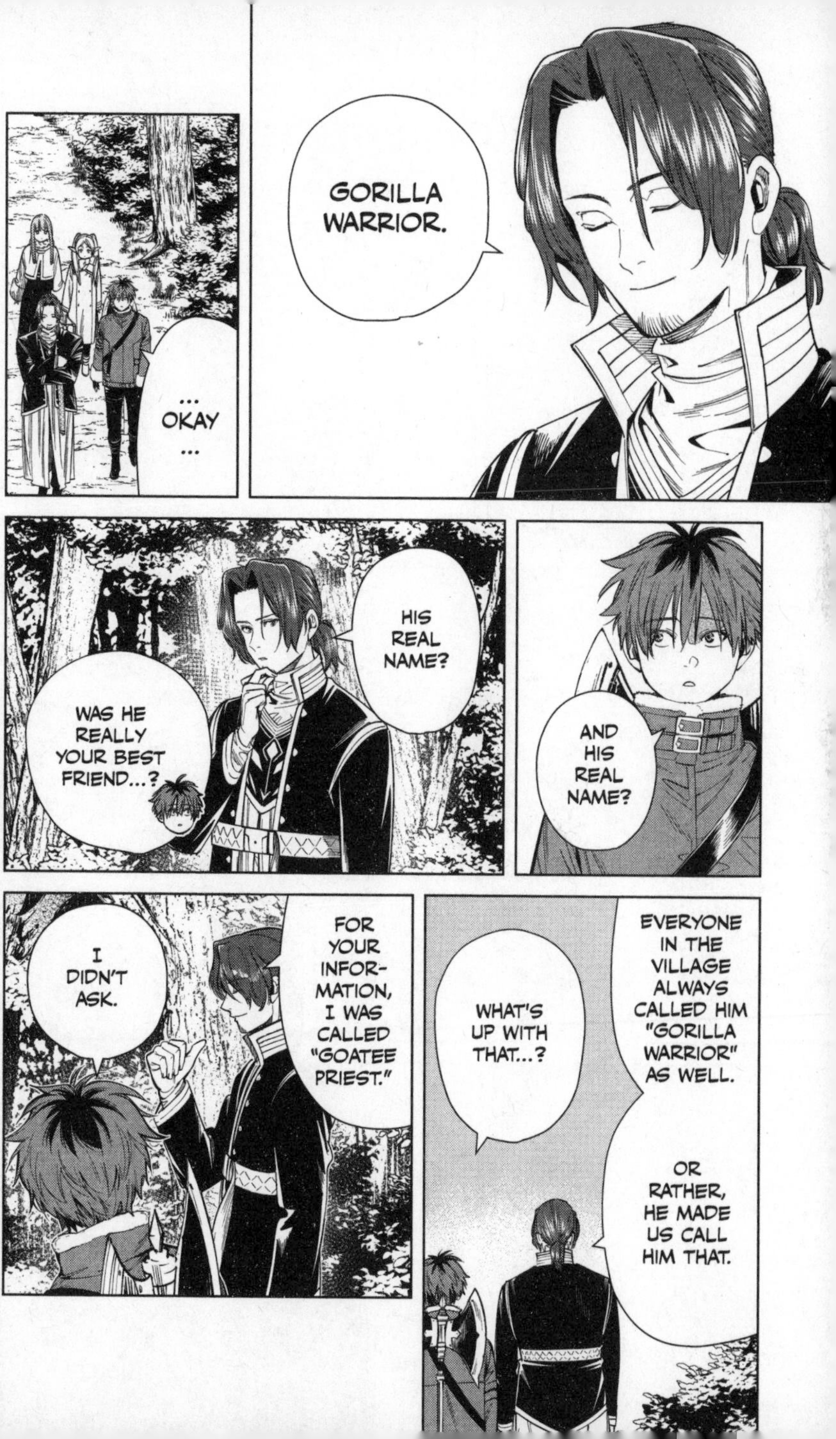
GORILLA WARRIOR.
... OKAY ...
AND HIS REAL NAME?
HIS REAL NAME?
WAS HE REALLY YOUR BEST FRIEND...?
EVERYONE IN THE VILLAGE ALWAYS CALLED HIM "GORILLA WARRIOR" AS WELL.
OR RATHER, HE MADE US CALL HIM THAT.
WHAT'S UP WITH THAT...?
FOR YOUR INFORMATION, I WAS CALLED "GOATEE PRIEST."
I DIDN'T ASK.

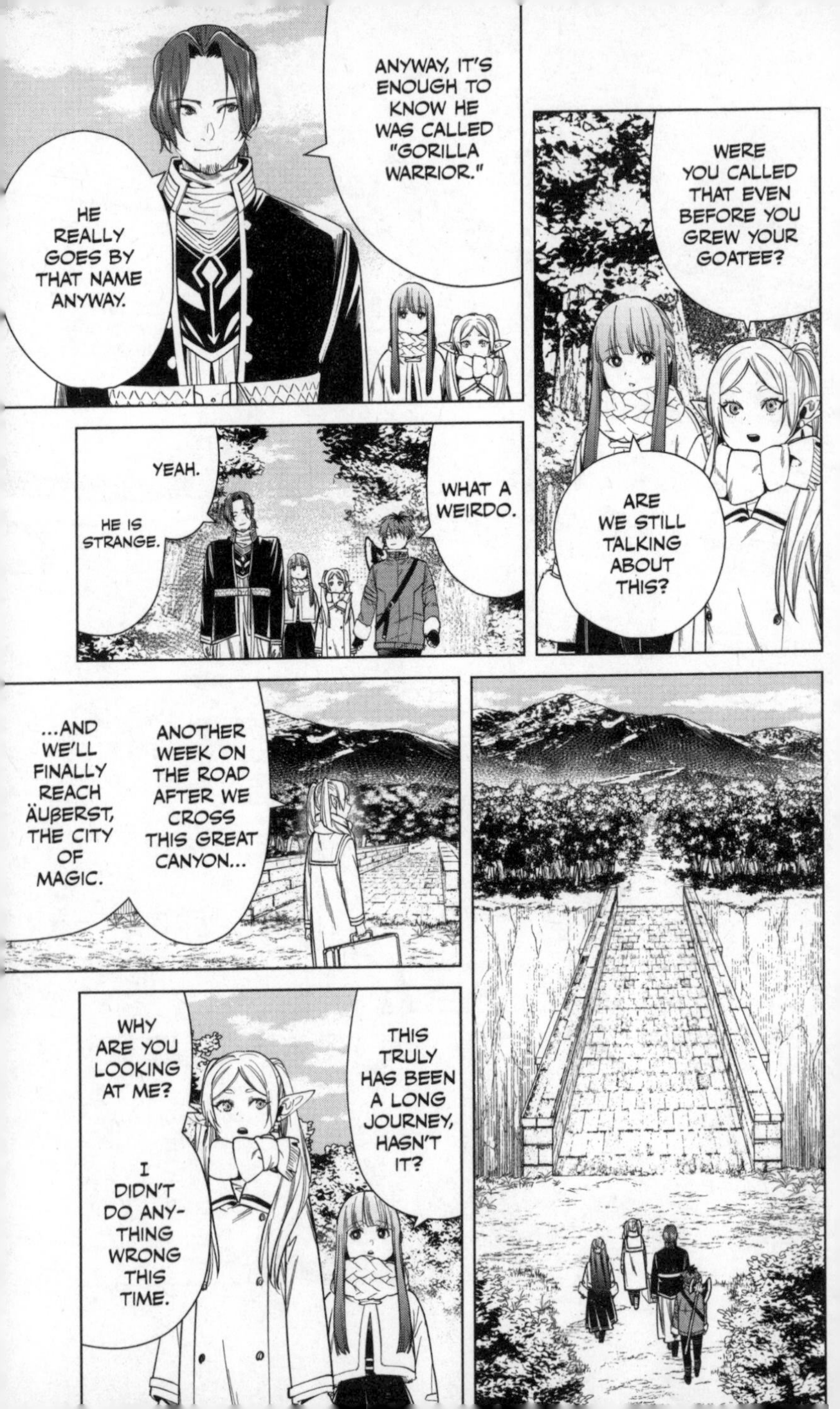
ANYWAY, IT'S ENOUGH TO KNOW HE WAS CALLED "GORILLA WARRIOR."
HE REALLY GOES BY THAT NAME ANYWAY.
WERE YOU CALLED THAT EVEN BEFORE YOU GREW YOUR GOATEE?
ARE WE STILL TALKING ABOUT THIS?
WHAT A WEIRDO.
YEAH.
HE IS STRANGE.
ANOTHER WEEK ON THE ROAD AFTER WE CROSS THIS GREAT CANYON...
...AND WE'LL FINALLY REACH ÄUßERST, THE CITY OF MAGIC.
THIS TRULY HAS BEEN A LONG JOURNEY, HASN'T IT?
WHY ARE YOU LOOKING AT ME?
I DIDN'T DO ANY-THING WRONG THIS TIME.

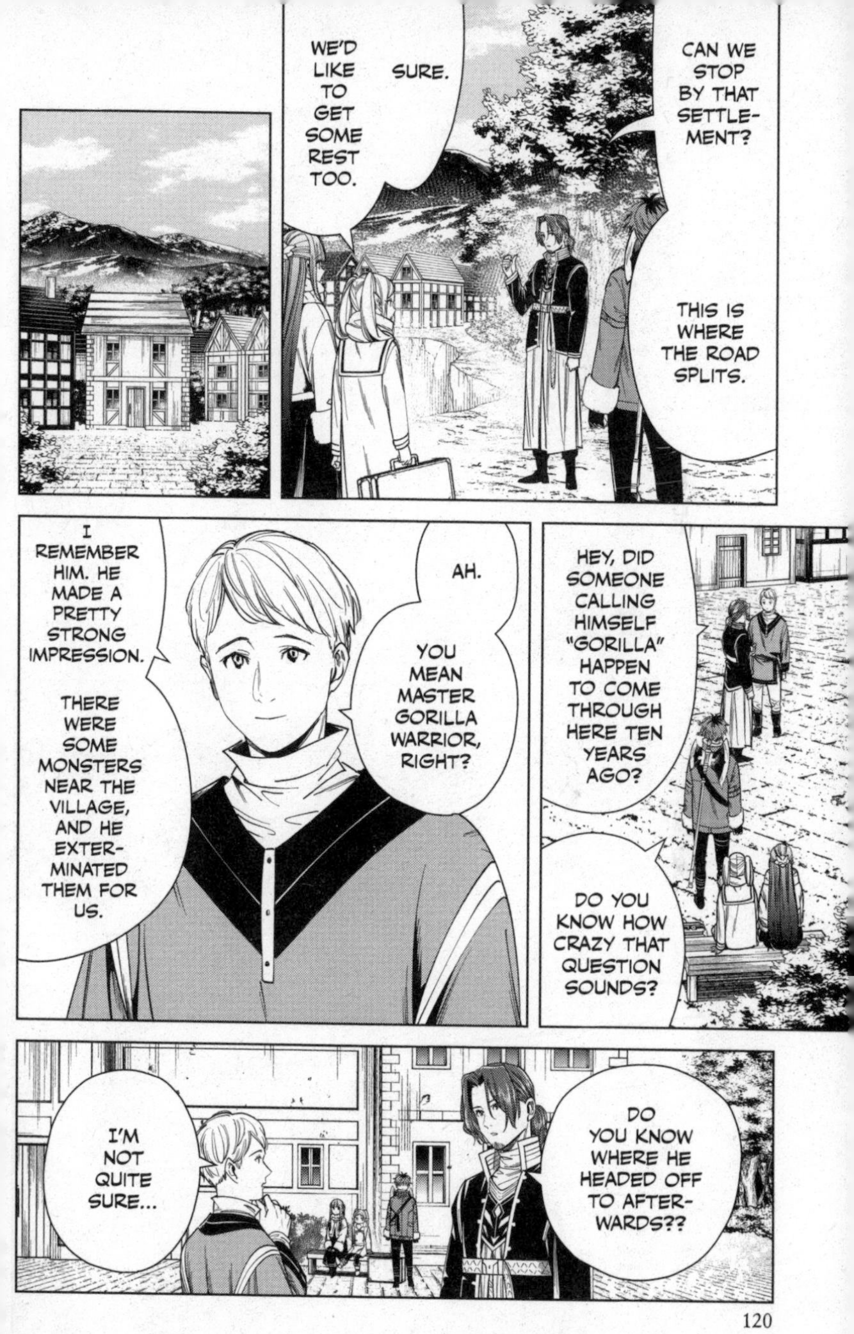
CAN WE STOP BY THAT SETTLEMENT?
THIS IS WHERE THE ROAD SPLITS.
SURE.
WE'D LIKE TO GET SOME REST TOO.
HEY, DID SOMEONE CALLING HIMSELF "GORILLA" HAPPEN TO COME THROUGH HERE TEN YEARS AGO?
DO YOU KNOW HOW CRAZY THAT QUESTION SOUNDS?
AH.
YOU MEAN MASTER GORILLA WARRIOR, RIGHT?
I REMEMBER HIM. HE MADE A PRETTY STRONG IMPRESSION.
THERE WERE SOME MONSTERS NEAR THE VILLAGE, AND HE EXTER-MINATED THEM FOR US.
DO YOU KNOW WHERE HE HEADED OFF TO AFTER-WARDS??
I'M NOT QUITE SURE...

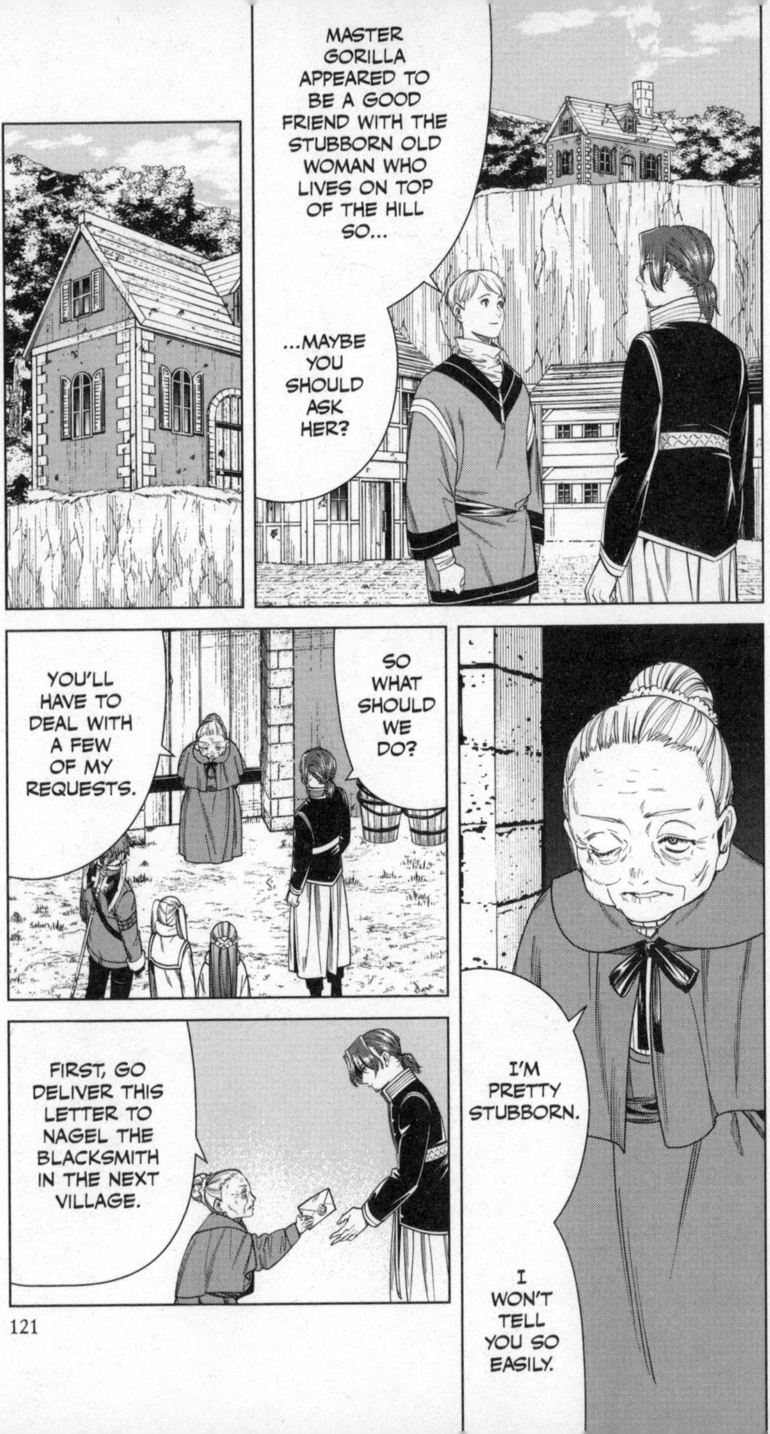
MASTER GORILLA APPEARED TO BE A GOOD FRIEND WITH THE STUBBORN OLD WOMAN WHO LIVES ON TOP OF THE HILL SO...
...MAYBE YOU SHOULD ASK HER?
I'M PRETTY STUBBORN.
I WON'T TELL YOU SO EASILY.
SO WHAT SHOULD WE DO?
YOU'LL HAVE TO DEAL WITH A FEW OF MY REQUESTS.
FIRST, GO DELIVER THIS LETTER TO NAGEL THE BLACKSMITH IN THE NEXT VILLAGE.

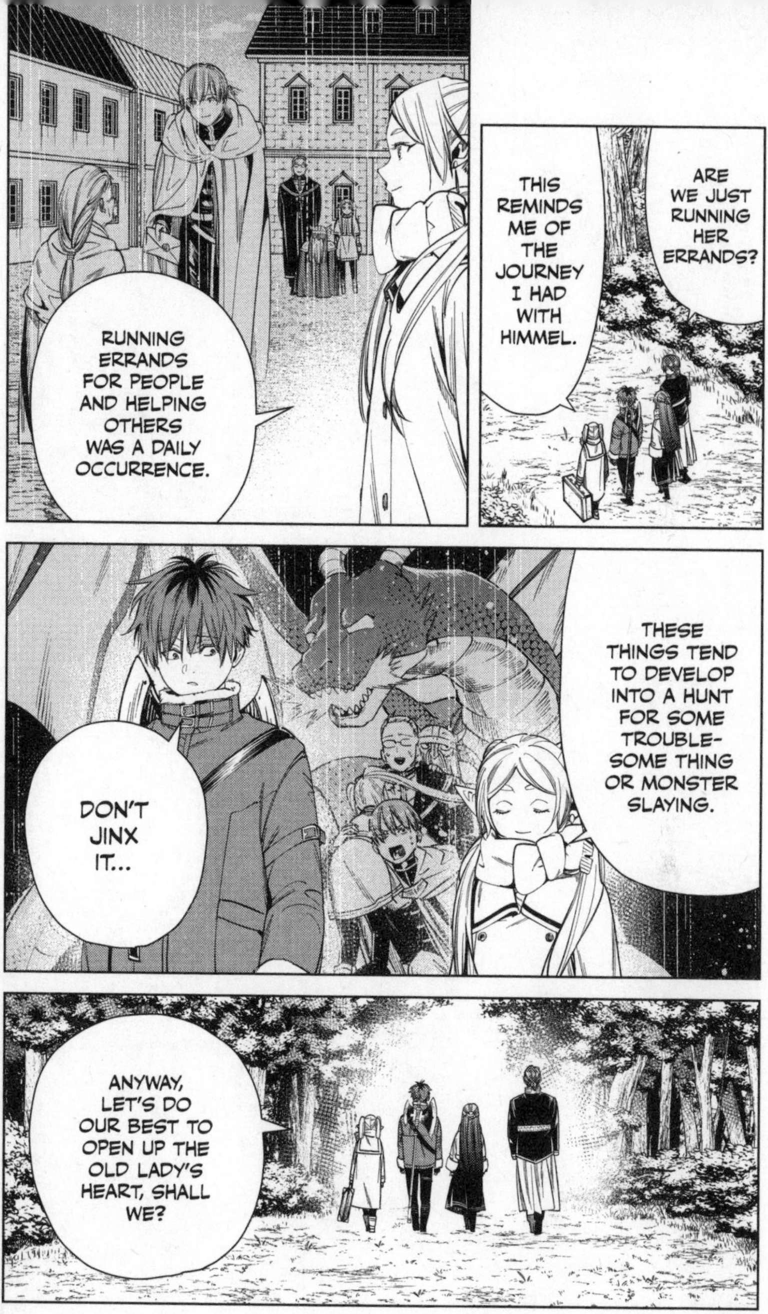
ARE WE JUST RUNNING HER ERRANDS?
THIS REMINDS ME OF THE JOURNEY I HAD WITH HIMMEL.
RUNNING ERRANDS FOR PEOPLE AND HELPING OTHERS WAS A DAILY OCCURRENCE.
THESE THINGS TEND TO DEVELOP INTO A HUNT FOR SOME TROUBLE-SOME THING OR MONSTER SLAYING.
DON'T JINX IT...
ANYWAY, LET'S DO OUR BEST TO OPEN UP THE OLD LADY'S HEART, SHALL WE?

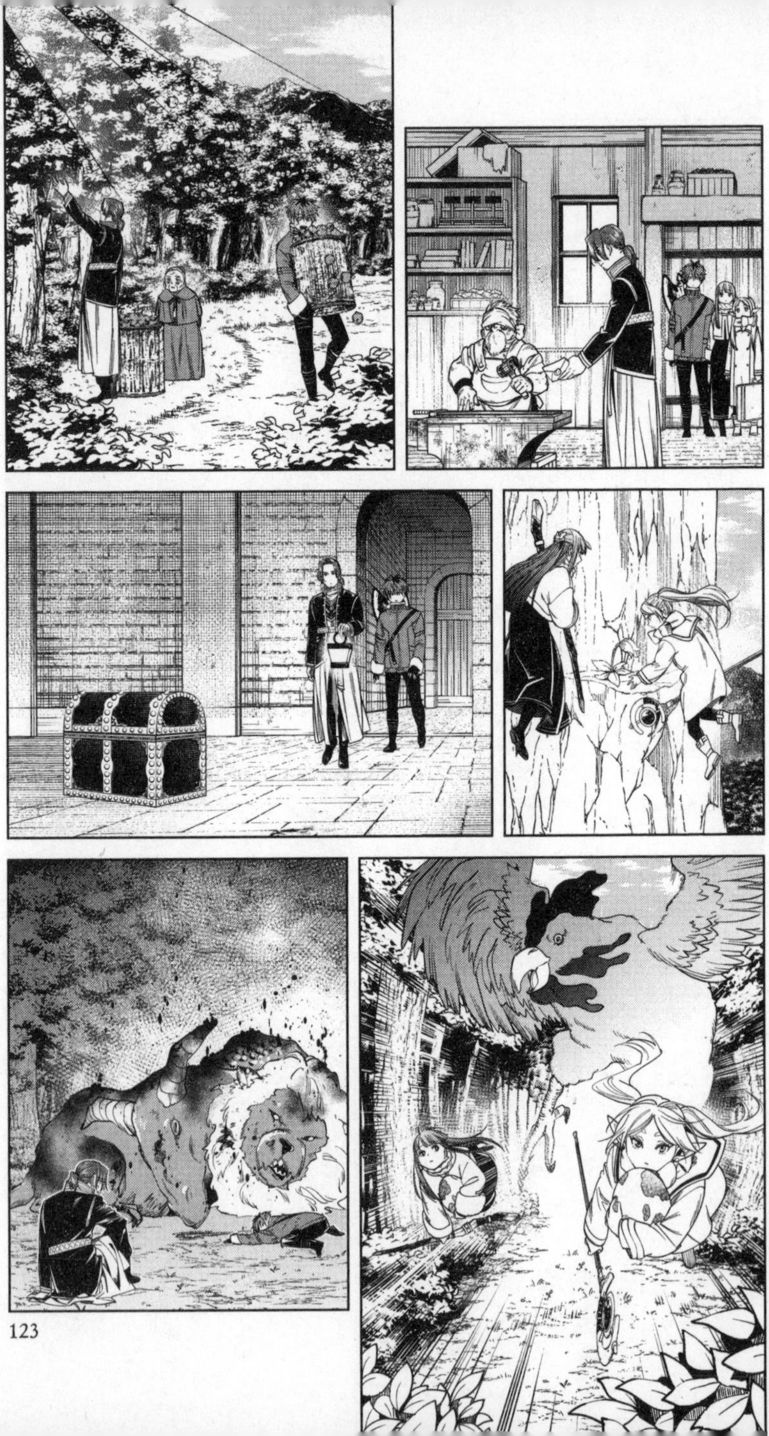

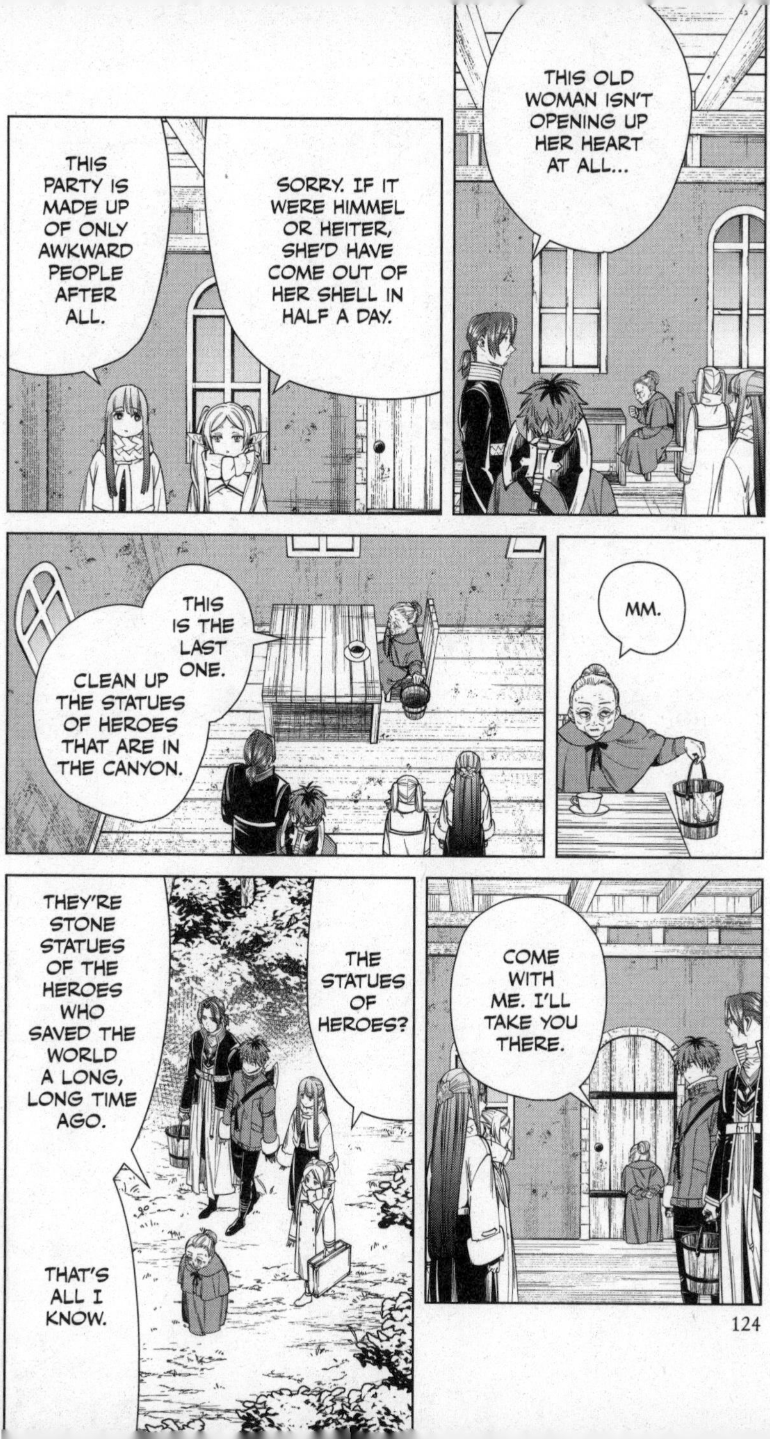
THIS OLD WOMAN ISN'T OPENING UP HER HEART AT ALL...
SORRY. IF IT WERE HIMMEL OR HEITER, SHE'D HAVE COME OUT OF HER SHELL IN HALF A DAY.
THIS PARTY IS MADE UP OF ONLY AWKWARD PEOPLE AFTER ALL.
MM.
THIS IS THE LAST ONE.
CLEAN UP THE STATUES OF HEROES THAT ARE IN THE CANYON.
COME WITH ME. I'LL TAKE YOU THERE.
THE STATUES OF HEROES?
THEY'RE STONE STATUES OF THE HEROES WHO SAVED THE WORLD A LONG, LONG TIME AGO.
THAT'S ALL I KNOW.

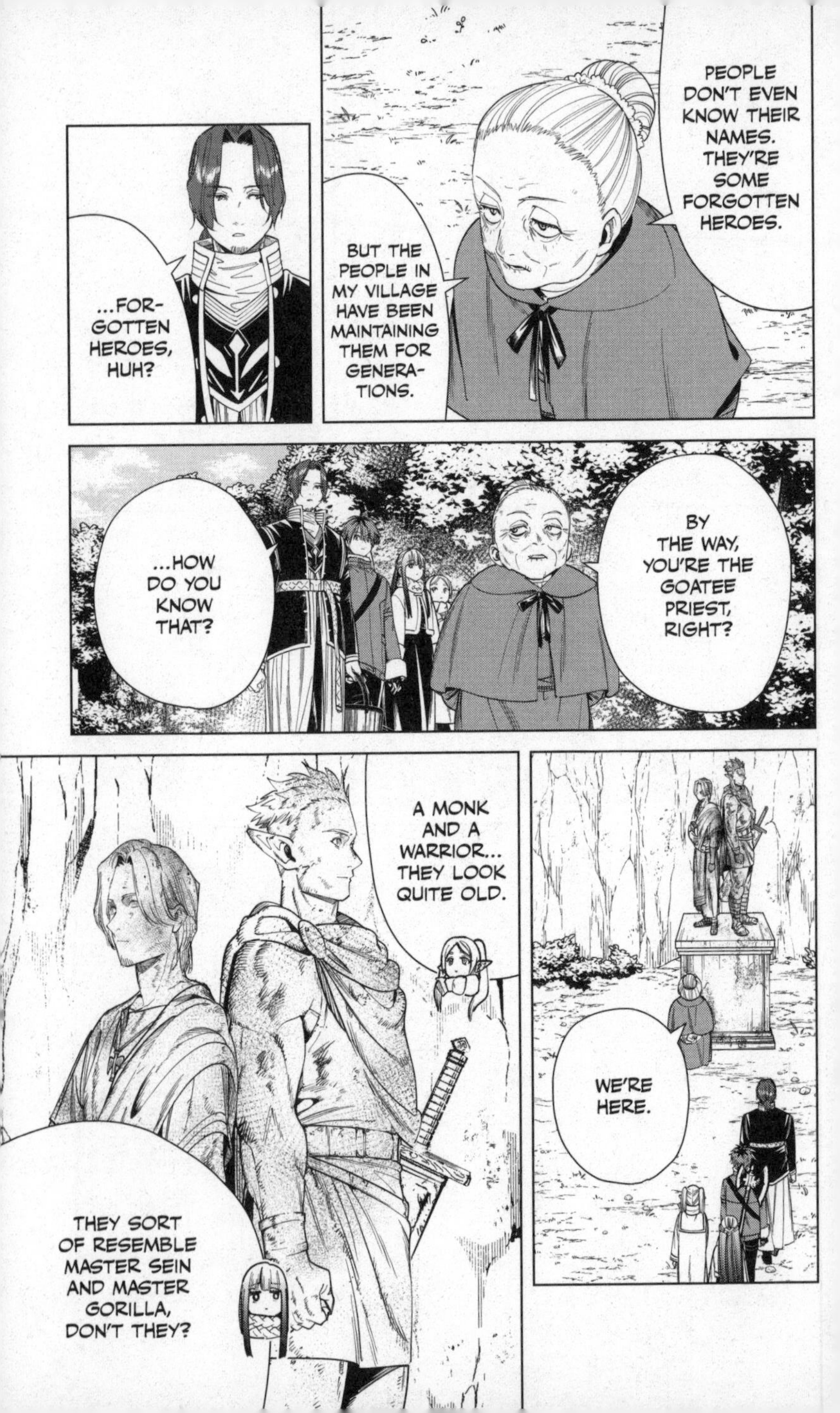
PEOPLE DON'T EVEN KNOW THEIR NAMES. THEY'RE SOME FORGOTTEN HEROES.
BUT THE PEOPLE IN MY VILLAGE HAVE BEEN MAINTAINING THEM FOR GENERATIONS.
...FORGOTTEN HEROES, HUH?
BY THE WAY, YOU'RE THE GOATEE PRIEST, RIGHT?
...HOW DO YOU KNOW THAT?
WE'RE HERE.
A MONK AND A WARRIOR... THEY LOOK QUITE OLD.
THEY SORT OF RESEMBLE MASTER SEIN AND MASTER GORILLA, DON'T THEY?

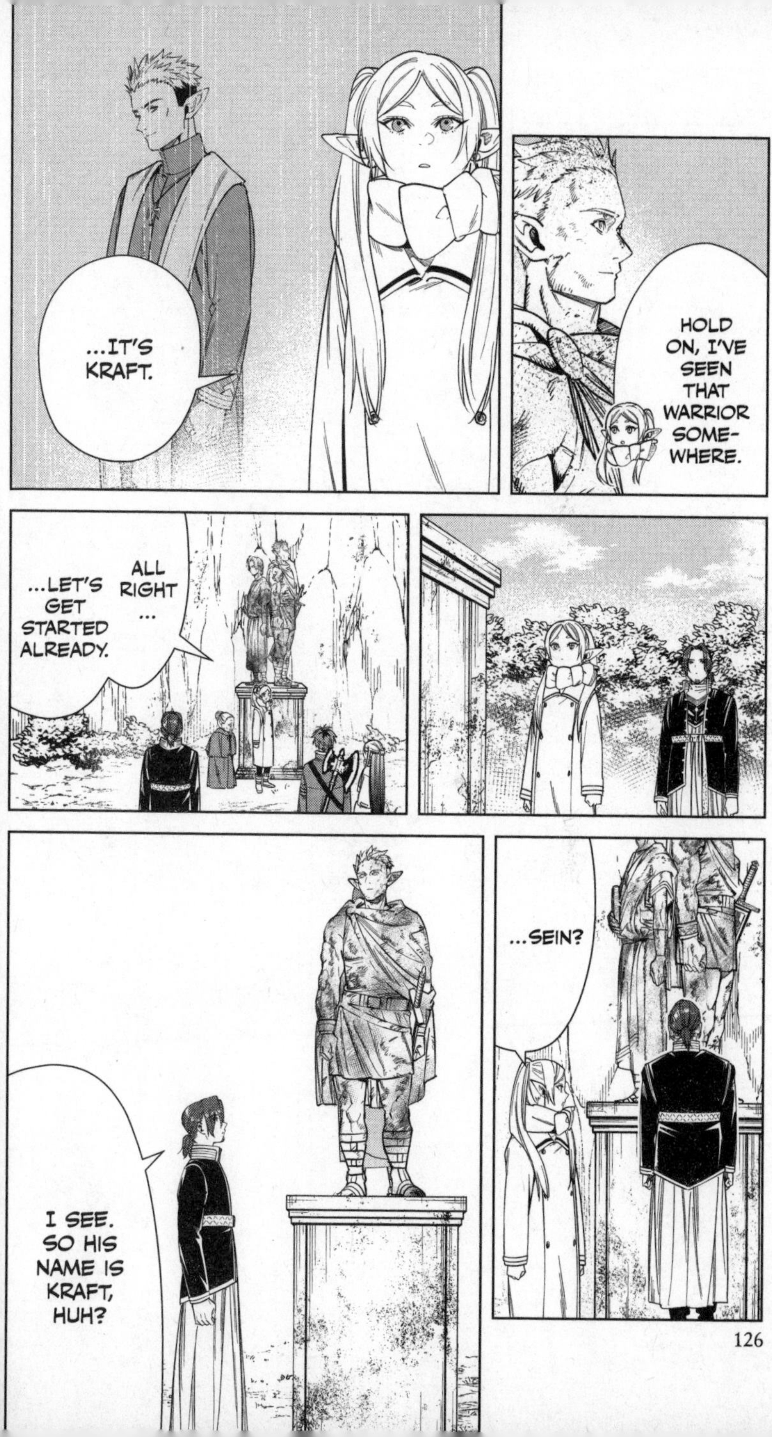
HOLD ON, I'VE SEEN THAT WARRIOR SOME-WHERE.
...IT'S KRAFT.
ALL RIGHT ...
...LET'S GET STARTED ALREADY.
...SEIN?
I SEE. SO HIS NAME IS KRAFT, HUH?

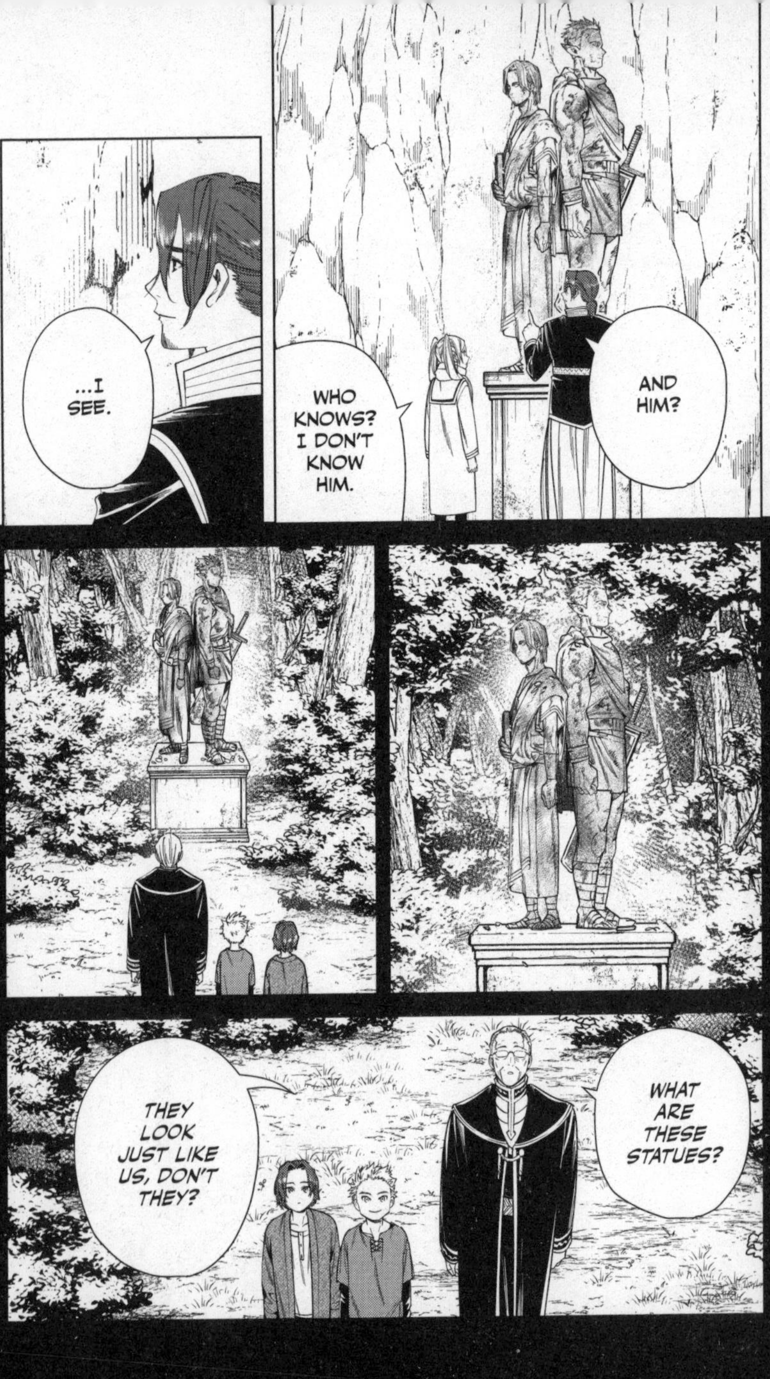
AND HIM?
WHO KNOWS? I DON'T KNOW HIM.
...I SEE.
WHAT ARE THESE STATUES?
THEY LOOK JUST LIKE US, DON'T THEY?

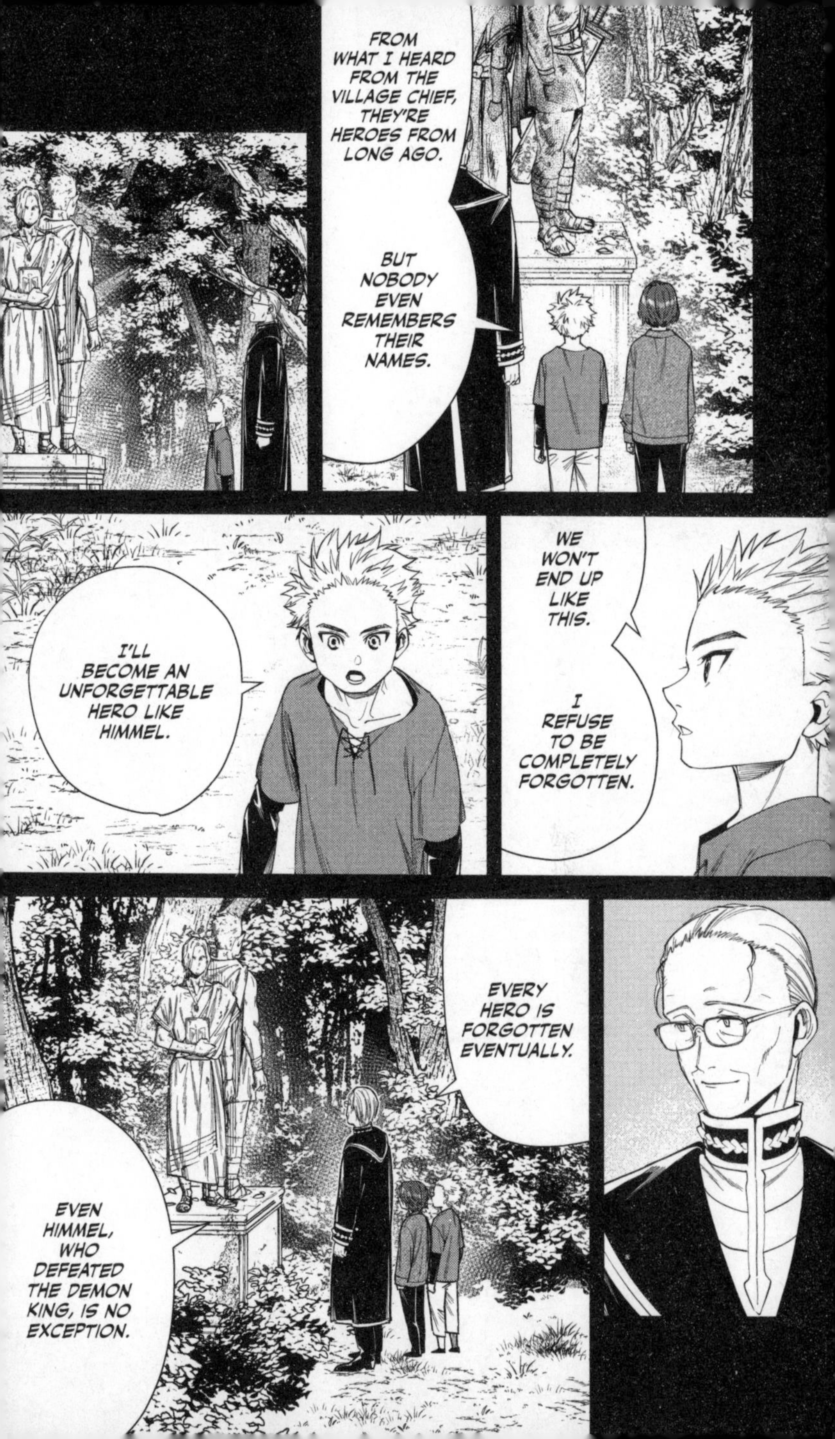
FROM WHAT I HEARD FROM THE VILLAGE CHIEF, THEY'RE HEROES FROM LONG AGO.
BUT NOBODY EVEN REMEMBERS THEIR NAMES.
WE WON'T END UP LIKE THIS.
I REFUSE TO BE COMPLETELY FORGOTTEN.
I'LL BECOME AN UNFORGETTABLE HERO LIKE HIMMEL.
EVERY HERO IS FORGOTTEN EVENTUALLY.
EVEN HIMMEL, WHO DEFEATED THE DEMON KING, IS NO EXCEPTION.

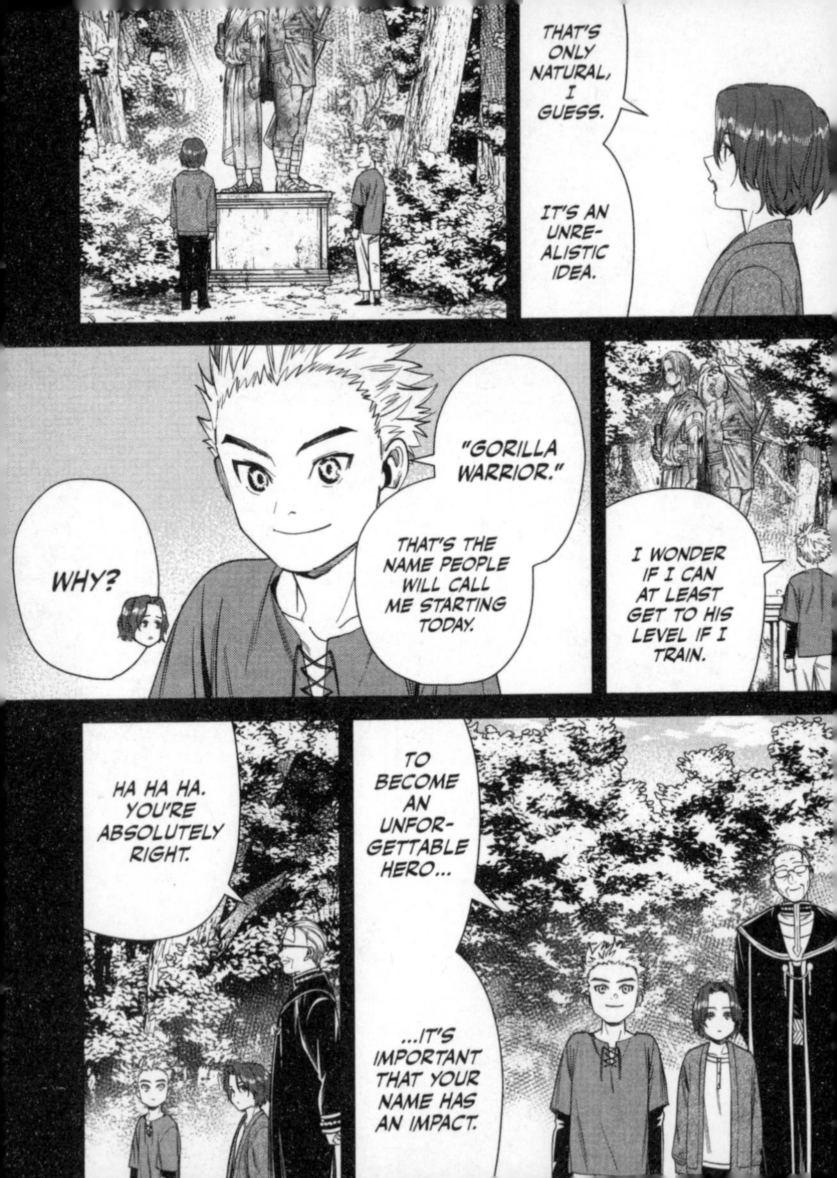
THAT'S ONLY NATURAL, I GUESS.
IT'S AN UNRE-ALISTIC IDEA.
I WONDER IF I CAN AT LEAST GET TO HIS LEVEL IF I TRAIN.
"GORILLA WARRIOR."
THAT'S THE NAME PEOPLE WILL CALL ME STARTING TODAY.
WHY?
TO BECOME AN UNFOR-GETTABLE HERO...
...IT'S IMPORTANT THAT YOUR NAME HAS AN IMPACT.
HA HA HA. YOU'RE ABSOLUTELY RIGHT.

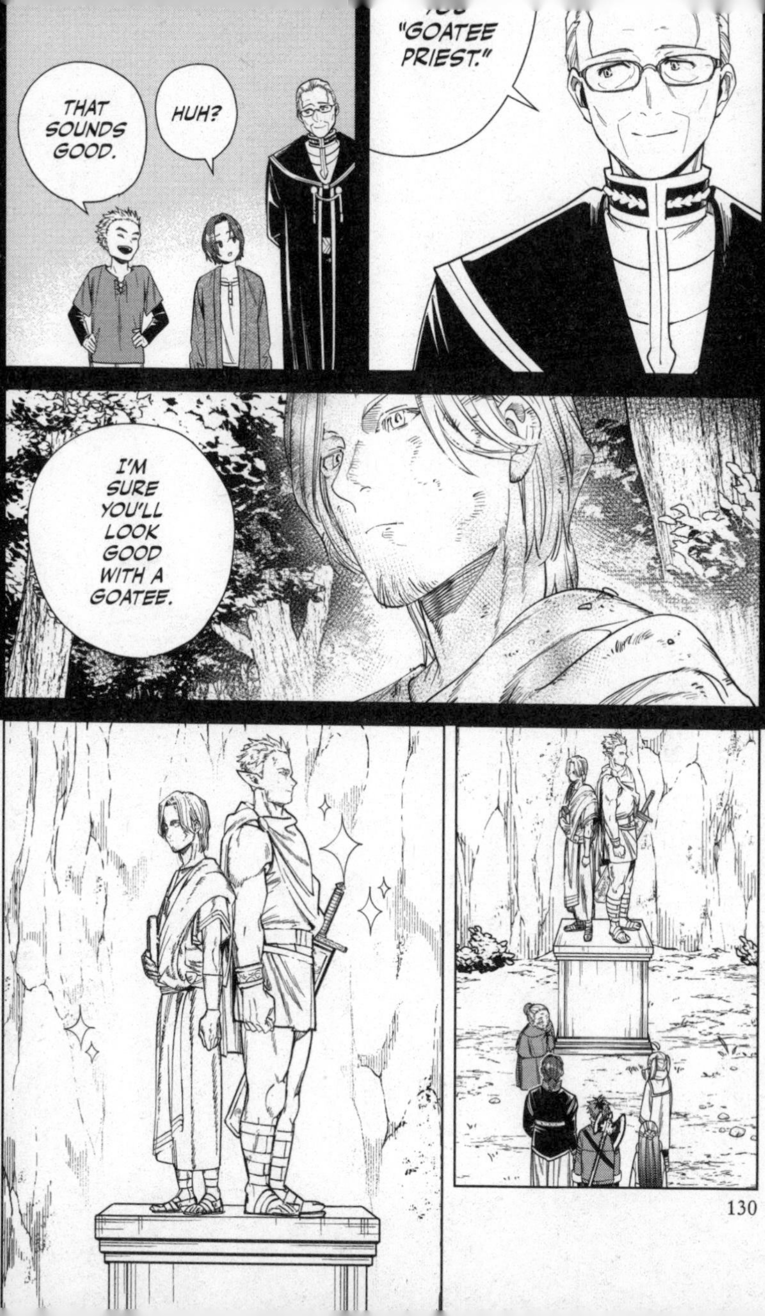
"GOATEE PRIEST."
HUH?
THAT SOUNDS GOOD.
I'M SURE YOU'LL LOOK GOOD WITH A GOATEE.

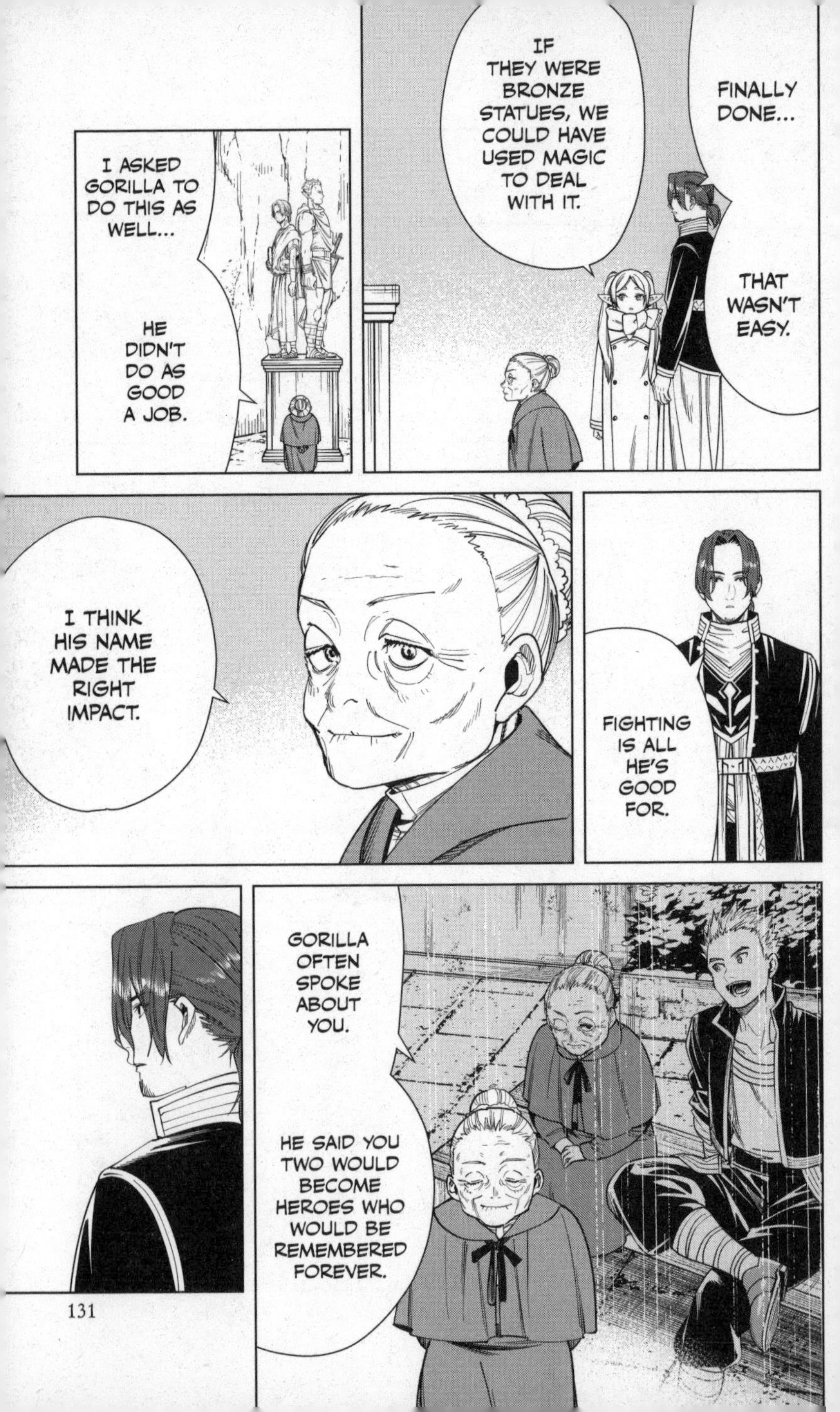
FINALLY DONE...
THAT WASN'T EASY.
IF THEY WERE BRONZE STATUES, WE COULD HAVE USED MAGIC TO DEAL WITH IT.
I ASKED GORILLA TO DO THIS AS WELL...
HE DIDN'T DO AS GOOD A JOB.
FIGHTING IS ALL HE'S GOOD FOR.
I THINK HIS NAME MADE THE RIGHT IMPACT.
GORILLA OFTEN SPOKE ABOUT YOU.
HE SAID YOU TWO WOULD BECOME HEROES WHO WOULD BE REMEMBERED FOREVER.

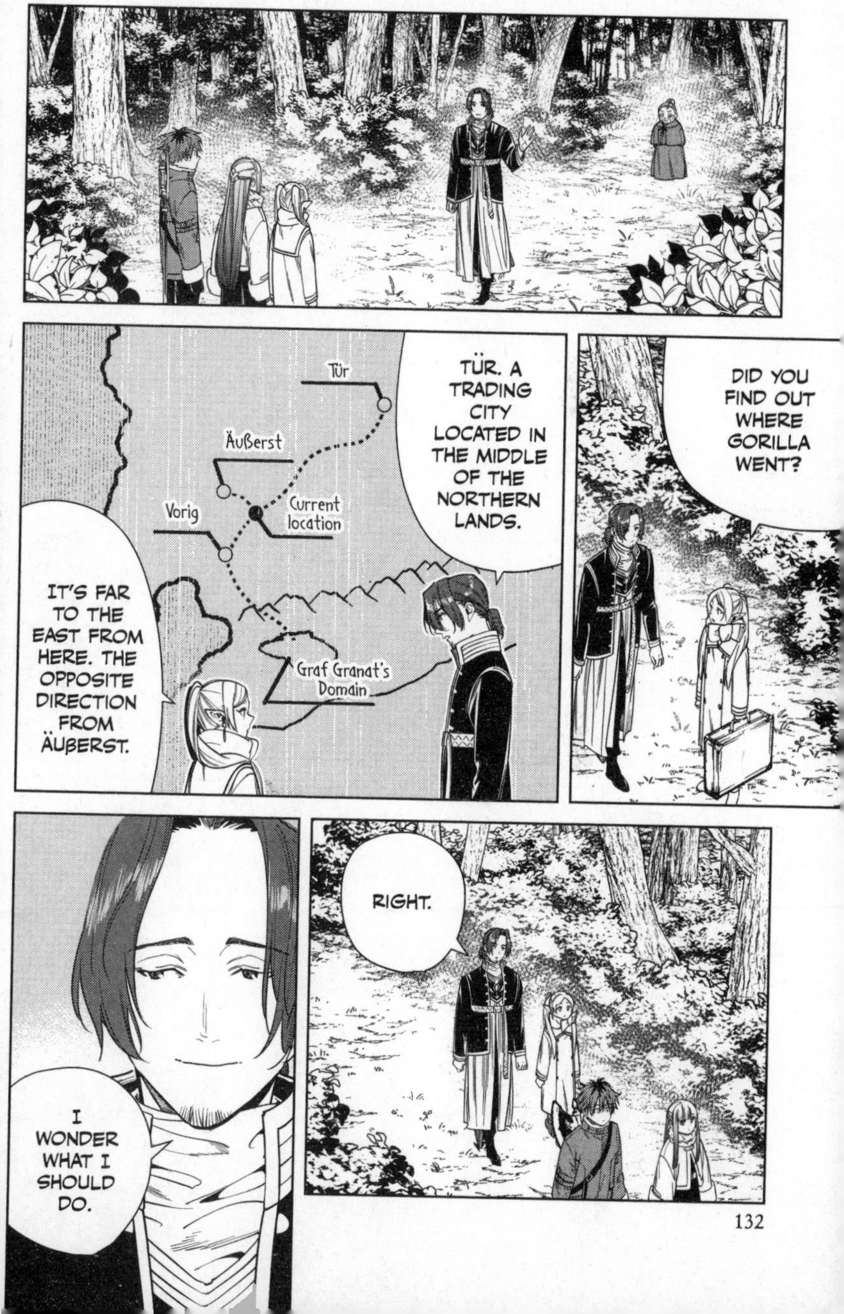
DID YOU FIND OUT WHERE GORILLA WENT?
TÜR. A TRADING CITY LOCATED IN THE MIDDLE OF THE NORTHERN LANDS.
Tür
Äußerst
Current location
Vorig
Graf Granat's Domain
IT'S FAR TO THE EAST FROM HERE. THE OPPOSITE DIRECTION FROM ÄUßERST.
RIGHT.
I WONDER WHAT I SHOULD DO.

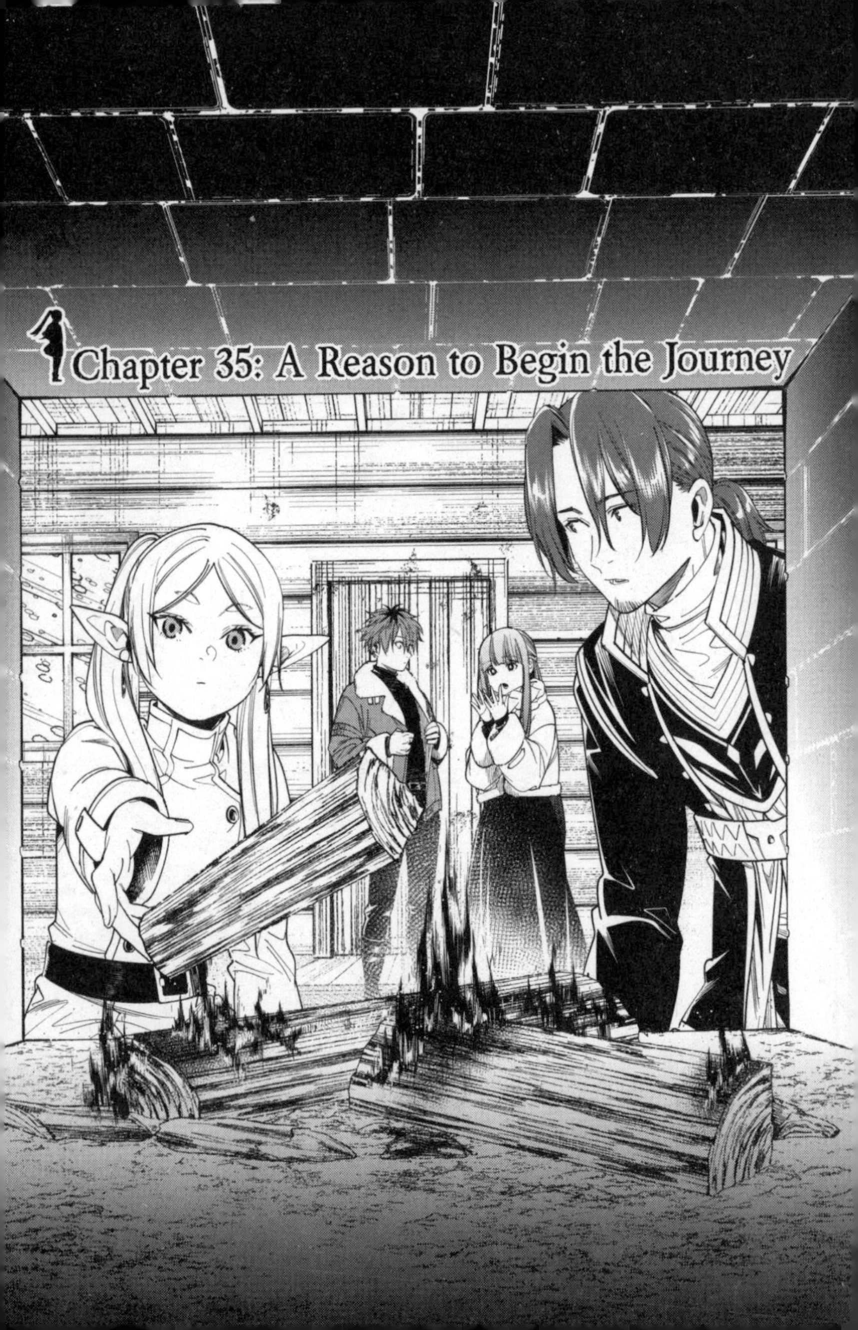
Chapter 35: A Reason to Begin the Journey

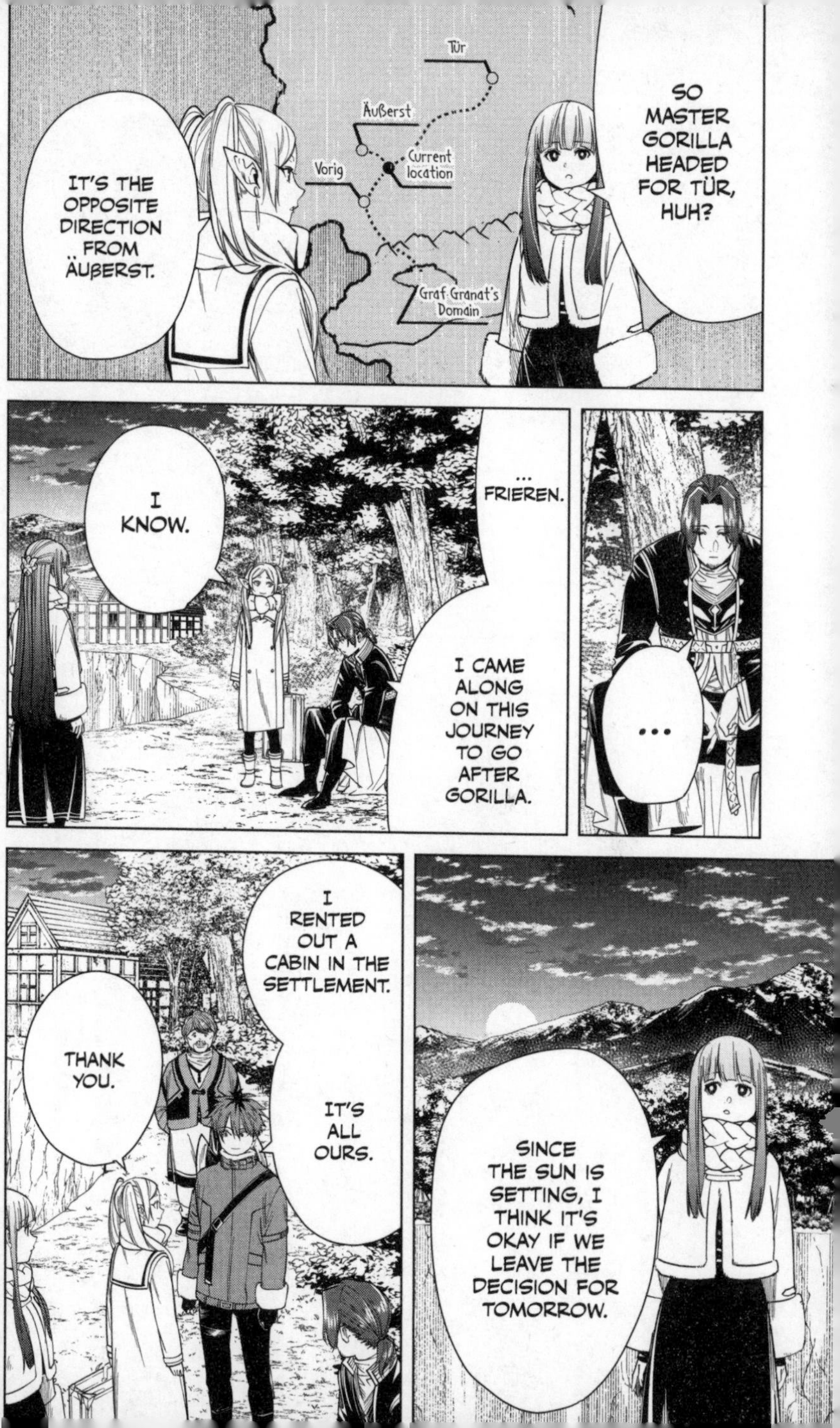
SO MASTER GORILLA HEADED FOR TÜR, HUH?
Tür
Äußerst
Current location
Vorig
Graf Granat's Domain
IT'S THE OPPOSITE DIRECTION FROM ÄUßERST.
...
... FRIEREN.
I CAME ALONG ON THIS JOURNEY TO GO AFTER GORILLA.
I KNOW.
SINCE THE SUN IS SETTING, I THINK IT'S OKAY IF WE LEAVE THE DECISION FOR TOMORROW.
I RENTED OUT A CABIN IN THE SETTLEMENT.
IT'S ALL OURS.
THANK YOU.

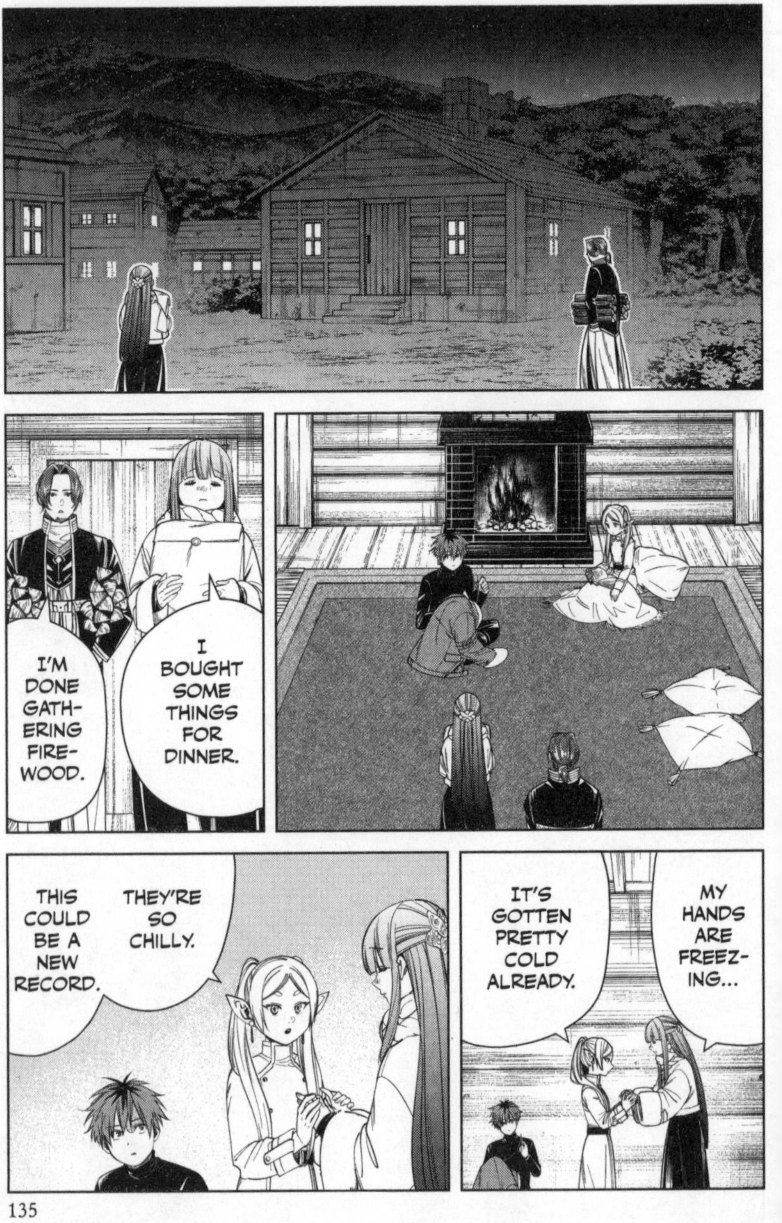
I BOUGHT SOME THINGS FOR DINNER.
I'M DONE GATHERING FIREWOOD.
MY HANDS ARE FREEZING...
IT'S GOTTEN PRETTY COLD ALREADY.
THEY'RE SO CHILLY.
THIS COULD BE A NEW RECORD.

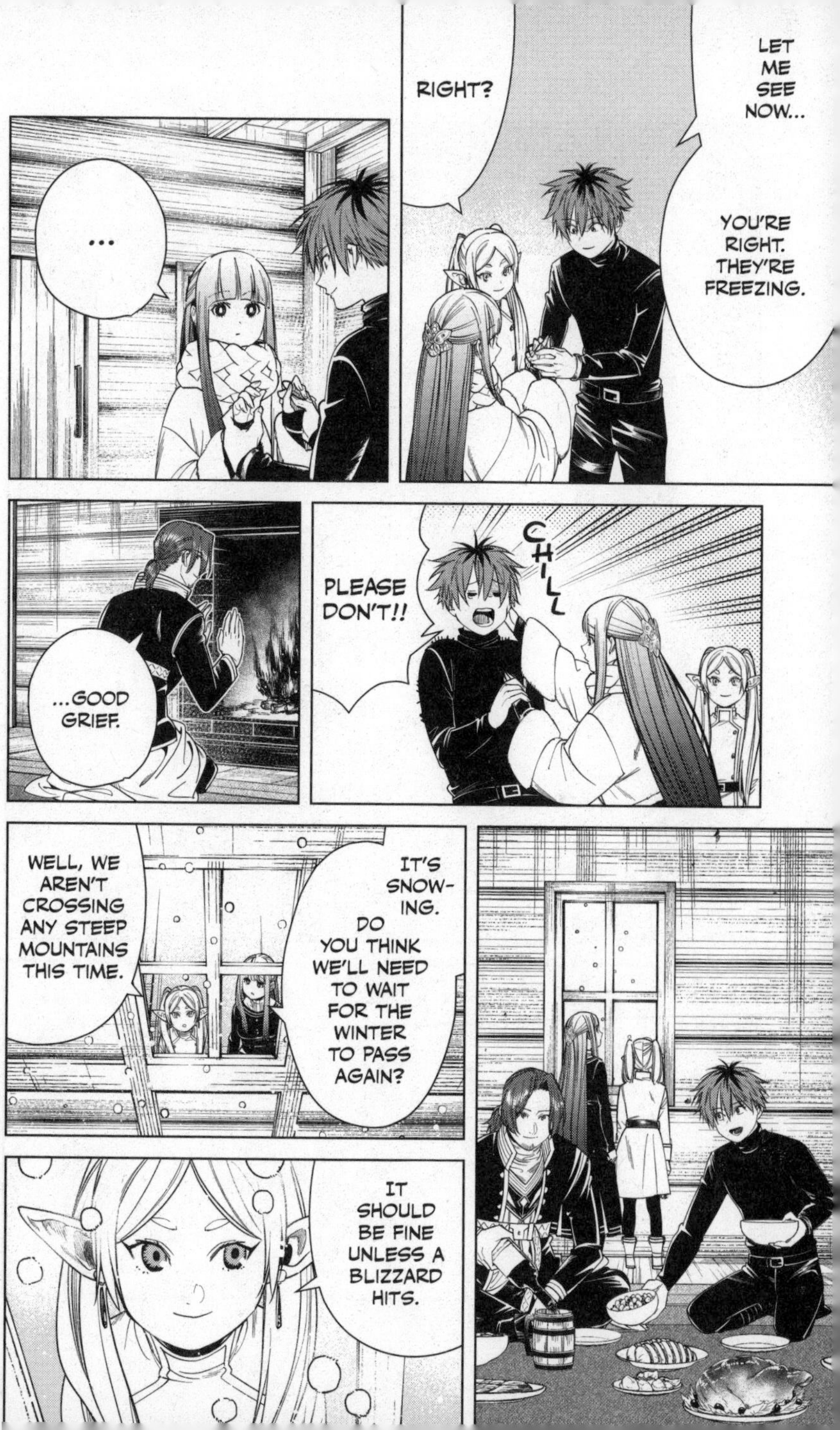
LET ME SEE NOW...
RIGHT?
YOU'RE RIGHT. THEY'RE FREEZING.
...
CHILL
PLEASE DON'T!!
...GOOD GRIEF.
IT'S SNOW-ING. DO YOU THINK WE'LL NEED TO WAIT FOR THE WINTER TO PASS AGAIN?
WELL, WE AREN'T CROSSING ANY STEEP MOUNTAINS THIS TIME.
IT SHOULD BE FINE UNLESS A BLIZZARD HITS.

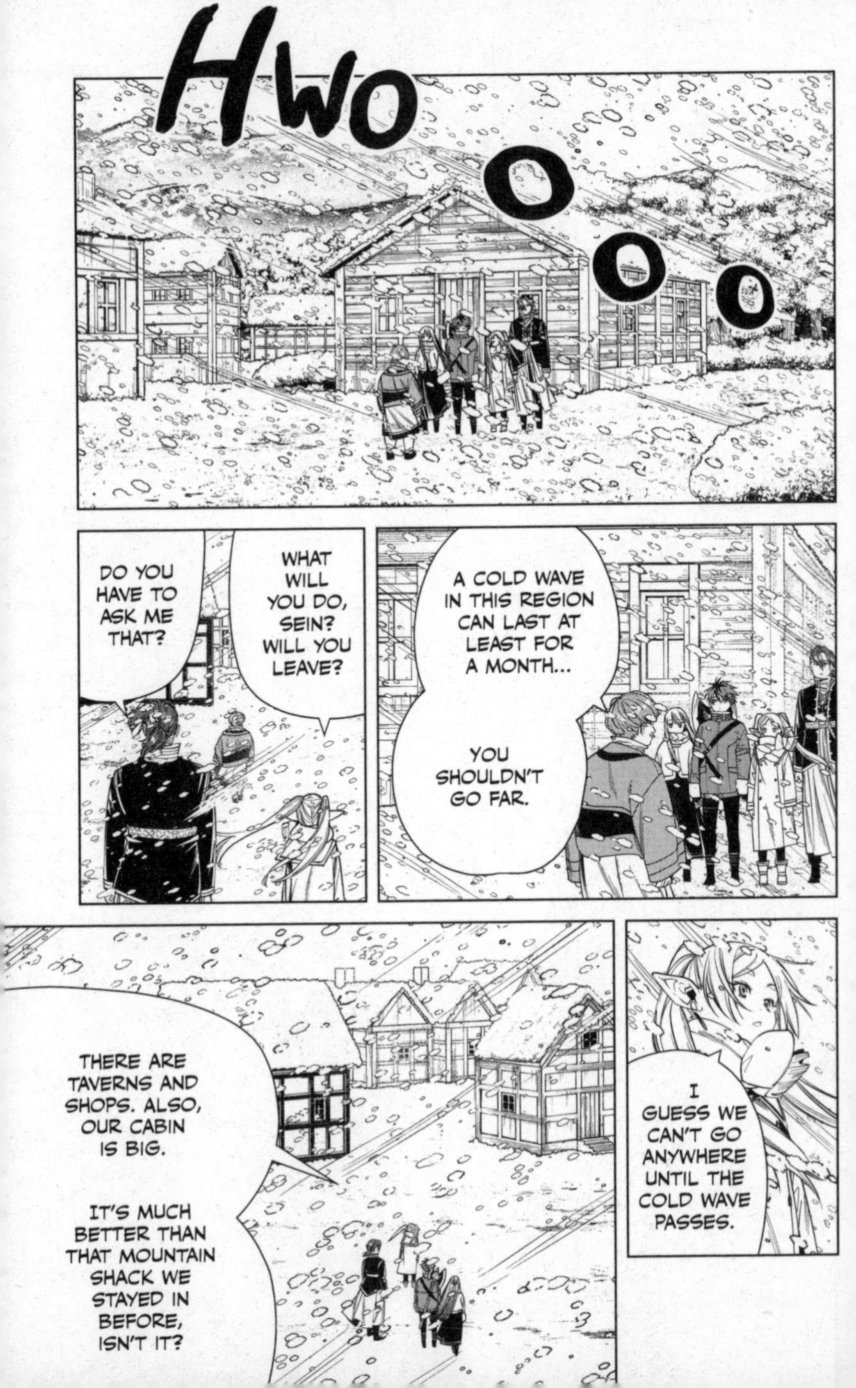
HWOOOOO
A COLD WAVE IN THIS REGION CAN LAST AT LEAST FOR A MONTH...
YOU SHOULDN'T GO FAR.
WHAT WILL YOU DO, SEIN? WILL YOU LEAVE?
DO YOU HAVE TO ASK ME THAT?
I GUESS WE CAN'T GO ANYWHERE UNTIL THE COLD WAVE PASSES.
THERE ARE TAVERNS AND SHOPS. ALSO, OUR CABIN IS BIG.
IT'S MUCH BETTER THAN THAT MOUNTAIN SHACK WE STAYED IN BEFORE, ISN'T IT?

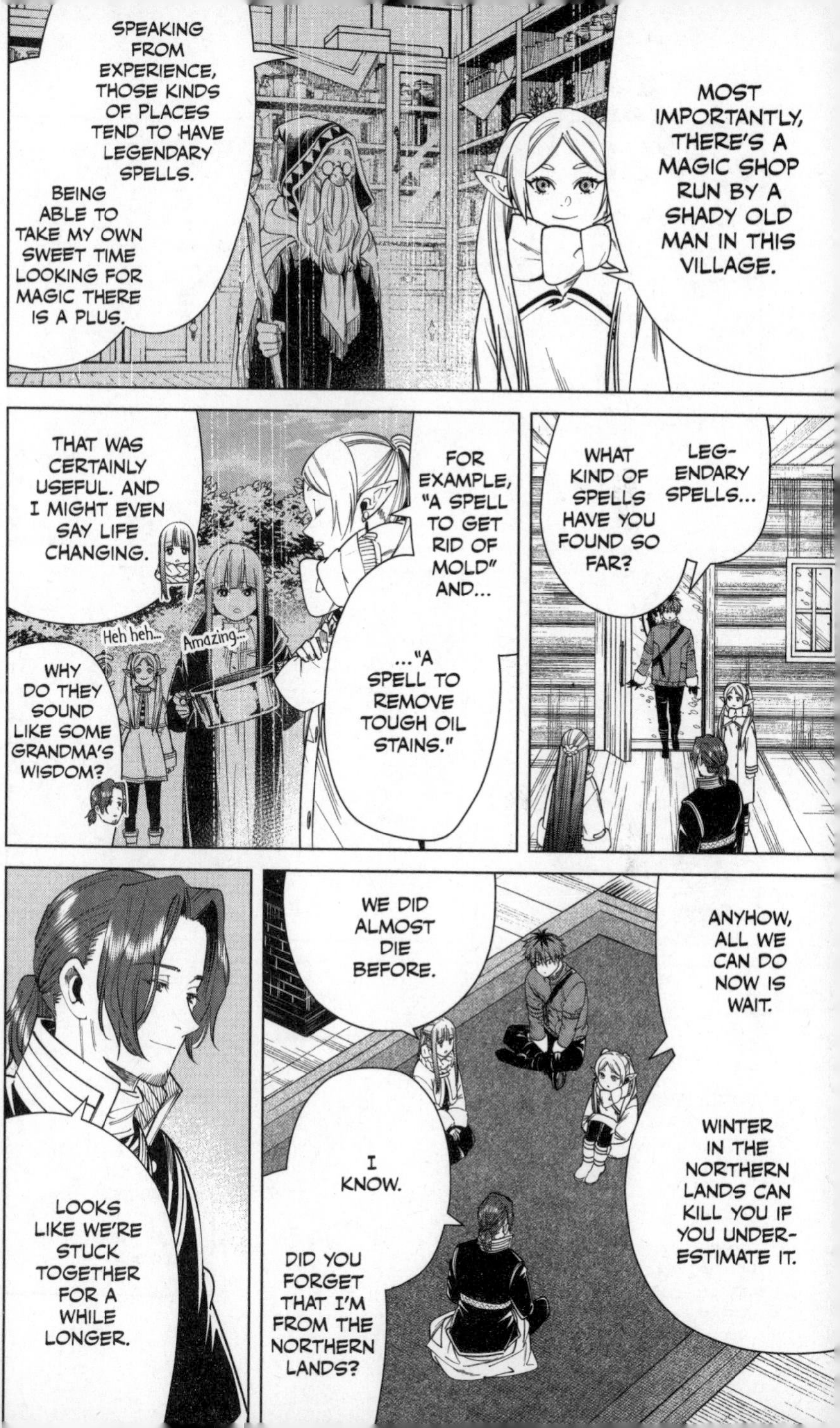
MOST IMPORTANTLY, THERE'S A MAGIC SHOP RUN BY A SHADY OLD MAN IN THIS VILLAGE.
SPEAKING FROM EXPERIENCE, THOSE KINDS OF PLACES TEND TO HAVE LEGENDARY SPELLS.
BEING ABLE TO TAKE MY OWN SWEET TIME LOOKING FOR MAGIC THERE IS A PLUS.
LEG-ENDARY SPELLS...
WHAT KIND OF SPELLS HAVE YOU FOUND SO FAR?
FOR EXAMPLE, "A SPELL TO GET RID OF MOLD" AND...
..."A SPELL TO REMOVE TOUGH OIL STAINS."
THAT WAS CERTAINLY USEFUL. AND I MIGHT EVEN SAY LIFE CHANGING.
Amazing...
Heh heh...
WHY DO THEY SOUND LIKE SOME GRANDMA'S WISDOM?
ANYHOW, ALL WE CAN DO NOW IS WAIT.
WINTER IN THE NORTHERN LANDS CAN KILL YOU IF YOU UNDER-ESTIMATE IT.
WE DID ALMOST DIE BEFORE.
I KNOW.
DID YOU FORGET THAT I'M FROM THE NORTHERN LANDS?
LOOKS LIKE WE'RE STUCK TOGETHER FOR A WHILE LONGER.

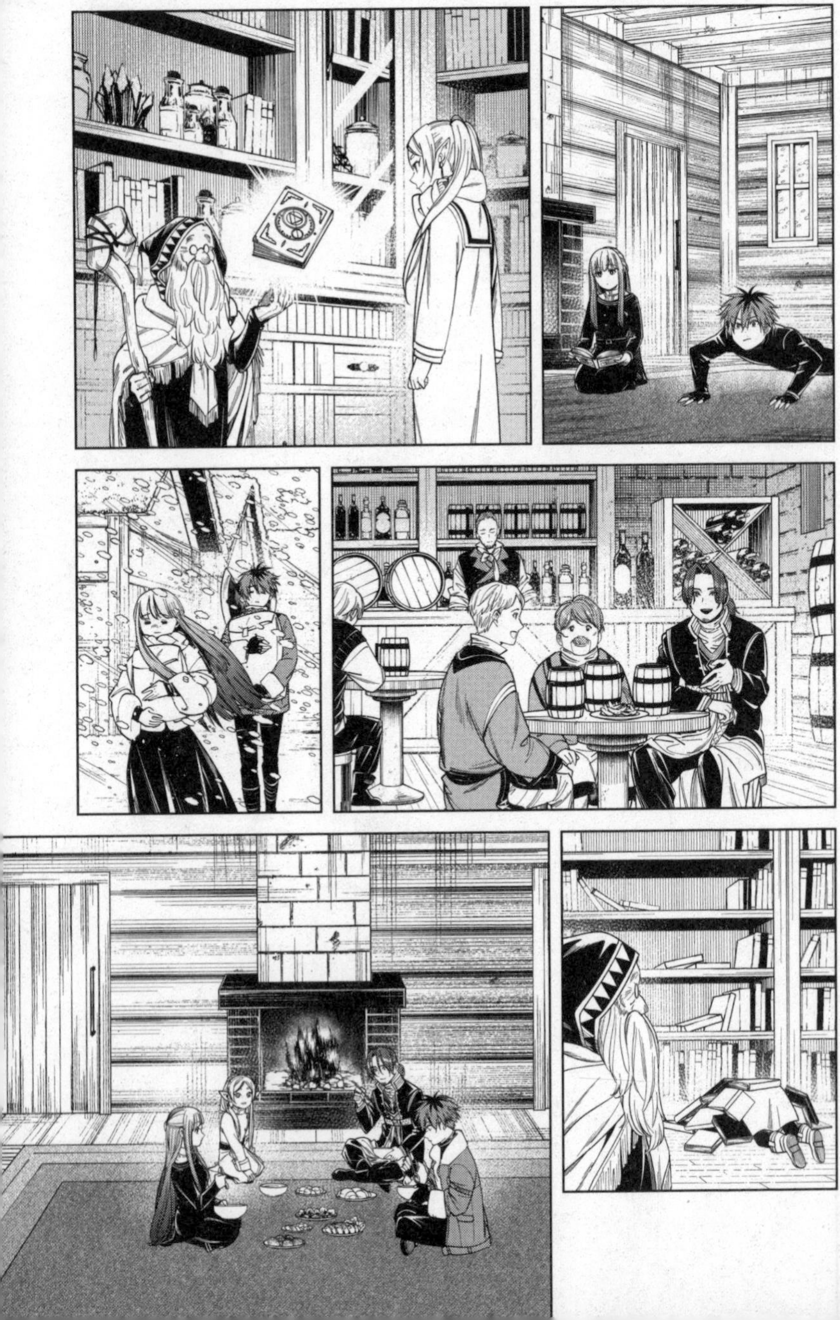

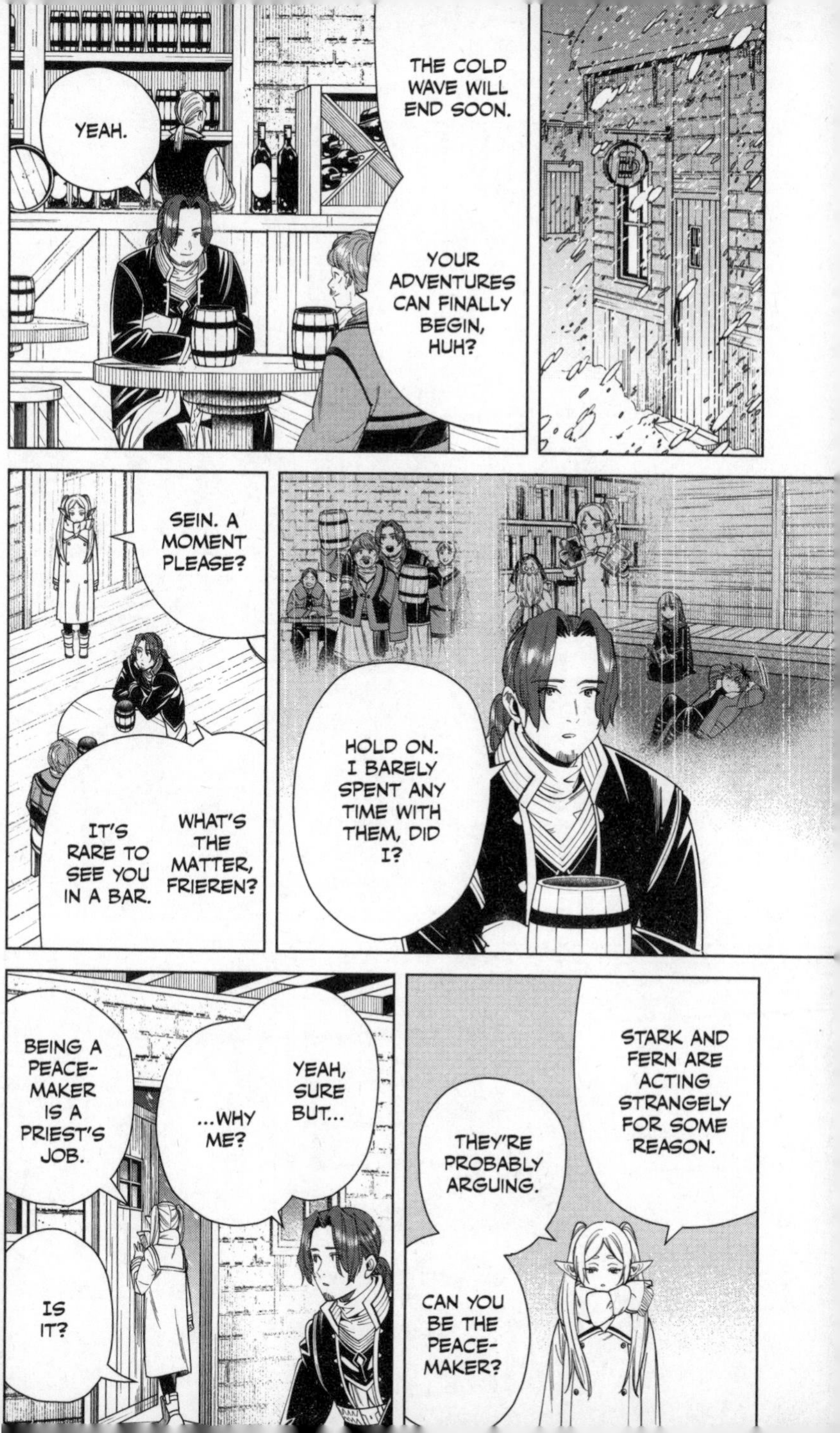
THE COLD WAVE WILL END SOON.
YOUR ADVENTURES CAN FINALLY BEGIN, HUH?
YEAH.
HOLD ON. I BARELY SPENT ANY TIME WITH THEM, DID I?
SEIN. A MOMENT PLEASE?
WHAT'S THE MATTER, FRIEREN?
IT'S RARE TO SEE YOU IN A BAR.
STARK AND FERN ARE ACTING STRANGELY FOR SOME REASON.
THEY'RE PROBABLY ARGUING.
CAN YOU BE THE PEACE-MAKER?
YEAH, SURE BUT...
...WHY ME?
BEING A PEACE-MAKER IS A PRIEST'S JOB.
IS IT?

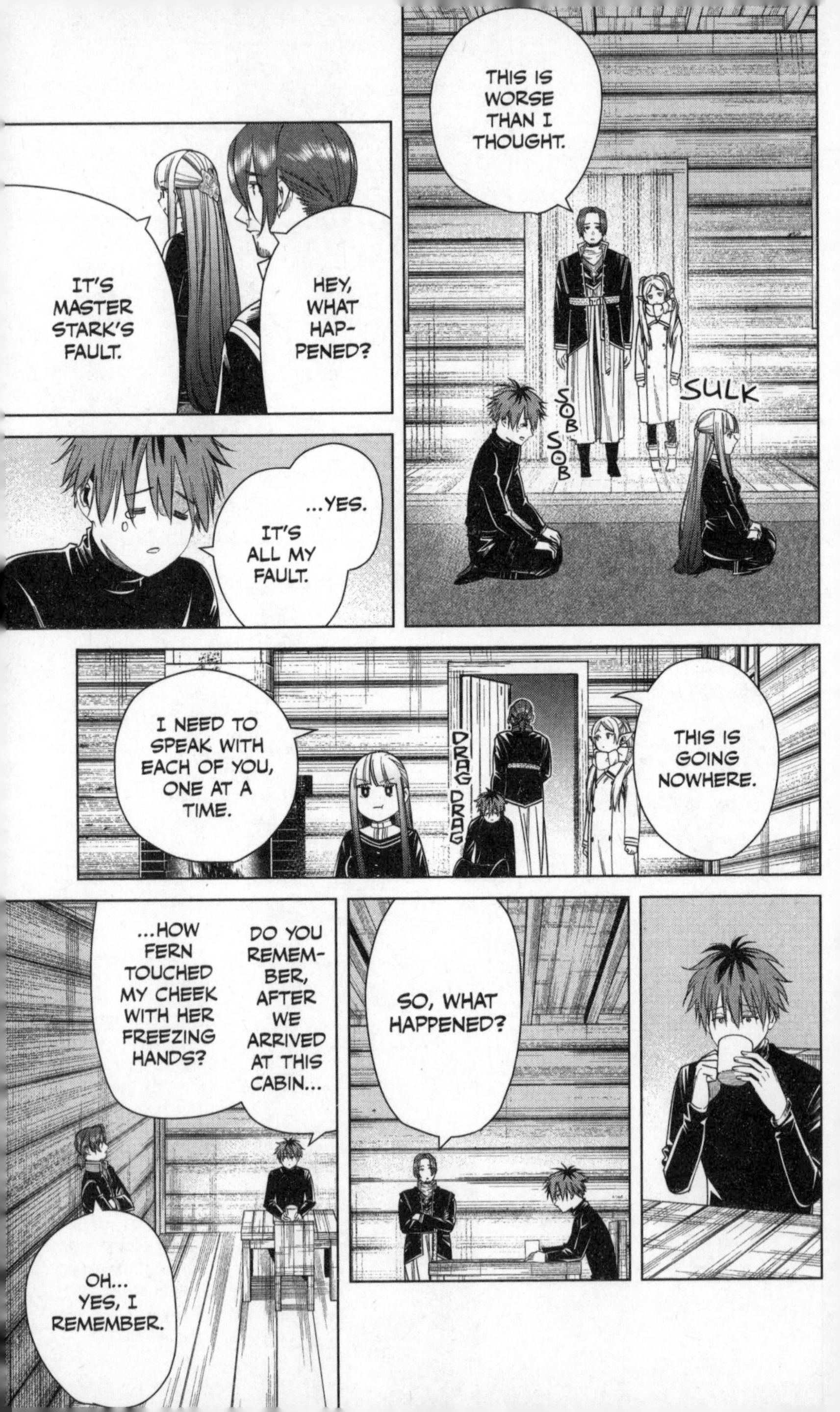
THIS IS WORSE THAN I THOUGHT.
SOB SOB
SULK
HEY, WHAT HAP-PENED?
IT'S MASTER STARK'S FAULT.
...YES. IT'S ALL MY FAULT.
THIS IS GOING NOWHERE.
DRAG DRAG
I NEED TO SPEAK WITH EACH OF YOU, ONE AT A TIME.
SO, WHAT HAPPENED?
DO YOU REMEM-BER, AFTER WE ARRIVED AT THIS CABIN...
...HOW FERN TOUCHED MY CHEEK WITH HER FREEZING HANDS?
OH... YES, I REMEMBER.

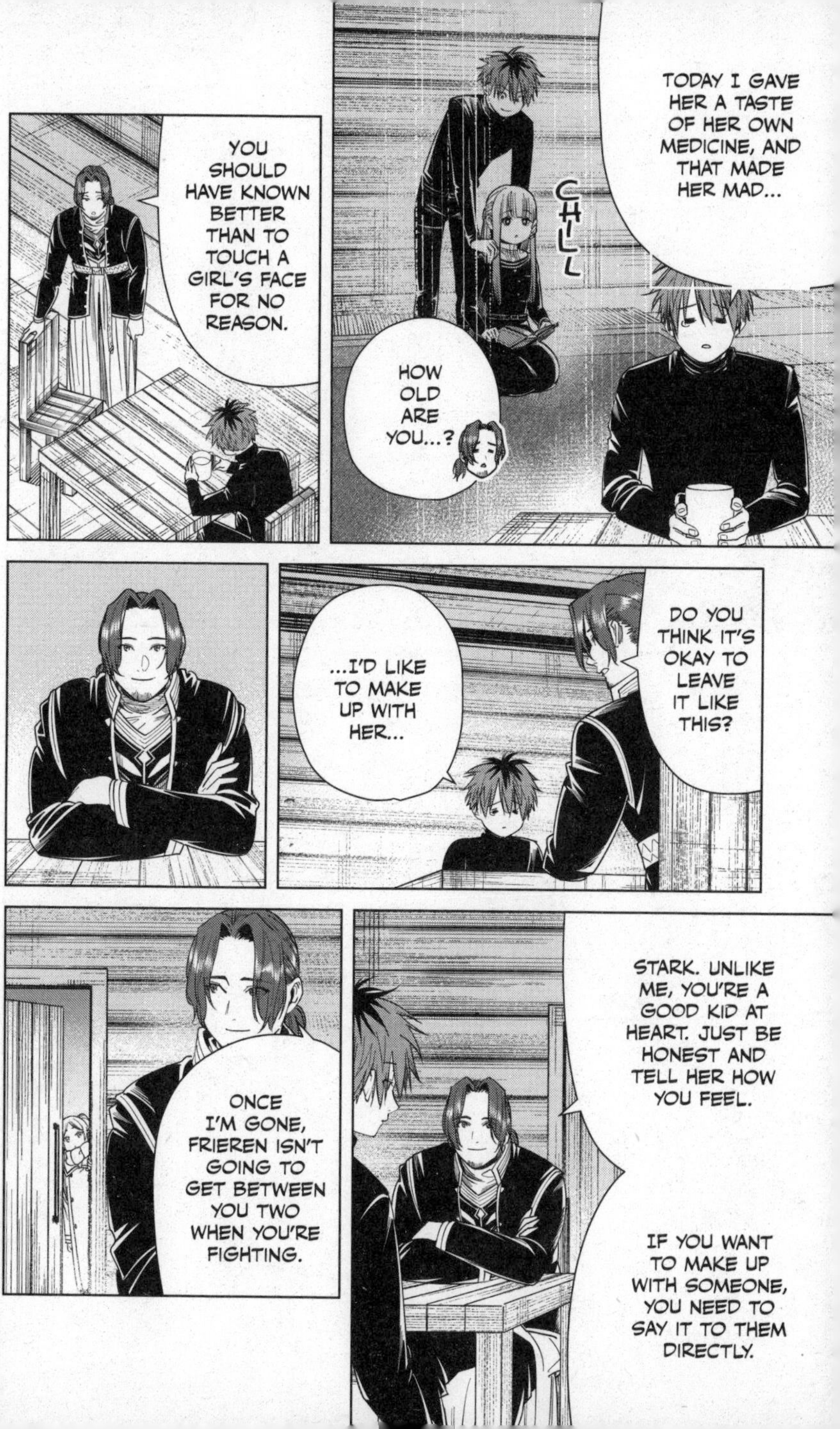
TODAY I GAVE HER A TASTE OF HER OWN MEDICINE, AND THAT MADE HER MAD...
CHILL
HOW OLD ARE YOU...?
YOU SHOULD HAVE KNOWN BETTER THAN TO TOUCH A GIRL'S FACE FOR NO REASON.
DO YOU THINK IT'S OKAY TO LEAVE IT LIKE THIS?
...I'D LIKE TO MAKE UP WITH HER...
STARK. UNLIKE ME, YOU'RE A GOOD KID AT HEART. JUST BE HONEST AND TELL HER HOW YOU FEEL.
IF YOU WANT TO MAKE UP WITH SOMEONE, YOU NEED TO SAY IT TO THEM DIRECTLY.
ONCE I'M GONE, FRIEREN ISN'T GOING TO GET BETWEEN YOU TWO WHEN YOU'RE FIGHTING.

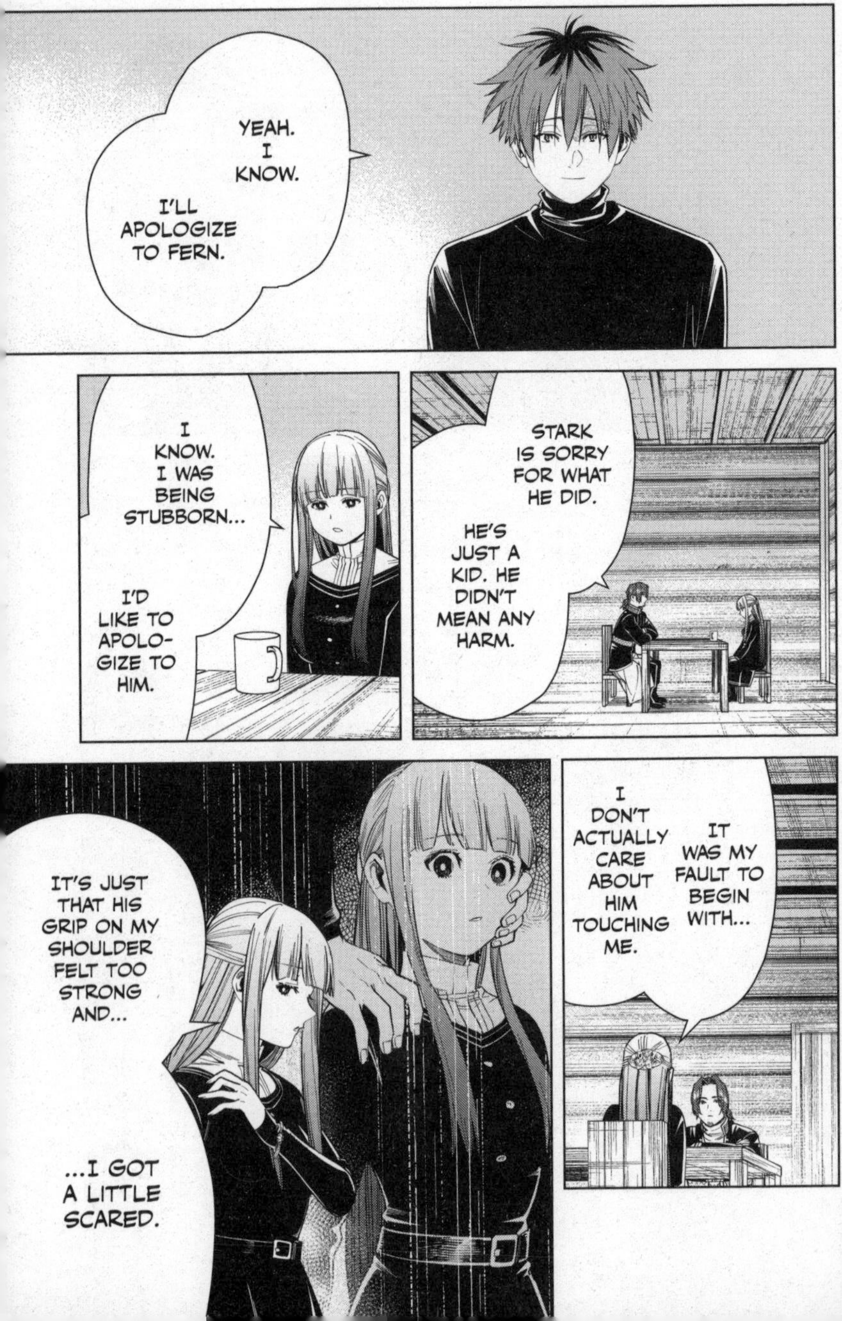
YEAH. I KNOW.
I'LL APOLOGIZE TO FERN.
STARK IS SORRY FOR WHAT HE DID.
HE'S JUST A KID. HE DIDN'T MEAN ANY HARM.
I KNOW. I WAS BEING STUBBORN...
I'D LIKE TO APOLOGIZE TO HIM.
IT WAS MY FAULT TO BEGIN WITH...
I DON'T ACTUALLY CARE ABOUT HIM TOUCHING ME.
IT'S JUST THAT HIS GRIP ON MY SHOULDER FELT TOO STRONG AND...
...I GOT A LITTLE SCARED.

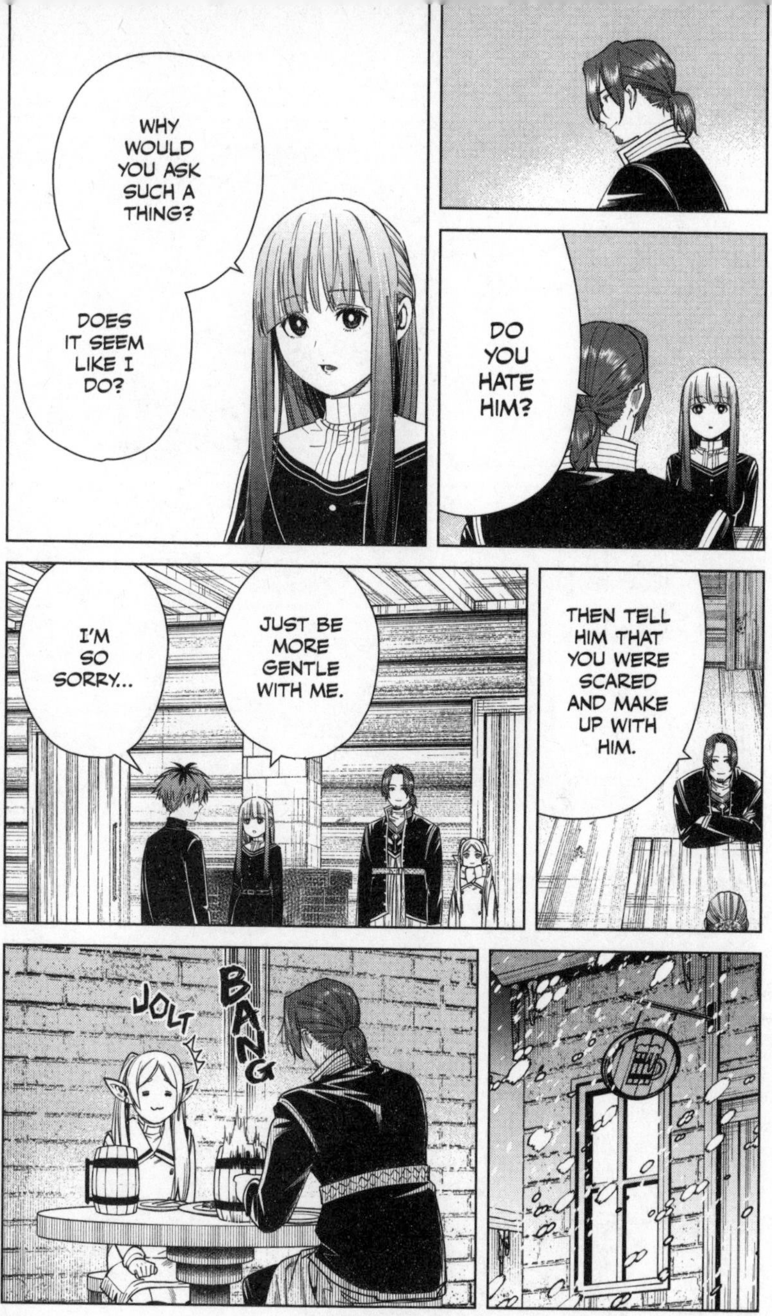
DO YOU HATE HIM?
WHY WOULD YOU ASK SUCH A THING?
DOES IT SEEM LIKE I DO?
THEN TELL HIM THAT YOU WERE SCARED AND MAKE UP WITH HIM.
JUST BE MORE GENTLE WITH ME.
I'M SO SORRY...
BANG
JOLT

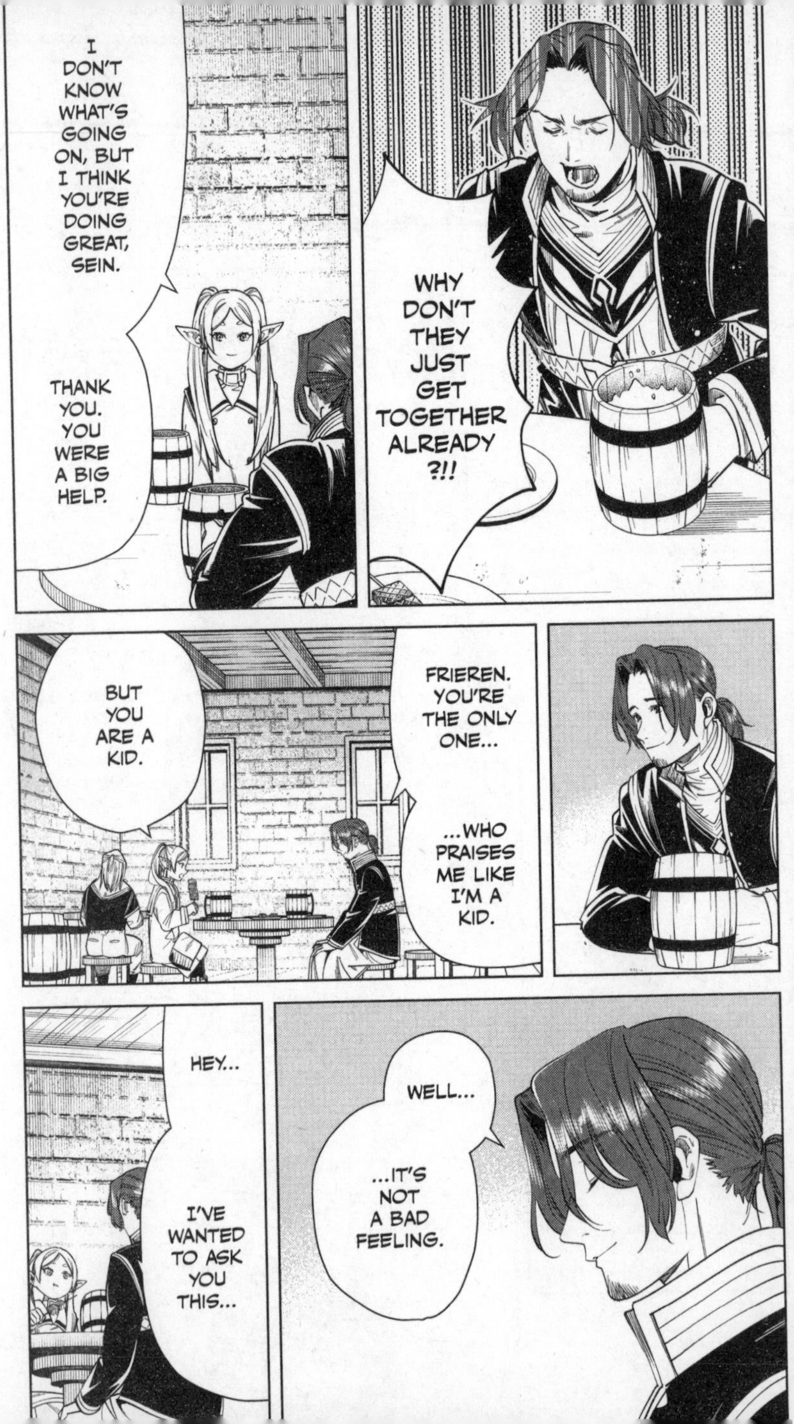
WHY DON'T THEY JUST GET TOGETHER ALREADY ?!!
I DON'T KNOW WHAT'S GOING ON, BUT I THINK YOU'RE DOING GREAT, SEIN.
THANK YOU. YOU WERE A BIG HELP.
FRIEREN. YOU'RE THE ONLY ONE...
...WHO PRAISES ME LIKE I'M A KID.
BUT YOU ARE A KID.
WELL...
...IT'S NOT A BAD FEELING.
HEY...
I'VE WANTED TO ASK YOU THIS...

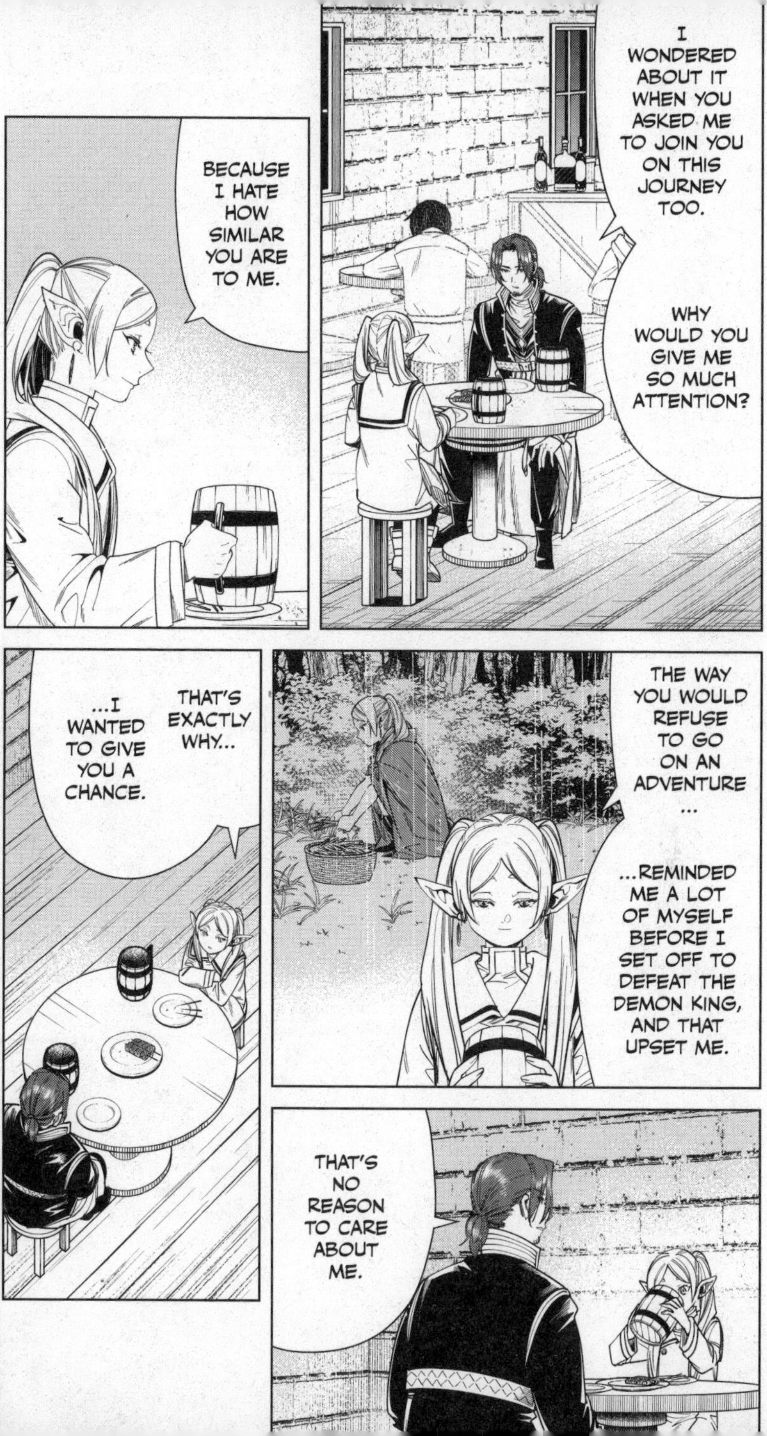
I WONDERED ABOUT IT WHEN YOU ASKED ME TO JOIN YOU ON THIS JOURNEY TOO.
WHY WOULD YOU GIVE ME SO MUCH ATTENTION?
BECAUSE I HATE HOW SIMILAR YOU ARE TO ME.
THE WAY YOU WOULD REFUSE TO GO ON AN ADVENTURE ...
...REMINDED ME A LOT OF MYSELF BEFORE I SET OFF TO DEFEAT THE DEMON KING, AND THAT UPSET ME.
THAT'S NO REASON TO CARE ABOUT ME.
THAT'S EXACTLY WHY...
...I WANTED TO GIVE YOU A CHANCE.

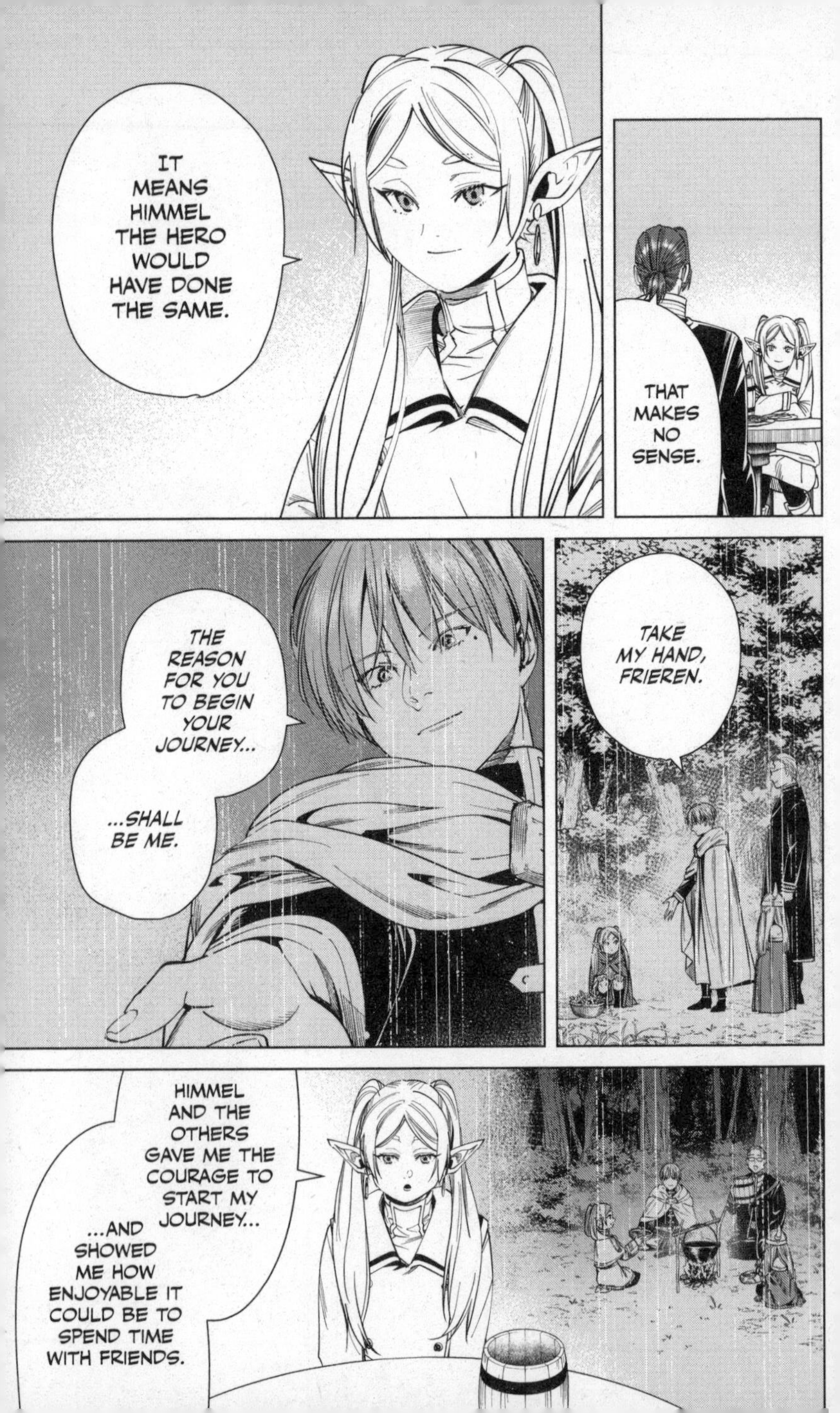
THAT MAKES NO SENSE.
IT MEANS HIMMEL THE HERO WOULD HAVE DONE THE SAME.
TAKE MY HAND, FRIEREN.
THE REASON FOR YOU TO BEGIN YOUR JOURNEY...
...SHALL BE ME.
HIMMEL AND THE OTHERS GAVE ME THE COURAGE TO START MY JOURNEY...
...AND SHOWED ME HOW ENJOYABLE IT COULD BE TO SPEND TIME WITH FRIENDS.

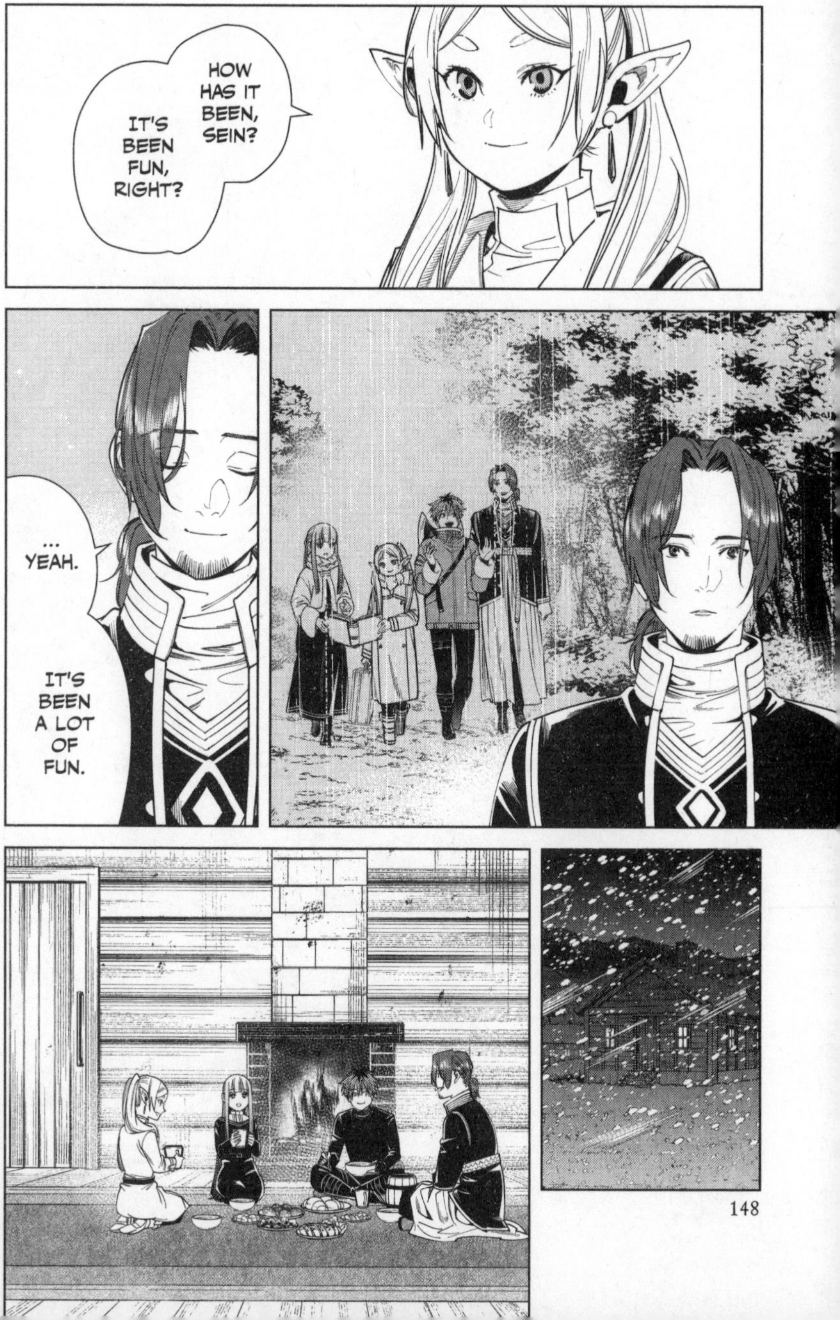
HOW HAS IT BEEN, SEIN?
IT'S BEEN FUN, RIGHT?
... YEAH.
IT'S BEEN A LOT OF FUN.

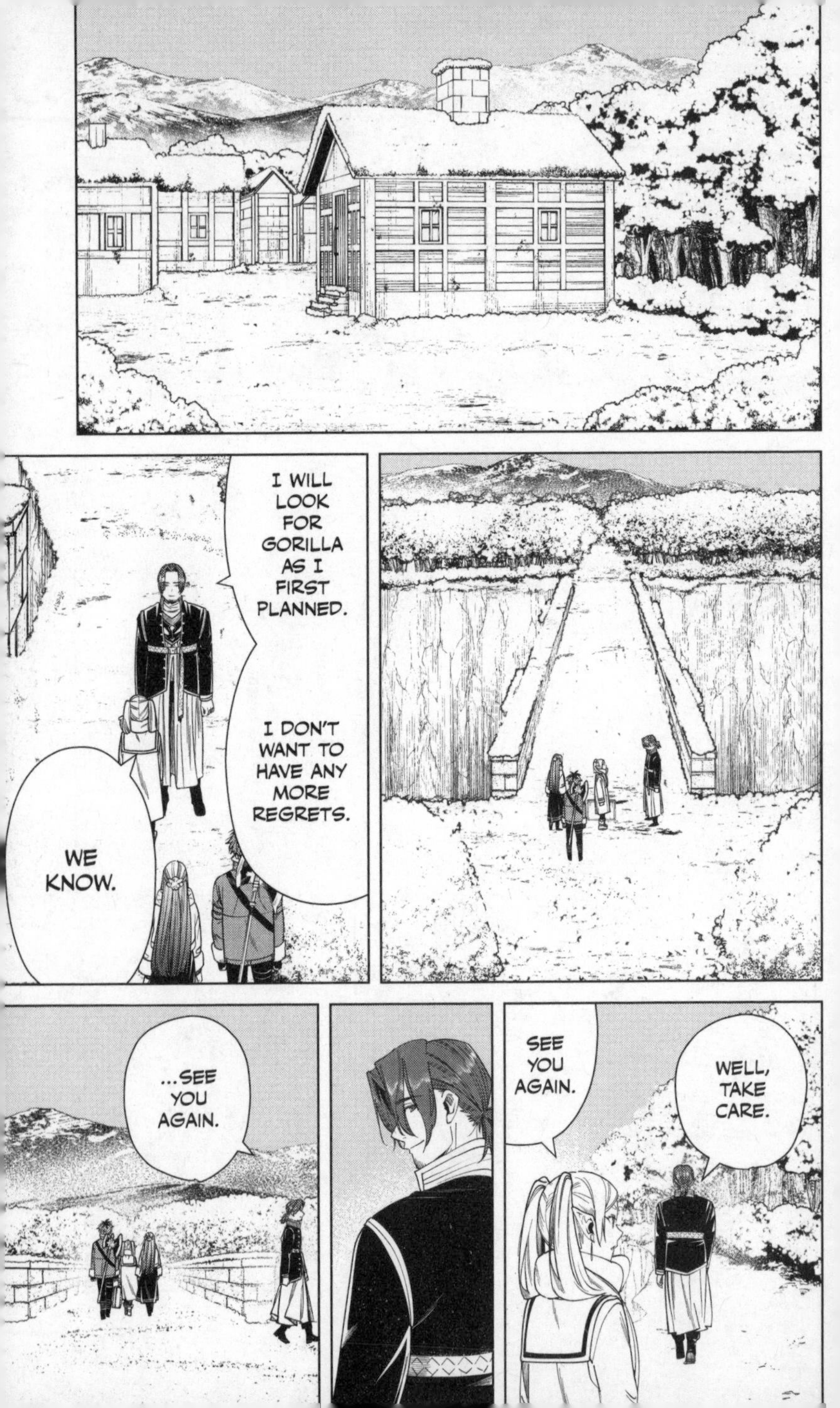
I WILL LOOK FOR GORILLA AS I FIRST PLANNED.
I DON'T WANT TO HAVE ANY MORE REGRETS.
WE KNOW.
WELL, TAKE CARE.
SEE YOU AGAIN.
...SEE YOU AGAIN.

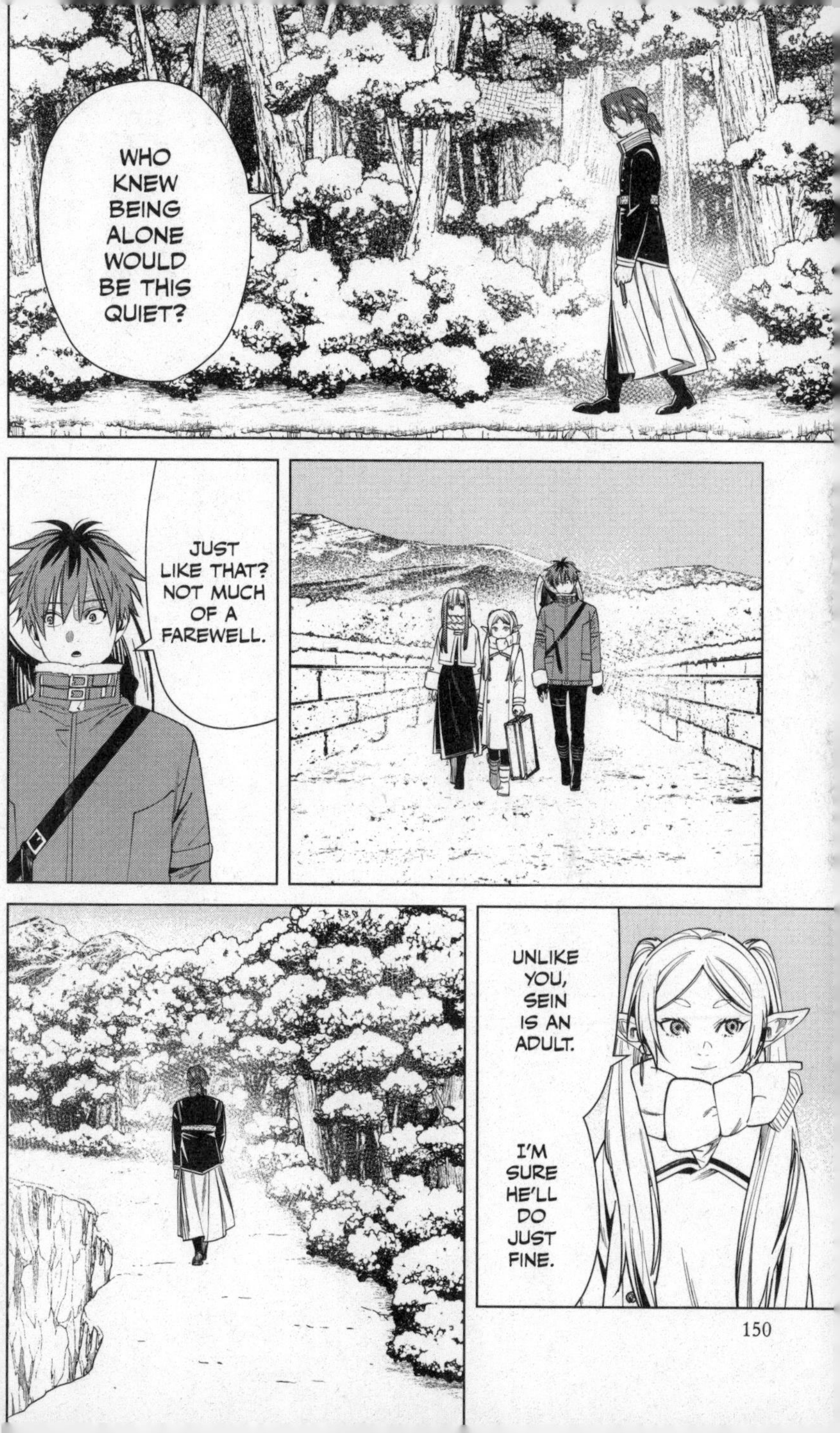
WHO KNEW BEING ALONE WOULD BE THIS QUIET?
JUST LIKE THAT? NOT MUCH OF A FAREWELL.
UNLIKE YOU, SEIN IS AN ADULT.
I'M SURE HE'LL DO JUST FINE.

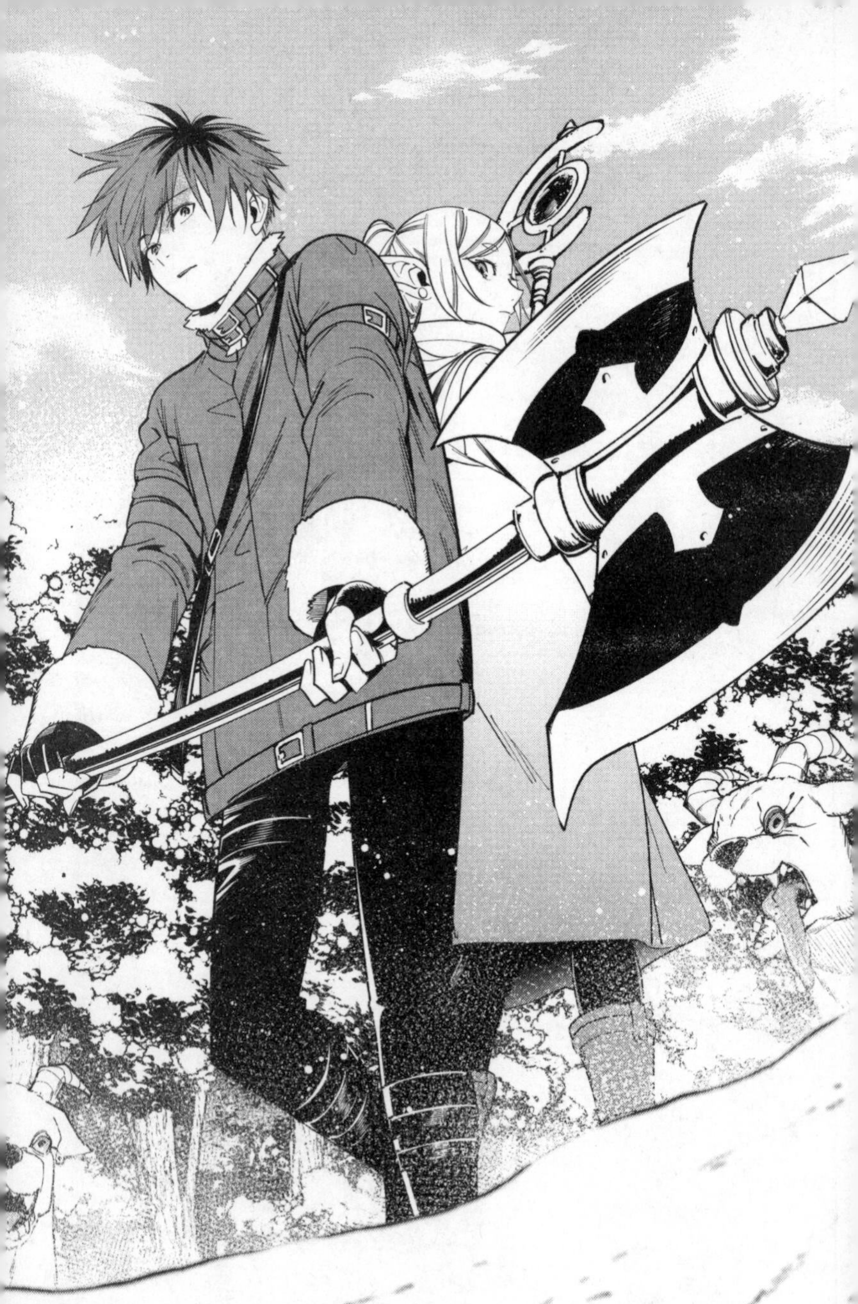

Chapter 36: Emotional Support

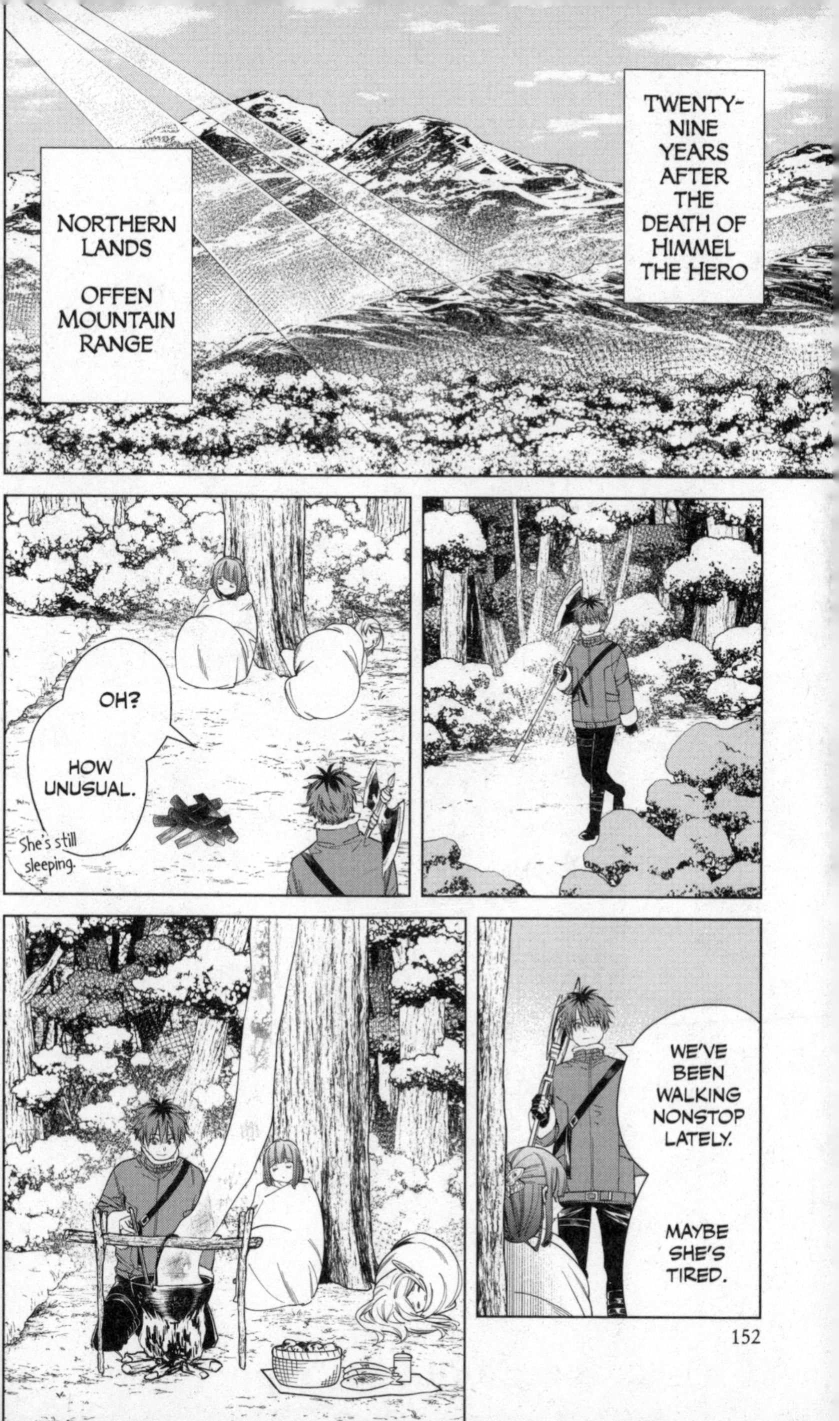
TWENTY-NINE YEARS AFTER THE DEATH OF HIMMEL THE HERO
NORTHERN LANDS
OFFEN MOUNTAIN RANGE
OH?
HOW UNUSUAL.
She's still sleeping.
WE'VE BEEN WALKING NONSTOP LATELY.
MAYBE SHE'S TIRED.

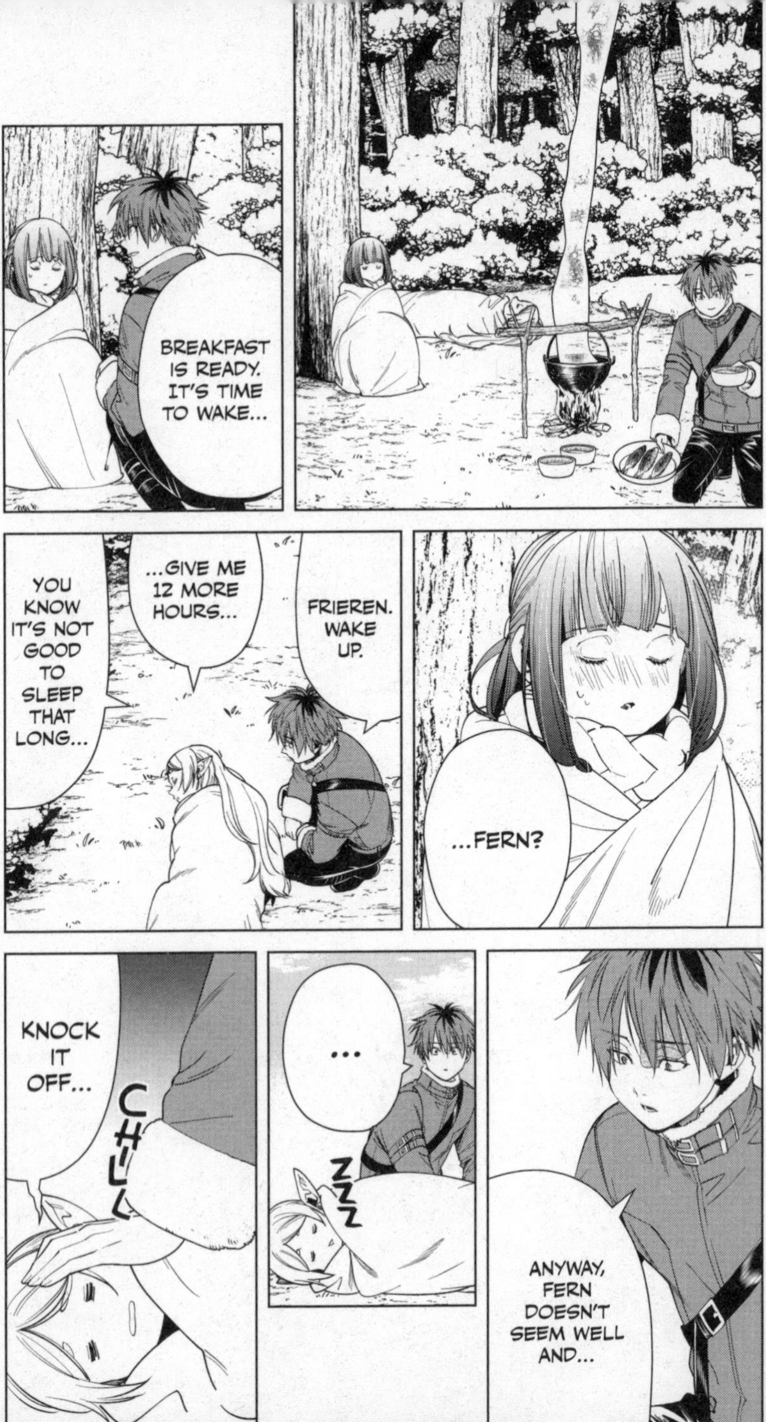
BREAKFAST IS READY. IT'S TIME TO WAKE...
...FERN?
FRIEREN. WAKE UP.
...GIVE ME 12 MORE HOURS...
YOU KNOW IT'S NOT GOOD TO SLEEP THAT LONG...
ANYWAY, FERN DOESN'T SEEM WELL AND...
...
ZZZ
KNOCK IT OFF...

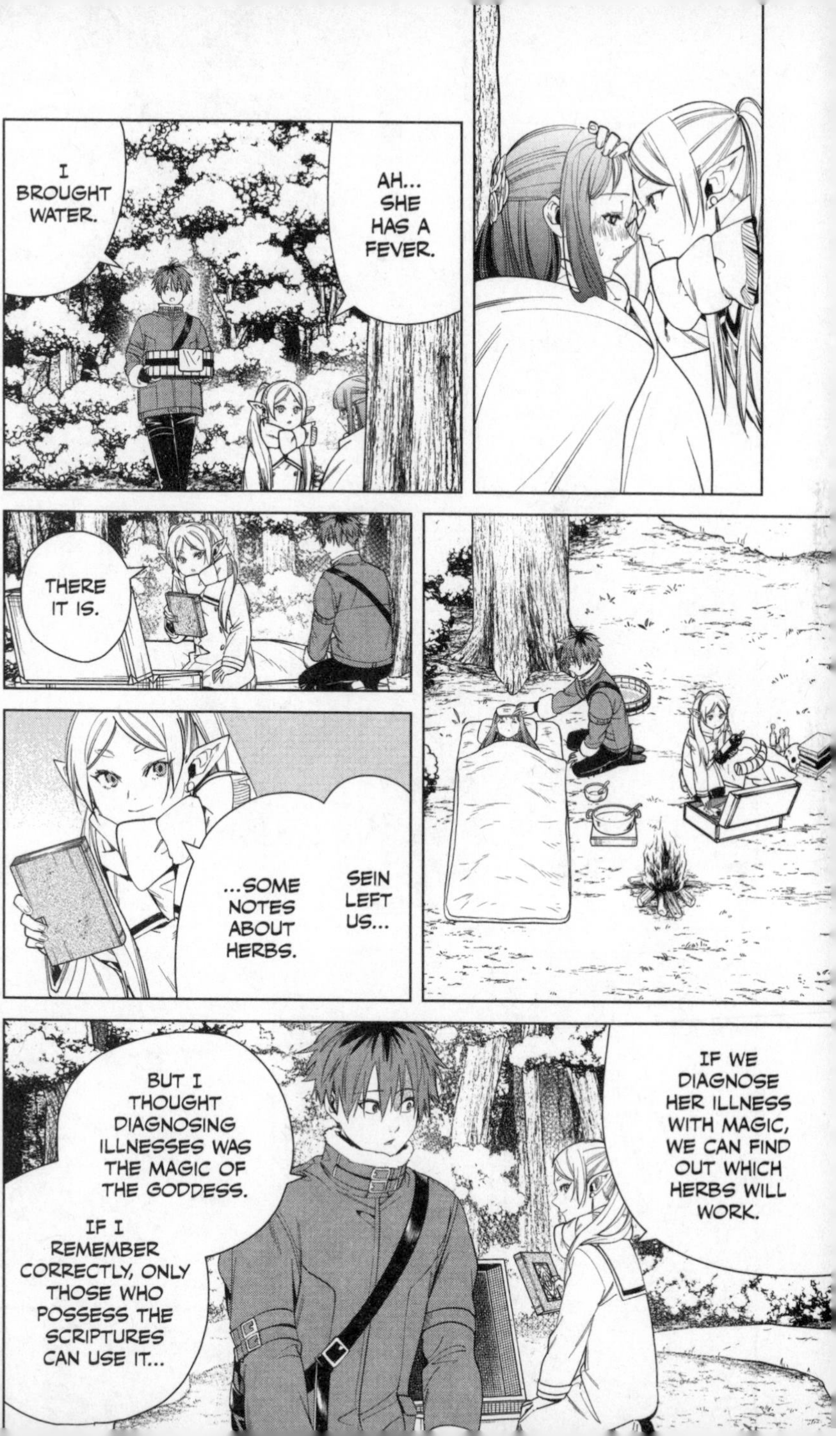
AH... SHE HAS A FEVER.
I BROUGHT WATER.
THERE IT IS.
SEIN LEFT US...
...SOME NOTES ABOUT HERBS.
IF WE DIAGNOSE HER ILLNESS WITH MAGIC, WE CAN FIND OUT WHICH HERBS WILL WORK.
BUT I THOUGHT DIAGNOSING ILLNESSES WAS THE MAGIC OF THE GODDESS.
IF I REMEMBER CORRECTLY, ONLY THOSE WHO POSSESS THE SCRIPTURES CAN USE IT...

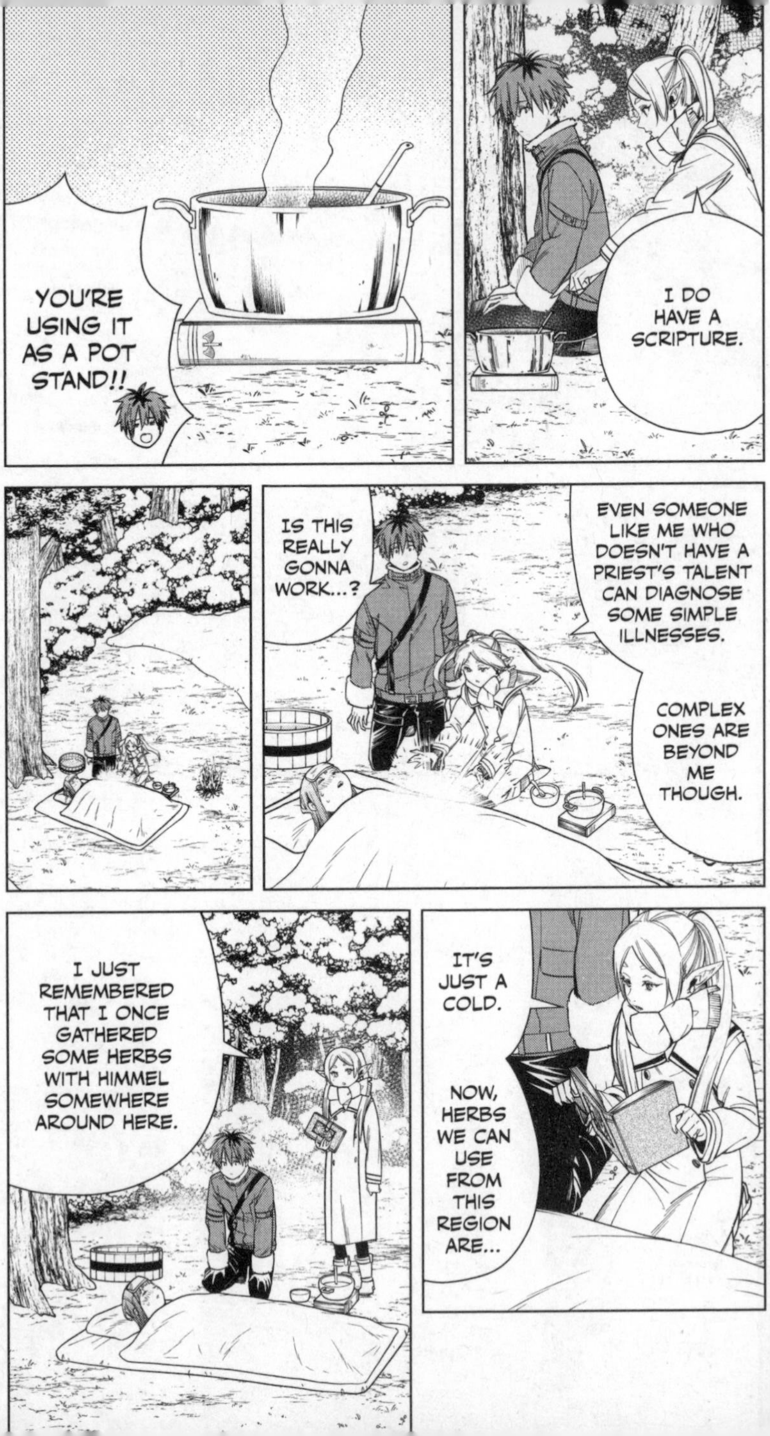
I DO HAVE A SCRIPTURE.
YOU'RE USING IT AS A POT STAND!!
EVEN SOMEONE LIKE ME WHO DOESN'T HAVE A PRIEST'S TALENT CAN DIAGNOSE SOME SIMPLE ILLNESSES.
COMPLEX ONES ARE BEYOND ME THOUGH.
IS THIS REALLY GONNA WORK...?
IT'S JUST A COLD.
NOW, HERBS WE CAN USE FROM THIS REGION ARE...
I JUST REMEMBERED THAT I ONCE GATHERED SOME HERBS WITH HIMMEL SOMEWHERE AROUND HERE.

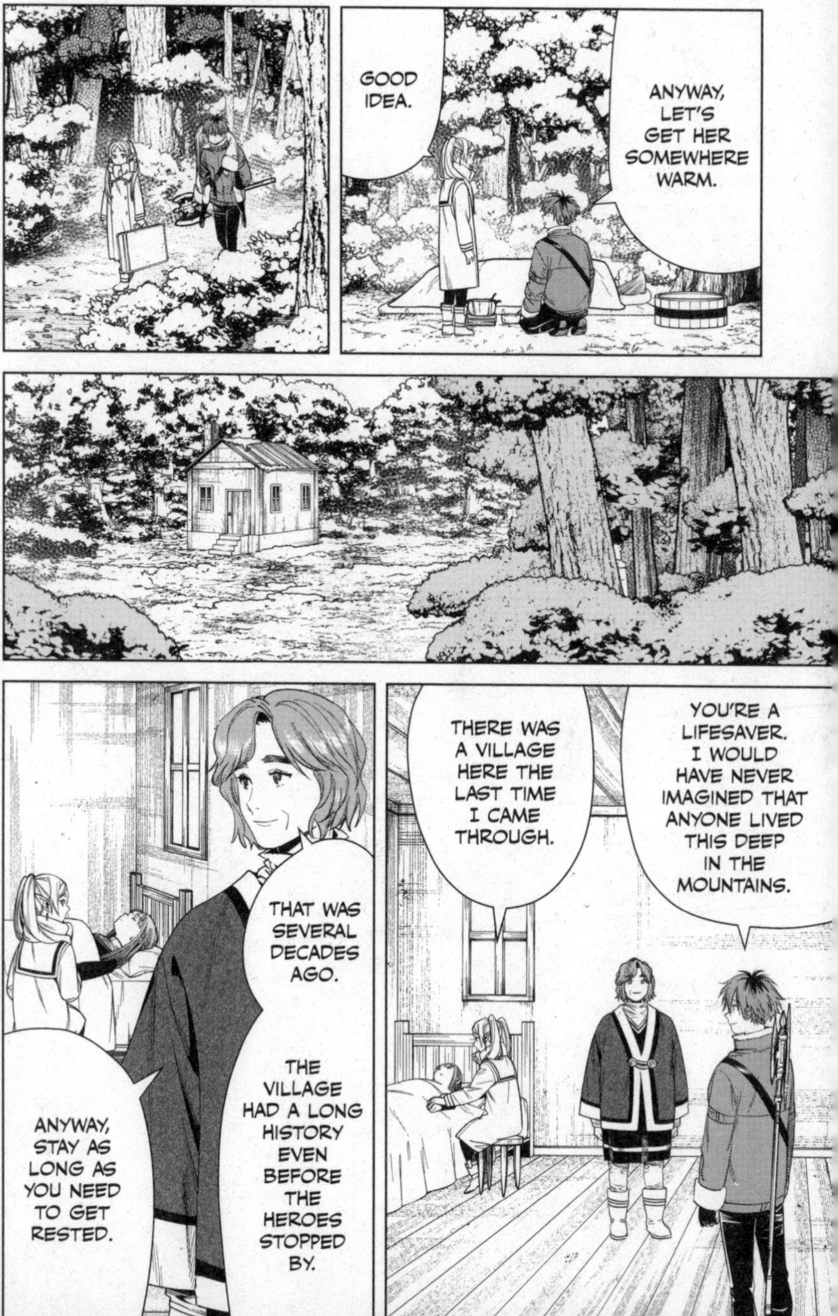
ANYWAY, LET'S GET HER SOMEWHERE WARM.
GOOD IDEA.
YOU'RE A LIFESAVER. I WOULD HAVE NEVER IMAGINED THAT ANYONE LIVED THIS DEEP IN THE MOUNTAINS.
THERE WAS A VILLAGE HERE THE LAST TIME I CAME THROUGH.
THAT WAS SEVERAL DECADES AGO.
THE VILLAGE HAD A LONG HISTORY EVEN BEFORE THE HEROES STOPPED BY.
ANYWAY, STAY AS LONG AS YOU NEED TO GET RESTED.

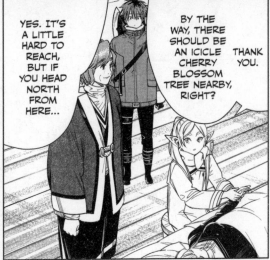

BY THE WAY, THERE SHOULD BE AN ICICLE CHERRY BLOSSOM TREE NEARBY, RIGHT?

THANK YOU.

YES. IT'S A LITTLE HARD TO REACH, BUT IF YOU HEAD NORTH FROM HERE...

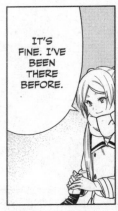

IT'S FINE. I'VE BEEN THERE BEFORE.

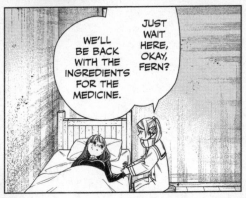

JUST WAIT HERE, OKAY, FERN?

WE'LL BE BACK WITH THE INGREDIENTS FOR THE MEDICINE.

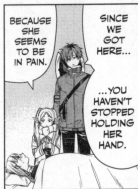

SINCE WE GOT HERE...

...YOU HAVEN'T STOPPED HOLDING HER HAND.

BECAUSE SHE SEEMS TO BE IN PAIN.

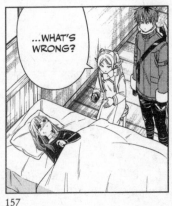

...WHAT'S WRONG?

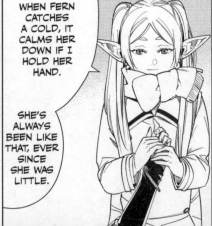

WHEN FERN CATCHES A COLD, IT CALMS HER DOWN IF I HOLD HER HAND.

SHE'S ALWAYS BEEN LIKE THAT, EVER SINCE SHE WAS LITTLE.

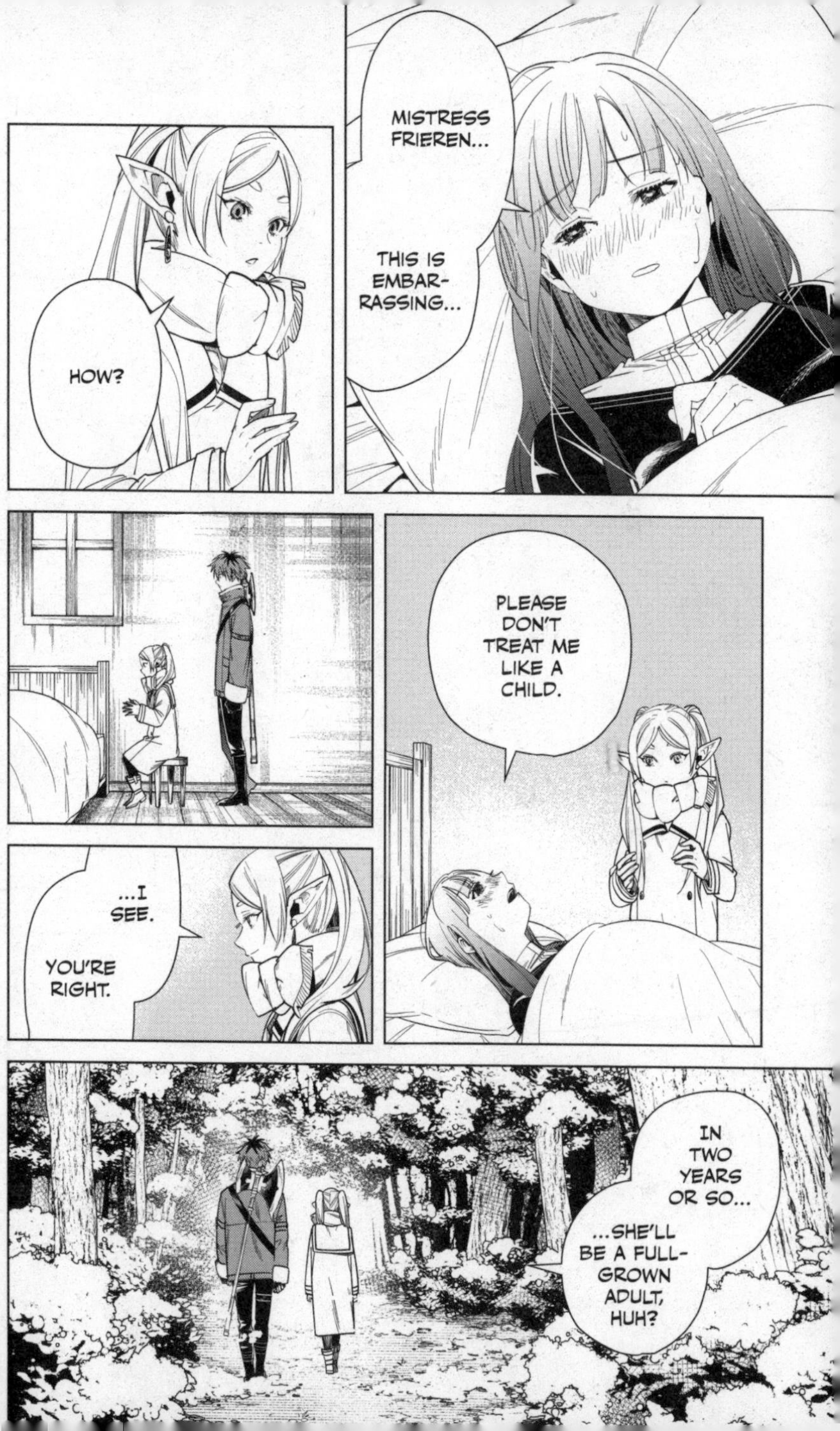
MISTRESS FRIEREN...
THIS IS EMBARRASSING...
HOW?
PLEASE DON'T TREAT ME LIKE A CHILD.
...I SEE.
YOU'RE RIGHT.
IN TWO YEARS OR SO...
...SHE'LL BE A FULL-GROWN ADULT, HUH?

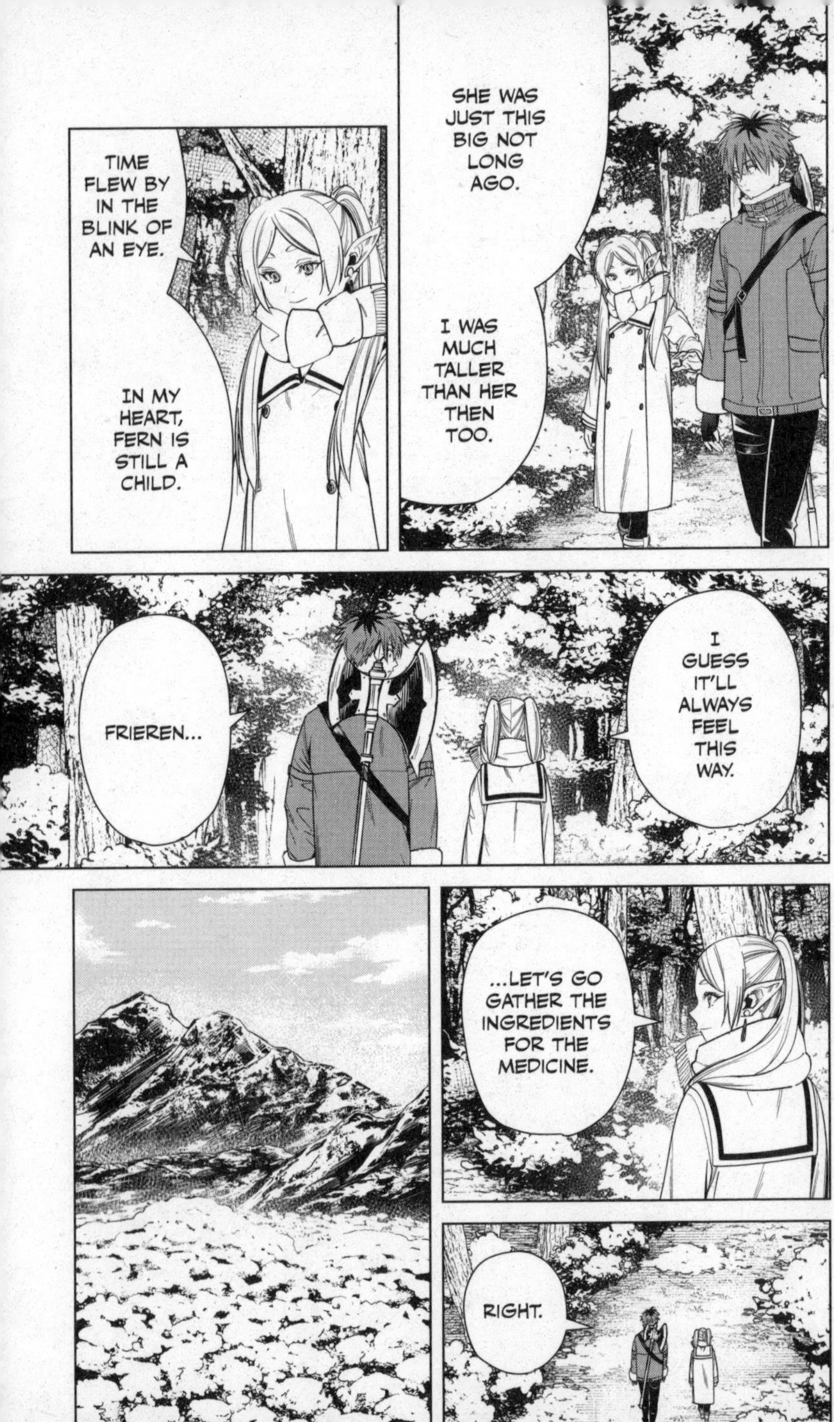
SHE WAS JUST THIS BIG NOT LONG AGO.
I WAS MUCH TALLER THAN HER THEN TOO.
TIME FLEW BY IN THE BLINK OF AN EYE.
IN MY HEART, FERN IS STILL A CHILD.
I GUESS IT'LL ALWAYS FEEL THIS WAY.
FRIEREN...
...LET'S GO GATHER THE INGREDIENTS FOR THE MEDICINE.
RIGHT.

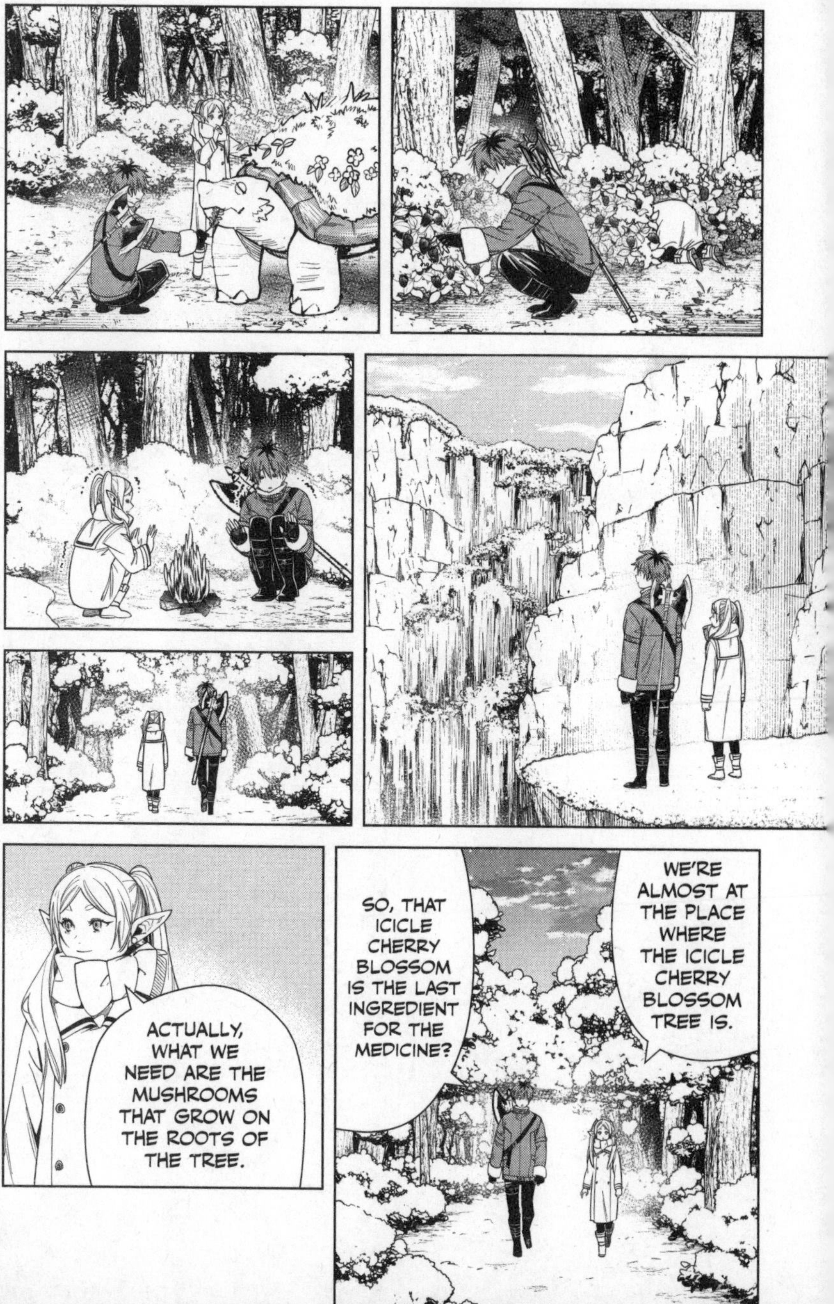
WE'RE ALMOST AT THE PLACE WHERE THE ICICLE CHERRY BLOSSOM TREE IS.
SO, THAT ICICLE CHERRY BLOSSOM IS THE LAST INGREDIENT FOR THE MEDICINE?
ACTUALLY, WHAT WE NEED ARE THE MUSHROOMS THAT GROW ON THE ROOTS OF THE TREE.

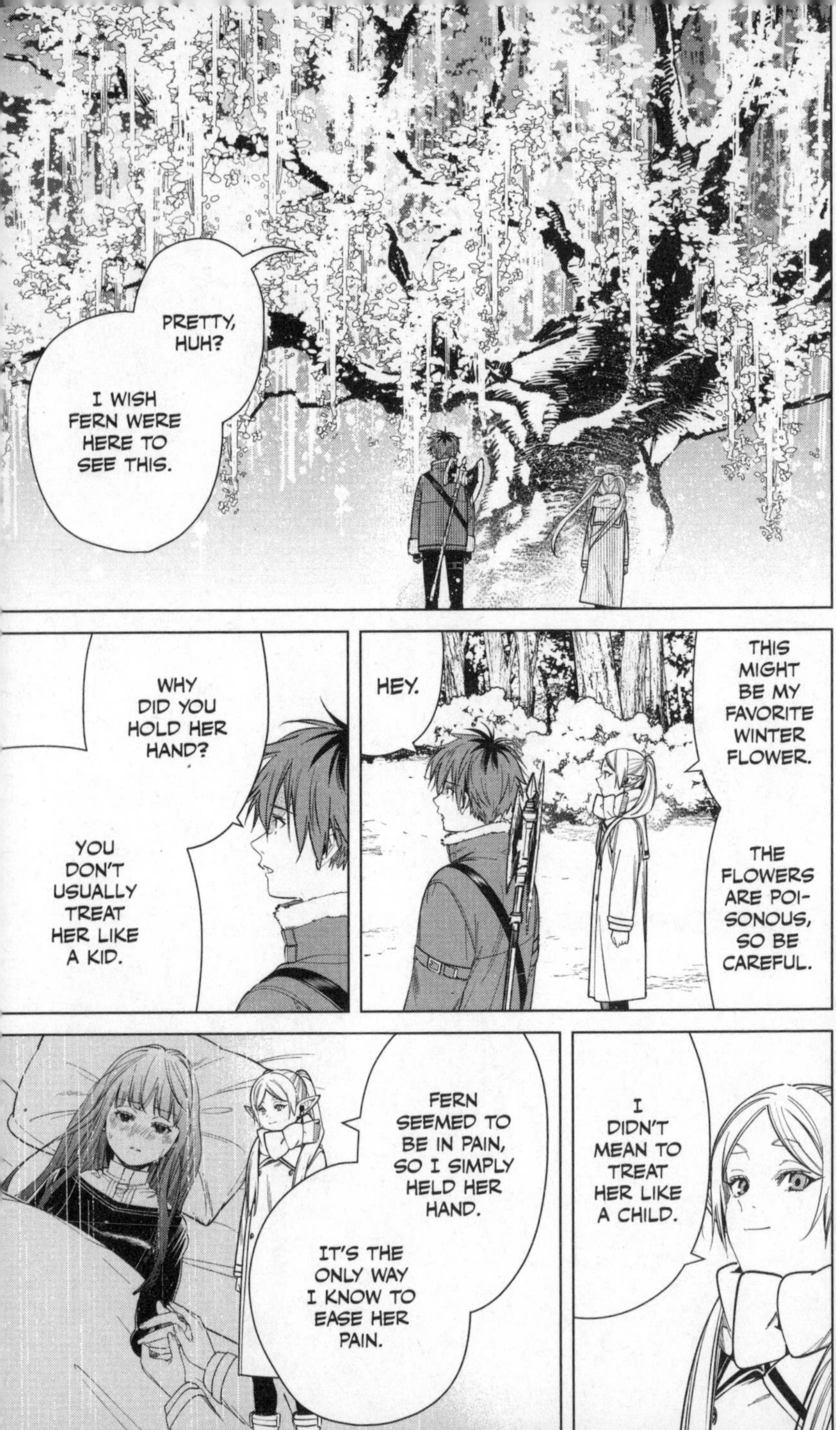

PRETTY, HUH?
I WISH FERN WERE HERE TO SEE THIS.
THIS MIGHT BE MY FAVORITE WINTER FLOWER.
THE FLOWERS ARE POI-SONOUS, SO BE CAREFUL.
HEY.
WHY DID YOU HOLD HER HAND?
YOU DON'T USUALLY TREAT HER LIKE A KID.
I DIDN'T MEAN TO TREAT HER LIKE A CHILD.
FERN SEEMED TO BE IN PAIN, SO I SIMPLY HELD HER HAND.
IT'S THE ONLY WAY I KNOW TO EASE HER PAIN.

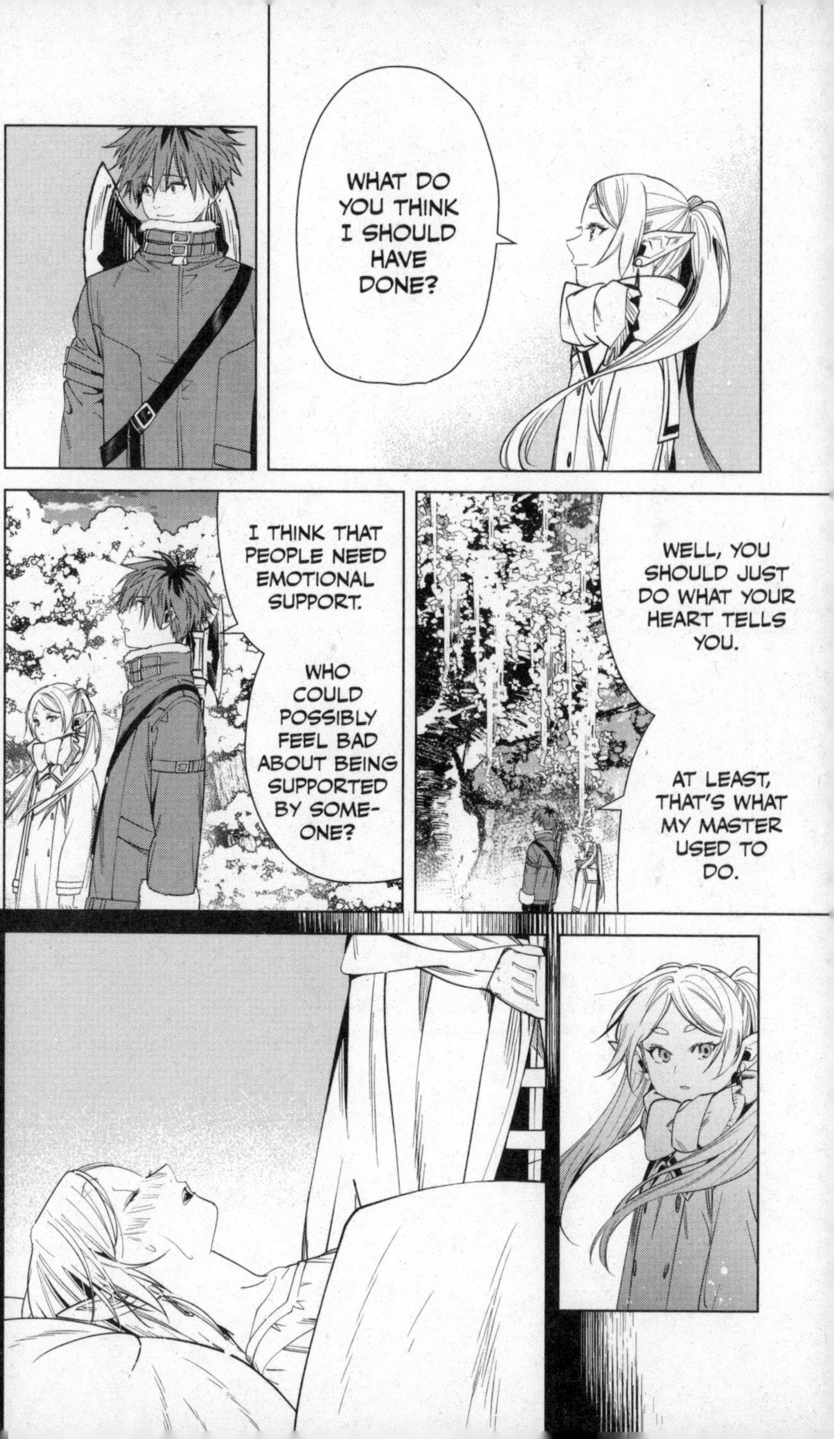
WHAT DO YOU THINK I SHOULD HAVE DONE?
WELL, YOU SHOULD JUST DO WHAT YOUR HEART TELLS YOU.
AT LEAST, THAT'S WHAT MY MASTER USED TO DO.
I THINK THAT PEOPLE NEED EMOTIONAL SUPPORT.
WHO COULD POSSIBLY FEEL BAD ABOUT BEING SUPPORTED BY SOME-ONE?

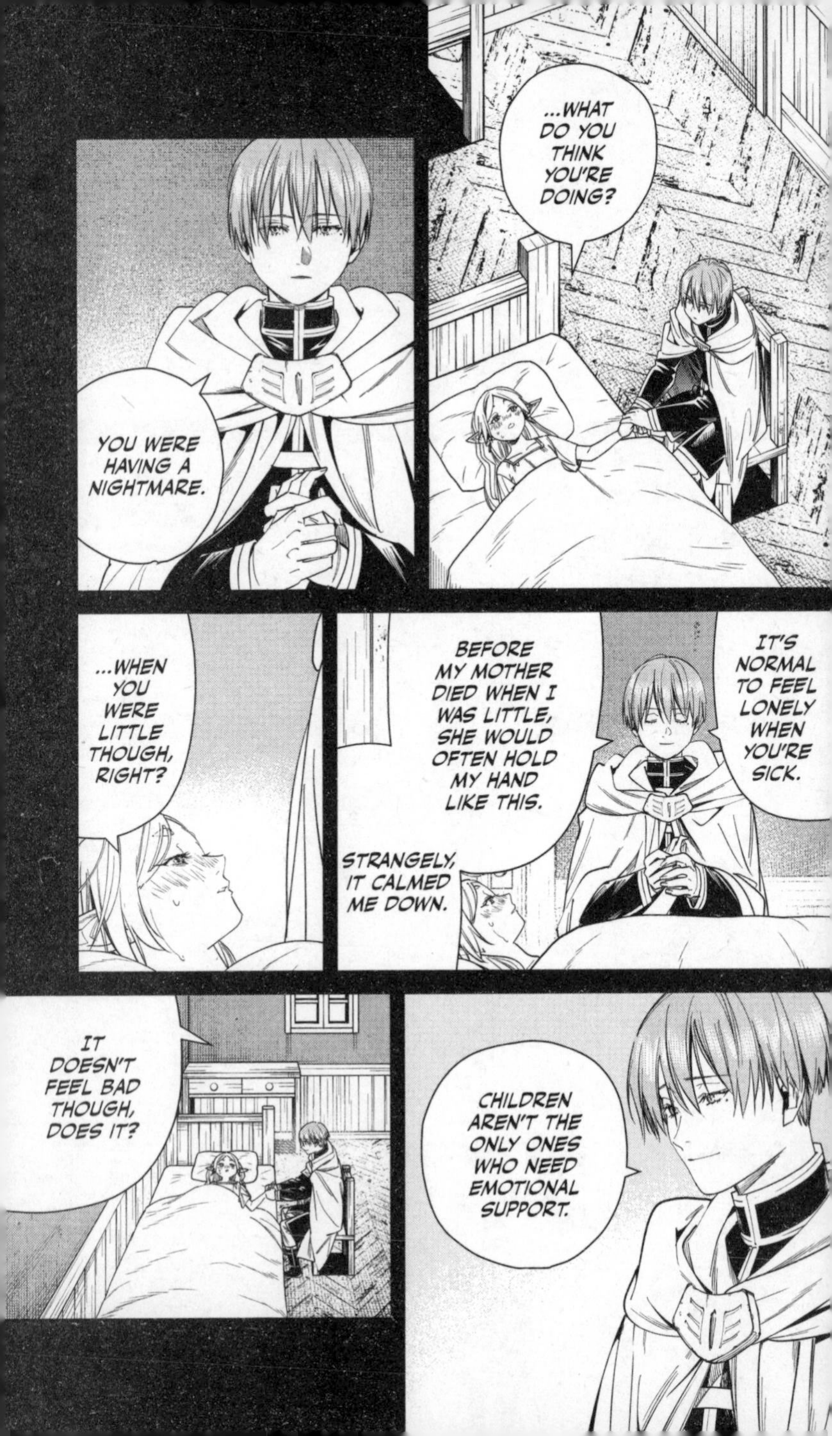
...WHAT DO YOU THINK YOU'RE DOING?
YOU WERE HAVING A NIGHTMARE.
IT'S NORMAL TO FEEL LONELY WHEN YOU'RE SICK.
BEFORE MY MOTHER DIED WHEN I WAS LITTLE, SHE WOULD OFTEN HOLD MY HAND LIKE THIS.
STRANGELY, IT CALMED ME DOWN.
...WHEN YOU WERE LITTLE THOUGH, RIGHT?
CHILDREN AREN'T THE ONLY ONES WHO NEED EMOTIONAL SUPPORT.
IT DOESN'T FEEL BAD THOUGH, DOES IT?

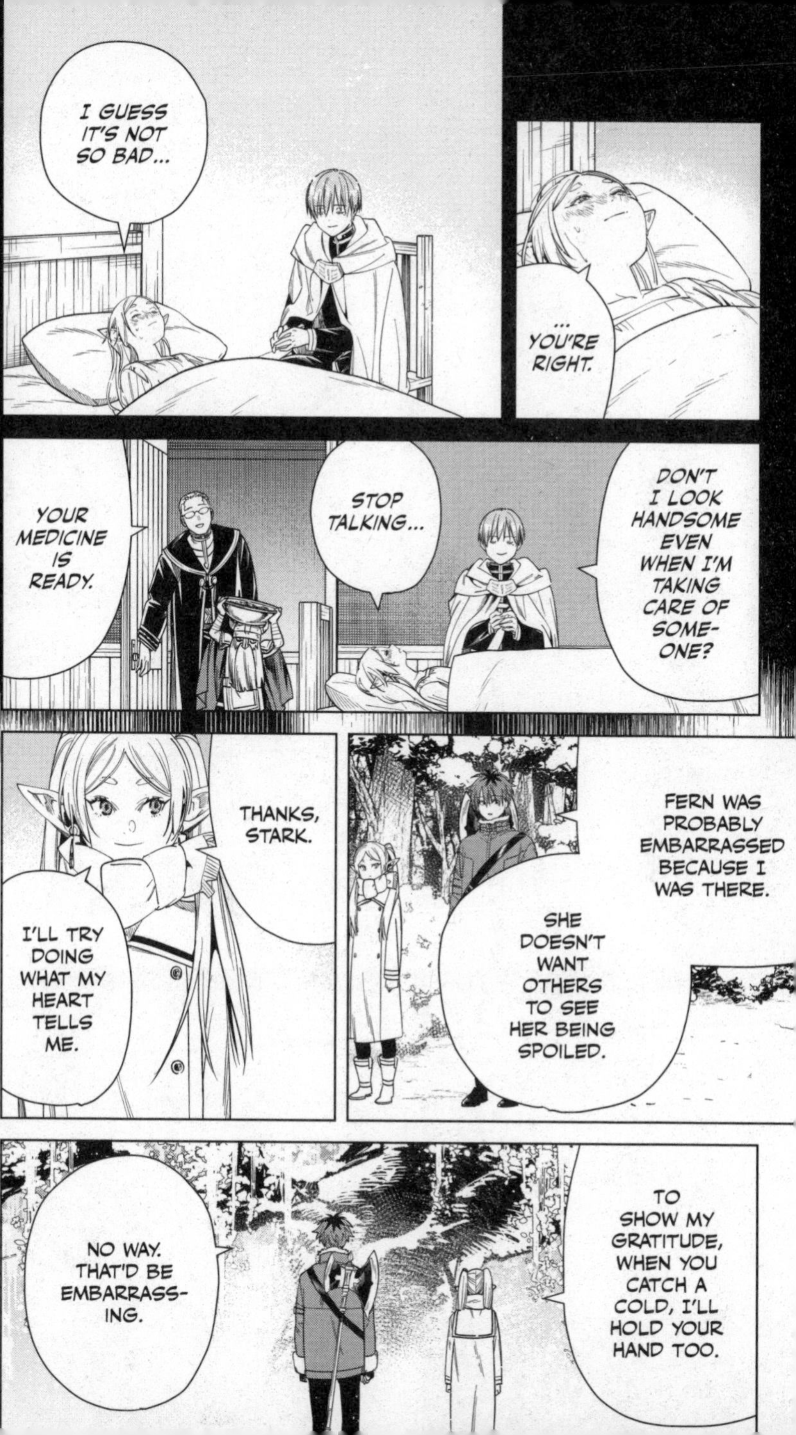
... YOU'RE RIGHT.
I GUESS IT'S NOT SO BAD...
DON'T I LOOK HANDSOME EVEN WHEN I'M TAKING CARE OF SOME-ONE?
STOP TALKING...
YOUR MEDICINE IS READY.
FERN WAS PROBABLY EMBARRASSED BECAUSE I WAS THERE.
SHE DOESN'T WANT OTHERS TO SEE HER BEING SPOILED.
THANKS, STARK.
I'LL TRY DOING WHAT MY HEART TELLS ME.
TO SHOW MY GRATITUDE, WHEN YOU CATCH A COLD, I'LL HOLD YOUR HAND TOO.
NO WAY. THAT'D BE EMBARRASS-ING.

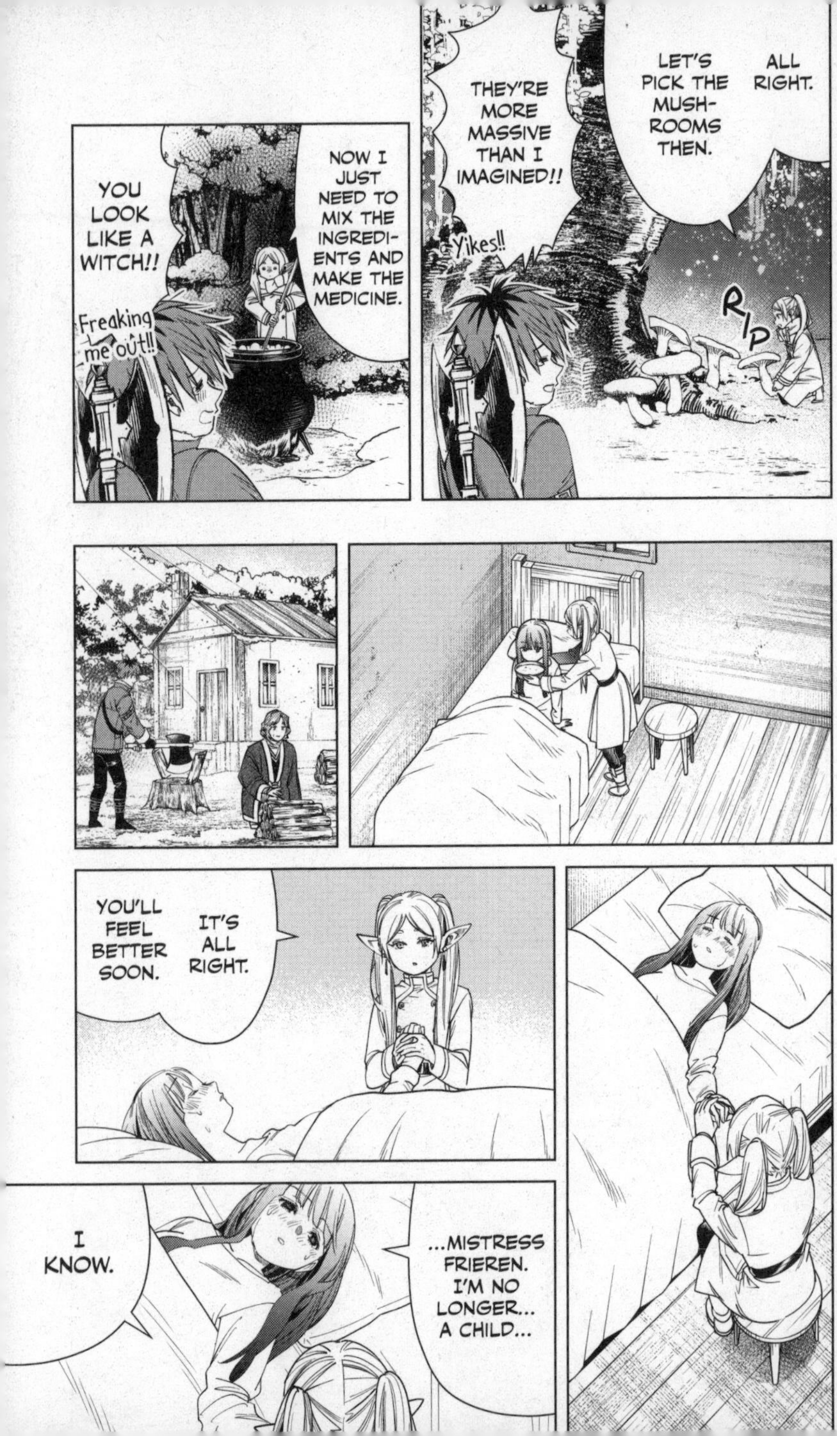
ALL RIGHT.
LET'S PICK THE MUSHROOMS THEN.
THEY'RE MORE MASSIVE THAN I IMAGINED!!
Yikes!!
RIP
NOW I JUST NEED TO MIX THE INGREDIENTS AND MAKE THE MEDICINE.
YOU LOOK LIKE A WITCH!!
Freaking me out!!
IT'S ALL RIGHT.
YOU'LL FEEL BETTER SOON.
...MISTRESS FRIEREN. I'M NO LONGER... A CHILD...
I KNOW.

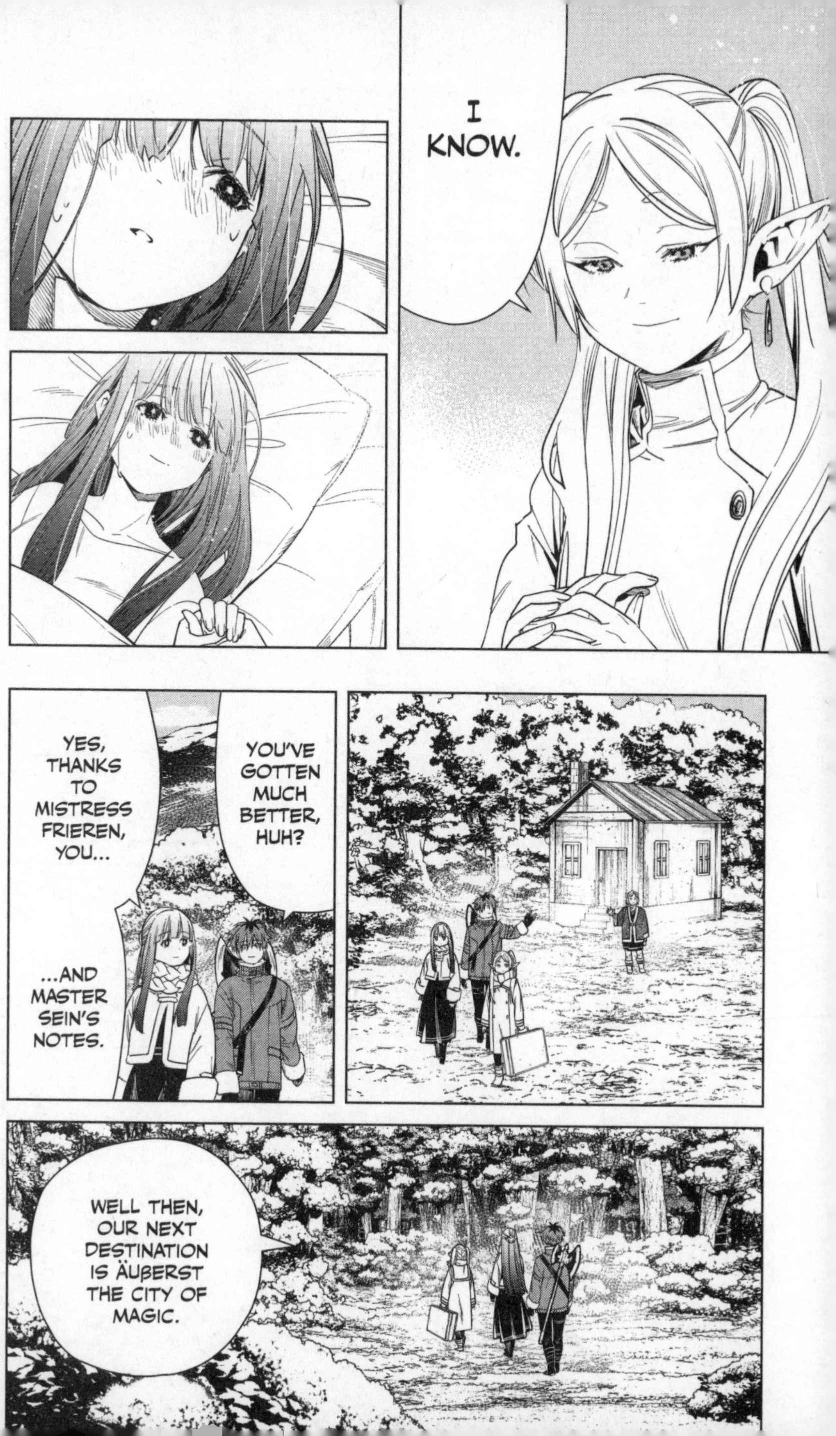
I KNOW.
YOU'VE GOTTEN MUCH BETTER, HUH?
YES, THANKS TO MISTRESS FRIEREN, YOU...
...AND MASTER SEIN'S NOTES.
WELL THEN, OUR NEXT DESTINATION IS ÄUßERST THE CITY OF MAGIC.

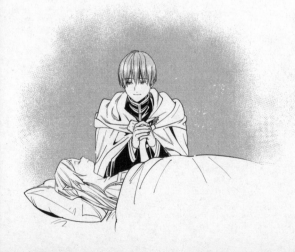

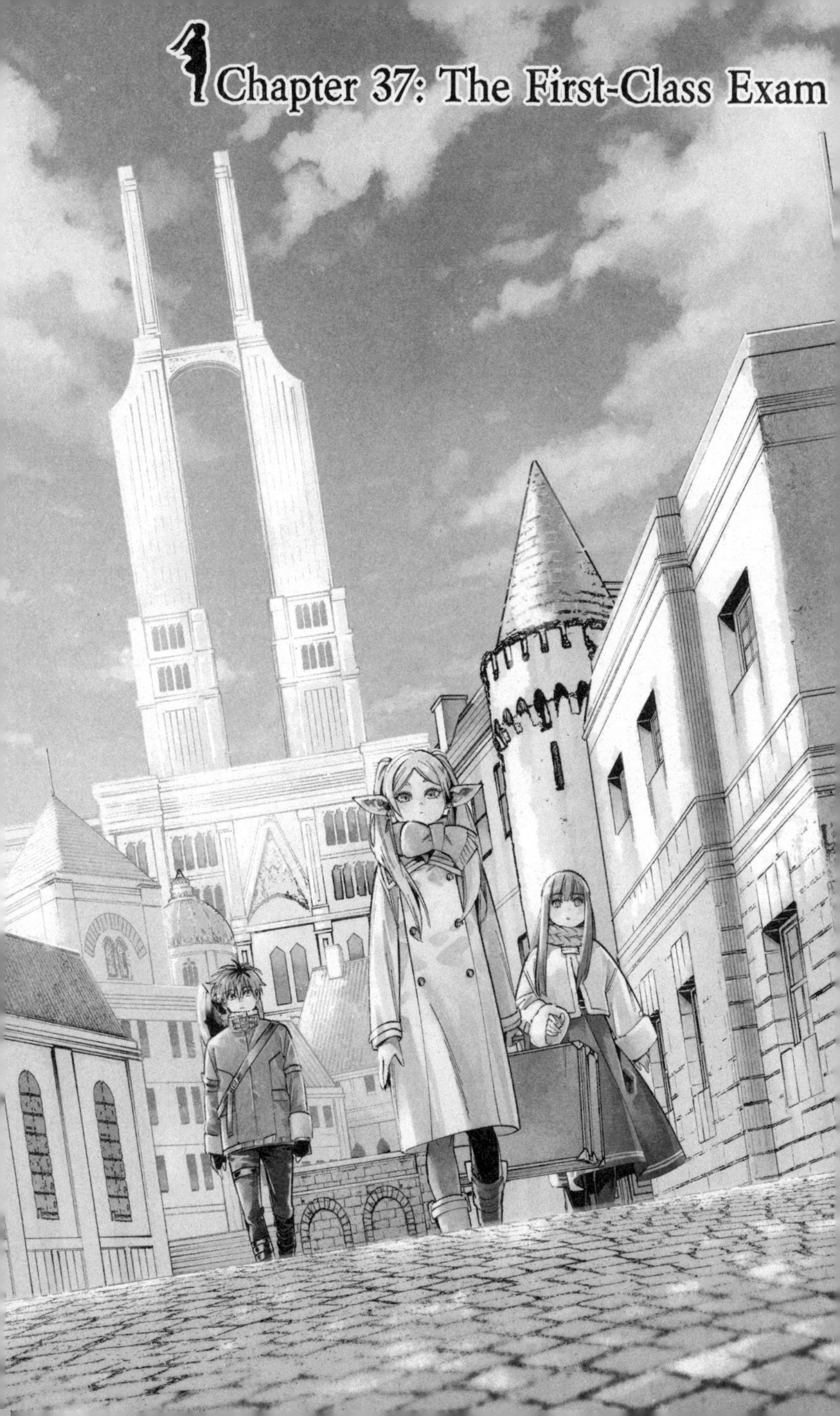
Chapter 37: The First-Class Exam

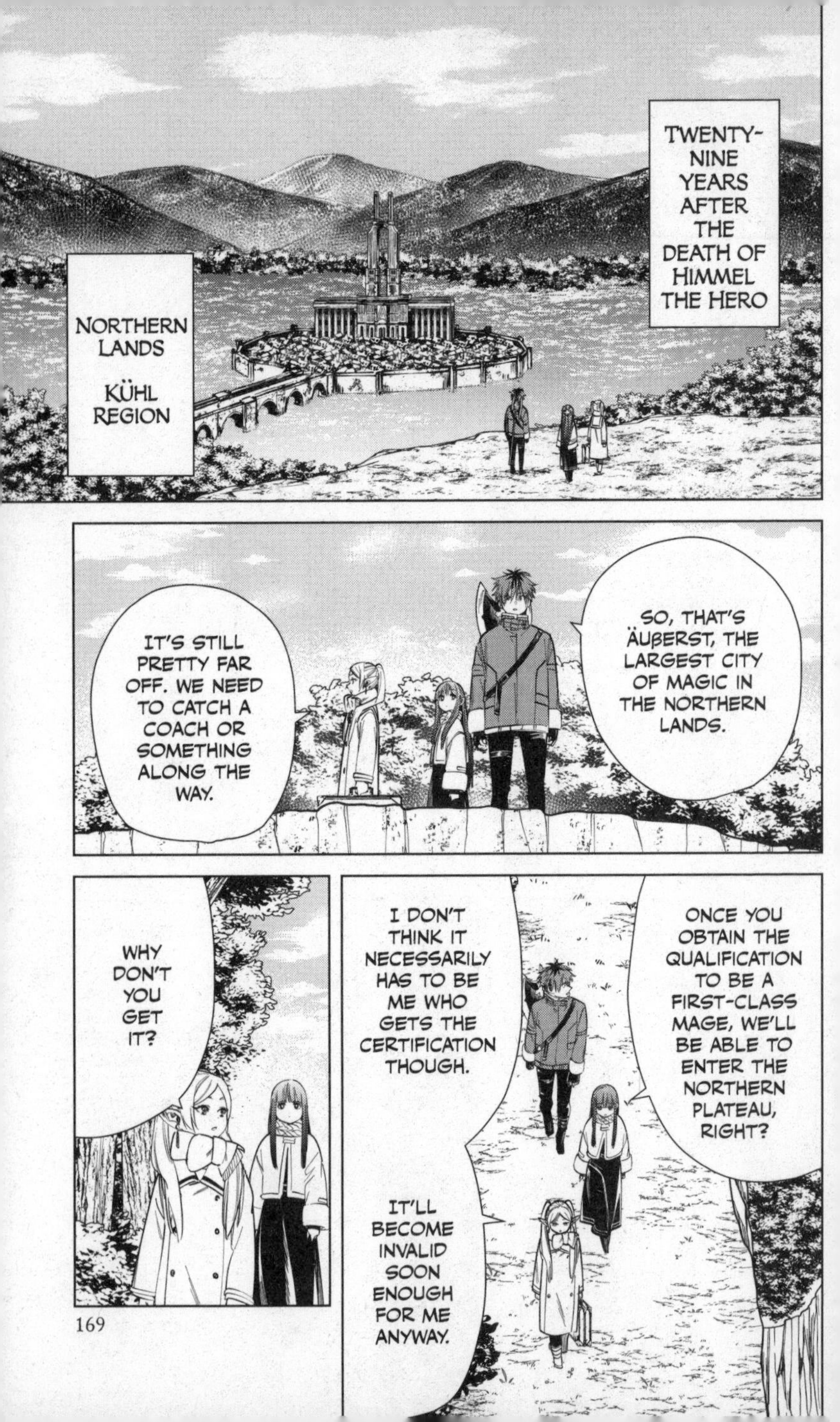
TWENTY-NINE YEARS AFTER THE DEATH OF HIMMEL THE HERO
NORTHERN LANDS
KÜHL REGION
SO, THAT'S ÄUßERST, THE LARGEST CITY OF MAGIC IN THE NORTHERN LANDS.
IT'S STILL PRETTY FAR OFF. WE NEED TO CATCH A COACH OR SOMETHING ALONG THE WAY.
ONCE YOU OBTAIN THE QUALIFICATION TO BE A FIRST-CLASS MAGE, WE'LL BE ABLE TO ENTER THE NORTHERN PLATEAU, RIGHT?
I DON'T THINK IT NECESSARILY HAS TO BE ME WHO GETS THE CERTIFICATION THOUGH.
IT'LL BECOME INVALID SOON ENOUGH FOR ME ANYWAY.
WHY DON'T YOU GET IT?

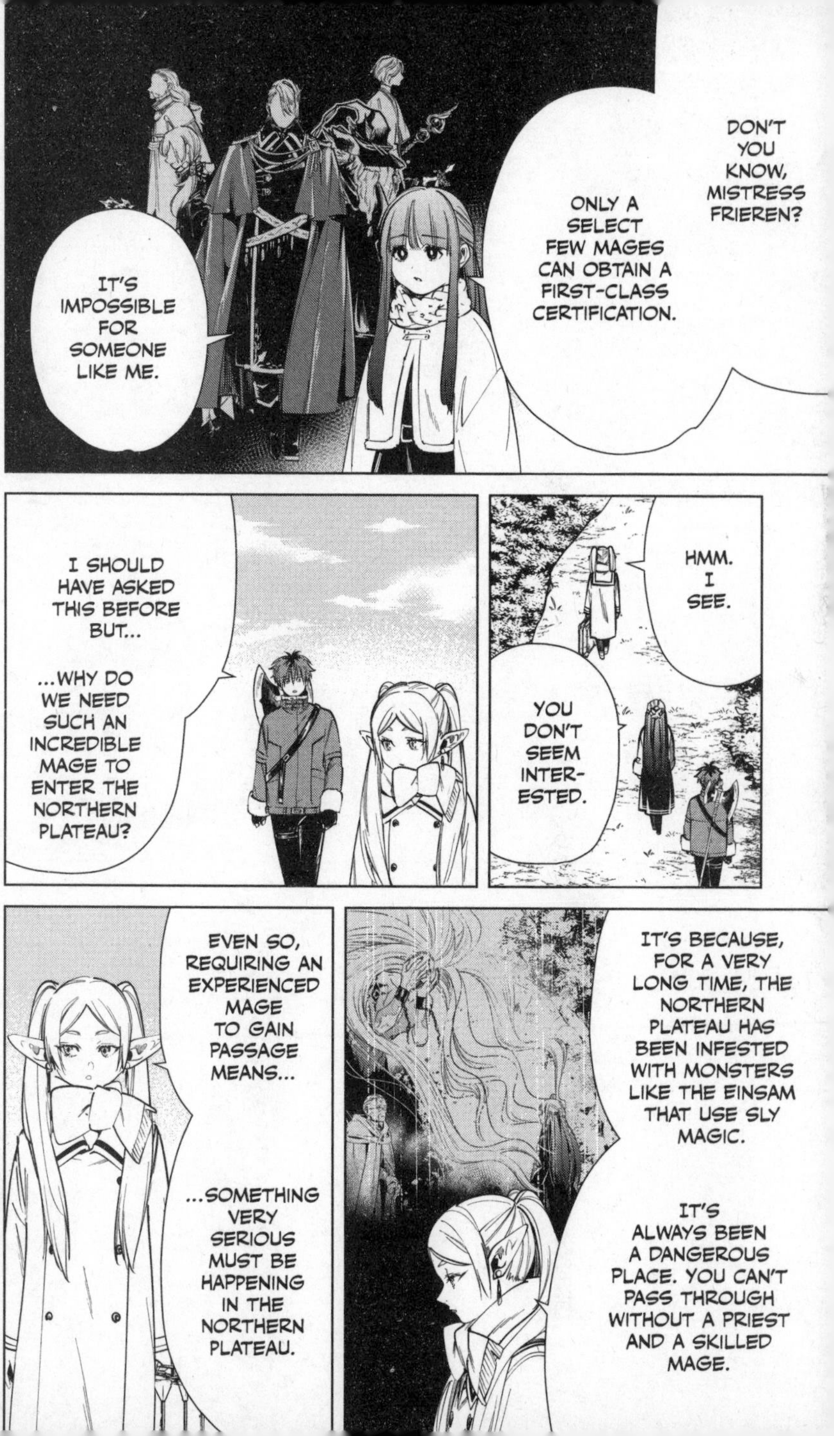
DON'T YOU KNOW, MISTRESS FRIEREN?
ONLY A SELECT FEW MAGES CAN OBTAIN A FIRST-CLASS CERTIFICATION.
IT'S IMPOSSIBLE FOR SOMEONE LIKE ME.
HMM. I SEE.
YOU DON'T SEEM INTER-ESTED.
I SHOULD HAVE ASKED THIS BEFORE BUT...
...WHY DO WE NEED SUCH AN INCREDIBLE MAGE TO ENTER THE NORTHERN PLATEAU?
IT'S BECAUSE, FOR A VERY LONG TIME, THE NORTHERN PLATEAU HAS BEEN INFESTED WITH MONSTERS LIKE THE EINSAM THAT USE SLY MAGIC.
IT'S ALWAYS BEEN A DANGEROUS PLACE. YOU CAN'T PASS THROUGH WITHOUT A PRIEST AND A SKILLED MAGE.
EVEN SO, REQUIRING AN EXPERIENCED MAGE TO GAIN PASSAGE MEANS...
...SOMETHING VERY SERIOUS MUST BE HAPPENING IN THE NORTHERN PLATEAU.

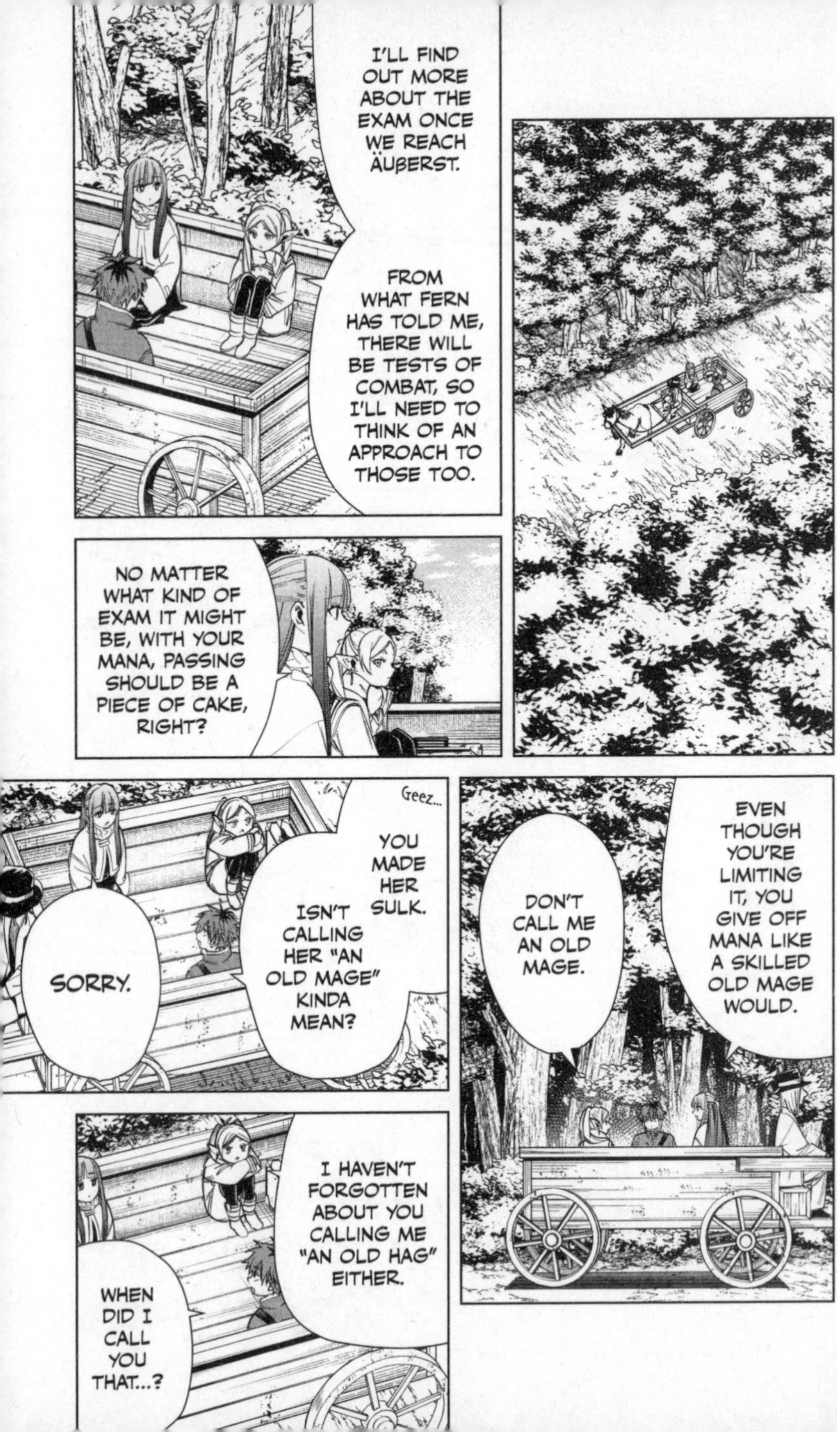
I'LL FIND OUT MORE ABOUT THE EXAM ONCE WE REACH ÄUẞERST.
FROM WHAT FERN HAS TOLD ME, THERE WILL BE TESTS OF COMBAT, SO I'LL NEED TO THINK OF AN APPROACH TO THOSE TOO.
NO MATTER WHAT KIND OF EXAM IT MIGHT BE, WITH YOUR MANA, PASSING SHOULD BE A PIECE OF CAKE, RIGHT?
EVEN THOUGH YOU'RE LIMITING IT, YOU GIVE OFF MANA LIKE A SKILLED OLD MAGE WOULD.
DON'T CALL ME AN OLD MAGE.
Geez...
YOU MADE HER SULK.
ISN'T CALLING HER "AN OLD MAGE" KINDA MEAN?
SORRY.
I HAVEN'T FORGOTTEN ABOUT YOU CALLING ME "AN OLD HAG" EITHER.
WHEN DID I CALL YOU THAT...?

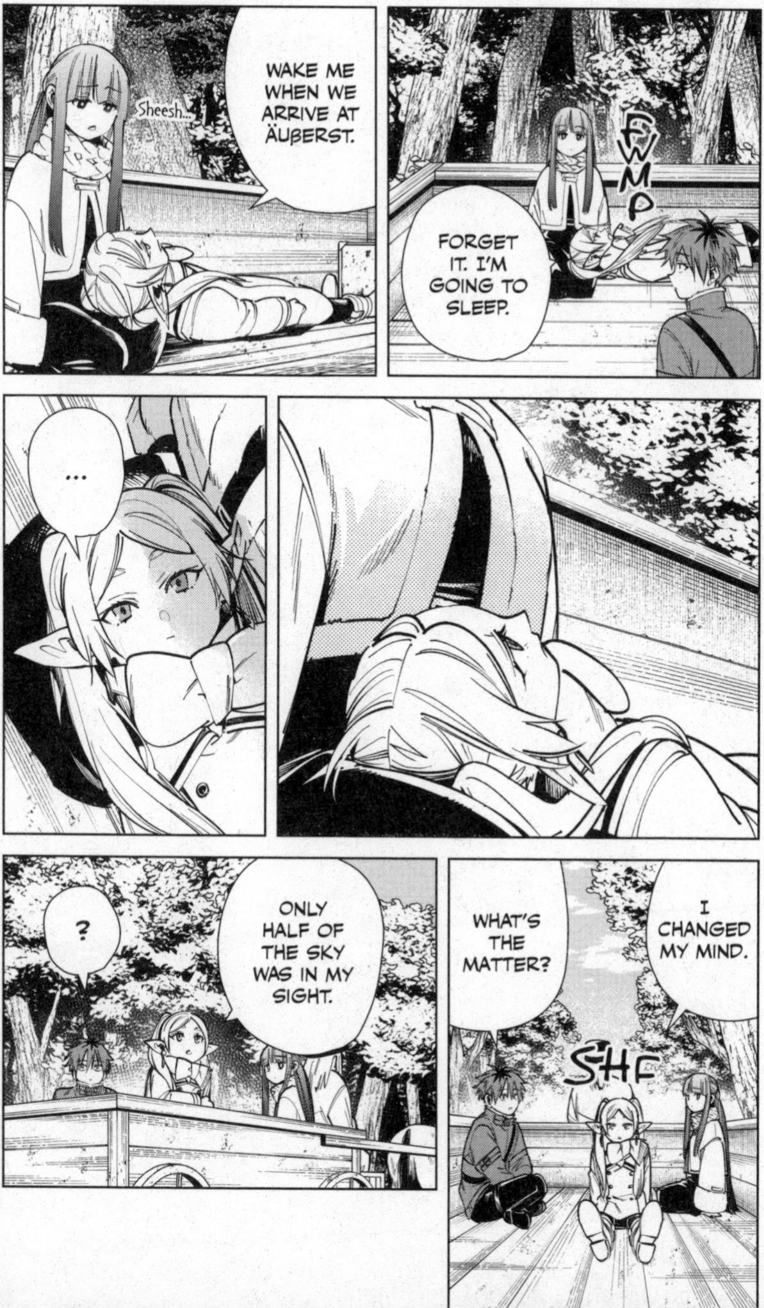
FWMP
FORGET IT. I'M GOING TO SLEEP.
WAKE ME WHEN WE ARRIVE AT ÄUßERST.
Sheesh...
...
I CHANGED MY MIND.
WHAT'S THE MATTER?
SHF
ONLY HALF OF THE SKY WAS IN MY SIGHT.
?

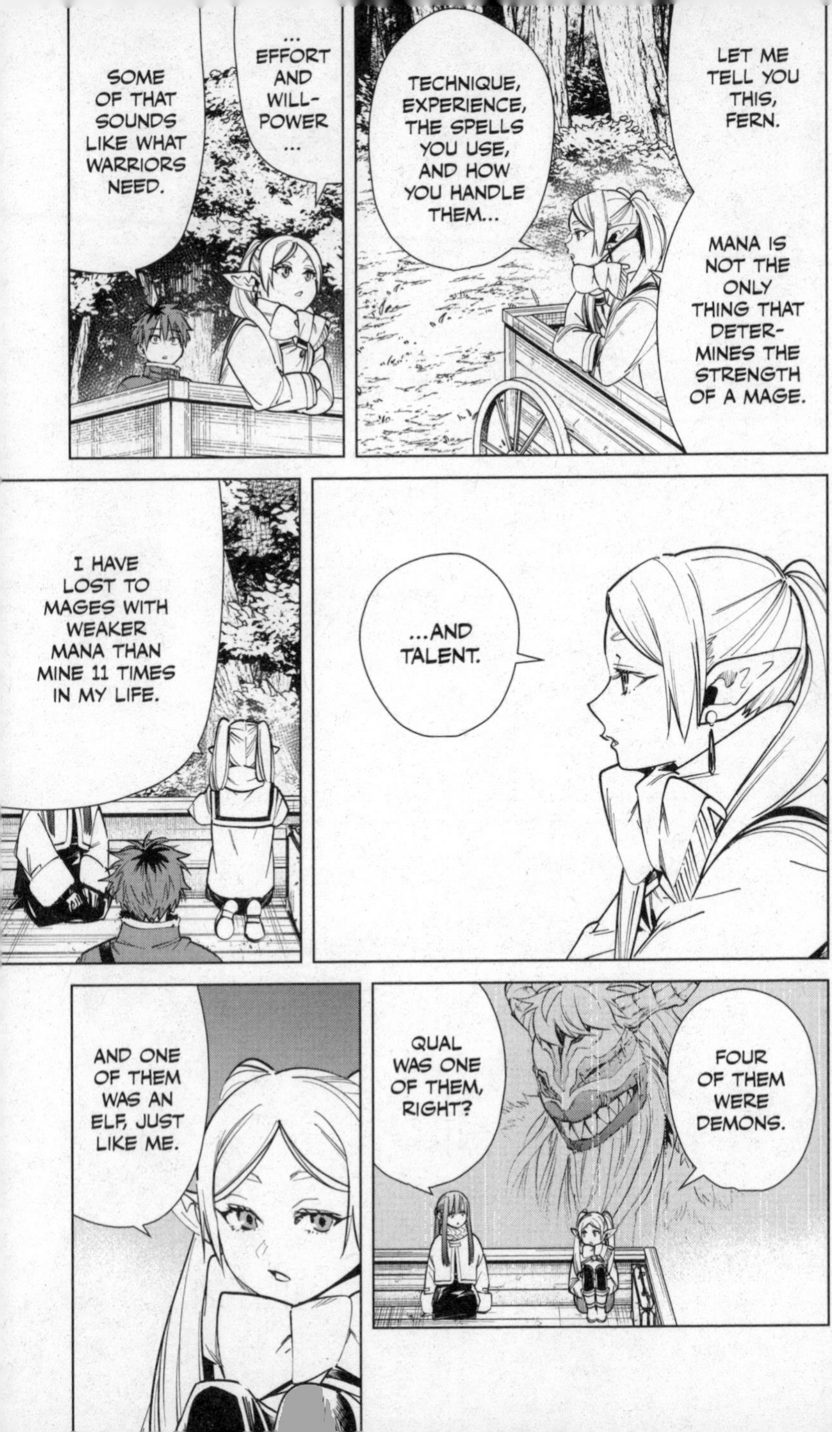
LET ME TELL YOU THIS, FERN.
MANA IS NOT THE ONLY THING THAT DETER-MINES THE STRENGTH OF A MAGE.
TECHNIQUE, EXPERIENCE, THE SPELLS YOU USE, AND HOW YOU HANDLE THEM...
... EFFORT AND WILL-POWER ...
SOME OF THAT SOUNDS LIKE WHAT WARRIORS NEED.
...AND TALENT.
I HAVE LOST TO MAGES WITH WEAKER MANA THAN MINE 11 TIMES IN MY LIFE.
FOUR OF THEM WERE DEMONS.
QUAL WAS ONE OF THEM, RIGHT?
AND ONE OF THEM WAS AN ELF, JUST LIKE ME.

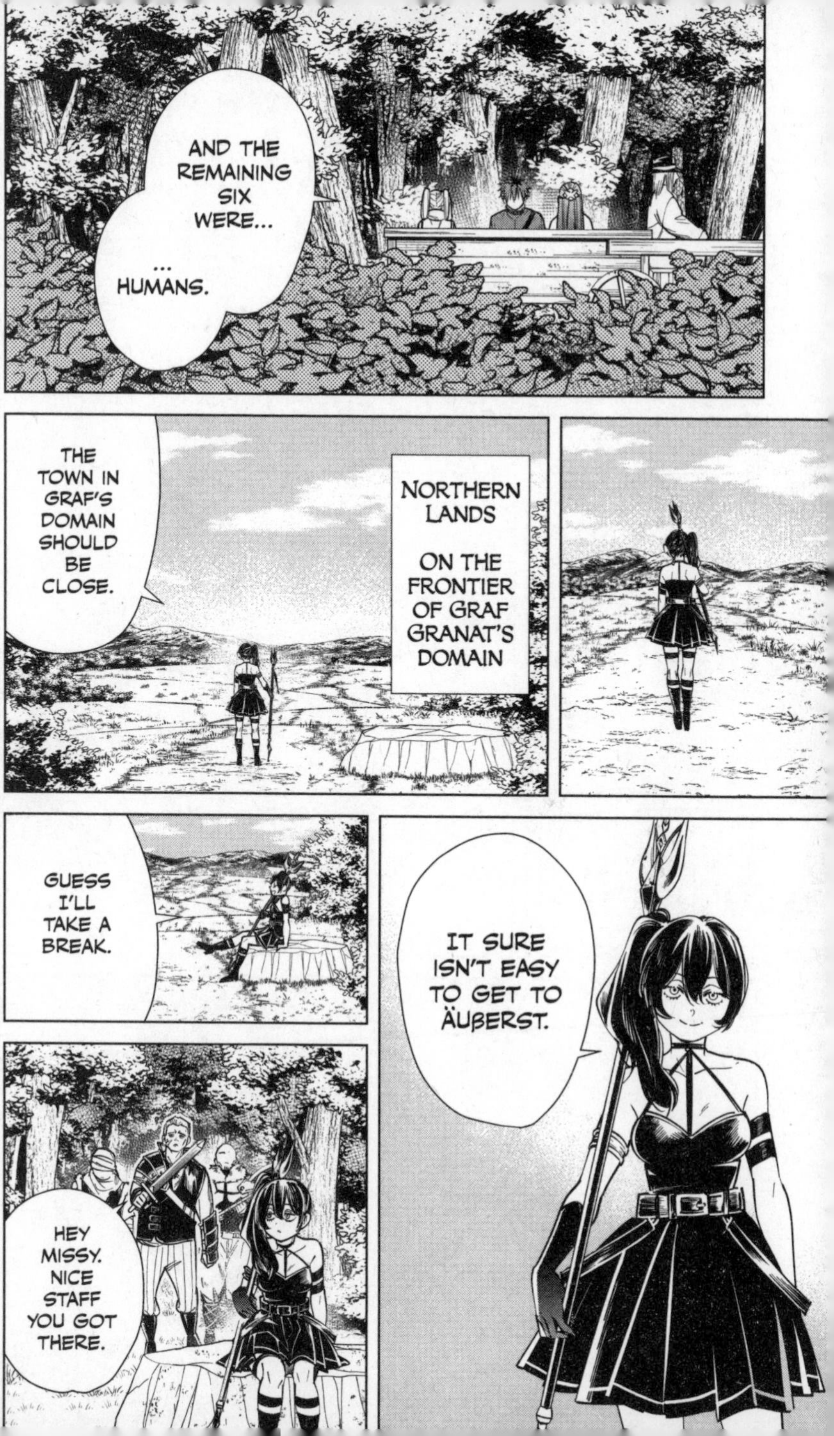
AND THE REMAINING SIX WERE...
... HUMANS.
NORTHERN LANDS

ON THE FRONTIER OF GRAF GRANAT'S DOMAIN
THE TOWN IN GRAF'S DOMAIN SHOULD BE CLOSE.
IT SURE ISN'T EASY TO GET TO ÄUßERST.
GUESS I'LL TAKE A BREAK.
HEY MISSY. NICE STAFF YOU GOT THERE.

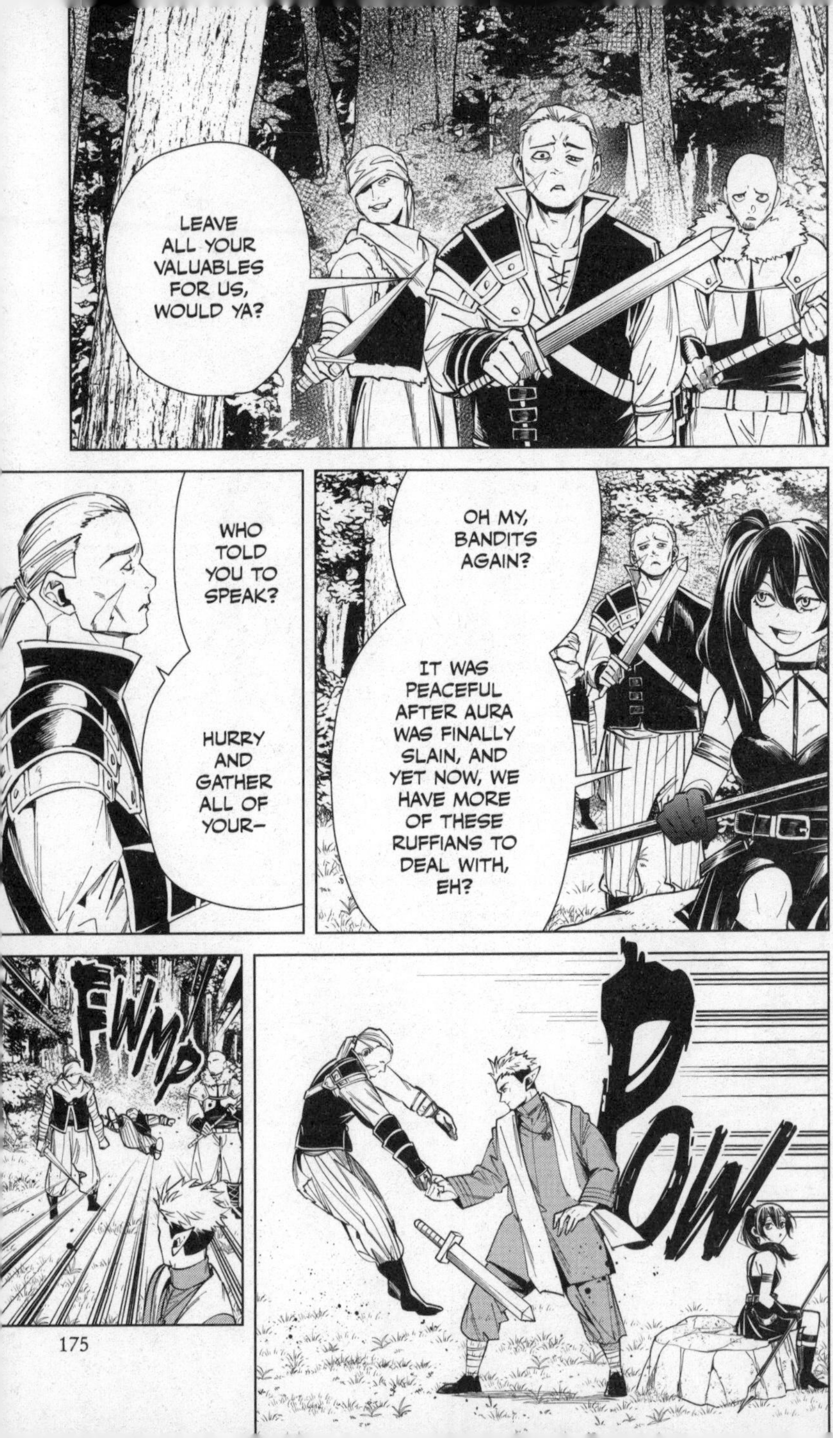
LEAVE ALL YOUR VALUABLES FOR US, WOULD YA?
OH MY, BANDITS AGAIN?
IT WAS PEACEFUL AFTER AURA WAS FINALLY SLAIN, AND YET NOW, WE HAVE MORE OF THESE RUFFIANS TO DEAL WITH, EH?
WHO TOLD YOU TO SPEAK?
HURRY AND GATHER ALL OF YOUR–
POW
FWMP

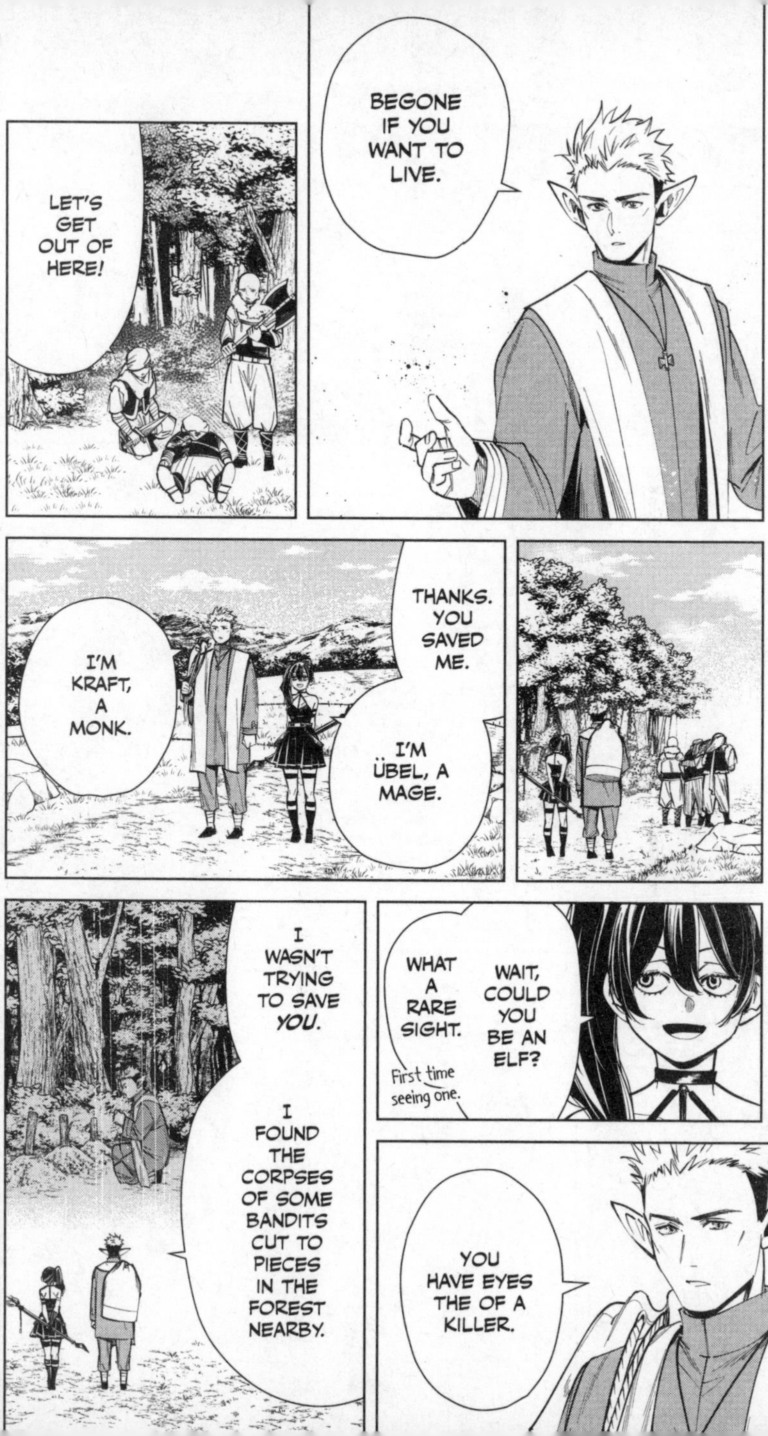
BEGONE IF YOU WANT TO LIVE.
LET'S GET OUT OF HERE!
THANKS. YOU SAVED ME.
I'M ÜBEL, A MAGE.
I'M KRAFT, A MONK.
WAIT, COULD YOU BE AN ELF?
WHAT A RARE SIGHT.
First time seeing one.
YOU HAVE EYES THE OF A KILLER.
I WASN'T TRYING TO SAVE *YOU*.
I FOUND THE CORPSES OF SOME BANDITS CUT TO PIECES IN THE FOREST NEARBY.

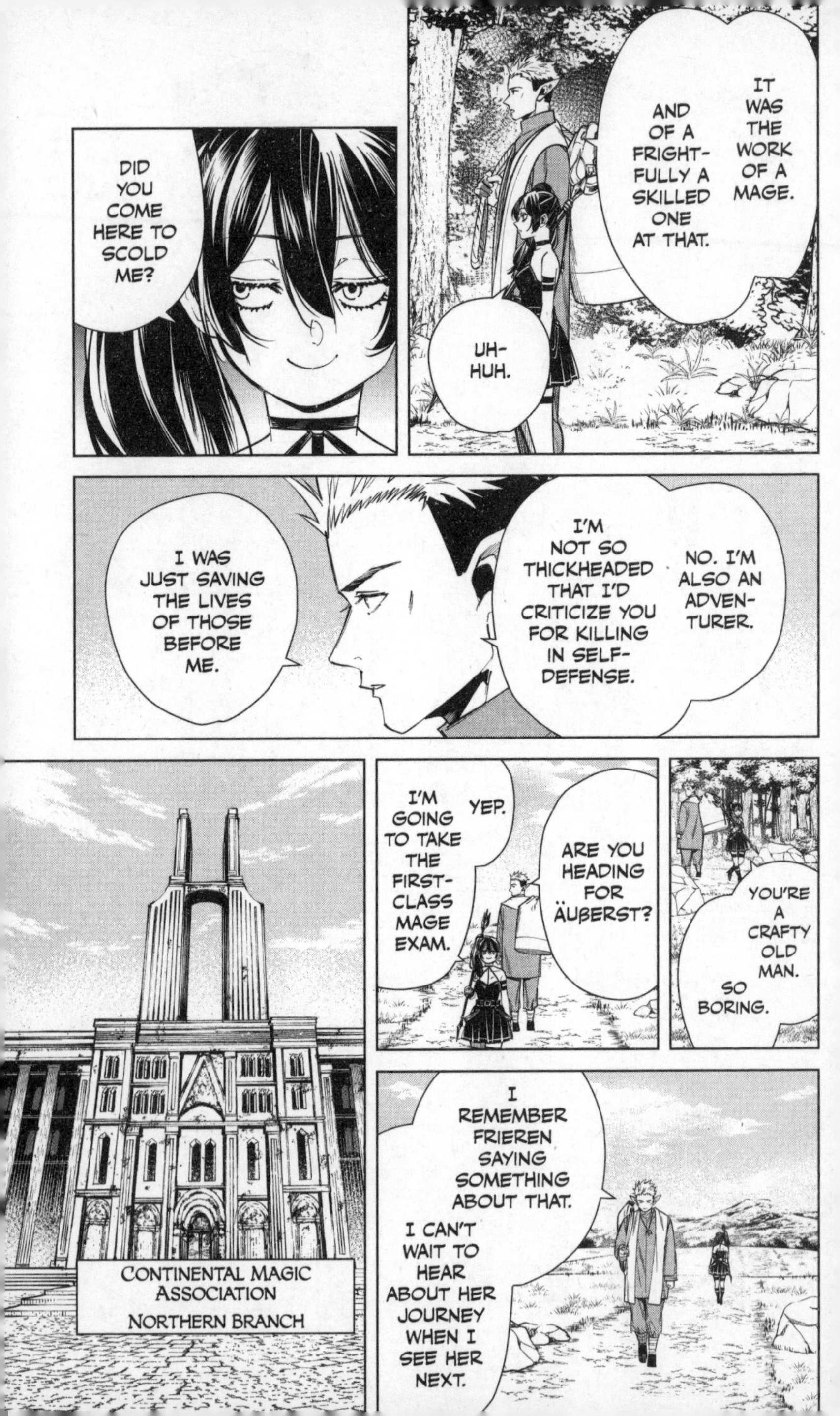
IT WAS THE WORK OF A MAGE.
AND OF A FRIGHTFULLY A SKILLED ONE AT THAT.
UH-HUH.
DID YOU COME HERE TO SCOLD ME?
NO. I'M ALSO AN ADVENTURER.
I'M NOT SO THICKHEADED THAT I'D CRITICIZE YOU FOR KILLING IN SELF-DEFENSE.
I WAS JUST SAVING THE LIVES OF THOSE BEFORE ME.
YOU'RE A CRAFTY OLD MAN.
SO BORING.
ARE YOU HEADING FOR ÄUßERST?
YEP.
I'M GOING TO TAKE THE FIRST-CLASS MAGE EXAM.
I REMEMBER FRIEREN SAYING SOMETHING ABOUT THAT.
I CAN'T WAIT TO HEAR ABOUT HER JOURNEY WHEN I SEE HER NEXT.
CONTINENTAL MAGIC ASSOCIATION
NORTHERN BRANCH

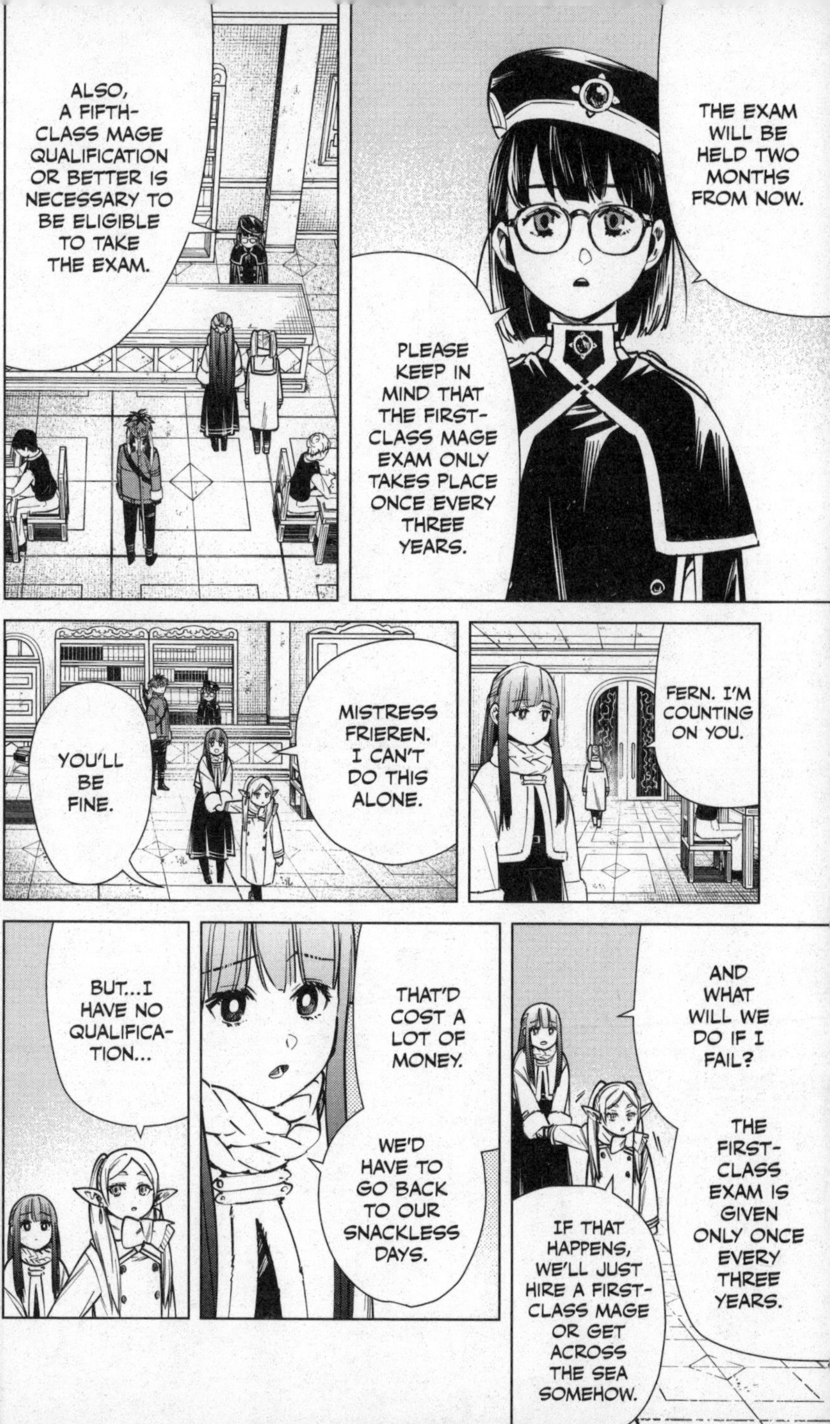
THE EXAM WILL BE HELD TWO MONTHS FROM NOW.
PLEASE KEEP IN MIND THAT THE FIRST-CLASS MAGE EXAM ONLY TAKES PLACE ONCE EVERY THREE YEARS.
ALSO, A FIFTH-CLASS MAGE QUALIFICATION OR BETTER IS NECESSARY TO BE ELIGIBLE TO TAKE THE EXAM.
FERN. I'M COUNTING ON YOU.
MISTRESS FRIEREN. I CAN'T DO THIS ALONE.
YOU'LL BE FINE.
AND WHAT WILL WE DO IF I FAIL?
THE FIRST-CLASS EXAM IS GIVEN ONLY ONCE EVERY THREE YEARS.
IF THAT HAPPENS, WE'LL JUST HIRE A FIRST-CLASS MAGE OR GET ACROSS THE SEA SOMEHOW.
THAT'D COST A LOT OF MONEY.
WE'D HAVE TO GO BACK TO OUR SNACKLESS DAYS.
BUT...I HAVE NO QUALIFICATION...

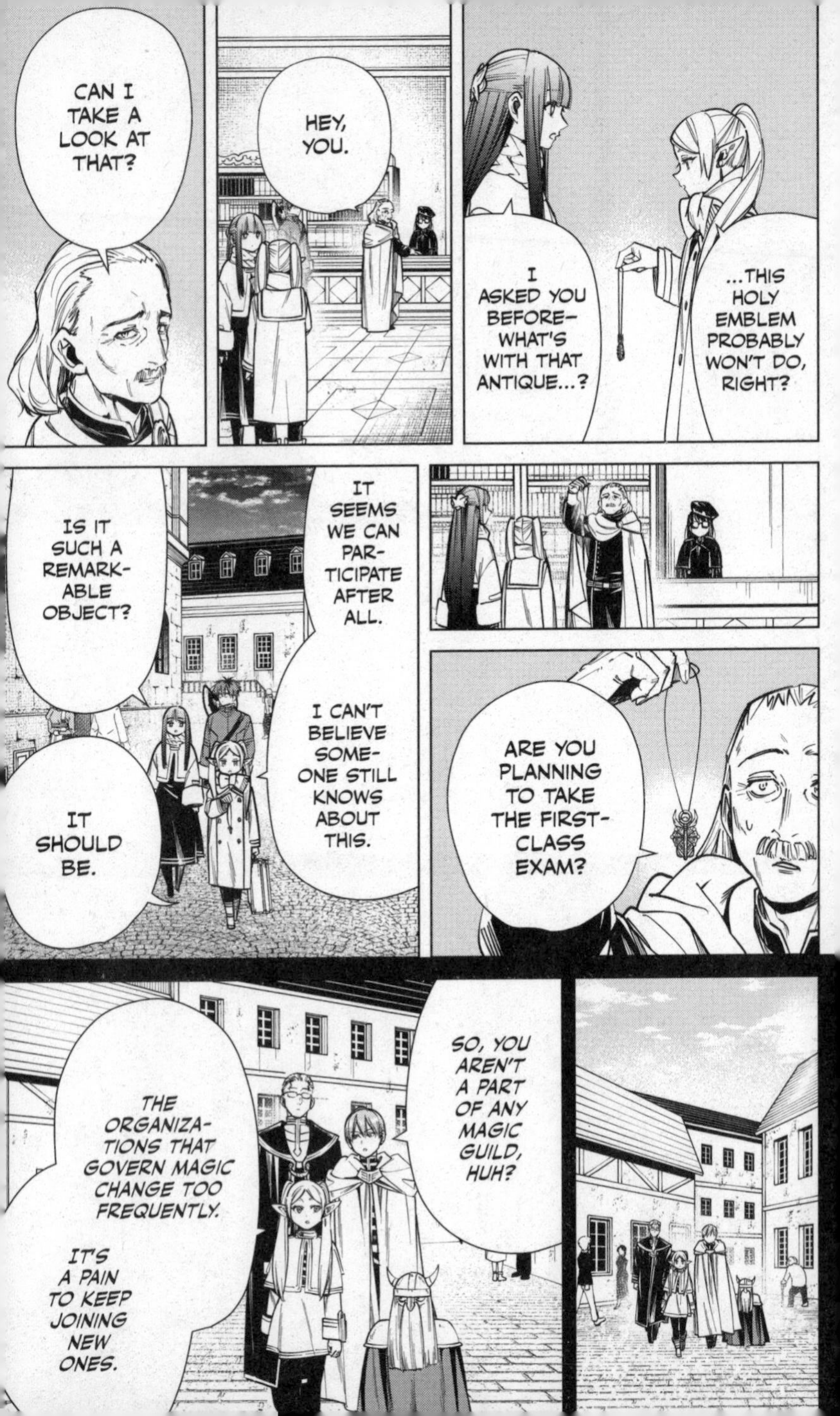
...THIS HOLY EMBLEM PROBABLY WON'T DO, RIGHT?
I ASKED YOU BEFORE—WHAT'S WITH THAT ANTIQUE...?
HEY, YOU.
CAN I TAKE A LOOK AT THAT?
ARE YOU PLANNING TO TAKE THE FIRST-CLASS EXAM?
IT SEEMS WE CAN PARTICIPATE AFTER ALL.
I CAN'T BELIEVE SOMEONE STILL KNOWS ABOUT THIS.
IS IT SUCH A REMARKABLE OBJECT?
IT SHOULD BE.
SO, YOU AREN'T A PART OF ANY MAGIC GUILD, HUH?
THE ORGANIZATIONS THAT GOVERN MAGIC CHANGE TOO FREQUENTLY.
IT'S A PAIN TO KEEP JOINING NEW ONES.

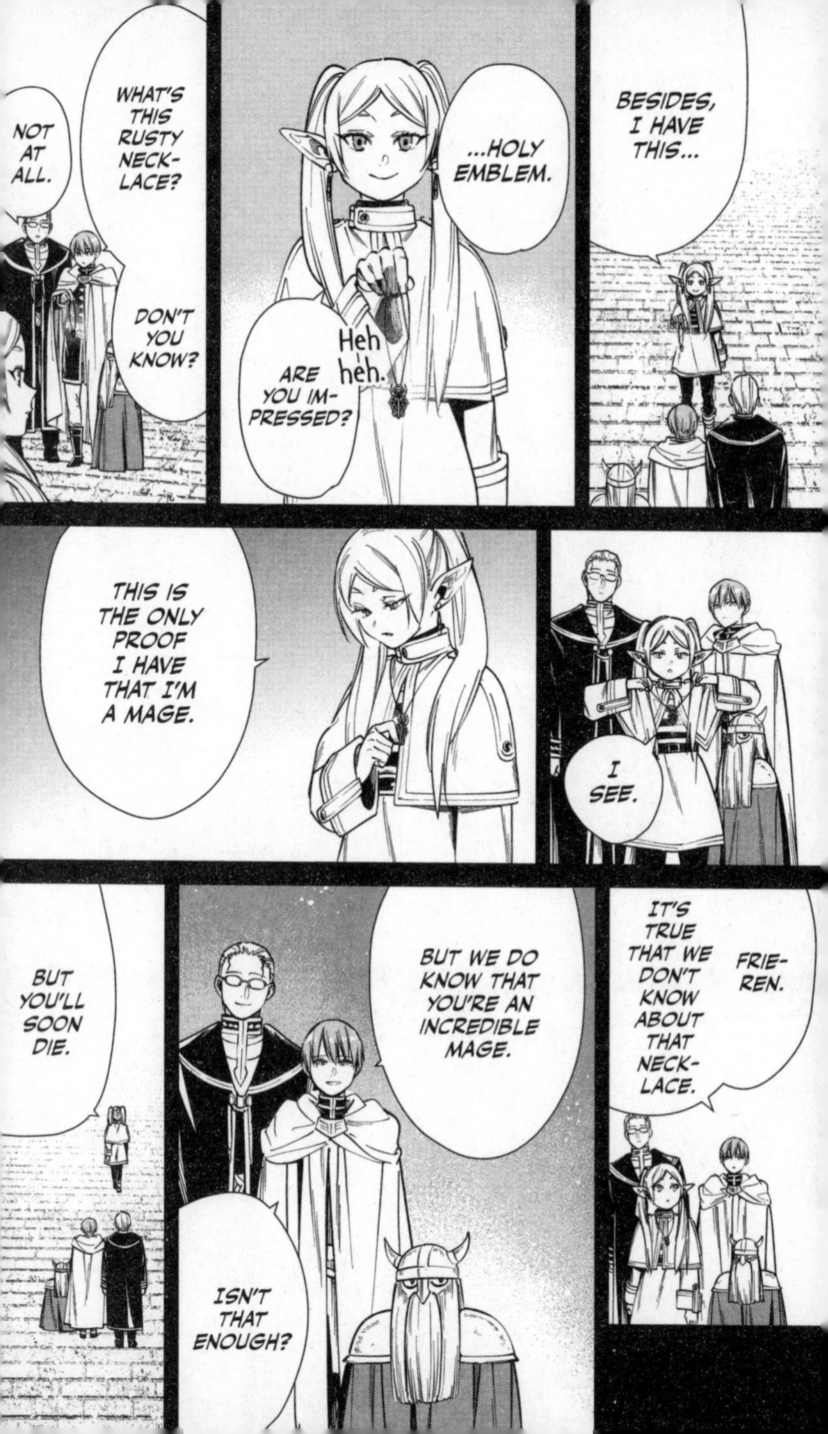
BESIDES, I HAVE THIS...
...HOLY EMBLEM.
Heh heh.
ARE YOU IMPRESSED?
WHAT'S THIS RUSTY NECKLACE?
NOT AT ALL.
DON'T YOU KNOW?
I SEE.
THIS IS THE ONLY PROOF I HAVE THAT I'M A MAGE.
FRIEREN.
IT'S TRUE THAT WE DON'T KNOW ABOUT THAT NECKLACE.
BUT WE DO KNOW THAT YOU'RE AN INCREDIBLE MAGE.
ISN'T THAT ENOUGH?
BUT YOU'LL SOON DIE.

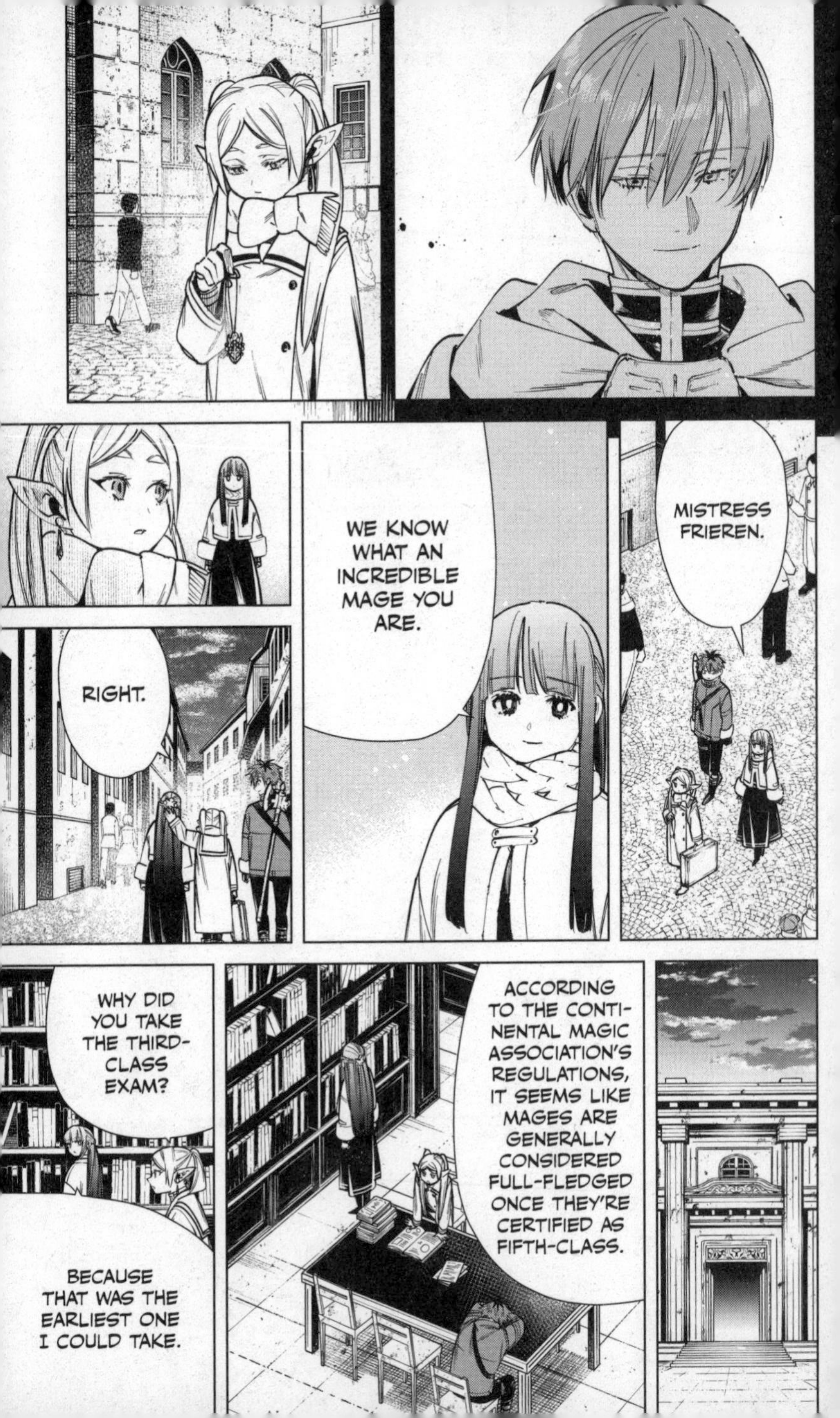
MISTRESS FRIEREN.
WE KNOW WHAT AN INCREDIBLE MAGE YOU ARE.
RIGHT.
ACCORDING TO THE CONTINENTAL MAGIC ASSOCIATION'S REGULATIONS, IT SEEMS LIKE MAGES ARE GENERALLY CONSIDERED FULL-FLEDGED ONCE THEY'RE CERTIFIED AS FIFTH-CLASS.
WHY DID YOU TAKE THE THIRD-CLASS EXAM?
BECAUSE THAT WAS THE EARLIEST ONE I COULD TAKE.

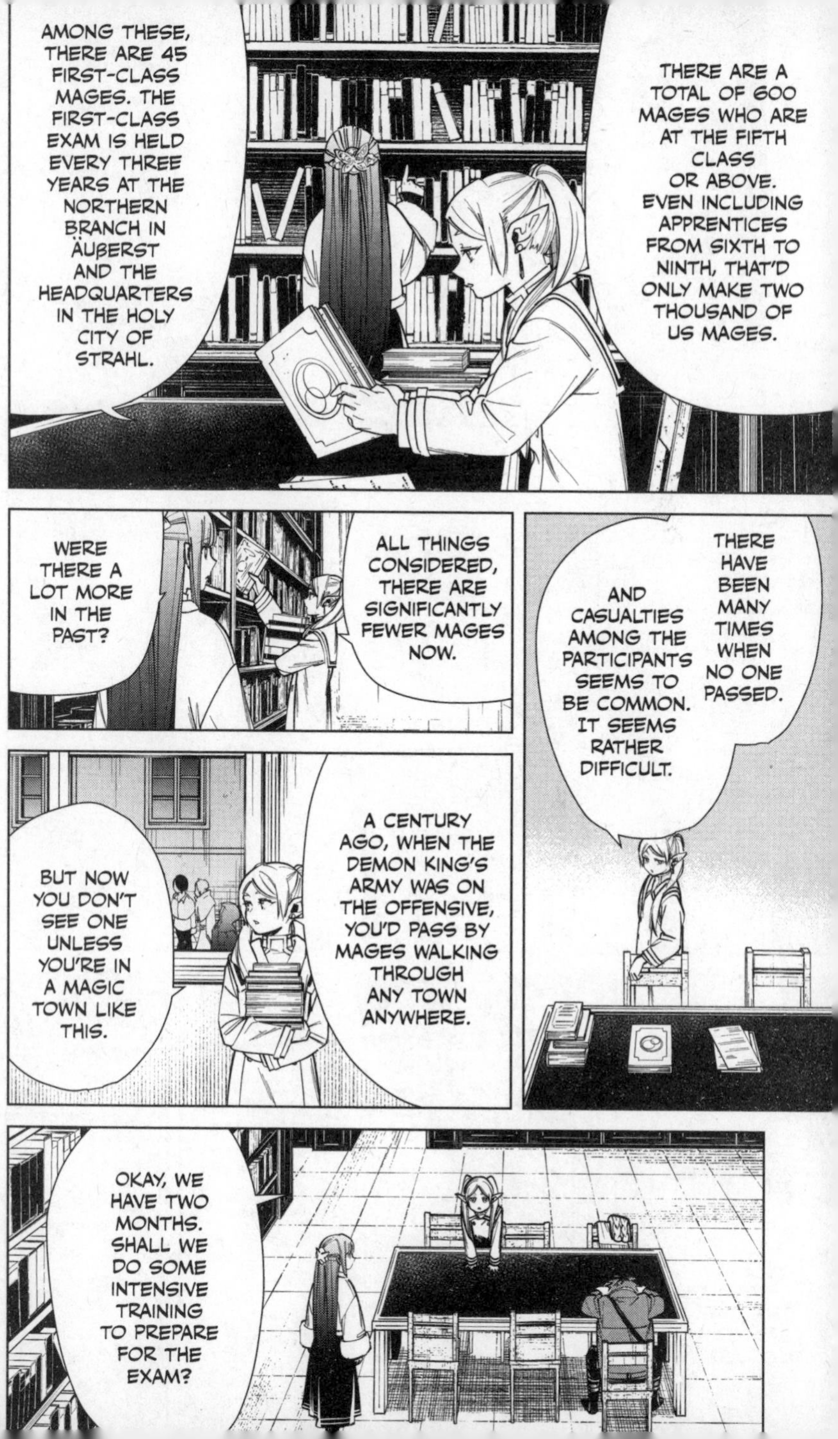
THERE ARE A TOTAL OF 600 MAGES WHO ARE AT THE FIFTH CLASS OR ABOVE. EVEN INCLUDING APPRENTICES FROM SIXTH TO NINTH, THAT'D ONLY MAKE TWO THOUSAND OF US MAGES.
AMONG THESE, THERE ARE 45 FIRST-CLASS MAGES. THE FIRST-CLASS EXAM IS HELD EVERY THREE YEARS AT THE NORTHERN BRANCH IN ÄUßERST AND THE HEADQUARTERS IN THE HOLY CITY OF STRAHL.
THERE HAVE BEEN MANY TIMES WHEN NO ONE PASSED.
AND CASUALTIES AMONG THE PARTICIPANTS SEEMS TO BE COMMON. IT SEEMS RATHER DIFFICULT.
ALL THINGS CONSIDERED, THERE ARE SIGNIFICANTLY FEWER MAGES NOW.
WERE THERE A LOT MORE IN THE PAST?
A CENTURY AGO, WHEN THE DEMON KING'S ARMY WAS ON THE OFFENSIVE, YOU'D PASS BY MAGES WALKING THROUGH ANY TOWN ANYWHERE.
BUT NOW YOU DON'T SEE ONE UNLESS YOU'RE IN A MAGIC TOWN LIKE THIS.
OKAY, WE HAVE TWO MONTHS. SHALL WE DO SOME INTENSIVE TRAINING TO PREPARE FOR THE EXAM?

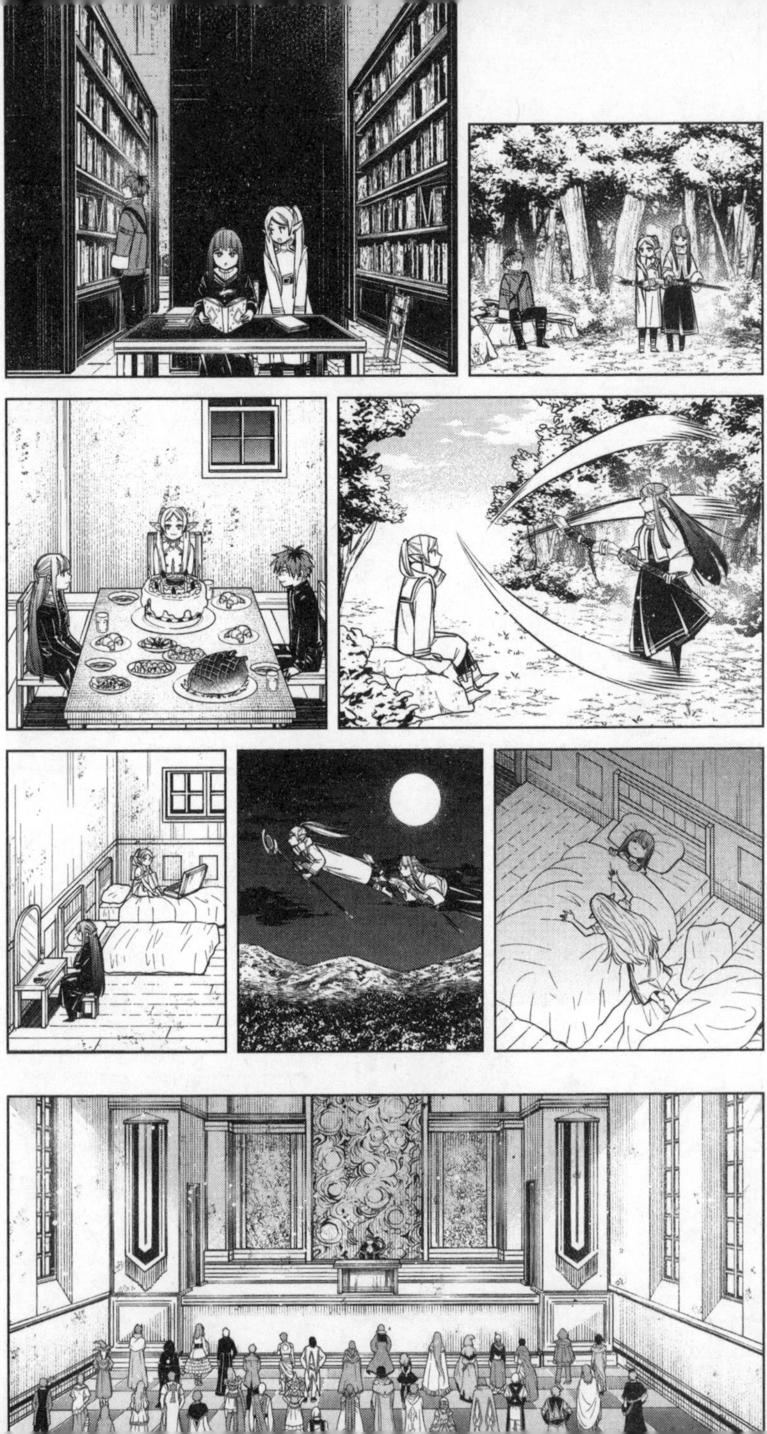

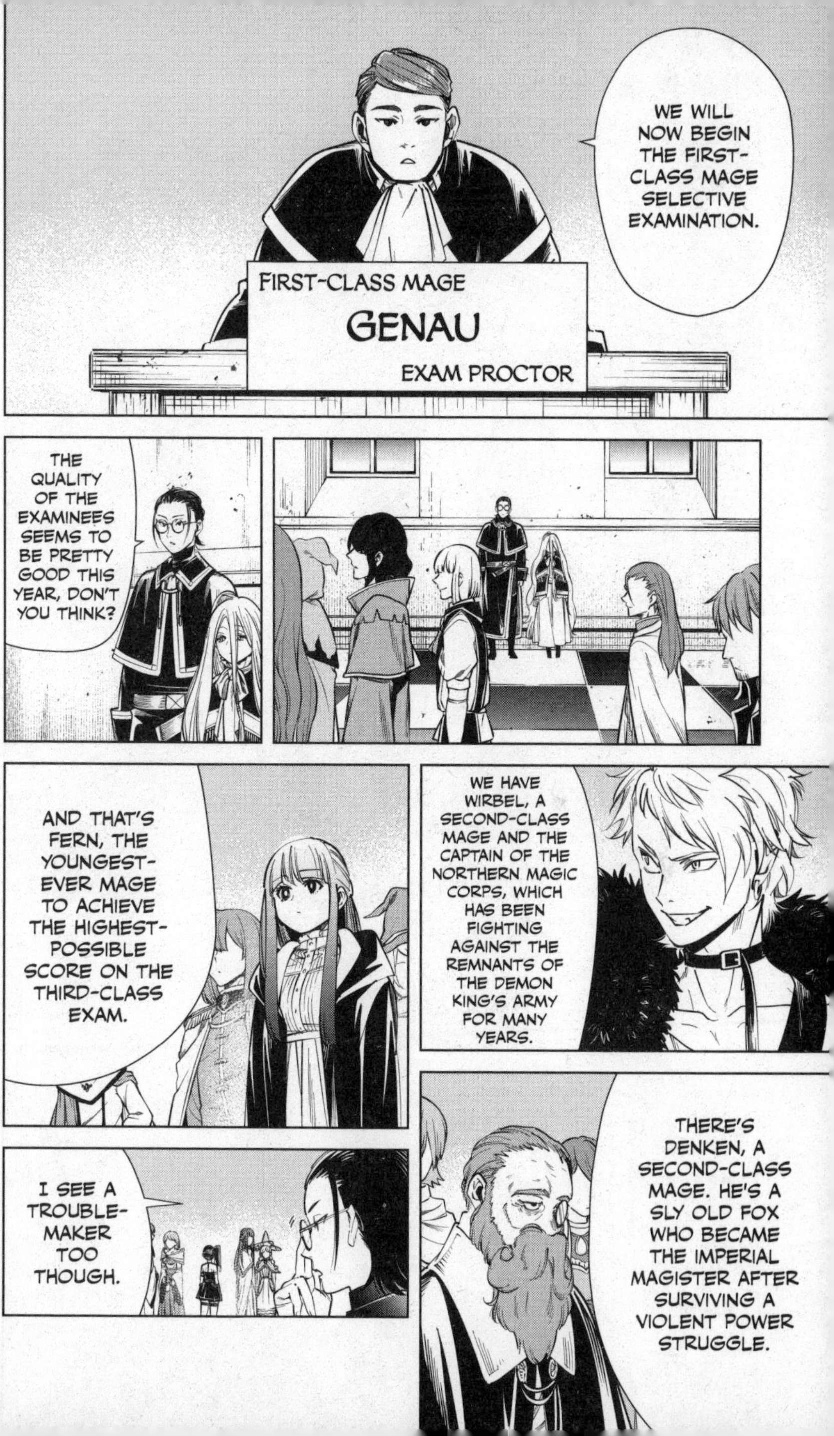
WE WILL NOW BEGIN THE FIRST-CLASS MAGE SELECTIVE EXAMINATION.
FIRST-CLASS MAGE
GENAU
EXAM PROCTOR
THE QUALITY OF THE EXAMINEES SEEMS TO BE PRETTY GOOD THIS YEAR, DON'T YOU THINK?
WE HAVE WIRBEL, A SECOND-CLASS MAGE AND THE CAPTAIN OF THE NORTHERN MAGIC CORPS, WHICH HAS BEEN FIGHTING AGAINST THE REMNANTS OF THE DEMON KING'S ARMY FOR MANY YEARS.
AND THAT'S FERN, THE YOUNGEST-EVER MAGE TO ACHIEVE THE HIGHEST-POSSIBLE SCORE ON THE THIRD-CLASS EXAM.
THERE'S DENKEN, A SECOND-CLASS MAGE. HE'S A SLY OLD FOX WHO BECAME THE IMPERIAL MAGISTER AFTER SURVIVING A VIOLENT POWER STRUGGLE.
I SEE A TROUBLE-MAKER TOO THOUGH.

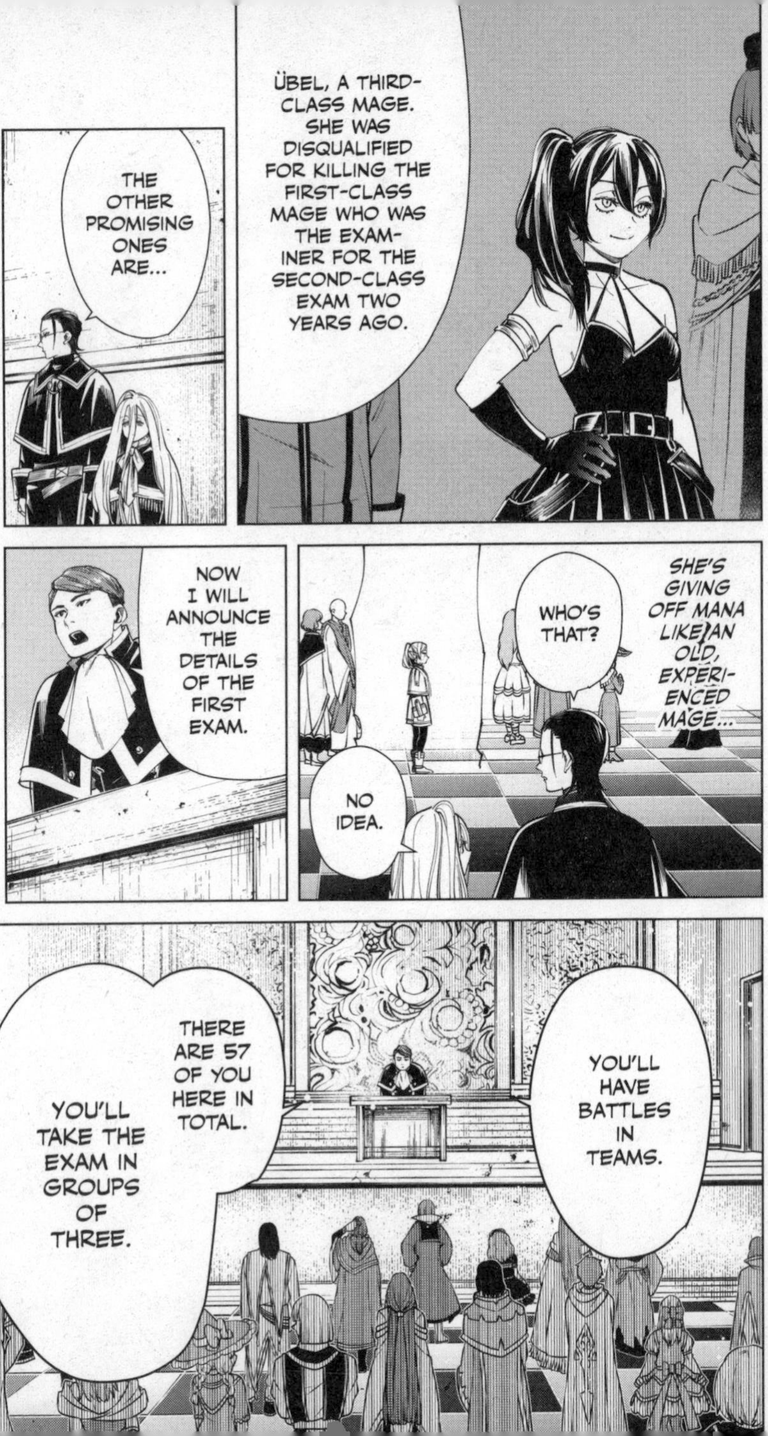
ÜBEL, A THIRD-CLASS MAGE. SHE WAS DISQUALIFIED FOR KILLING THE FIRST-CLASS MAGE WHO WAS THE EXAMINER FOR THE SECOND-CLASS EXAM TWO YEARS AGO.
THE OTHER PROMISING ONES ARE...
SHE'S GIVING OFF MANA LIKE AN OLD, EXPERIENCED MAGE...
WHO'S THAT?
NO IDEA.
NOW I WILL ANNOUNCE THE DETAILS OF THE FIRST EXAM.
YOU'LL HAVE BATTLES IN TEAMS.
THERE ARE 57 OF YOU HERE IN TOTAL.
YOU'LL TAKE THE EXAM IN GROUPS OF THREE.

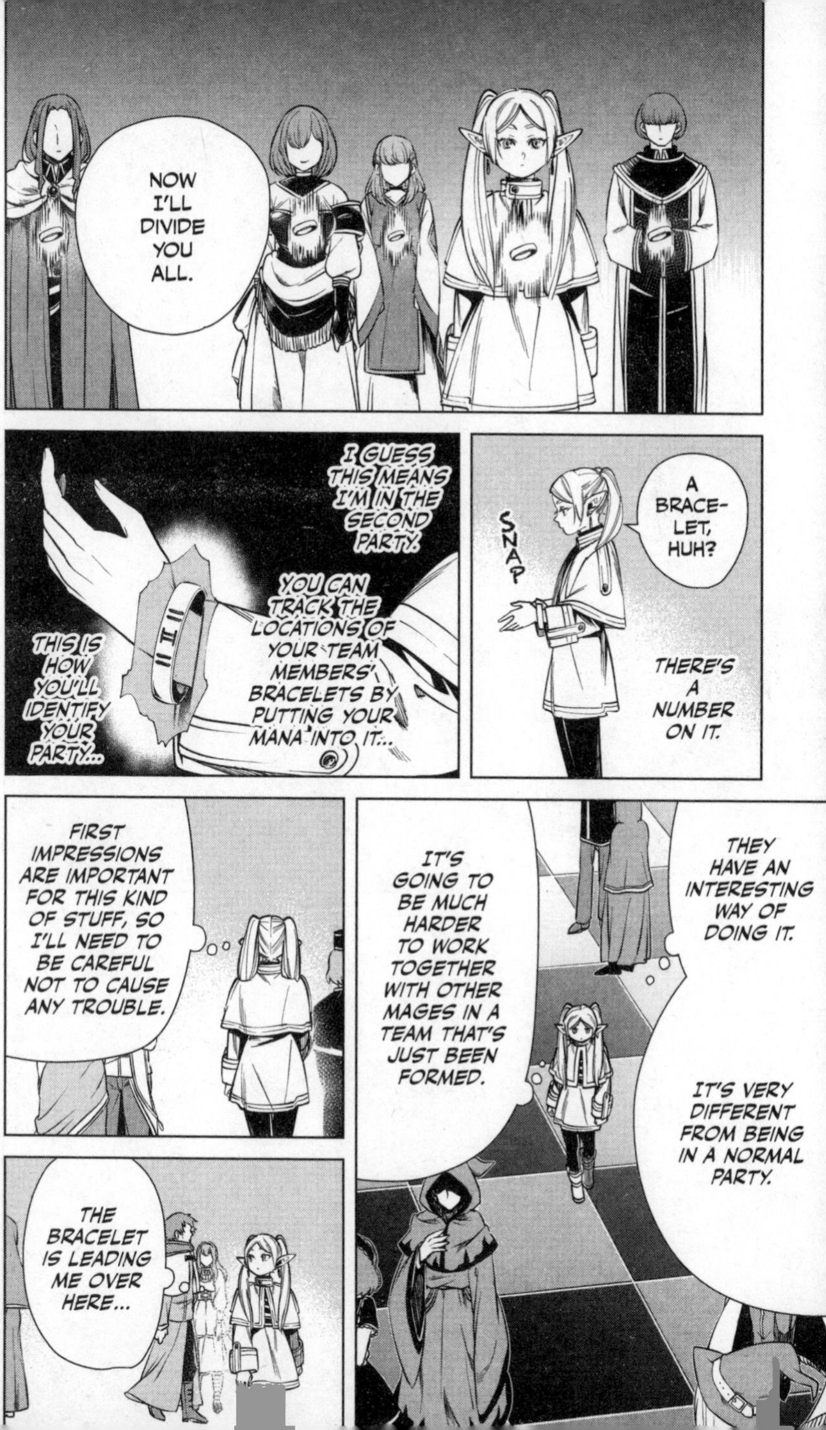
NOW I'LL DIVIDE YOU ALL.
A BRACE-LET, HUH?
SNAP
THERE'S A NUMBER ON IT.
I GUESS THIS MEANS I'M IN THE SECOND PARTY.
YOU CAN TRACK THE LOCATIONS OF YOUR TEAM MEMBERS' BRACELETS BY PUTTING YOUR MANA INTO IT...
THIS IS HOW YOU'LL IDENTIFY YOUR PARTY...
THEY HAVE AN INTERESTING WAY OF DOING IT.
IT'S GOING TO BE MUCH HARDER TO WORK TOGETHER WITH OTHER MAGES IN A TEAM THAT'S JUST BEEN FORMED.
IT'S VERY DIFFERENT FROM BEING IN A NORMAL PARTY.
FIRST IMPRESSIONS ARE IMPORTANT FOR THIS KIND OF STUFF, SO I'LL NEED TO BE CAREFUL NOT TO CAUSE ANY TROUBLE.
THE BRACELET IS LEADING ME OVER HERE...

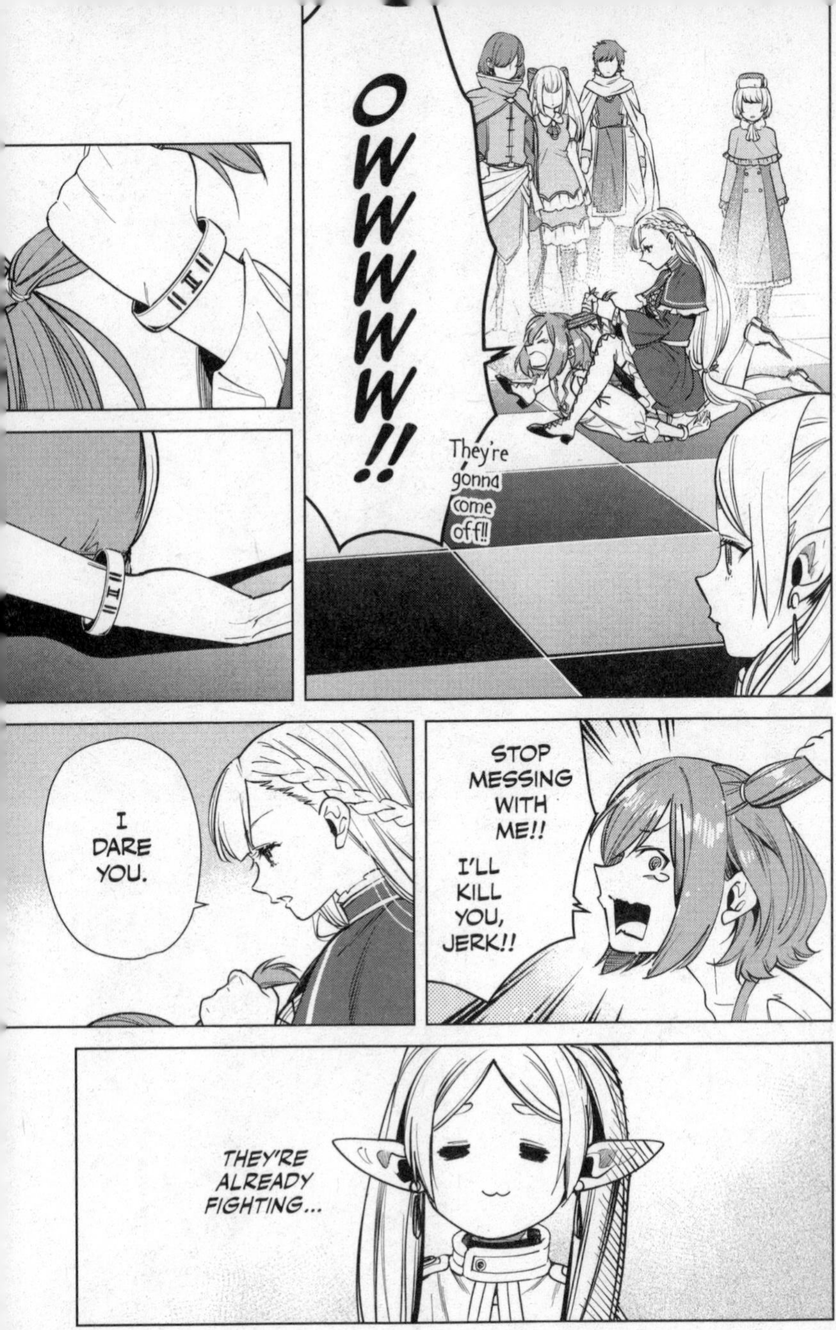
OWWWWW!!
They're gonna come off!!
STOP MESSING WITH ME!!
I'LL KILL YOU, JERK!!
I DARE YOU.
THEY'RE ALREADY FIGHTING...

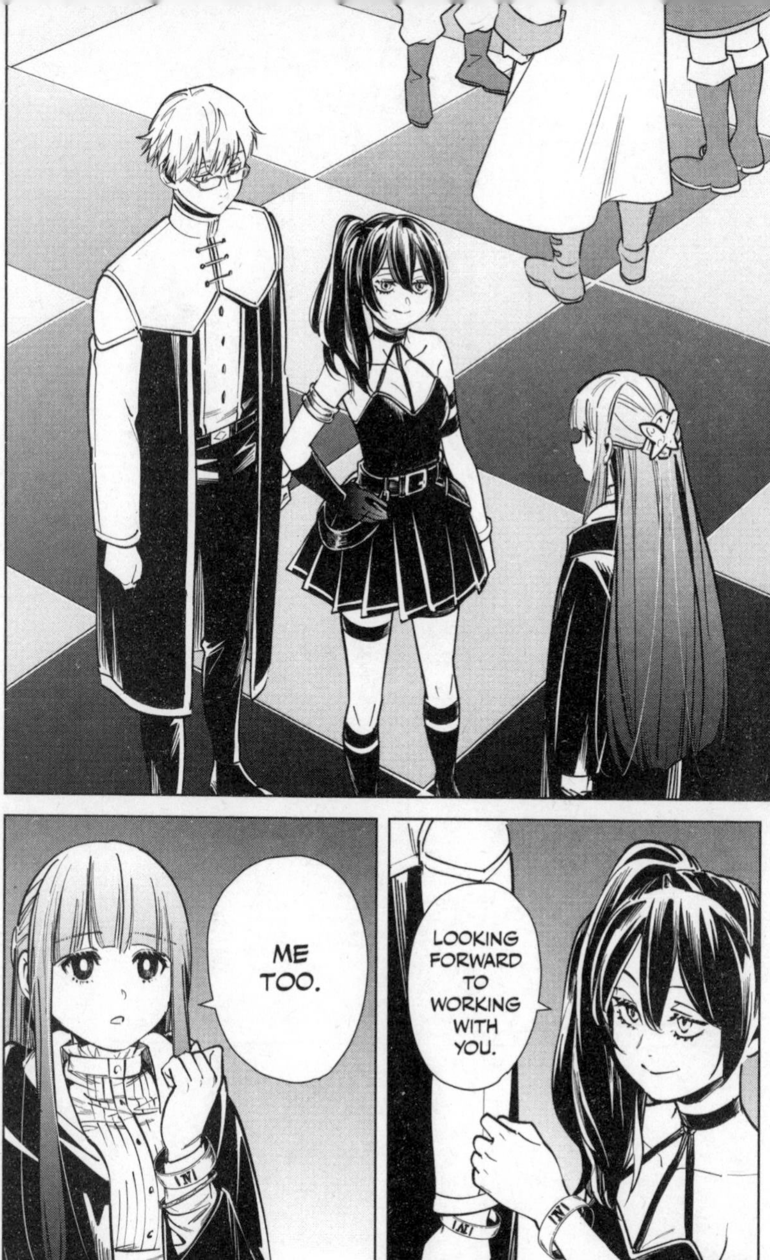
LOOKING FORWARD TO WORKING WITH YOU.
ME TOO.

Frieren: Beyond Journey's End – Vol. 4 - End

Kidnapped by the Demon King and imprisoned in his castle, Princess Syalis is...bored.

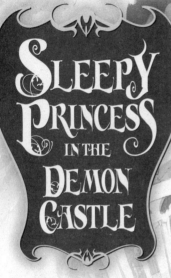

SLEEPY PRINCESS IN THE DEMON CASTLE

Story & Art by
KAGIJI KUMANOMATA

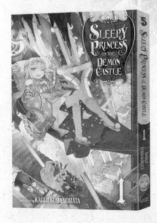

Captured princess Syalis decides to while away her hours in the Demon Castle by sleeping, but getting a good night's rest turns out to be a lot of work! She begins by fashioning a DIY pillow out of the fur of her Teddy Demon guards and an "air mattress" from the magical Shield of the Wind. Things go from bad to worse—for her captors—when some of Princess Syalis's schemes end in her untimely—if temporary—demise and she chooses the Forbidden Grimoire for her bedtime reading...

Hey! You're Reading in the Wrong Direction!

This is the end of this graphic novel!

To properly enjoy this VIZ graphic novel, please turn it around and begin reading from right to left. Unlike English, Japanese is read right to left, so Japanese comics are read in reverse order from the way English comics are typically read.

This book has been printed in the original Japanese format in order to preserve the orientation of the original artwork. Have fun with it!

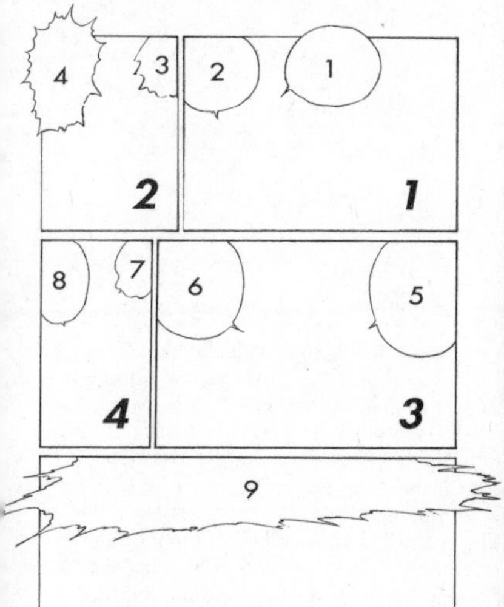
1
2
3
4
1
2
5
6
7
8
3
4
9
5

Follow the action this way

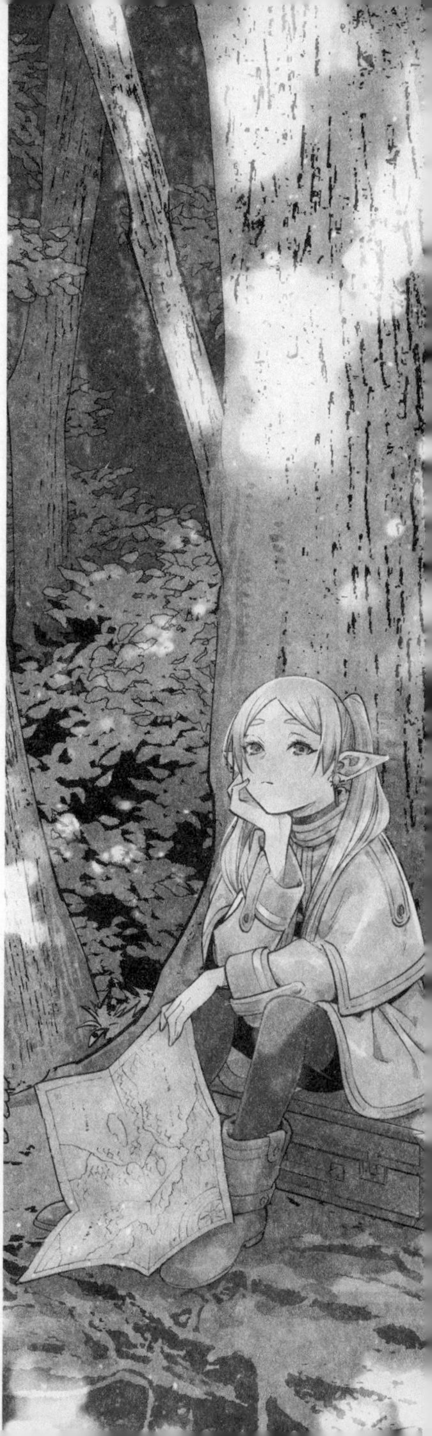

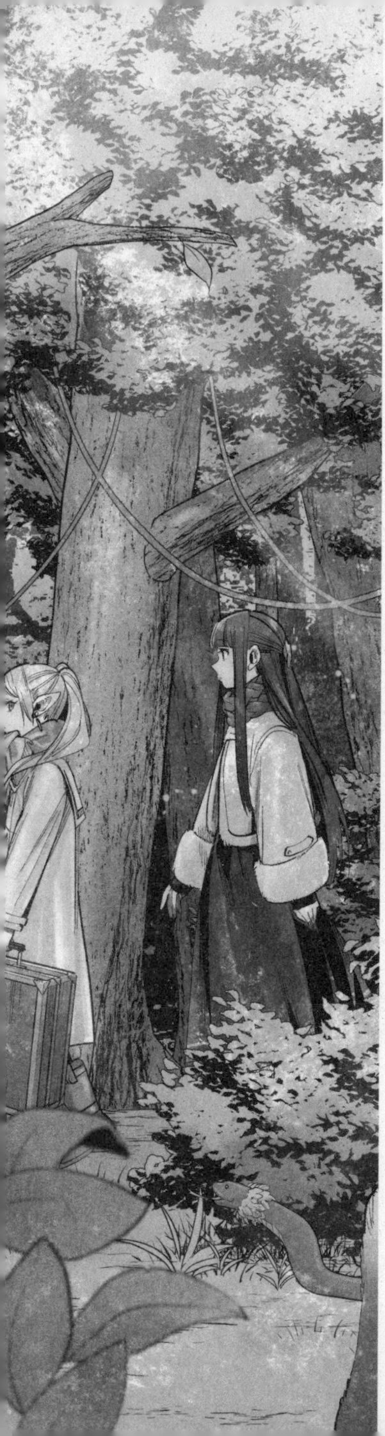

Frieren: Beyond Journey's End

VOLUME 4

Shonen Sunday Edition

STORY BY
KANEHITO YAMADA

ART BY
TSUKASA ABE

SOSO NO FRIEREN Vol. 4
by Kanehito YAMADA, Tsukasa ABE

Original Japanese edition published by SHOGAKUKAN.
English translation rights in the United States of America, Canada, the United Kingdom, Ireland, Australia and New Zealand arranged with SHOGAKUKAN.

Original Cover Design: Masato ISHIZAWA + Bay Bridge Studio

Translation/Misa 'Japanese Ammo'
Touch-up Art & Lettering/Annaliese "Ace" Christman
Design/Yukiko Whitley
Editor/Mike Montesa

Printed in the U.S.A.

Published by VIZ Media, LLC
P.O. Box 77010
San Francisco, CA 94107

10 9 8 7 6 5 4 3 2 1
First printing, May 2022

ratings.viz.com RATED T TEEN

PARENTAL ADVISORY
FRIEREN: BEYOND JOURNEY'S END is rated T for Teen and recommended for ages 13 and up. This volume contains fantasy violence.

VIZ MEDIA
viz.com

shonensunday.com